W9-AXI-889

327.51
L57

Modern China's Foreign Policy

OTHER BOOKS BY WERNER LEVI

American-Australian Relations
Fundamentals of World Organization
Free India in Asia

PUBLISHED BY THE

DS740.63
L48

MODERN CHINA'S
FOREIGN POLICY

by Werner Levi

UNIVERSITY OF MINNESOTA PRESS, MINNEAPOLIS

48597

MAR '55

Copyright 1953 by the

UNIVERSITY OF MINNESOTA

All rights reserved. No part of this book
may be reproduced in any form without
the written permission of the publisher.
Permission is hereby granted to reviewers
to quote brief passages in a review to be
printed in a magazine or newspaper.

PRINTED AT THE NORTH CENTRAL PUBLISHING CO., ST. PAUL

Library of Congress Catalog Card Number: 53-10470

PUBLISHED IN GREAT BRITAIN, INDIA, AND PAKISTAN BY
GEOFFREY CUMBERLEGE: OXFORD UNIVERSITY PRESS, LONDON, BOMBAY, AND KARACHI

TO

Harold S. Quigley

TEACHER AND FRIEND

Preface

THE main purpose of this book is to analyze and interpret Chinese foreign policy, both in the course of its development over the past century or so and in its present-day manifestations. China, not the countries with which she has had dealings, is the focus of the study. Consequently other nations and their activities are considered only as they have been or are now the object of Chinese foreign policy and throw light upon it. Internal Chinese developments are treated at some length, as important determinants of foreign policy.

A detailed account of every move that China has made in the past in the conduct of her foreign affairs has not been aimed at. This limitation, mainly one of choice, will extenuate, I hope, my failure to use sources in the Chinese language — an omission that might justly be considered inexcusable if the purpose of the book were not analytical rather than descriptive. It will also explain why many books that have contributed to a general knowledge of international relations in the Far East have not been utilized and are not acknowledged by title in the Notes.

This study was begun long before the so-called Great Debate on Far Eastern politics was heard in the public forums, and I hope I have not been affected by it. My purpose is not forensic. Fully aware of the risks involved (in view of the present temper of American politics), I have tried to keep the analysis and interpretation objective and not to depart from facts. The resulting picture may not have the virtuosity that marks so much of our contemporary political landscape- and portrait-painting. I hope, however, that it will give some sense of having been drawn in perspective. It can hardly fail to impress one, at any rate, with the relative permanence of national interests, goals, and ambitions — of political methods, even, at times — regardless of the differing political regimes in control of the government and regardless of what outside attempts are made to influence them.

I wish to thank the Graduate School of the University of Minnesota for several grants enabling some of the research for this study.

Table of Contents

Modern China's Foreign Policy

The Inadequacy of Old Practices

MANY decades of intense Western impact upon China were needed before an appreciable number of Chinese began to realize that the invasion of their country by the Western "barbarians" was different from all earlier ones. Paradoxically, the event which contributed the most toward making this realization crystallize was Japan's attack upon China in 1894. Up to that time the Chinese had had difficulty in comprehending that the Westerners and their ways had come to the Orient to stay and that there was no possibility of absorbing them into Chinese culture. Taking in the actual fact of Western permanence was a disturbing experience. The Chinese still conceived of themselves as the Middle Kingdom — not necessarily in a spirit of conceit, but as part of their world view. In the universe at large, they, highly developed in their civilization, lived at the center; surrounding them were tribes inferior and less developed. The standard by which the quality of other peoples was judged was the degree to which they patterned themselves culturally after the more fortunate Chinese.

The idea of the Middle Kingdom was therefore the expression of a pattern of culture which needed adjustment before a *modus vivendi* with the Westerners could be developed. Since the Westerners approached the Orient with similar ideas of superiority and had equally little understanding of the Chinese and their thoughts, the stage was set for interminable misunderstandings and frictions.[1] In the circumstances, friendly, let alone mutually beneficial, contacts were impossible. The prerequisite of normal channels of communications had still to be fulfilled.

The difficult process of adjustment was aggravated by the memories which the Western visitors of the sixteenth and seventeenth centuries had left with the Chinese.[2] These memories were refreshed, not changed, by the behavior of the visitors of the late eighteenth and early nineteenth centuries. These returning Westerners were no Confucian gentlemen,

3

a fact alone sufficient to make them contemptible to the Chinese. Many of them were not gentlemen from anybody's standpoint. Their rudeness, brutality, lack of cultural refinement, overbearing attitude, and undisguised greed shocked the officials. They lacked respect for things Chinese and had none of the humility of the customary tribute-bearers from the Asian countries under Chinese suzerainty. When the Westerners finally forced themselves upon the Chinese by the wars of 1839 to 1842, 1856 to 1858, and 1860, the Chinese did not acknowledge military defeat as Western superiority. On the contrary, the use of force merely confirmed their opinion of the barbaric nature of the Westerners. They therefore saw no reason to dignify the new invaders by departing from the methods traditionally applied to invading barbarians. But these methods had not been devised to deal with such insistent, stubborn, and militarily superior "barbarians" as the Westerners turned out to be.

The problem was most puzzling to the Chinese. There was no provision in the organization of the Chinese government for the conduct of foreign relations in the Western sense. There were no such relations. In fact, the Book of Rites ordained that "the officials of the Empire shall have no intercourse with foreigners." The China of the Manchu dynasty, beginning with 1644, dealt with neighboring states as a conqueror. She imposed conditions, exacted tribute, always passed judgment upon the rulers, and sometimes appointed them. The regular tribute payments to Peking, the key to the whole Chinese system of control, symbolized Chinese suzerainty and usually exhausted the duties of the inferior state. Dependencies such as Mongolia and Tibet were under the jurisdiction of the Board of Dependencies, the Li-fan Yuan, while tributary states such as Korea and Annam were dealt with by the Board of Rites and Ceremonies, the Lee Pu.[3] The rare negotiations with nations on an equal footing, such as Russia, were handled by the Board of Dependencies and the Ministry of Rites. In the absence of a proper office, the relations between China and Western countries from 1842 to 1858 were handled mainly by the viceroy of Kwangtung and Kwangsi, in whose territory Canton was located. Because of the importance of his task he received the additional title of Imperial Commissioner.

That the conduct of political and commercial relations with other peoples was left by the central government to viceroys and other provincial authorities was in part due to the unimportant and undignified nature of these relations in the eyes of the Chinese. This administrative

4

arrangement did not mean, however, that the central government was unaware of such relations. On the contrary, provincial officials acted on the authority of the central government and were strictly supervised. But they had a reasonably free hand in negotiations. When, for instance, Grand Secretary Yeh Ming-ch'en negotiated with the British in 1857 to prevent the occupation of Canton, an imperial edict stated that "the Viceroy has been in office in Kwangtung for a long time and is familiar with the barbarian state of affairs. He must be able to find means to restrain and handle the barbarians satisfactorily so as not to give cause for trouble. Here, at a distance, we shall abstain from interference." [4]

The corollary of this freedom of action was responsibility for success. It happened often that a viceroy lost his rank, and sometimes his head, if negotiations with the Westerners ended unfavorably for China. This strict control lasted until the end of the T'ai-p'ing Rebellion in 1865. Thereafter, owing to a shift of political power in favor of the viceroys during the rebellion, some of them — for instance, Tseng Kuo-fan and Li Hung-chang — became stronger and more influential than the government in Peking and began indeed to conduct their own foreign policies. Chinese foreign policy was then difficult even to speak of at times, for it was a composite of several individual or regional policies. [5]

The strong emphasis upon the personal freedom of action and the responsibility for success of the individual negotiator sprang immediately from the attitude that foreign relations were a matter of little significance. But it stemmed, more fundamentally, from the individualistic Chinese view of the nature of society. The Chinese found it difficult to conceive that an individual should be the mere mouthpiece of a collective unit called the state, that he should speak for an institution, in view of the fact that institutions exist to serve human beings and not vice versa. They also felt it unwarranted to interfere in the performance of a task before the end product was delivered.

This cultural, essentially Confucian background, led the Chinese to view and to conduct foreign relations as a highly personal affair. To de-individualize a man to the point where he became the spokesman of a group appears to have been repulsive to Chinese patterns of thought about the value of the human being, the nature of the human community, and the relation between the two. [*]

[*] It should always be remembered that these patterns of thought dominated only the educated class. The masses did not study Confucius, though through the

5

Individual psychology was therefore an important tool of Chinese diplomacy. To the Confucian statesman international relations, like all social relations, were relations not between groups as such but between the individuals who conducted them. He felt, moreover, on much safer ground handling them on that level. For he knew little about the political conditions of the world and a good deal about human nature and human relations. The ideal of the Chinese had for centuries been the integration of man into the harmonious order of the cosmos, an integration a man could achieve by perfecting himself into a balanced and harmonious person. The Chinese had thus acquired a deep insight into the nature of man and had become experts in handling and judging people. This stress upon the importance of the individual had led to the conviction that the solution of social problems must be found in the manipulation of human beings, treated as individuals.

Applying this conviction to their international relations, Chinese officials regarded a knowledge of human nature, not of world politics, as the most requisite tool of foreign policy. They felt that they must aim at satisfying foreign diplomats personally if they wanted to satisfy the diplomat's nation. This concept explains the long and detailed descriptions of the characters of diplomats which can be found in the official reports of Chinese negotiators. It also explains the practice of personally rewarding or punishing individual diplomats in the attempt to obtain results in international negotiations.[6]

It is not surprising that this manner of handling contacts with the aggressive Westerners should considerably limit the success of Chinese policy.[7] The Chinese could hardly help noticing the inadequacy of their approach.[8] Its continuation was due partly to the difficulty of changing centuries-old habits, partly to incomprehension of the new situation, and partly to some virtues which the Chinese discovered in it.

The indirection resulting from conducting foreign relations through the periphery instead of from the center of government proved to be the saving grace of the Chinese approach, so much so that the viceroys refined it further by using officers inferior to themselves, at times down

influence of their rulers they may have acted according to the same moral doctrines. Since the educated class was also the ruling class, Chinese politics were dominated by Confucian doctrines. Cf. Lily Abegg, *The Mind of East Asia* (London, 1952), pp. 104–105; C. P. Fitzgerald, *Revolution in China* (London, 1952), p. 152; Junyu Kitayama, *West-Östliche Begegnung* (Berlin, 1942), p. 36; Otto Franke, in Alfred Bertholet and Edvard Lehmann, *Lehrbuch der Religionsgeschichte* (Tübingen, 1924), p. 255.

to personal servants, in negotiating with foreign diplomats. This hierarchy of officials served as a buffer between the foreigners and the central authorities ultimately responsible for foreign policy. Reliance on it was extremely helpful as a delaying tactic. The officials could do reconnaissance without committing anybody. They could prolong the bargaining process and assist in the petty tricks and annoyances with which they sought to soften up the adversary. Above all, they could reduce foreign pressure upon Peking in the process of its transmission. The whole treatment weakened the personal status of the foreigner and permitted the central government to remain complacent, superior, and undisturbed. But the viceroys were often pushed from both sides and so bore the brunt of the situation. They could rarely determine policy according to their own light and better knowledge of the foreigner, for fear of reprisals from Peking. In many instances, therefore, their role became that of mediator between two contending forces rather than that of representative for the one side.[9]

Through this system, direct access to Peking was barred to foreigners, physically as well as diplomatically. Until 1860 foreigners were restricted to sojourn in the five ports opened by the war of 1842. They found the situation humiliating, as it was, of course, intended to be, and ultimately intolerable. They decided that for reasons of prestige and the fullest utilization of commercial possibilities, their direct contact with the highest officials in Peking was necessary.[10]

Such an arrangement, it appears from later events, would probably have been more favorable to the Chinese as well. But they could hardly have recognized that at the time. Only those actually negotiating with the foreigners had begun to realize that the "barbarians" wanted trade rather than conquest and that by a different Chinese policy a compromise might be reached. But when they advocated policies to this end, they got into difficulties with Peking because Peking still acted in the belief that the foreigners were aggressors and conquerors and that only a policy of denial and defense could be successful. There was such an abysmal ignorance at the capital that some officials even believed Westerners to be physically different from themselves.[11]

The behavior of the Westerners did nothing, of course, to alleviate Peking's suspicions, born of ignorance and fear, and to disclose the almost purely commercial motivations behind the Westerners' presence in China. How could the Chinese officials guess that the foreigners

7

wanted trade when they waged wars, cooperated with Chinese spies, traitors, and opponents of the regime, seemed inaccessible to bargaining propositions, were always ready to fight, and made inexhaustible demands?[12]

To the minds of most Peking statesmen the situation was clear. China was faced with unwarranted aggression, to which the only answer was outright opposition. Suspecting the physical superiority of the aggressor, Peking aimed therefore at keeping relations with him to a minimum or, if possible, to have none at all. Every means that promised fulfillment was welcome: procrastination, intrigue, deceit, obstruction, interruption of contacts, little tricks of all kinds, personal embarrassments to the foreign diplomats, appeasement, even occasional generosity, and, above all, inciting rivalry among the foreigners themselves. "Using barbarians to control barbarians" was an old rule in the Chinese textbook on politics. Its application was discussed as soon as the insistence of the Westerners upon staying in China proved impossible to overcome.

Commissioner Lin Tse-hsu, whose unfortunate task it was around 1840 to keep foreign opium out of China, used the jealousies among the foreigners in Canton to arouse one against the other. He suggested the policy — quite beyond China's means to execute — of inducing Russia to attack India, and of getting France and the United States to attack Great Britain. Another official, a little later, advocated the opening of more ports to foreign residents in the hope that their dispersal might weaken their solidarity. France received concessions in her first treaty with China in 1844 as a bribe for French aid against Great Britain. In short, the idea of playing one power against the other came in Chinese minds to be an important element in foreign relations.[13]

All methods of frustrating and circumventing the intruders were employed with a great show of politeness. Occasionally generosity was added to politeness in the hope that the magic of example* might yet induce foreigners to comport themselves in the same manner. More often, however, Chinese behavior had little of the magnanimous about it, magnanimity being entirely unwarranted. Foreigners therefore called it immoral, unjustifiably, though understandably in view of the cultural

* This was the application to international relations of the general principle strongly held by the Chinese that example has a great influence on the character of a person — good or bad, depending on the nature of the example. Following Wilhelm Richard, "magic" rather than the more common "virtue" is used here for the Chinese term.

differences between the Chinese and them. These differences lay not in the substance of any particular moral concepts but rather in their applicability.

To the Westerner, in theory at least, morality is total in the sense that it should govern human behavior at all times in all situations. To be moral is a matter between the individual and God. It is an absolute and eternally existing obligation. To the Confucian Chinese, morality is applicable to specific personal relationships recognized by Confucianism as in sum composing society. Relationships outside these categories, those between officials and diplomats among them, are amoral. Moral judgment cannot be applied to them.

The basis of Chinese conduct in matters relating to foreigners, therefore, was not a code of ethics but a conception of human nature. Depending upon what in their judgment the situation demanded, the Chinese might antagonize and annoy foreign diplomats or they might be kind to them, flatter them, and try to oblige them by sheer kindness. They would not hesitate to create relations of cordial intimacy, even joviality, if that served their political purpose. While they were acting thus out of expediency and a spirit of condescension, the foreigners usually congratulated themselves on their clever handling of the Chinese and thought they had been accepted.[14]

The impression should nevertheless not be gathered that the Chinese had a master-plan for dealing with the foreign threat and that all their actions were based on an ingenious scheme. Scheming was indeed what many foreigners suspected at the time. Had they been able to look behind the scenes, they would have found confusion and bewilderment in which the only stable factor was the desire to avoid contact with the Westerners. In governmental councils there was perennial vacillation between peace and war, between appeasement and opposition. The Peking officials had great difficulty in moving out of their traditional patterns and meeting the new challenge with new policies.[15]

When the foreigners began to sense the fundamentally negative and antagonistic attitude of the officials, they abandoned peaceful diplomacy in most cases and developed the habit of applying force or the threat of force to get their way. This practice was rationalized on the grounds that the Chinese "yielded nothing to reason, but everything to fear," as Lord Elgin expressed it, or that "diplomatic intercourse," as the American minister reported home, "can only be had with this government at the cannon's mouth," or, as the Russian minister Ignatieff formulated the same idea, that China had to be taught a "lesson of force." [16] To the Chinese, who did not think that they were unreasonable at all but who merely wanted to be let alone, this approach by the foreigners was just another reason to reduce Sino-Western relations to a minimum.

Because of ignorance, different habits, and relatively superficial cultural differences, therefore, the first two decades of Sino-Western relations set an unfortunate pattern for the future. Yet misunderstandings and the absence of channels of communication were not the only cause of the tensions that arose. They arose partly also from clashes of interest, though these were less real than they appeared on the surface. The Chinese felt threatened in the sphere of their political-strategic interests, on which they had definite and inflexible views. The interests of the foreigners were very largely commercial, but were expressed in political terms. The major interest of each side was thus in a different, not necessarily conflicting, sphere, but it was pursued almost entirely in the political sphere. The resulting conflict appeared much more difficult of reconciliation than in reality it would have had to be.

Relations might have developed more smoothly had the foreigners made clear that their demands and activities were intended to be essentially commercial. The Chinese were used to these and had few objections. Trade was below their dignity, it was despised and not deserving their serious attention. Merchants were useless and nonproductive people with little standing in Chinese society. Self-respecting people would not degrade themselves by dealing with them. "The petty affairs of commerce are to be directed by the merchants themselves, the officers have nothing to hear upon the subject," stated the governor of Canton to his emperor.[17] As long as the merchants, native or foreign, stayed within their bailiwick, they could presumably pursue their interests undisturbed.

The Chinese government never regarded international trade as a means of enrichment and never sponsored it until westernization had made considerable progress in China. But it knew that the barbarians of the border states were anxious to trade, and so it happened that their desire was used as a political means to keep them under control through the modification (over a period of centuries) of the tribute system.

In return for trading privileges the neighboring tribes and peoples paid tribute to China. The advantages accruing to China through this arrangement were many. Relations with neighbors were peaceful, and the Chinese in the border regions were protected against raids. Security was achieved in a more politic and cheaper way than by fighting. Tribute payments implied a recognition of the superior status of the Chinese emperor and the Chinese way of life and permitted a type of peaceful and effective control which could not otherwise be had. The tribute-bearers brought valuable news, and on trips to dependent countries Chinese officials could gather it. On such visits they could also exercise influence in crucial political matters — for instance, in the selection of a new ruler while they attended the funeral ceremonies for his deceased predecessor. So the tribute system was a useful diplomatic mechanism. It was a tool for colonial administration. It was an instrument of governmental power in the category of "Awards and Punishments." It had functioned successfully for centuries because the desire for trade among the "barbarians" was endless, and the more keenly the "barbarians" wanted to trade, the better did it function. According to Chinese interpretation, therefore, it was bound to work best with the Western "barbarians." For they, so the Chinese believed, could not get along one day without Chinese silks and rhubarb, whereas foreign articles entering China, Commissioner Lin informed Queen Victoria, "can only be used as toys. We can take them or get along without them." [18]

Economically, the tribute system was a deficit enterprise for the government. The tribute-bearers were feasted at court. Imperial gifts were bestowed upon them while their companions traded in the frontier provinces. Occasionally the system represented a program of aid to needy neighbors, similar to the Point Four Program, and founded to a large extent on the same principle: to keep the neighbors satisfied and obviate the need of raids into the more prosperous Chinese territory.

For the most successful functioning of the system, the trade had to be controlled by the government. Riots that might be caused by unscrupulous merchants had to be prevented. Military information had to be withheld from merchants crossing the borders. Trade had to be made rewarding enough to the "barbarians" to retain its value as bait, in application of the ancient rule "Covet nothing of far-off lands and peoples of far-off lands will submit themselves to you." * A further reason for the

---

* There was a basic hypocrisy in the whole system. While the literati despised trade, they must have known that trade needs two parties. While the government maintained the system as a political-diplomatic mechanism, it recognized the existence of Chinese merchants by regulating their activities. The merchants and officials

control of trade, not directly related to the tribute system, may have been the desire of the ruling class to preserve an agrarian, self-sufficient society. Such a society did not need trade, which could only lead to its destruction.

Because the tribute system as a diplomatic device had been effective for centuries — even when applied to the visiting Portuguese in the sixteenth century — the Chinese had got the idea that it was adequate to handle every kind of "barbarian." They had developed a false sense of security, and they hung on to the system with great tenacity after 1842, when objectively the conditions for its survival were changing completely. Their growing awareness that the ambitions of the Westerners and the new kind and volume of their trade would force the abandonment of the tribute system had no immediate effect upon their traditional conduct of affairs. The spirit of the tribute system permeating Chinese officialdom long outlasted the conditions of its successful application.[19]

From the traditional mentality sprang many of the maneuvers of the Chinese to cope with the problem the Westerners posed: the attempts at "control by negotiation," the measures to regulate trade, the restricting of foreigners to residence in open ports, the constant reminders to them of the unlimited economic opportunities offered by China, the suggestion (in 1858) that free trade be granted to prevent aggression. Fear and general uneasiness were produced by the failure of these time-tested approaches effectively to control the Westerners. The difficulties in negotiating the first treaties were less owing to the demands of the foreign powers for commercial privileges or extraterritoriality than to their requests for such things as permission to reside in Peking — requests that ran counter to Chinese mores. The viceroy negotiating a treaty in 1844 with the American Caleb Cushing was instructed by imperial edict to announce that Americans could not go to the capital, that "in controlling barbarian peoples the Celestial Empire always follows old rules," and to explain this "kindly and refuse their requests by just reasoning." [20]

Political relations were viewed by the Chinese in an altogether different light from economic relations. Tributary relations were the only political type they had known for centuries. They had not had and did

in the localities visited by the tribute-bearing people were anxious to trade. Trade was a great help in filling the local private and public purses. Some details of this trade with Great Britain are discussed in Michael Greenberg, *British Trade and the Opening of China 1800–42* (Cambridge, 1951), pp. 75–103.

not want international relations in the Western sense. These were considered a nuisance if not an actual danger to the Empire. This conception had originated in the eleventh and twelfth centuries when China was weak and harassed by northern tribes. The very understandable reaction to these events had been the development of the dogma that "national security could only be found in isolation and . . . that whoever wished to enter into relations with China must do so as China's vassal, acknowledging the supremacy of the Chinese emperor and obeying his commands, thus ruling out all possibility of international intercourse on terms of equality." [21] This dogma, stemming from very concrete interests, fitted neatly into the doctrine of the harmonious order of the universe, of which China was the Middle Kingdom. By the time the Westerners came to China, the refusal to establish equal political relations had become a matter of ideology as well as of interest. Such relations simply did not fit into the Chinese view of the world, they could not exist. They were contrary to the preordained order of things. The Chinese could hardly understand either why anybody should object to the arrangement. In return for their submission, the "barbarians" received imperial compassion as a reward. If they did not comprehend or appreciate this arrangement, if they did not like it, all they had to do was to stay away from China.[22]

Behind the obstinate Chinese refusal to alter ancient political customs lay an additional, more materialistic consideration. The demand for equal treatment by the foreigners struck at the roots of Chinese society and threatened to undermine the position of the ruling classes.

The emperor, ruling by the Mandate of Heaven, was above all men and equal to none. "As there is but one Sun in the visible heavens to rule the day, so there can be but one man to rule all the people." When the emperor condescended to extend his benevolence to his own people or foreigners, it was only fitting that the recipients of such favors should show their gratitude, just as the emperor showed his to Heaven. The symbol of this action was the kowtow, which was interpreted by the Chinese not as a degradation but as a recognition of the natural order of things.[23] The granting of equality to foreign diplomats at the court would overthrow the whole social order, would indeed amount to a social revolution. Its consequences for the social hierarchy were unforeseeable. They had to be prevented at their point of origin. Foreigners could not be treated as equals.

The Chinese officials could see very quickly that if a barbarian was equal to an official, many Chinese were as well. The class structure which supported the officials' pre-eminent position would collapse. Furthermore, the officials realized soon that the infiltration of Western ideas would endanger the foundation of their preferred status, which consisted in a monopolistic knowledge of the classics. As Chester Holcombe has pointed out, Confucius was the literati's only capital and stock in trade. "Reduce Confucius to his proper level, as a wise man twenty-five centuries ago, but antiquated and valueless when compared with the needs and the leaders of modern days — do this, and the entire Chinese literary aristocracy is made bankrupt." [24]

The literati's vested interest in the *status quo* was threatened by the aggressiveness of the foreigners and especially by the demands for equality. There was no escape, as there had been for the ruling class of Japan, in accepting Western ways. For the ruling class in China was not a closed corporation. It could be joined by anybody who presented the passport of classical knowledge and passed the examinations. To obtain this passport was difficult enough to make the monopoly reasonably tight. But the literati feared — and they feared quite rightly* — that with the infiltration of the Westerners would infiltrate new ideas.[25] When an intellectual proletariat should arise, possessing ideas and knowledge more useful for the solution of contemporary problems than the literati possessed, they knew that they would lose their monopoly of political power.

To make the establishment of friendly contacts between Chinese and Westerners even more difficult, the structure of the Chinese government, as well as the character of the people who controlled it in the middle of the nineteenth century, represented a serious handicap. There existed — although sometimes only in theory — a few traditional features of government which would be called liberal from the standpoint of a modern democracy and which should have resulted in some flexibility. An emperor could be deposed if he had lost the Mandate from Heaven, a provision which meant, in practice, if conditions in the country were unsatisfactory.† There were censors to criticize the actions of the govern-

---

* Not all the literati were motivated by egoistic considerations. Many had a strong pride in their culture and tried to protect it against foreign subversion.

† The emperor's rule by Mandate of Heaven was primarily a device to control, not to strengthen, that rule. For the criteria by which it was decided whether the emperor still possessed the Mandate were his good example and the country's wel-

ment. The civil service was open to all qualified candidates. The villages had a large measure of self-government. These features, however, had little effect upon the conduct of foreign policy; they did not make governmental procedures more adaptable to the requirements of the day. More important, they did not affect the fundamentally authoritarian nature of the emperor's position and the highly concentrated power of the central government. The presence of a few enlightened, progressive officials in the provinces had little influence upon the policies emanating from the court as long as the court's power lasted. And while it lasted it was strong. The barriers to strict central control represented by long distances and poor communications were overcome by clever organizational devices: frequent changes of officials, a system of checks and balances within the administration, the planting of spies and informers. The emperors, or whoever in fact took their place at the center, reigned and ruled.

Unfortunately the emperors of the nineteenth and twentieth centuries were mostly antiforeign and were, by education and training, steeped in tradition and fixed in rigid forms of behavior. These characteristics were good politics at the time the Manchu dynasty took over in 1644. In its anxiety to conciliate the Chinese, it preserved everything in China as it found it. But in the course of centuries this devotion to the past became empty and detrimental formalism. The arrival of the Westerners in the middle of the nineteenth century created irrevocably new conditions. Yet it was fifty years before the residents of the imperial palace were ready to accept this fact and adjust to the situation.

The more politic and far-seeing imperial advisers, who may also have been antiforeign but who were shrewd enough to realize the Westerner was not going to go home, usually lived away from the capital and in parts of the country where they had an opportunity to study foreigners. It was difficult for them to influence decisions at the court. Besides, tendering advice was risky, for any suggestion contrary to the policies which had guaranteed success for centuries would have been considered

fare. For these he was responsible to Heaven. Since Heaven spoke and acted through the people, he was in reality responsible to the people. Because of this concept, Chinese rulers have been sensitive to the Voice of the People, notwithstanding the absence of modern channels for the expression of public opinion. See Eduard J. M. Kroker, "Die Legitimation der Macht im chinesischen Altertum," *Sinologica*, III (1952), 129–144; E. V. Zenker, *Geschichte der chinesischen Philosophie* (Reichenberg, 1926), I, 56; and *Soziale Moral in China und Japan* (München, 1914), p. 29.

damaging to the foundations upon which Chinese society rested. There were officials who had recognized the futility of physical resistance to foreigners twenty years before the British started the first war against China.[26] Ideas such as Commissioner Lin's in 1842 to translate Western books, to modernize the army, to build shipyards and arsenals, were revolutionary and unacceptable, for they implied that the barbarians had something worth imitating.[27] Most officials with ideas running counter to the court's did not dare to speak up forcefully. They confided only in their most intimate friends. Their fortune depended upon the emperor; they had nothing to expect from the people. And the emperor was surrounded by reactionaries whose clamor for war and against the appeasement of foreigners drowned out the few guarded hints of some progressive and daring provincial officials that changes and reforms were needed.[28] The chances of these officials to get a hearing* improved only after the T'ai-p'ing Rebellion had weakened the central government[29] and after the military defeats by the Westerners in 1842, 1858, and 1860 had persuaded even the most reactionary Chinese that thought would have to be given to a constructive policy to meet the new conditions.

These defeats showed that the haphazard methods, the use of palliatives, the temporizing, the treatment of foreign relations as an obnoxious side issue were no longer possible. The signing of the treaties of Tientsin in 1858 was in part a result of this realization. These treaties opened up further cities to residence by foreigners, improved the opportunities for commercial and missionary activity, and above all finally established the foreigners' right to equal treatment, proper diplomatic representation, and direct access to the highest offices of the Empire at the capital. The growth thereafter of Sino-Western contacts and of the need to regularize them could easily be foreseen. The British in their settlement at Tientsin therefore obtained a promise from the Chinese that a high officer would be nominated with whom business might be transacted. Out of this agreement developed an agency resembling a foreign office.

The creation of a foreign office was suggested by H. N. Lay, a British interpreter at the time the Tientsin treaties were concluded and later the first inspector-general of the Chinese Customs. Prince Kung and some of his colleagues, who knew foreigners from past negotiations, sent a

* As a result of the defeat in 1842 the court showed, for a moment, some signs of realizing that ships were needed for defense. It must be remembered that aggression from the sea was something new to the Manchu dynasty.

memorial to the emperor in which they advocated the creation of a foreign office. They pointed out that the "barbarians" had evacuated the capital after securing their treaties. They "really do not covet our land and people; they can still be managed with faith and justice; their nature can still be tamed." These pleadings were resisted only feebly by the war party at the court, which had been subdued by the military defeat, and they overcame the court's desire to grant the foreign powers a status no better than that of Korea and Annam. In 1861 the Tsungli Yamen, an office devoted to dealing with foreigners and international relations, was created. Prince Kung, uncle of Emperor T'ung Chih, assisted by two high officials, became the first head. Major policy decisions, however, remained the prerogative of the Grand Council.[30]

One problem arising immediately was the shortage of people qualified in foreign languages, educational background, and diplomatic skill to handle the day-to-day business of international relations. It was solved by the establishment of the T'ung Wen Kuan in 1862. This institution started as a school for interpreters. Five years later, through the addition of other disciplines, especially Western sciences, it developed into a college for the training of officers for the foreign service.

The creation of machinery for dealing with the Westerners by no means indicated a fundamental change of heart on the part of the Chinese rulers. The most potent argument in support of it had been that one must know one's enemy in order to defeat him. Prince Kung pointed out in his memorial asking for the interpreter's school that a knowledge of English was the "sole means to protect ourselves from becoming victims of crafty imposition."[31] There is plenty of evidence that animosity was still the fundamental motivation of the Chinese.

In order to negotiate the peace treaties of 1858 and 1860, and before the creation of the Tsungli Yamen, an office, the Fu Chu, was created as a branch of the Department of Territories. "Fu" here signified the government in its paternalistic implications, a sign that the emperor continued to harbor ideas of superiority. A trace of this could be found also in the long full name of the Tsungli Yamen, which was, strictly speaking, an office to regulate commercial relations with foreigners — relations, in other words which in Chinese eyes did not have the dignity of political relations. The office was not listed in the official directory of Metropolitan and Provincial State Offices (The Red Book) until 1890.

The spirit permeating the Tsungli Yamen and dominating its officials

17

further confirmed foreign suspicions that the creation of the office did not signal an altogether new era in China's foreign relations. The board members of the office, from seven to ten in number, were all high officials, many of whom were also connected with the Grand Council, the highest organ of the state. This distinguished membership, however, was not a way of honoring foreigners. For invariably the officials considered their Tsungli Yamen positions inferior and less important than their others and even undesirable. Their task of denying foreign demands and at the same time of avoiding any serious consequences from such denials was superhuman, and was certainly unpleasant and unrewarding. Consequently the turnover in the membership of the Tsungli Yamen was rapid, and not one official left without a loss of prestige and influence. Occasionally appointment to the office was a punishment, especially for those who had criticized the Tsungli Yamen and who were to be shown how difficult it is to get along with foreigners. The officials soon concluded that the easiest way to remain on good terms with the court was to elude responsibility, to tergiversate, to prevent results. Their efforts to this effect were facilitated by the rules that all members of the Tsungli Yamen had to pass on every decision, that at least three members had to be present during negotiations, and that (so it was maintained) no member was permitted to speak first. Among foreigners the office got the reputation of being an institution for the prevention of business transactions.

Even when there was willingness to negotiate, results were difficult to achieve. The meetings were extremely formal. Chinese officials were ignorant of foreign affairs. There were no social contacts between Chinese and foreign diplomats, so that informal talks for formal agreements could not take place. To an extent, therefore, the inefficiency of the Tsungli Yamen was due to the novelty of the situation. But, one cannot help feeling, it was at times also deliberate. For when action was expedient from the Chinese standpoint, the office could be remarkably efficient. Nevertheless, during the first two or three decades of its existence, the Tsungli Yamen meant only a very slow change in official attitudes toward relations with the West.[32]

For a much longer period, the efficiency of the Tsungli Yamen was greatly reduced by the decentralization of political power which resulted from the T'ai-p'ing Rebellion (1851–1864). The viceroys emerged as powerful figures from the event and began to conduct their own, local foreign policy, often in competition with, sometimes in opposition to the Tsungli Yamen, though almost always maintaining a semblance of obedience to Peking. Such paradoxical situations resulted as that a foreign government quarreled with a Chinese province while being on good terms with Peking, that it was at war with a viceroy and friendly with his people, that a major city was being bombarded by foreign gunboats while official intercourse with the capital remained undisturbed.[33] The viceroys took advantage of this situation — for their own or the country's benefit — by accepting responsibility for decisions or shifting it to the center, as the occasion demanded.

The foreigners, after fighting for decades for access to Peking, began to appreciate the value of dealing with provincial officials, increasingly so as certain progressive viceroys became amenable to Western arguments and certain corrupt ones to bribes. The weakening of the central government facilitated foreign penetration of the whole country. The foreign mercantile community, especially the British, enjoyed and fostered this split between the central and provincial authorities. Yet for fear that the country might actually fall apart, foreign governments much of the time supported the central authority as a countermove.[34] A bewildering situation developed in which the Peking government, the viceroys, the foreign merchants, and the foreign governments each pursued their own policies.

To the contemporary outside observer, the Chinese scene was further confused by the conflicting popular attitudes taken toward foreigners throughout the nineteenth century and by his ignorance of the causes. The vast mass of the Chinese people had no contacts with foreigners at all. Where there were contacts, they were usually friendly. Clashes seemed ordinary only because they received much publicity. To interpret them as a crude form of foreign policy conducted on a disorganized mass basis would certainly be erroneous. Such an interpretation assumes the existence of a public opinion based upon a set of facts which were entirely inaccessible to the Chinese public in the second half of the nineteenth century.*

As far as the masses were concerned, the effects of centuries of seclusion continued deep into the nineteenth century. The results of the new conditions — in the form of opium-smoking or unemployment due to the

---

* Occasionally, it is true, antiforeign riots were inspired and organized from above.

importation of foreign goods — were usually felt before people ever knew about the change. How could they know about it? Their government did not inform them. A Chinese press did not develop until the 1870's. The official gazettes were read mostly by those who were officials or who expected to be and perhaps by some merchants. Very little information on China's foreign relations could be gathered from them anyhow. The newspapers and magazines which began to appear in the last quarter of the century had, at least until about 1895, only a few hundred readers, the majority of whom were foreigners and Chinese merchants dealing with foreigners. They contained gossip about officials, local news, poems, advertisements of amusements, and practically no important news about internal or external politics. What political news there was originated with the government and could not be commented upon. The closest approach to an expression of public opinion came from the Public Readers, wandering from town to town, or was to be found in the placards stuck on the walls in villages and cities. These placards were usually anonymous, unrestrained, and provocative in language, criticizing the government or foreigners, but offering little news. They were often a very effective means of propaganda for the personal grievances of those who paid for them, and they dealt with the affairs of a geographically limited area, but they were not informative.[35]

In the face of this general lack of information, any explanation of antiforeign riots on the basis of centralized instigation and nation-wide organization is unlikely to be true. In most riots there was no noticeable prearranged coordination. If at times they covered a relatively large area of the country, the reason is that they spread like contagious disease because local grievances made people ready for them. Typically these riots were local, turning upon local issues, and usually participated in by only a small section of the local population. Their causes can be found in local complaints of an economic and social kind, occasioned mostly by nature, bad government, the influx of foreign goods and ideas, or all three combined. Traditionally the wrath of the people was directed against their rulers. Now the rulers, national or local, sometimes found in the foreigners a convenient scapegoat to deflect that wrath.

Very frequently, antiforeign violence was an attempt to prevent a real or imagined interference with local life. The village of the average Chinese was his world. When the foreigner disturbed that world, he ran counter to a strong sense of local autonomy and feeling for tradition and was resisted. Anybody, foreign or Chinese, coming from the outside and behaving as the foreigner did, would have received the same treatment. Foreigners usually fared no worse than imperial messengers meddling in local communities.

There is little need to look for deeper causes than these to explain most of the antiforeign riots in the nineteenth century.[36] It is even doubtful whether the riots were directed against foreigners as foreigners rather than as disturbers of the traditional way of life. Most certainly concern over the preservation of China's sovereignty did not incite the people to violence. That concept had as yet no meaning to them. China was still a civilization rather than a nation. Nationalism and the sense of national community that it implies were totally absent.

During the first few decades of Chinese contact with the West in modern times, the role of the people was essentially that of pawns in the game. The international implications of antiforeign feeling among the people and of antiforeign riots were apparent only to the foreigners, the government, and those provincial officials who occasionally provoked them or had to suppress them. Most Chinese were preoccupied with their own daily troubles in the local sphere. They were glad to leave national strategy to the rulers to whom was assigned the task of running the country. Many years were to elapse and many shocks to be administered to China before the Chinese people began to develop a unifying national consciousness. Only then could the government and the governed unite in a common front against foreign aggression. Only then could there be that reliance on popular support without which the government could not successfully develop a new approach to the country's international problems. In the meantime the government, with the help of a small group of the literati and the gentry had to rely upon its own inadequate resources and limited imagination to formulate and execute policies that might guarantee the continued existence of a peaceful Chinese Empire.

Any audit of China's international account between 1842 and 1899 must have shown the government how pitiful its efforts in this direction had been. The country lost three wars against combined Western powers, had to cede the Amur region to Russia, lost Annam to France, Burma to Great Britain, and the suzerainty over the Liu-ch'iu Islands; was defeated by Japan, with serious consequences to its financial and territorial status; and had to grant unheard of favors and privileges to foreign powers on its own territory. These spectacular events highlighted the failure of governmental attempts to cope with the foreign problem and stimulated thought among ever widening circles about more effective policies and the creation of internal conditions to secure their execution. The fact that an international problem existed for China simply forced itself at last upon the Chinese people, the educated first and the uneducated soon after.

2

Developing a Foreign Policy

THE recognition that the traditional methods of dealing with foreigners were inadequate and the search for new ones led the Chinese quite naturally to an examination of the Western culture that was proving so indigestible and superior in many respects. Their approach, even after formal channels of communication had been created in the 1860's, remained hostile and resistant to acculturation or change of attitude. The hostility was by no means always an obstinate affectation of contempt or a rationalization for the maintenance of vested interests. It often rested upon a genuine belief in the higher values of Chinese culture. But the force of circumstances made the penetration of new ideas inevitable. Certain progressive Chinese began to show a willingness to accept Western achievements, especially of the technical kind. They began to re-examine traditional concepts and beliefs. This softening of the old rigid refusal to dignify anything Western even by giving it attention was the first step toward sounder relations with the West.

For a long time, however, no change in foreign policy resulted. In its early stage the appreciation of Western achievements was not comprehensive enough to include Western peoples. Years would have to elapse before appreciation broadened to that extent.[1] As always in the contact of cultures, it was easier to accept technical advances than to adjust psychologically to the new. The innovations which the Chinese leaders accepted from the West, slowly and hesitantly between 1840 and 1860, more quickly in the decades following, were used to bolster old Chinese policies rather than to alter their substance. The central government renovated and westernized its façade, but only to appease foreigners and to hide better its continuing opposition to foreign contacts. Peking still wished to have nothing to do with foreign powers. The spirit of its policy changed much slower than its means and methods, and throughout the 'sixties and 'seventies the old antagonism prevailed.

The determination of the court to have nothing to do with the West was reinforced by the events of the T'ai-p'ing Rebellion, the peasant revolt which occurred between 1851 and 1864. Though the rebellion, fundamentally the expression of misery of many kinds, was primarily an internal affair, international relations were involved both through the aims of the rebels and the role foreigners played. The rebels fought under the banner of certain pseudo-Christian doctrines and social, partly Western-inspired, reforms. To the orthodox Confucians at the court and among the literati this banner was a red flag. Their hatred of the rebels extended to the Westerners, because without Western influence — so they reasoned — there would have been no rebellion.[2] This opinion seemed substantiated by the sympathy the Western powers showed for the rebels at first. Though in the later course of the rebellion the Chinese government, for selfish reasons, asked for foreign help, which was granted, also for selfish reasons, this help did not ingratiate the foreigners any further with Peking.* On the contrary, the Manchus hated foreigners even more for having to depend upon their assistance. Dependence hurt their pride and lessened still more their waning prestige.

Weakness and fear deepened the inherent dislike felt toward the intruding West. During the period from the Tientsin treaties in 1858 to the time, twelve years later, when their renewal was due, China's foreign policy remained characterized by uncertainty regarding the aims of foreigners in China and by resistance felt to be futile even by those offering it. In 1858 a high Chinese official summed up the situation prevailing then and for many years to come when he wrote to a friend regarding foreigners, "As I estimate the situation, if we grant their requests, then we bow our heads and take their orders; if we do not grant them, then they will do whatever they want to do."[3]

Yet the defeats of 1858 and 1860 and the intensification of Western impact hastened the gradual breaking down of psychological resistance to the West. The more progressive and enlightened officials dared to expound their ideas with greater frankness, although they still had to hedge and apologize profusely.† The 1860's became the years of "self-strengthening" and even the imperial palace was touched by the new

* Foreigners here initiated the policy of supporting in China whoever promised them the greatest advantages together with the best chances of realizing them. This usually turned out to be the "strong man."

† After every major defeat that China suffered the court appeared more liberal and progressive. This was usually, however, the opening of a safety valve rather than a real change of heart.

24

atmosphere. A good indication of what appeared to be a new spirit was the "secret correspondence" which took place in 1867 and 1868 between the Tsungli Yamen and a number of high officials of the Empire in which the nature of China's future foreign policy was discussed.[4]

The Yamen's letter was divided into several sections. The first dealt with the advisability of granting foreign envoys an audience with the emperor. The Yamen favored it and so did the majority of the officials, though many included the proviso that the step should be postponed until after the regency was terminated and the young emperor had come of age. The second section dealt with the usefulness of permanently stationing Chinese diplomats abroad. The Yamen favored this too, on the ground that you should "know your enemy as yourself," an idea which had already motivated a Chinese negotiator of the Treaty of Nanking in 1842 to befriend the foreigners.[5] Most of the officials also were favorable, but it took seven more years before plans were made.[6]

The third section of the Tsungli Yamen's letter dealt with the right of foreigners to construct railways and telegraph lines. The Yamen felt such rights should be denied, and the officials shared this opinion. The fourth section concerned the demand of foreigners for permission to open warehouses and business offices outside the treaty ports and navigate inland waterways with their steamships. These demands were opposed by the Yamen and, in general, by the officials. Their main arguments were that such an arrangement might be harmful to Chinese merchants and would make it difficult to keep foreigners under control. The fifth section dealt with the right of foreigners to mine salt and coal. There was general refusal to grant the right regarding salt, because the government's monopoly was an important source of income. The majority were also opposed to foreign mining of coal. However, some of the more progressive officials, Li Hung-chang among them, could detect some advantage in letting foreigners modernize coal mines and coal production, provided that foreign activity could be kept within bounds.

The final section of the letter dealt with the prospect of expanded missionary activity in China. The Yamen complained that too often missionaries had gone beyond the limits set by the treaties. The letter may have suggested that missionary activity should secretly be counteracted. That this was the meaning of some cryptic remarks in it appears from the fact that antimissionary activities began to increase at this time. Most officials were opposed to an expansion of missionary activity, though their reasoning differed. Many resented missionaries as trouble-makers. Many recognized the high quality of Christian principles but felt that the disadvantages in having the missionaries present outweighed the advantages. Basically these officials did not seem to take very seriously the effectiveness of missionary activity, and there was as yet little fear of any social disruption due to the influx of new ideas.

These Chinese leaders seemed willing to make concessions to the foreigners which would presumably not affect any considerable section of the population. But they were worried about popular reaction and anxious to prevent anything which might arouse the public. This concern to leave the public undisturbed was widely shared and appears over and over as a factor in determining decisions on a high level. None of the officials involved in the "secret correspondence" could be called radical. Fundamentally their attitude was cautious, in many respects even negative. Yet the discussion certainly gave evidence of ideas that would have been considered heretical a few decades earlier. Progress was undeniable. It was even more noticeable in philosophical debates and in the adoption of technical innovations during the period 1860 to 1900. Developments in these fields benefited greatly from the freer atmosphere resulting from the T'ai-p'ing Rebellion and the consequent loss of power by the court and from the challenge the rebellion presented to the two-thousand-year-old political and social system.[7]

The philosophies which were being developed during this period ended eventually in the reform movement and a modernization of Chinese life. They all were erected upon Confucianism, which retained its strong hold over the literati. The anti-Confucianism of the T'ai-p'ings was unique and did not represent a trend. In fact, their "un-Chinese" ideology, while raising false hopes among Western missionaries, antagonized the literati and was probably a major cause of their failure. The literati dissociated themselves from the rebels, and the masses could not be lured away from their traditional values and beliefs by the mixture of Christian and primitive-communist ideals offered by the T'ai-p'ings. Confucianism remained the ideological foundation of Chinese culture. But it began to be reinterpreted in several different ways and to be used by some of the leaders for purposes of their own.

All the new variations of Confucian doctrine, however, showed some similarities. They invariably struggled with the problem of intercourse with the West. What the Chinese found most difficult to adjust to was the restlessness and insecurity which accompanied technological progress. Had the technology of the West been a static pattern, they might have made a supreme effort to absorb it and relax. But the unending change was most disturbing — what seemed to them the subordination of life to technical progress especially so. Life never seemed permitted to settle down in the West. Yet the moral and contemplative life was what the Chinese wanted to preserve at all cost and what they felt was the price the West had paid for its material progress. They would not abandon it and felt certain they did not have to.

They did not doubt the basic compatibility of Confucianism with Western technical means and institutions. To strengthen a China founded on Confucian teaching was their object in favoring Western innovations. China's weakness was felt to be strictly economic and military, capable of being overcome with the help of Western achievements. Thereafter, other things being equal, the moral superiority of Confucian doctrine over anything the West had to offer (of which the Chinese knew little) would reassert itself. Indeed, the great moral weaknesses of the West, its materialistic outlook, its class struggles, its religious conflicts, its nationalistic rivalries, would of themselves lead to the triumph of Chinese teachings. After reason had regained control over man,* the progress of mankind would continue, but it would be a moral progress whose last stage would be world peace and world unity. The reconciliation between Western material, mechanical achievements and the Chinese way of life was eventually rationalized through recourse to the traditional philosophical concepts of the dichotomy of root and ramification or the dualism of substance and function. For, as Hellmut Wilhelm put it, "To acknowledge western superiority in the sphere of the ramifications leaves Chinese superiority in the sphere of the root intact." [8]

That the creation and use of the coveted technical achievements might be an integral part of an altogether different culture seems at first to have occurred to a few Chinese only at rare moments. Many did, how-

---

* How important Chinese ideas on the "unreasonableness" of foreigners were for the conduct of Chinese foreign relations can be seen from the words of Marquis Tseng, spoken on the eve of his departure as minister to England and France: "The difficulty in the treatment of foreign affairs lies in the inaccessibility of foreigners to reason . . ." (Quoted by A. Vissière, "L'Audience de congé du Marquis Tseng à Peking," Revue d'histoire diplomatique, XVI (1902), 183.) The Western diplomats in Peking had the same complaints about the Chinese.

ever, realize, especially after China's defeat by Japan in 1895, that westernization could not take place in the material sphere of life without some adjustment in the spiritual. Upon the degree of this adjustment, then, turned the debate.[9]

All shades of opinion were represented. There were reactionaries who advocated modernization only up to the point where a renewed seclusion of China could be made more successful; on the other hand, there were radicals who wanted to create a new China with the retention of only the most fundamental philosophical aspects of purest Confucianism. There were even a few revolutionaries who wanted to discard Confucianism altogether. However, when the end of the century came, the extremists on either side were only small minorities, and early in the twentieth century the reactionaries disappeared.

The middle group could be divided according to the degree of their desire to retain features of Confucianism and their willingness to accept Western institutions. K'ang Yu-wei, Liang Ch'i-ch'ao, T'an Ssu-t'ung, and others of the group responsible for the foundation of reform associations and reform parties in various parts of the country, favored the retention of Confucian ethics and an application of Confucianism in the light of the practical experiences of everyday life. Government was to be a tool, not a testament; it must adjust to the ever changing conditions of life. These men had very eclectic theories, attempting a synthesis of the elements from Confucianism, Christianity, and Western philosophy that might be most desirable for their country. Their specific proposals for a new political order amounted largely to a retention of the forms suggested by Confucian doctrine (as interpreted by them) and the introduction of the substance of Western political institutions.

Another group, with Chang Chih-tung and Ku Hung-ming as members, were more conservative. They were willing to accept Western technical achievements but wished to retain Confucian ethical and political ideals (as interpreted by them). The need of changes in China's spiritual life, which they admitted, could be fulfilled, they thought, by a return to pure Confucianism, cleaned of all the falsities and perversions to which it had been subjected in the course of more than two thousand years.[10] Most of the officials and the men in power at Peking could be placed to the right of this conservative group.

Where these differences originated can only be guessed. Philosophizing had been an old pastime in China. The spiritual roots of many reformer-philosophers went centuries deep. Practical application of thought had been the spirit of almost all philosophy under the Manchu dynasty [11] and it was particularly apropos at this juncture in Chinese history. The urgency of finding a practical answer to China's problem and the fact that many of the philosophers were simultaneously acting statesmen blurred the dividing line between philosophy and practical politics. Considering the temper of the period, objectivity and abstract theorizing became an impossibility. The personal involvement of the individual in the political events of the day was bound to color his opinions.

Many Chinese felt that the defense of Confucianism, however understood, against a foreign culture claiming equality, if not superiority, was vital for the survival of the country. To them, the permissible degree of change became a matter of life and death to China. Others defended Confucianism knowing that if Chinese learning and the old institutions diminished in importance, their own positions of respect could not be maintained. Yet others pretended adherence to Confucianism to maintain a popular following. "We do not really believe in Confucius," a high official once confided in Chester Holcombe, "but the ignorant masses hold him in the most profound regard, and hence we appear to worship him, and we quote his sayings, in order by these means to hold the populace in subjection." [12]

But whatever motivated the individual and however much expediency may have influenced his philosophy, the debate showed in every case an awareness that the traditional views were bankrupt and that adjustment was necessary. In its early stages, the debate took place on a high level and among only a few, though important, Chinese. But as it moved on and as the danger to China's existence from abroad increased, it became more pragmatic and interested wider circles, leading eventually, toward the end of the century, to the Reform Movement and the modernization of China.

As the radius of the philosophical debate grew wider, changes, more easily observed, were taking place also in the fields of technology and defense during this period of 1860 to 1900. They were accompanied by much less controversy. It was easier to win acceptance of, or at least acquiescence in, technological innovations than it was to create a hospitable atmosphere for Western ideas. Technological advance was less objectionable to the conservative Chinese, and it affected only a small

29

fraction of the population. To superimpose these innovations on the existing pattern without disturbing traditional concepts and customs seemed not impossible. Even reactionaries could see the conveniences and benefits to themselves in the use of some of the new science. Besides, the innovations were on such a small scale that they did not constitute a ferment of any social consequence. They were not worth any resistance by the leaders; yet they were adequate in many instances to strengthen the personal regime of those who created and controlled the factories, arsenals, and shipyards.

"Industrialization" was at first the enterprise of a few forward-looking individuals, prominent among them Chang Chih-tung when he became governor-general of Wuchang in 1889. He established the Han-Yeh-P'ing iron and steel works and several cotton mills, silk factories, and tanneries. Other factories were similarly the creation of a few aggressive, and frequently selfish, officials. The mass of the Chinese were untouched by these developments. According to uncertain estimates in 1896, none of the factories, including the twelve cotton mills, had more than thirty employees. And many of them belonged to foreigners and were operated in the ports.[13]

Some advances toward industrialization were made in the field of communications. With a view to improving the defenses of the country, railroads and telegraph lines were constructed, and a postal system was introduced. Defense, at any rate, was the argument advanced to overcome the resistance of local officials who objected to modern communication systems either because they feared that stricter central political control would result or because they were superstitious and distrustful of modern gadgets. In 1896 China had approximately 250 miles of railroad.

Somewhat more notable as examples of industrialization were the numerous arsenals and navy yards built in many parts of the country. Their construction was mostly an aftermath of the T'ai-p'ing Rebellion, when the central government was weakening and local lords were developing regional centers of power by the creation of their own private armies.* But though political motives and not a desire for modernization lay behind their getting built, the arsenals and navy yards did represent a step toward industrialization. Quite unexpectedly and indirectly they

* The government gave its first approval for the building of warships on July 14, 1866.

also contributed to modernization. Their functioning required trained manpower. Consequently schools were attached to them in which foreign languages were taught so that Western technical books might be used. For the training of officers, especially the naval personnel, Western treatises on history and international law were translated. And so, while the schools produced mostly generals and admirals, a few scholars were turned out as by-products. These scholars were responsible for the introduction of many important Western works in philosophy and the social sciences.[14] In the course of time students began to attend Japanese and Western universities in ever larger numbers. They were usually sent to study the useful arts, but they could not avoid bringing back subversive social ideas. Many a reformer and revolutionary arose from the ranks of these young men, sent abroad by a conservative government for the purpose of learning how to defend the country and the established order against enemies from within and without.

In the face of perennial attacks by the modern armies and navies of the foreign powers, many Chinese officials realized the woeful inadequacy of their own national defenses. They devoted themselves to the improvement of the Chinese forces whose efficiency alone would justify the expense for arsenals and navy yards.

The idea for a Chinese navy was born during the T'ai-p'ing Rebellion, though a few Chinese had advocated the building of ships in China as early as the 1840's. In order to check the supply of arms to the rebels, the government had chartered foreign vessels, manned by foreign officers. In 1862 the suggestion was made to the government to organize a navy in order to fight the T'ai-p'ing rebels, and H. N. Lay, then inspector-general of Customs, was instructed to buy on behalf of the Chinese government a small fleet of British warships and man them. Overstepping his instructions in good faith, he enlisted British sailors and made them responsible to himself alone. He thereby offended Chinese national pride as well as disturbed internal power relations. The ships, and soon thereafter Mr. Lay, were sent home.[15]

This episode did not discourage the sponsors of a Chinese navy, mainly Li Hung-chang and Tseng Kuo-fan. They continued to work for the idea, and in 1885 a Board of Admiralty was created. To give it a *raison d'être* a few ships were bought. "The fleet," however, was and remained in pitiful shape. Empress Dowager Tsu Hsi used most of the money appropriated for the building of the navy for the reconstruction of the summer palace. Jealousy among the officers was intense, and they enjoyed the defeat of a colleague more than a victory of their own. The sailors would hesitate to obey the orders of a superior not from their home province. There was among them, foreign observers reported, no sense of tradition "to render them useful, no martial spirit, no disgrace for the coward, no honour for the valiant." They obviously were influenced, in spite of personal courage, by the Chinese adage that one can do many things upon meeting the enemy but the best is to run away.[16]

The spirit of the common soldier was about the same, and the organization of the army contributed little to its improvement, though attempts in that direction were made between 1860 and the end of the century. At the time the T'ai-p'ing Rebellion broke out, in 1851, the formal organization of the military establishment was hardly different from what it

China and adjoining areas

was in the days when it was created by Emperor K'ang Hsi at the turn of the seventeenth century. The army of the Manchu dynasty, the Bannermen, was the core of the garrison forces in Peking and the key provinces. It was supplemented by the Chinese provincial armies, the Green Standards (originally composed of rebels and volunteers anxious to defeat the Ming dynasty). Their total strength was estimated from the payrolls — traditionally padded for the sake of larger appropriations — at not quite 300,000 Bannermen and a little over 600,000 Green Standards. Their main function was to defend the country and the dynasty. Yet, when they had to fight foreign armies or local rebels, they usually performed miserably. One of their generals had this explanation, "The army has never recovered from the disorganization caused by the want of success in the 'barbarian affairs' [Opium War] so that the troops do not attend to order; regard retreat on the eve as 'old custom'; and the abandonment of places they should hold as an 'ordinary affair'." [17] This decay among the troops had its parallel in the chain of command from the Ministry of War down to the provincial governors and commanders who were responsible for the armies in their bailiwick. The army decayed with the decay of the administration in general.

The inefficiency of the governmental troops led to the creation of local forces as the need arose. Sometimes the government itself used these forces, sometimes they were used against the government. In the T'ai-p'ing Rebellion, as soon as the gentry took a stand against the rebels, they were used on behalf of the government. As the rebel armies were growing, these local forces proved inadequate. Li Hung-chang and Tseng Kuo-fan, advised by General Gordon and the British diplomat Sir Harry Parkes, supplemented them with new regional armies, the Hunan and Anhwei forces, organized on a militia basis. These two new armies, the Braves, were the first Chinese forces to resemble a modern army. They were recruited from farm boys and from among the younger professional soldiers willing to fight. In return they received better pay than the regular "soldiers," and a strong indoctrination of Confucian ideology. The government never succeeded in gaining control over these regional armies. Together with the local forces, they became a challenge to the central power and contributed greatly to its weakening and to the increased strength with which the provincial governors emerged from the T'ai-p'ing Rebellion. The growth among them of an *esprit de corps*, modernization with the help of Western advisers, and relatively

33

honest and unselfish leadership made them fairly effective.* They could not, however, compare with Western armies.[18]

These first steps in the modernization of China between 1840 and 1895 were largely the work of a few highly placed individuals, assisted occasionally by well-meaning and sometimes overoptimistic Western friends.† They were undertaken essentially for the purpose of supporting an as yet poorly defined and mostly traditional foreign policy. This purpose they failed to fulfill. They affected very few Chinese. The technical improvements were minuscule compared to China's needs and completely negligible as a factor in foreign relations. But since they were remarkable from the standpoint of Chinese cultural traditions, they got much contemporary attention. The spiritual struggles among the Chinese elite and the consequent changes in concepts and attitudes were less spectacular and received less notice. Nevertheless, in the long run these turned out to be more important and to have more lasting effects. To this period belong the conception and the first stirrings of a new spirit which was destined eventually to improve China's status among the powers. But the spirit was born, and in time developed into an effective force, only through the defeat which China suffered at the hands of Japan and the humiliations to which she was subjected by the Western powers between 1898 and 1921.

* These armies were pulverized during the Sino-Japanese war in 1894–1895. The army which was reorganized thereafter was a return to the system of provincial forces.

† For example, the Burlingame mission to the West on behalf of China in 1868.

3

Foreign Impact and Reform

THE unhappy course of Sino-Japanese relations during the second half of the nineteenth century, culminating in the war of 1894–1895, was a great disappointment to the Chinese. They were persuaded to sign a treaty of friendship and commerce with Japan in 1871 in the hope that it would lay the foundations for close and friendly relations with a neighbor and fellow sufferer. They felt then, as they have often felt since, that the Western nations were the common enemy of both countries. Japan, they feared, would be made a Western base of attack against China. Cooperation between them would improve the chances of both to resist foreign aggression. In no case, so the Chinese argued at the time, must they pursue a policy which would drive Japan into Western arms. Japan's proposal for the treaty must therefore be accepted while it was made in a friendly spirit. Otherwise, the Chinese were given to understand, Japan might force itself upon China with the aid of the Western powers. This unfriendly hint turned out to be only a prelude to most unfriendly acts. The Chinese, who had hoped to learn from Japan's westernization by close association and cooperation, learned indeed, at great expense to themselves, what Western influence had made of Japan.[1]

In 1874, a year after the ratification of the Sino-Japanese treaty of 1871, the Japanese engaged in a succession of expansionist drives which ended in war within twenty years. They organized a punitive expedition to Formosa against some natives who had allegedly maltreated shipwrecked sailors from Japan and the Liu-ch'iu Islands, over which the Japanese claimed control. As a consequence, a dispute arose between China and Japan over the suzerainty of these islands. It was settled in 1881 when China acquiesced in Japan's claim.

To the Chinese these affairs had their greatest importance mainly in relation to Korea. Korea was the cornerstone of China's policy toward Japan at that time. While there was a good deal of helplessness, wavering, and indecision in Chinese foreign policy, there was never any doubt in the minds of the Chinese statesmen that Korea must be kept out of the hands of all powerful nations, whether Japan, Russia, or any other. Its strategic position as the gateway to Manchuria, hence to northern China, was fully appreciated. Korea was the wall protecting China's three eastern provinces, said Li Hung-chang in 1879; it was "the lips protecting the teeth." An invasion of Korea was feared more than one of some coastal province of China proper. China's naval building program was patterned to match that for the Japanese fleet with a view to protecting Korea. Li Hung-chang consistently warned the Tsungli Yamen about the Japanese (and Russian) menace to Korea. Even the war with France over Annam and Tonkin in 1884 and the Russian temporary occupation of Ili in Sinkiang in 1871[2] were to the government less important concerns than the potential dangers to Korea were.

In the dispute over the Liu-ch'iu Islands, Li Hung-chang had stated to the Tsungli Yamen that in themselves they were "insignificant," but that a firm stand was important because "the precedent of aggression might be applied to Korea later." Regarding Formosa he thought – in the optimistic vein typical of many Chinese statesmen of the period – that Japan was "not likely to resort to war without first negotiating with us," but that war, if Japan wanted it, was "more likely against Korea." He even went so far as to consider the possibility of a preventive war to safeguard Korea.[3]

But China was in no position to undertake any such adventure. On the contrary, her policy had to be based on weakness, and the Chinese statesmen were aware of that fact. On that premise, close friendship with Japan was most desirable. The ambition of Japan, however, frustrated this desire, and China had to ward off her bellicose neighbor by diplomacy. This was of a characteristic kind. She engaged in attempts at appeasement by offering Japan economic concessions. There was procrastination through endless negotiations and exchanges of notes. There were eternal consultations within the Chinese government between the reactionary and progressive factions of Chinese officialdom, with the inevitable indecision on policy. Above all there was an undue reliance upon foreign aid. This was solicited in the form of mediation, as, for instance, when General Grant was asked to intervene in the Liu-ch'iu case and the Russians were similarly approached in the Korean crisis shortly before the outbreak of war, or it was in the form of tempting foreign interests to settle in areas threatened by an aggressor, as in the case of Korea.* The sudden show of firmness in sending an army to Korea in 1884 and in the inauguration of a "strong" policy — short of war — to reassert Chinese control over Korea was an unusual and quite temporary phenomenon. The step itself could succeed at the time only because the Japanese were not yet ready to oppose it.

Most of the time, and especially in the crucial initial stages of the Korean crisis, Chinese policy was half-hearted, owing presumably to weakness. But there were other reasons, though they may not have been more than rationalizations. The Chinese desired to maintain the traditional policy of noninterference in Korea and not to go beyond the discretion befitting a suzerain. They were averse to increased contacts with Western powers via Korea. They also wanted to spare Korea the curse of unequal treaties which, they thought, would descend upon that country if they took too prominent a part in Korean affairs. They decided, therefore, that it would be preferable to influence Korea's policy secretly toward an avoidance of conflict with Japan.

They were well aware that this policy was not the most desirable. Forthright action on behalf of Korea, if need should arise, was dictated not only by the strategic importance of the area but also by the bad precedent which would be created if China failed to protect a dependent state. But they were also aware of the complete unpreparedness of the country to wage war, in spite of some tough talk by Li Hung-chang to the effect that China would rather go to war than let Korea be taken over by another power.

When war appeared inevitable, Li took stock of the Chinese position. He found Japan well prepared and China's forces inadequate. But he also realized that after the Formosa and Liu-ch'iu affairs another appeasement of Japan would be useless. Sooner or later the Japanese would be after Korea and Manchuria. Since the reactionary court officials were convinced of China's military superiority and since there was some justified hope of foreign, especially British, assistance in a war, Li reluctantly chose war with Japan.[4]

* The belated Chinese offer to the American government early in the 1880's to arrange a treaty between Korea and the United States was not so much an attempt to attract American interests to Korea, however, as a countermove to the prior offer of Japan to the same effect. The Japanese were working hard to undermine Chinese suzerainty over Korea, and to be recognized as an intermediary by the United States would have been a great success.

The diplomacy and conduct of the war had many of the features characteristic of China to this day. In the negotiations leading up to the conflict, the Chinese expected too much from others and too little from themselves. Any willingness of Japan to discuss or negotiate was taken as weakness and the advantage pushed to an extreme. The risk of a break was chanced in the expectation of foreign intervention. China miscalculated by assuming that foreign antagonism against Japanese methods would overcome selfish national considerations and would outweigh foreign sympathy with the purported reformist aims of Japan in Korea. She did little to prepare for the emergency or to cope with it even while it existed. Time and Patience were expected to settle the matter. The usual shock leading to outcries, recriminations, and general excitement but rarely to constructive action was in this case provided by the defeat at the Yalu River and the crossing of Japanese troops into Manchuria. Li Hung-chang was blamed, the intervention of foreign powers was solicited, and the festivities for the celebration of the empress dowager's sixtieth birthday anniversary were called off. That was all.

Lord Curzon summed up the situation, which was to recur many more times in China's history: "From the Palace downwards there was no centralization of authority or responsibility, no unity of counsel, no agreement as to action, no plan of campaign. Stupefied bewilderment, helpless inertia, or arrogant contempt for the invader prevailed alternately, sometimes simultaneously in every Yamen. Each man was absorbed in the effort to get the better of somebody else, and to make something for his own pocket out of so paying a concern as a campaign. Viceroys swindled governors, governors swindled generals, generals swindled subalterns. There were infinite and delicately shaded grades of peculation. Of patriotism or enthusiasm for the war, or loyalty to the dynasty, or self-respect for the race there was not a sign. Chinese telegraph clerks sold important information to the Japanese. Chinese officers accepted bribes to retreat or to surrender. Nobody thought of China. In the first resort a man cared only to save his face, in the last . . . to save his skin," and so Curzon goes on.[5] There was nothing to show for the millions of taels spent on building up an army and navy. As a high Chinese official put it to Sir Robert Hart, "The lid has been taken off the box, and there's nothing in it," but some "very big folk" were making money.[6]

Shocked by the evils disclosed during the war, many Chinese joined the ranks of the reformers, who felt encouraged to bring the issues before the people. They declared westernization responsible for Japan's success. The argument strengthened the hand of those reformers who advocated a minimum of Confucianism and a maximum of Western institutions. They were given some freedom to agitate for their ideas as a safety valve for an aroused "public opinion," which meant the small group of educated Chinese. They also had some support in high circles. Many officials favored reform. They and their sympathizers encouraged the emperor by sending petitions to him, asking for all kinds of reform.[7] Some of them even hoped that Japan might occupy Peking in the course of the war and force the court to introduce reforms and open the country to trade and residence by foreigners. The peace treaty of Shimonoseki (1895) disappointed them, mostly for what it did not stipulate. They were afraid its provisions* would not affect the mass of the people, hence not arouse them to demand changes. The opening of only a very small number of ports to foreigners demanded by the Japanese would not materially enlarge contacts with foreigners and would leave the country as a whole unaffected.[8]

The reformers could, however, take some fleeting encouragement from the fact that the empress dowager seemed to have become somewhat sympathetic toward reforms, perhaps remembering her younger days when she was not disinclined toward moderate changes. She called Prince Kung back to the highest office in the Tsungli Yamen during the war, though he was known to favor many reforms.† When the Grand Council nullified all his reform schemes, she went further and appointed him president of the Council, a step which enabled him to force the schemes upon that unwilling group.[9]

The chief reform agitators were the scholars and propagandists K'ang Yu-wei and Liang Ch'i-ch'ao, who were gaining fame just when Sun Yat-sen was failing in organizing the first uprising of his revolutionary societies in Canton in 1895. They were actively supported by many younger Chinese and had the benevolent patronage of older progressives, such as Chang Chih-tung. Their literary output was enormous. It was

* Korea was to be granted independence (a first step toward its annexation by Japan in 1910), Formosa and the Pescadores went to Japan, the Liaotung peninsula was temporarily lost (it was later returned to China, thanks to the intervention, in China's favor, of Russia, France, and Germany), and damages were imposed upon China.

† It is also true, however, that it was customary for the court to change responsible officials when a given policy had failed and a different policy was to be tried.

augmented by the many periodicals which made their appearance at this time. K'ang Yu-wei's motto was characteristic and quickly put into practice, "It is better to share learning with a group than to have learning by oneself, and it is better to share this learning with the millions of the masses than to share it with a group." [10] The reformist press, of various shades of opinion, flourished and penetrated into all parts of China. The reformers had recognized the value of the press for their cause. Unfortunately for them, so had the reactionaries at the court in Peking, and they quickly attempted to ban the publication of these periodicals. Though they did not succeed, their influence was still sufficiently strong for the time being to prevent any substantial reforms from being introduced.

The conservative rulers did not permit the defeat by Japan to benefit fully the reformers. They tried to counteract any deep impression the defeat might have made upon the people. It was either explained away as the result of natural and unavoidable disasters or actually falsified into a story of victories — a type of propaganda which made it easy for large sections of the people to remain self-complacent. Many officials outwardly assumed the same attitude, though well aware of the disaster's real significance. Unpleasant facts were overcome by rationalizations, and face was saved toward critical foreigners by pointing out that in spite of defeat and the absence of reforms, the European powers were eager to trust the Chinese with large loan funds — sufficient proof of the Empire's sound condition.[11]

Generally speaking and as far as action was concerned, the Sino-Japanese War brought no awakening to Peking. The central government gave no indication that the lesson had been learned. Some observers doubted whether the rulers had the capacity to understand recent events. "A more hopeless spectacle of fatuous imbecility made up in equal parts of arrogance and helplessness, than the central government of the Chinese Empire presented after the actual pressure of war had been removed, it is almost impossible to conceive," reported the London *Times* correspondent, and a Frenchman remarked, "Avant la guerre la Chine dormait sur une oreille; aujourd'hui elle ronfle sur les deux oreilles." [12]

Many of the officials who had originally favored some reforms even turned against the reform movement, adjusting to a postwar trend which they thought they sensed in high circles. Conceivably, as some observers maintained, the reformers missed a good opportunity for their cause during the war by weakening the dynasty and its advisers, the strongest opponents of reform. The Manchus were under pressure and the feeling against them, which was supposed to prevail especially in south China, might have been mobilized to drive the reactionaries from the court. On the other hand, the split between the Chinese and the Manchus may have been exaggerated in European minds, anti-Manchu agitation was still a risky enterprise, and the reformers were not opposed to the perpetuation of the Manchu monarchy as such. In other words, they may not have wanted to use that kind of opportunity to introduce their reforms.[13] At any rate, the reform movement lost many adherents and much of its impetus in the years following the war. Only the enthusiastic K'ang Yu-wei and his disciples kept it alive. Their endurance was rewarded in 1898 and 1899, when the scramble of foreigners for concessions and privileges administered a new shock to official China and pleas from reformers fell on fertile soil.

This was the moment when it was widely assumed that the end of China as an independent nation had arrived. The Chinese melon was being carved up in one of the worst cases of unadulterated imperialism in modern times. With the brutal methods they had become accustomed to using in dealing with China, the Western nations — Russia, Great Britain, France, Germany especially — and Japan forced the Chinese to grant leaseholds of territory along the coast, which became wedges for the creation of spheres of interest in the hinterland. The foreigners then forced the granting of rights to develop and exploit these areas as they saw fit, without regard to Chinese interests. At times economic control was accompanied by political influence and the behavior of Western nations was hard to distinguish from colonialism. Agreements between the Chinese and foreigners, usually unwillingly entered into by China anyway or obtained by bribes, were nominal and merely served as pretexts for the most outrageous demands by the latter. On occasion, foreign nations made agreements with one another concerning Chinese affairs without even consulting China.

Young Emperor Kuang-hsu, reigning in Peking but ruled over to a considerable extent by his aunt, Empress Dowager Tsu Hsi, was greatly concerned about the Empire's integrity when the scramble for concessions began. Many educated Chinese shared his concern and they flooded him with petitions to resist the incessant demands of foreign powers. At this opportune moment, K'ang Yu-wei was brought before the emperor and permitted to influence him in favor of very radical reforms. The situation seemed most favorable for change, and the public temper, so it appeared to these enthusiastic young leaders, was ready for it. "In the spring of 1898, all the younger members of the mandarinate and the gentry were reformers." [14] Many advocated cooperation with the foreigners in order to use their superior methods and weapons against them,* a policy which was often confused by foreigners with pro-Westernism. They favored inviting British and American technicians to advise them because they felt that these two nations, being most sympathetic to China's aspiration for modernization, would be the least selfish. They even suggested a military alliance with Great Britain.

The emperor and his friends paid special attention to Japan, where developments had led so rapidly to liberation from foreign controls. They were anxious to learn "the secret" of Western superiority which Japan, apparently, had found out. Chinese-Japanese relations became friendly. The Japanese were willing to assist their neighbors toward emancipation. Of the many means which were employed to establish closer ties and to overcome Chinese postwar hatred of Japan, none was probably more significant than the creation, toward the end of the century, of the "Society for the Common Culture of Eastern Asia." Western influence in a perhaps more palatable orientalized form thus percolated to China through Japan. The Japanese succeeded in rapidly converting their erstwhile enemies, the reformist literati, into admirers, if not followers. [15]

The Japanese Count Ito, however, on a good-will tour in China, realized better than the reformers that the pace of innovation was too rapid and that vested Chinese interests were being antagonized. He advised the emperor to slow down his reforms. [16] But the advice came too late. After one hundred days of continuous reform legislation, [17] the empress dowager and the older conservative court officials engineered a *coup d'état* in 1898 by which the young emperor became a prisoner, many reformers lost their heads, and most others had to flee the country.

Several reasons may underlie the failure of the Hundred Days Reform. Changes were introduced fast, probably too fast for a culture so tradition-bound as the Chinese. Enlightened literati, motivated by convictions, not selfish interests, opposed the changes as contravening traditional Confucian doctrine. Government, they argued, was based on

* This idea was suggested in Chinese writings as early as 1844.

personal example; men govern, not laws. Since laws cannot stand by themselves, a reform which merely changed laws, orders, regulations could do no good. The Chinese government was founded upon institutions established by wise and perfect royal ancestors, and the present rulers could not change it. Based upon moral force, the force of all forces, it could not be improved upon by the mechanical ways of the West.

This debate highlighted the difficulties of reform in general but hardly explains its failure in 1898. For it proceeded on a high, philosophical plane and among a small group. Indeed, the whole question of cultural change through reforms was unimportant, for the reforms did not even potentially affect the masses and never had a chance actually to affect anybody. Their failure can better be explained on several more practical grounds. The direct cause of the *coup d'état* appears to have been that the empress dowager learned of the emperor's plan to seize her. Support in the enterprise came to her from many members of the mandarinate and the gentry who had been antagonized by the reforms. Even those who had originally shown sympathy for the emperor's activities turned against him when they realized the price of the reforms to themselves. Finally, the behavior of the foreigners did nothing to help matters. Instead of meeting the emperor's desire for cooperation, they brought to a peak their demands for concessions, rights, and privileges, thus supporting the argument of the conservative officials that an appeasement of foreigners would only induce them to make further claims.

A *coup d'état*, however, could not reverse the trend of which the Hundred Days Reform was an expression. The Reform was more than an isolated and inorganic incident in China's history. It might be considered the counterpart, on the intellectual plane, of the T'ai-p'ing Rebellion on the plane of mass action. The later upheavals and catastrophies and the eventual introduction of reforms in the quieter days of the early 1900's by the very persons who opposed them in 1898 are proof enough that the time was ripe for changes. Impolitic handling and the clash of personalities, more than basic differences of opinion on the need of reform, were responsible for the failure of the emperor and his friends.[18]

The final outcome could hardly have been otherwise. After the many shocks China had suffered at the hands of foreign powers, almost any educated Chinese was bound to become sympathetic toward reforms. The inability of the government to hide from the masses China's humilia-

43

tion pushed it in the same direction. The increasing impact of Western culture inexorably destroyed the system of government which had resulted from Confucian teachings. The absence of political responsibility on the part of the governing had created self-complacency in them and indifference in the governed. While contact between official and citizen was slight and government affairs were of little consequence to the individual, the maxim that "Inaction is the secret of Government" could operate well enough to escape challenge.[19] But the situation was tolerable only as long as China was undisturbed from the outside and not seriously endangered by any aggressor. By 1900 conditions had changed. This time the attack was upon the very existence of the country, and the attacker could no longer be coped with by absorbing him into China's culture. If China was to survive, new methods of dealing with disruptive forces had to be devised. The gradual growth of this conviction on the part of rulers and ruled alike was the greatest single force propelling China down the path of reform and modernization.

The progress of reform was, however, delayed by the defeat of the leaders in the movement. The damage might have been more serious but for the fact that the doctrines had been picked up by the merchants, mostly the compradores, in the important trade centers. They represented the bulk of China's middle class. Like their counterparts in other nations at comparable stages of political development, they carried on the movement for reform (with the help of the original reformers, who had escaped and found refuge in Japan).

The material welfare of these merchants was closely tied up with foreign trade. They realized that a return to the good old days of seclusion would mean the end of their business. Their influence in Chinese politics was considerable, if somewhat localized. They were organized; they knew their aim; they were financially strong; and they were vocal. When, after the Hundred Days Reform, their country was threatened by imperialism from without and by reaction from within, they acted. They held meetings, especially at the time of Lord Beresford's stay in China, during the winter of 1898–1899, to discuss a Chinese program of action. Presumably without any outside influence, they assembled in many places and approved Lord Beresford's suggestions for China's salvation: administrative reorganization, a foreign-drilled army, and a policy favoring the Open Door and territorial integrity.[20]

Most of these influential merchants were domiciled in the center and south of China, for many centuries the seat of the more forward-looking part of the population. Between the *coup d'état* and the Boxer Rebellion, they were the only important group that dared to continue advocating reforms along Western lines. Influential officials who sympathized with the reformers — Chang Chih-tung, Tuan Fang, Yuan Shih-k'ai — had withdrawn to safety in time or had chosen the "right" side at the last moment. Another group of high officials who had been too clever to take a definitive stand and had tried to compromise with all sides, Li Hung-chang and Prince Ch'ing among them, remained silent and waited for the storm to blow over.

After the *coup d'état* the empress dowager surrounded herself with all the enemies of Western reform. Men like Prince Tuan, Kang Yi, Li Ping-heng were swept into positions of great influence. In the flush of success the official policy in Peking became rapidly antiforeign and extremely conservative in tone. But not quite so in action. There is some evidence that the strictly anti-Western terminology of the government was a reaction to the Hundred Days Reform rather than an absolute conviction that Western methods were inapplicable to China. After all, the hanging of the reformers had to be justified by a policy which seemed opposite to theirs. The empress dowager admitted in an edict of 1899 the superiority of the West in military, agricultural, mechanical, and commercial matters. These, of course, were matters below the dignity of the Chinese. Nevertheless the policy and the methods inaugurated by her government showed traces of the reformers' influence, even though they were designed to maintain the ruling groups in power. The main aim of eliminating foreign influence in China and preventing further aggression was now approached along four main avenues. The government initiated the development of an efficient army; it passed legislation to curb foreign activity in China; it made every possible use of friction between foreign powers; and it attempted to enlist the help of every nation whose aims happened to coincide with China's.

Reorganization of the army was accepted by the Peking government as its foremost task. As foreign intervention became more determined and importunate, the literati became aware of the inadequacy of the armed forces. They realized that an inability to defend the nation meant at the same time an inability to pursue an independent foreign policy. But the task of creating an efficient instrument of defense was encumbered with unusual difficulties, the results of a culture pattern thousands

45

of years old, and all the government's attempts to build a unified armed force failed.

None of the political, economic, and social conditions that before the war with Japan had made a national army impossible had by 1900 really changed. A principal factor in the failure of attempts to strengthen China's position had always been, and still was, the decentralization of Chinese military power and the spirit of provincial and local particularism prevailing. An episode occurring in 1895, at the end of the war with Japan, illustrates the anomalous position in which the government was put as a result of the lack of any central authority. In arranging details for the capitulation and surrender of the Chinese navy to the Japanese, a Chinese official found that among the ships to be handed over was the Kwang-ping, the only surviving vessel of three which had come north from the south before the war to participate in a naval review. The Kwang-ping belonged to Kwangtung, a province which had not participated in the war. The Chinese official therefore requested the Japanese to release the ship so that the rights of neutrals might be preserved! [21] The weakness resulting from this administrative decentralization was the crux of China's predicament in handling international affairs.

To overcome the disadvantages of decentralization, which by this time were fully understood, the Peking government toward the end of the century took various steps, most of which, however, had only the force of urgent appeals. The command over the troops around Peking was concentrated in one hand. The viceroys and governors were exhorted to mobilize men and materials to provide for emergencies. The provincial officials were invited to resist by force the encroachments of foreigners. They were asked not to cherish the fallacy that foreign demands could be satisfied peacefully. Rather, they should fight and not think of peace; they should unite behind the throne and offer a common front, irrespective of provincial jurisdiction or particular interest. Of a country which had not known nation-wide unity of action for centuries,[22] to ask such cohesion was to ask the impossible, and of course mere exhortation produced little effect.

At the end of the century the quality and size of the provincial armies varied considerably and usually depended upon the governor or viceroy. In its attempt at reorganization, Peking tried to improve the quality especially of those troops stationed in the areas the most likely to be attacked from abroad. The result was rather disappointing. The provincial armies, for the most part, remained inefficient, resembling an armed rabble more than a military organization. They could not be used outside a province without the governor's permission. Many of the governors used funds levied for the army for their own purposes, and the soldiers considered their jobs sinecures. Li Hung-chang, Chang Chih-tung, and Yuan Shih-k'ai were only exceptions to the rule. The dynasty itself supported an army, which was sometimes considered a national army because its support came from Peking. But in character it was a provincial army. By 1898 there were perhaps six armies in China which could be said to have military value. These were the armies of Chihli, of the three Manchurian provinces, of the northern frontier, and of Kwangsi, Yunnan, and Nanking. These few armies had European drilled cadres, and in an emergency the formations could be brought up to full strength by volunteers drawn from the provinces.[23]

The government was anxious to enlist foreign help for the education of the army. Prince Ch'ing, for instance, agreed with Lord Beresford upon the hiring of British military instructors for troops in the Yangtse Valley, although the empress dowager was opposed to the scheme. She feared both Lord Beresford's intentions and the reactions of other Western powers. Among high officials there was more sympathy with the idea of inviting Japanese military instructors. Peking actually requested the Tokyo government to send officers, provided that Japanese conditions were reasonable, and accepted a Japanese offer to establish a military academy in Peking.

The Japanese seemed as anxious as the Chinese government to see China's power of resistance grow. So eager were they, in fact, that some publicists suggested the protection of China by the combined Anglo-Japanese fleet until she should be strong enough to defend herself.[24] The assistance given by the Japanese, however, was motivated not by altruism but by expansionist ideals. They feared that a break-up of China into colonial areas might frustrate their ambitions on the Asiatic mainland and become a threat to their own security. Hence their solicitude for China's integrity at this time and for several years following.

Peking's second line of approach to the handling of the foreign problem, curbing the activity of foreigners, was foredoomed to failure in view of its inability to enforce its will. The government hoped to cure two great evils, the failure of the foreigners to develop concessions and their overexpansion of granted rights, by refusing to concede any further privileges and by strictly defining those already given. In December 1898 the government forbade all further concessions until all the old ones were exploited. In November of the same year new regulations concerning mining rights and railway enterprises were promulgated and made more stringent in August 1899. According to these regulations, permits to construct railways could not include mining or other rights along the railway line, and vice versa. The locality of a concession was to be strictly delimited and was not to include a surrounding, vaguely defined area. At least one half of the capital of any business was to be Chinese, and, irrespective of the amount of Chinese capital, the control of the enterprise was to be in Chinese hands. Any new concession had to be exploited within ten months from the grant. In 1899 a central bureau was established for the control of all railways and mines throughout the country. But neither the bureau nor the perennial renewal of such legislation * improved the situation very much,[25] nor has it unto this day.

This legislation presumed, as a very minimum, cooperation from provincial officials. It presumed that these officials would give up the profitable business of handing out concessions and would transfer this source of income to the central government. A very naive presumption. These edicts were never lived up to fully and certainly not at all in the first years of their existence. During that period foreigners ignored them and Chinese officials paid respect to them as expediency dictated. Besides disregarding internal conditions, such legislation ignored the dynamics of contemporary imperialism, which could not be stopped by action no stronger than paper edicts.[26]

The only method that worked at all well in preventing foreigners from accumulating further privileges was used by Peking in regard to treaty ports. According to Chinese interpretation, the special favorable treaty-regime governing foreign settlements had to be conceded only if a port was opened in fulfillment of treaty obligations. If a port was opened voluntarily, the Chinese retained the right to determine the regime. So, occasionally, when the Chinese felt that a demand for the opening of a new port was likely to be made, they anticipated the request and opened the port themselves.[27]

Altogether, the Chinese were not very successful in their attempts to preserve their interests by legislation. Too often they were either unable

* The latest, March 1944; see *New York Times,* March 20, 1944.

or unwilling to enforce what they had decreed. Foreigners certainly had no scruples about contravening the laws when the Chinese themselves did so, and the conscientious foreigner merely lost out to his less conscientious competitor and the venal Chinese official. The situation generated much dissatisfaction among all concerned and was favorable to none.[28]

That China was saved the fate of disappearance as a nation was to some extent due to the third of the policies she adopted in the attempt to preserve her integrity. This was the deliberate exploitation of the rivalries and suspicions existing among the various competing nations with interests in China. The foreign powers were jealously watching one another's activities. Mutual distrust was the outstanding characteristic of their relations. In this atmosphere of intrigue, secret diplomacy, and tortuous politics Peking could easily pit one nation against the other. The game was not new, but circumstances at the time of the scramble were favorable to playing it, and it was played now with a greater skill.

As a solution to China's problems, it was far from ideal. The policy was a costly one. But Peking's choice of political means was restricted, and a balance-of-power policy became standard in China from now on. Unable to restrain the powers herself, China tried to make them restrain each other. Unfortunately for her, in the end she suffered from such quarrels between other nations, and whichever of them won, she lost. For whenever one of them had acquired an advantage, the others consoled themselves by wresting new privileges from her and compensated themselves at her expense. The foreign powers seemed always to be able to find new ways of satisfying their imperialistic appetites. Sometimes they treated China with complete neglect and disdain in settling their rivalries. An early example of this was the Scott-Muravieff agreement of 1899 between Great Britain and Russia, which specified that these two nations would respect each other's sphere in the development of railroads in China. On this occasion the feeling of frustration and annoyance habitual to the Chinese government burst into open complaint. It refused to acquiesce in the principle that two nations could enter into arrangements concerning China without consulting the Chinese government.[29] The slur upon China's sovereignty implied in such behavior became the more painful as China's national consciousness developed, but this did not keep foreign powers from continuing it, and deals regarding China have since become common practice among the nations. Yet whatever the humiliation and the cost to China in this policy of hers of attempting to maintain some balance of power among the nations with designs upon her, without it she probably would have suffered a worse fate. The intentions of every aggressor were reduced by fear of what another power might do, as they would not have been by any consideration of the merely Chinese reaction. The ability to play upon such fears was often what saved China.

The fourth policy of China, an obvious one for her to adopt, was to enlist the help of nations which seemed friendly or which, at least, had shown an interest in the maintenance of her territorial integrity. The Chinese had no illusions about the meaning of "friendship" in international relations, though they often tried to exploit it to its utmost limits. They knew quite well that such friendship has a price. Usually, however, they were willing to pay it, though such consent was never arrived at without preceding long and bitter debate in the inner circles of the government.

Between the years 1898 and 1900, the Japanese seemed to be the most friendly of all foreigners to China and a *rapprochement* was attempted, largely for reasons of state, but also for reasons of personal interest to the empress dowager. Close relations with Japan seemed politically reasonable in view of the solicitude Japan was showing for China's fate and the assistance she was willing to give to Chinese endeavors to modernize. Her ulterior imperialistic aims were overlooked (except by the anti-Japanese faction led by Li Hung-chang and Jung Lu) in favor of the immediate benefits expected from the policy. The reformers particularly favored a Japanophile policy. But the reformers now had a different membership from the pre-*coup d'état* days. They lacked personal integrity and honest patriotism and were more intent upon securing their own advantage. Thus the motive of personal interest entered into policy-making. This was especially true of the empress dowager, who sided with the pro-Japanese because she hoped to obtain for the Manchus the help of the Japanese dynasty against both internal and external foes. Since she and not the Tsungli Yamen determined foreign policy, a pro-Japanese policy was attempted.[30]

On July 8, 1899, two Chinese commissioners left for Japan, ostensibly on a commercial mission. They carried valuable presents to the emperor and credentials entitling them to discuss an alliance. They hoped to secure China against foreign aggression by this alliance, though they were not without fears that serious protests would be provoked from other nations. They were correct. Russia informed Peking that an alliance with Japan might have the "most serious" consequences for China.

The Tsungli Yamen denied all knowledge of the mission. Tokyo declared all rumors of an alliance baseless and elaborated that the growing friendship between Japan and China would not be used for a racial war against the West but was only calculated to bring China into the comity of nations as a full-fledged member. The mission left Tokyo without having achieved its aim. The empress dowager thanked the mikado for his good wishes and for the friendly reception granted the mission. She pointed out that she was in great difficulties. The European powers were pressing her to give up certain portions of her country and she did not know how to satisfy their greed. England, she maintained, was the worst. England wanted the Yangtse Valley, encouraged Italy to demand Fukien, and forbade China to turn to Russia for help. The empress was now therefore turning to Japan with a plea for help and an alliance. In requital, she was prepared to accept Japanese officers for the Chinese army and navy and to give freedom of trade to Japanese ships and merchants.

This generous offer was not accepted. Freedom of trade, if it had been given to Japan, would have accrued to all nations having the most-favored-nation clause, whereas later Japanese policy showed that Japan wanted exclusive privileges. An alliance would have been a liability rather than an asset at this time, China being weak and Japan unready for military action. The consequence of the falling through of this alliance was typical. The empress dowager withdrew her sympathy from the pro-Japanese faction and bestowed it upon the pro-Russian faction.[31]

A few high officials continued to advocate a pro-Japanese policy. But to most it had become perfectly clear by 1900 at the latest that the westernization of Japan had proceeded to a point where Japanese imperialism equaled anything the West had to offer, that for China to tie herself to Japan was impossible even for the sake of learning Western ways that might enable her to resist aggression from elsewhere.[32] Finding no nation to which she could appeal for unselfish assistance, she looked forward with great interest to the development of an Open Door policy as obviating the need to woo any one nation.

4

Territorial Integrity or the Open Door?

T HE Open Door policy suited China for a number of reasons, not all of which were ideally compatible with the spirit of that policy. But then, every nation sought its own advantage in the policy, not the least its official originator, and China had no reason for being better than anybody else.

Possibly China's first contact with a policy under this name was in connection with the Li-Lobanoff treaty of 1896, in which Russia obtained the right to build the Trans-Siberian railroad to Vladivostock through Manchuria. Reportedly upon Chinese request, the treaty contained a defensive alliance against Japan, and an agreement was reached between the two powers to combat an Open Door policy in China. This information, as well as the nature of the understandings reached when the agreement was signed, is still subject to doubt.[1] But whatever the Chinese government's policy toward an Open Door may have been in 1896, there was no opposition to it in 1899 and 1900.

Early in November 1899 news leaked out about Secretary of State Hay's Open Door notes, in which he asked that nations having spheres of interest in China not interfere with the vested interests of other states, that customs duties be in accordance with the Chinese tariff, and that no preferential harbor dues or railroad charges be granted to citizens of the state having the spheres. Since replies had not yet come in, Hay refused to elaborate on the notes, but other officials confirmed the first reports as "substantially correct."

Uncertainty regarding the steps undertaken by the State Department gave rise to an abundance of rumors. The Russian ambassador, Cassini, was supposed to have brought with him from Europe an invitation to the United States to cut a slice off China so that the break-up could proceed undisturbed. Very mysteriously he neither confirmed nor denied the story. Another rumor was that the United States, Great Britain, and China had concluded an alliance to protect the Open Door in China.

52

Yet another was that the United States intended to ask for concessions in China if the powers should give negative replies to the Open Door notes. The last turned out to be more than a rumor.[2]

The Chinese government naturally was intensely concerned. Minister Wu Ting-fang in Washington watched closely over the goings-on between America and Europe. Peking feared that America's action might mean the final — favorable or unfavorable — decision on China's fate. Wu called on Hay asking for moral support of his country's struggle to preserve its integrity. Hay declined to promise such support, but took the occasion, apparently for the first time, to inform Wu about the notes. He told the minister that he had requested of the various powers with interests in China that there should be no interruption of American trade through treaty ports or anywhere in the interior of China. This was less reassuring to Wu than a guarantee of China's integrity would have been, and the fact that he put to Hay a request for assistance permits the conclusion that there had been no understanding between the American and Chinese government prior to the sending of the notes, and that the Chinese authorities were not consulted on the policy. This conclusion is further supported by the fact that the American minister in Peking, Conger, read of the Open Door notes in the newspapers before Hay's official information reached him on January 9, 1900. After he saw the news, he expressed pleasure in a letter to Washington and wrote that "so far as China is concerned, she is now and is likely to remain powerless in the matter, and attempted negotiations with her would be useless." [3]

In an interview Wu Ting-fang stated that he did not believe the United States would make territorial demands even if the replies to the Open Door notes should be unfavorable. On the contrary, he thought, the notes implied an American warning to the powers not to encroach further upon Chinese territory. American-Chinese relations had always been friendly and he was satisfied that the United States did not intend to obtain a foothold on the Asian mainland. In his opinion the American action was motivated by a desire to maintain friendly relations between the two countries and to preserve American interests in China.[4]

This interpretation was in part correct; in part it was either wishful thinking or a trial balloon to discover American intentions. If the references to friendship are written off as diplomatic verbiage, the accurate statement that the United States was acting in her own interest remains.

That interest was primarily to save as much as possible at this late date out of the progressing deterioration of China. To be sure, the United States government would rather have seen China free than a colony of European powers. But the Open Door notes of 1899 were not expected to prevent the worst. Rather they were intended to safeguard American interests even in the case, clearly envisaged by the State Department, that further spheres of interest might be created. Beyond and above that, so much the better if the notes in effect provided a brake to the dynamics of the sphere-of-interest system, if they served as a stop to the further acquisition of special privileges. In that event the United States might eventually catch up with the progress of other nations in China. Whatever might thus be saved by the notes could serve as a basis for developing a situation more favorable to the United States. For the chance that the Open Door policy might eventually be expanded by interpretation beyond its original modest three points was not overlooked in Washington.[5]

No particular endeavor to preserve China's integrity can be read into the correspondence of the State Department with other countries or its own representatives abroad. Wu's opinion that the Open Door notes were a warning against further encroachments upon Chinese territory was therefore anticipating things somewhat. This brave step was not undertaken by Hay until about six months later. In the meantime there was a good chance that the United States herself might ask for leases and concessions in China and disprove Wu's optimistic interpretation of the Open Door notes.

The uneasy minister Wu wanted to reassure himself further.* On diplomat day, November 9, 1899, he asked Hay whether America would follow the example of other nations if the Open Door policy should prove unsuccessful. In answer, Hay remarked that the acquisition of Chinese territory would be contrary to American policy. America wished to prevent China from falling into the hands of other powers. Wu, anxious to stop all rumors unfavorable to his country, induced Assistant Secretary of State Hill to deny them all, and especially the one concerning an Anglo-American-Chinese alliance.[6]

Chinese anxiety to learn American intentions in the Far East was not merely caused by rumors. American policy in the Philippines seemed

---

* It was said that Wu talked to Hay until he was woozy, while Hay talked to him until he was hazy.

rather untraditional. The Chinese had expected an American demand for a concession at Amoy as a supply base for the Philippines, a demand that had not eventuated simply because the American merchants in Amoy felt they could not afford one.[7] This apparent self-denial permitted the Chinese to relax and enjoy more the inauguration of the Open Door policy.

The reaction in China was favorable, especially among the progressive Yangtse viceroys. By an optimistic interpretation of the policy, particularly by emphasizing the implication of the notes rather than relying on their exact text, the Chinese permitted themselves to hope for American support in their endeavors to stop foreign aggression. They felt, in fact, that United States policy was now paralleling their own centuries-old policy of equal treatment of foreigners. They never had made fine distinctions, they claimed, between the various nationalities. The red-haired barbarians all looked alike and were to be treated alike.[8]

Equality of treatment, particularly equal restraint, fitted well into China's policy, especially when the restraint was mutually enforced by the powers upon themselves. The Open Door policy, to which China did not legally become a party until 1921 in the Nine-Power Treaty, rarely prevented the Chinese from continuing their favorite policy of playing one nation against the other. On the contrary, it introduced a new balancing force which the Chinese could bring into play by subtly disturbing the balance at their own convenience and with complete legality. Even while the policy was in the making, and at its very inauguration, the Chinese tested its usefulness by offering special favors to chosen nations. In 1899 the empress dowager offered the Japanese freedom of trade in return for an alliance.* In October 1899 the British government received only a noncommittal answer from Peking when it wanted a guarantee that uniform rates would apply when the French began operating their railroad into Yunnan. In a speech at Cincinnati Wu Ting-fang very cleverly pointed out that whoever treated China best in the Boxer settlement could expect to get most of the concessions which would no doubt be handed out after the Boxer incident was settled [9] — a kind of enticement typically offered by the Chinese. To play upon exaggerated Western ideas of the economic possibilities in China in order to drive the powers against each other or to obtain concessions from them has long been standard Chinese tactics. Even Chiang K'ai-

* See the previous chapter.

shek on Formosa, with nothing but liabilities to give away, dangled them before his foreign friends.

The fact is that, in 1900 or at any other time, China's primary interest was not equal treatment of foreigners but the maintenance of territorial and administrative integrity. Hay's circular of July 1900, in which he added the guarantee of China's integrity to the Open Door, appealed to the Chinese much more than the earlier notes. The anxious inquiries of Wu Ting-fang and the discussions on foreign policy in China dealt almost exclusively with aspects of China's integrity. Indeed, adherence to strictly equal treatment of foreigners would have robbed the Chinese of their best tactical weapon. In 1900 as well as later, the Chinese preferred sacrificing equal treatment to integrity, whereas with most foreigners the choice was reversed. It was reversed with the Americans, as their policy shows.

For instance, in 1900 the United States planned to acquire a coaling station in Fukien, but withdrew after the Japanese protested in the name of the American Chinese-integrity-policy! During the Boxer Rebellion the American government instructed Conger that it favored "securing foreign rights at treaty ports by adequate foreign concessions, either as an international settlement or as separate concessions to the interested nations," but not by forcible acquisition. In 1903, when Conger informed the State Department that the Russians were establishing their own customs service in Manchuria, Secretary Hay felt that this was no ground for American action as long as the duties charged were the same as everywhere else in China. And in questions of securities for foreign loans, the American government frequently approved of measures which came close to the denial of Chinese administrative autonomy.[10]

Luckily for China, the avarice of the foreigners could always be satisfied without a complete sacrifice of her territorial or administrative integrity. There is, in fact, some evidence that in order to avoid breaking the country up, the avarice was on occasion controlled. The message of the Hay notes of 1900 asking for the maintenance of China's integrity was an expression of a previously existing consensus among the Western powers rather than the inauguration of a brand-new policy. The exceptions were Russia, which had immediate plans for expansion, and Japan, which had no long-range intentions of adhering to such a policy, though for the moment she was interested in China's integrity.[11] Great Britain, with interests spread all over the country and preoccupied with the

Boer War, preferred a whole to a partitioned China. Germany and France did too. The French ambassador in Berlin reported on June 14, over two weeks before Hay's circular, that he had found von Bülow in complete agreement with the French Chinese policy — to wit, absolute accord among the powers during the Boxer crisis and, once calm was restored and the security of foreigners assured, an endeavor to maintain the *status quo ante* and the integrity of the Chinese Empire.

On July 2, one day before the date of Hay's notes, the French Foreign Minister Delcassé sent a circular to various Western nations summarizing and confirming what he had found to be the general accord among the powers in regard to China. Agreement existed on the following points: (1) a guarantee of the welfare of foreign nationals in China, (2) maintenance of the territorial *status quo*, (3) guarantees against a repetition of uprisings. This message was answered by Hay in the form of his circular. And while Hay had to be satisfied with a cursory note of reply from England only, the Frenchman received acknowledgments from every nation he approached.[12]

There were many reasons why China was not divided up into colonial territories. First of all, official reactions to the demand for China's integrity were bound to be positive. International conditions had not yet deteriorated to such a degree (nor policies become so clumsy) that nations would admit ahead of time their plans to establish a colony on Chinese territory. Second, the interests of many nations were dispersed, and in case of partition some holdings would have been lost. Third, in the mad scramble for concessions and privileges there was no time to determine their value, and no decision was possible, therefore, which ones would be most worth retaining. Fourth, European conditions were becoming tense, and political and military attention was beginning to focus there. Complications in the Far East appeared undesirable. Fifth, though militarily weak, China still was a colossus, and the prospect, to even the most imperialistic power, of having to control such a country was discouraging. Sixth, in various nations a liberal public opinion, very weak and uninfluential as yet, but growing and destined to become very useful to the Chinese cause, was making itself felt against any further imperialism in China and actually demanded the surrender of all ill-gotten gains.[13]

In other words, the constellation of circumstances was favorable to the survival of China, but mostly without China's active contribution.

Her own policy of playing the powers against one another would probably not have succeeded if selfish considerations on their part had not
played into her hand and if the strong attacks marking the closing years
of the nineteenth century had not somewhat abated. Any comfort China
could take from the situation was therefore not great. She was to have
to pass through several crises yet before she should be treated as anything but an international pawn, and it is arguable whether she
has ever been able to abandon that status altogether. One of those
crises was the Boxer Rebellion. This was similar to the T'ai-p'ing Rebellion in the mixture of motives underlying it, but was more specifically
directed against foreigners. It was one of those spectacular events which
caused great suffering to the people and brought defeat by foreign
powers, but which in the long run helped to improve China's international position.

5

Rebellion against the West

THE Boxer Rebellion was explained by one high official, Prince Chun, as a spontaneous protest against the behavior of foreign powers toward China. "It is natural that even a peaceable people should turn at last," he said. "The people of China have been gradually worked up by the recent loss of territory around Wei-hai-wei, Port Arthur, and other places, as well as the Catholic missionaries having been granted rights and honours by the officials." He maintained that during the Boxer Rebellion the Chinese behaved no worse than the French during their "celebrated" revolution.[1] Quite apart from the rather unfortunate choice of the French Revolution as a parallel, Chun's explanation of the reasons for the rebellion was most incomplete, and his contention regarding the degree of popular support for it, very much exaggerated.

With the exception of the province of Shantung, and to some extent Chihli, there was no general support of the Boxers in the country. Even in Peking neither the whole population nor even all the armies stationed there participated in the rebellion. In reality the "movement" consisted of a series of local outbreaks in different parts of the Empire. Outside of Peking, and especially in the interior of the country, the population was hardly aware of the meaning of the Boxer struggles and the issues involved. The people believed foreign troops to be honored guests from afar. Within the area affected by the fighting, many Chinese stoically accepted foreign troops as bands of brigands and robbers who, like their numerous Chinese predecessors, would one day disappear again.[2]

At the end of the rebellion pictures appeared in stores and shops all over the country, even in cosmopolitan centers like Shanghai, depicting such scenes of Chinese success as victorious troops throwing foreigners into the sea. These pictures apparently convinced the masses.[3] In the light of this prevalent ignorance, the Boxer Rebellion can hardly be interpreted as a well-thought-out political maneuver by the people. The truth is that it was a symptom of the extreme dissatisfaction reigning

59

in various localities and sprang from numerous local sources. The motivations of the participants varied greatly. One was economic distress, caused largely by the introduction of foreign goods and production methods; another was resentment against interference in local affairs; yet another, very rare, was fear for China's survival as an entity. In many cases there was no rational kind of motivation at all, but only superstition and mass psychosis, suggestive of the spirit animating revival meetings and equally contagious. The behavior of foreigners was only one, and apparently a minor, motivation among many. Quite in accord with these primarily local causes, the leadership of the Boxers was, at first, decentralized, and the rebellious groups functioned separately in different localities.

There was a distinct difference in character between the events in the north and south, and the Peking government treated them quite differently. The empress dowager and her advisers distrusted the loyalty of the central and southern provinces and were convinced that the trend of events there confirmed these areas once again as the traditional seats of revolution.[4] The southern uprisings were caused primarily by natural or by local political misfortunes: droughts and inundations, bad officials, bad laws. Christians and foreigners had little part in causing them, and they took on significance as an antidynastic revolt only after certain revolutionaries and adventurers gained control over and organized them. In contrast, the northern upheavals, influenced by the Peking atmosphere, had a political tendency from the beginning. Their slogans quickly became: support of the dynasty, expulsion of foreigners, eradication of Christianity. In answer to diplomatic protests against the antiforeign and anti-Christian outbreaks late in 1899, the Peking government offered only reluctant cooperation. This reluctance was not surprising in view of the antiforeign court atmosphere and the uncertain nature of the outbreaks — uncertain, that is, from the standpoint of their possible usefulness to the court. Once the ruling group in Peking discovered this usefulness, it took over the rebellion for its own purposes, and the rebellion assumed more of an over-all goal and a broader regional character.[5]

Unfortunately for China's international relations at that moment, this group was composed of extremely antiforeign persons, led by Prince Tuan, who had little difficulty in drawing the empress dowager into their scheme of using the Boxers for their benefit. The considerations motivating these political manipulators of the rebellion, however, were only a little less diverse than those of the rebels. In the atmosphere of intrigue at the court, it was not easy to discern what moved the empress dowager or any of her advisers. There may have been strong concern for the welfare of the country, and there was most assuredly concern for personal power and prestige as well as a desire for revenge. Some of the politics were purely personal and related to the internal affairs of the imperial palace. Part had national implications and related to the split between conservatives and reformers or to the rivalry for power raging between high court officials and the viceroys in the Yangtse Valley and the southern provinces. Yet another part was connected with the problem of international relations. Not until early 1900, when the rebellion was well on its way, did the situation crystallize.

The tenser the atmosphere became in the north, the more provocative proved every foreign diplomatic act to the Chinese, and the more hostile was their reaction to it. But as late as June 1900, counsels of moderation could still be heard in the meetings of the government. No all-out support of the Boxers had yet been agreed upon. After the decision was finally made, the diplomats, in ignorance of it, still were in doubt about what the government's attitude toward the Boxers might be. They were also uncertain about the exact meaning of the rebellion, though they were fairly well convinced that it was antidynastic as well as antiforeign and that therefore they would be able to obtain the collaboration of the empress dowager. The Peking statesmen fostered this uncertainty because it was politically useful and because it delayed foreign intervention. How successful they were in misleading foreign diplomats is shown by the information the American and French ministers sent back advising their home offices that because the Boxer Rebellion was antidynastic and the government depended upon the foreign powers for its very existence, the time was opportune to press it for reformation.[6]

After the foreign attack on the Taku forts on June 17, 1900, the lines were drawn more sharply. The government had no further hesitancy in throwing its support wholeheartedly to the Boxers and silencing all opposition.[7] Even then it did not give its cooperation entirely in the open, in order that diplomatic relations and other advantages might continue for Peking.

Events leading to the outbreak of hostilities in and around Peking had moved in a vicious circle. Foreign representatives felt justified in taking extensive precautions, while the Boxers and their sympathizers considered every new precaution another provocation of China. The Peking government attempted for a long time to pursue a conciliatory policy, but was finally driven into a position where a stand had to be taken. It would have welcomed a victory of the Boxers over the foreigners but realized early in the fighting that the foreigners would eventually be victorious. It was therefore reluctant to be too brusque with either the Boxers or the foreigners. Practical considerations required a policy making a reasonable peace possible. The government, or at least the empress dowager, always left a door open for an understanding by never making clear exactly how far collaboration with the Boxers went. Fortunately this imperial policy suited Western diplomacy.

The situation in the central and southern parts of China was more unequivocally favorable to foreigners. The population there was friendlier. The literati were more familiar with and appreciative of Western thought. The merchants of the important cities had profitable Western trade. Viceroys Chang Chih-tung and Liu K'un-i were the leaders in this vast region. These two *Realpolitiker* represented the moderately modernized type of Chinese, and their vigorous policy attracted the support of most southern viceroys.[8] Their greatest concern during the Boxer troubles was the maintenance of China's integrity (in addition, of course, to their own position). This concern was also that of Peking. But the policies of the north and south differed greatly. Peking, either voluntarily or forced by supporters, followed a policy antagonistic toward foreigners; the viceroys in the center and south maintained friendly relations with foreigners throughout the difficult period.

From the beginning of the rebellion the viceroys exerted themselves to protect foreigners. They suggested a treaty in which Western powers should receive a guarantee of safety for the lives and property of their nationals in return for a promise to cease military and naval activity in the south altogether or restrict it to an absolute minimum. This was a reasonable proposal. The military activities of the Boxers and foreigners had contributed greatly to the actual outbreak of hostilities in the north. The situation in the south was tense. The presence of foreign warships in the southern ports and on the Yangtse made the natives fear the customary indiscriminate reprisals for the killings of missionaries which might occur in the interior. But the viceroys felt that they could control the existing situation if no more warships arrived or troops were landed.

The Western powers declined to conclude a treaty. They did not recognize the viceroys as a government with which treaties could be made. More important reasons for their refusal were, first, that they were suspicious of the viceroys' friendship and, second, that the suggested treaty stipulations were contrary to some existing treaty rights which they refused to sacrifice. The viceroys had to be satisfied with a promise that as long as they proved able to maintain peace and order in their regions no new troops would be landed in southern China.[9]

Throughout the fighting in the north the viceroys reverted to this point. The prevention of an increase in foreign military activity in their area was the basis of their policy. Under no pretext would they permit the Western powers to augment their contingents. They politely declined a British offer of military assistance "as being calculated rather to make difficulties for Chinese authorities than to aid them." They repeatedly announced that they would decline all responsibility for the outbreak of antiforeign riots unless foreigners refrained from "obtrusive demonstrations" or military activity. They even warned the British government that the landing of new troops in Shanghai might force them into the antiforeign camp.

The anxiety of the viceroys was based on several considerations. One was fear that an extension of the northern troubles might provide the pretext for breaking up the country. Another was that even though China's existence might not be threatened, new troop landings would further infringe upon Chinese sovereignty. Finally, new foreign encroachments would reflect upon the viceroys' ability to exercise proper control within their jurisdiction. In every respect, therefore, the viceroys' policy was a Chinese policy and not one to accommodate foreigners.[10]

The viceroys, like the Peking government, were caught between two possibilities. On one side were the foreigners, whom the viceroys recognized as strong, whose assistance would be needed for the modernization of China, and whose trade was valued by the merchants residing in the viceroys' territories. These factors weighed in favor of a policy of collaboration. On the other side were doubts, especially after the experience of the reformers in 1898, regarding the amount of foreign support the viceroys could expect against the powerful reactionaries in Peking if they showed friendliness toward foreigners during the fighting and sympathy with modernization during the peace negotiations. These considerations suggested a careful policy toward foreigners, and Peking officials did not let the viceroys forget them.[11]

63

The viceroys solved the dilemma by following a line essentially in agreement with their convictions, yet one that would not antagonize either the empress dowager or the foreigners too much. Foreign powers were promised security. The promise was kept, although not all Western powers kept theirs regarding military activity in southern China. In many petitions to the court the viceroys denounced the anti-Christian and antiforeign policies of some Peking officials. Often appeals were made to Peking for peace between China and the foreign powers. On the other hand, the viceroys ostensibly complied with Peking edicts asking for assistance against foreigners. They sent many thousands of troops north, but they were raw troops, badly armed, needing many months to arrive in the Peking region.[12]

The cleverest policy of the viceroys was a declaration that the Boxer activities were strictly a rebellion in which the dynasty was not involved. They insisted throughout on this interpretation of events in the north. They demanded assurances on several occasions that the Western powers would pay proper respect to the empress dowager and the emperor and would "not even frighten" them, that both rulers would remain free, and that the empress dowager would remain in undisturbed possession of her power. They denied that the empress dowager held her position illegitimately and maintained that they were acting upon imperial instructions in protecting foreigners.[13]

This attitude enabled the viceroys to ignore any orders from Peking which they disliked by declaring that the orders lacked imperial sanction. They could thus pretend that they never faltered in their loyalty to the dynasty and yet could disregard orders incompatible with their general policy. Once peace was re-established, the empress dowager would not be made personally responsible for events, and the viceroys hoped to receive grateful credit for this. The method permitted the viceroys to insist to foreigners that the local rebellion in the north did not justify war against the whole of China. The most serious threat to Chinese integrity could thus be averted.

This balance-of-power game by the viceroys exposed them to alternate wooings and threats from Peking and the foreign envoys. Edicts poured forth from the imperial palace imploring the viceroys to help in the struggle against foreign enemies; then supplications became orders.[14] When neither approach brought results, the execution of some progressive officials in Peking caused the intended shock to the southern viceroys, but did not produce the desired policies. Indeed, the viceroys were so impressed that they asked for protection from the British consul in Shanghai.[15]

From that moment on, August 1900, the reactionary officials in Peking planned to oust the southern viceroys from their positions in order to eliminate their progressive influence. When outright relegation from office failed, owing to foreign protests, for which the viceroys had asked, Peking tried the subtler method of undermining the viceroys' position by appointing antiforeign and reactionary officials within their jurisdiction. This scheme also failed owing to foreign protests.[16] Thanks to an interference in China's administration which they themselves, patriotic champions of China's integrity, had solicited, the viceroys stayed in power.

The pressure from Peking was countered by pressure from the foreign powers desirous of retaining the viceroys' friendship. The United States in particular went along with the viceroys in declaring the empress dowager innocent, since otherwise the existence of a state of war could hardly have been denied. A further consideration persuading the foreign powers to uphold the empress dowager was apparently that a new government could decline responsibility for the events in the north and refuse to acknowledge the settlement of the Boxer incidents.[17]

In two most important points, then — avoidance of war and retention of the ruling dynasty — the policy of the powers and that of the viceroys coincided. Consequently relations between the consular representatives in the center and south and the viceroys were friendly. Early in July the consular body in Shanghai decided to send identical telegrams to their respective governments requesting support of the viceroys of the Yangtse and the south.[18] The Hay circular of July 3, reaffirming the Open Door policy and adding a request for the guarantee of China's territorial and administrative integrity, was intended, in part, to boost the viceroys' morale and to support their stand in favor of neutrality. In a letter to the French chargé d'affaires, furthermore, Hay mentioned his government's readiness to support every effort of the Chinese provincial authorities to protect foreigners and their possessions.[19]

The British government sustained the viceroys in a similar way and gave them every assurance they required. Early in August 1900 it went even further. Upon an urgent demand by Chang Chih-tung, supported by the British consul, the government made a loan of £75,000 to the viceroy with which to pay his troops and strengthen his friendship.[20] The loan coincided with the landing of British troops in Shanghai and the execution of the progressive officials in Peking and was undoubtedly calculated to cushion the shock of both happenings.*

The settlement finally made of the Boxer Rebellion pleased no one very much. In the protracted discussions which led to it, the Chinese representatives, though they tried to keep to a minimum the demands that were the condition of peace, had little to say. The compromise the foreign representatives reached among themselves left none of them entirely satisfied. All Chinese, of course, found the terms too harsh, although reactions differed in intensity. Feelings ranged from disappointment to disgust.[21]

In many ways the lack of foresight and imagination shown in the Boxer settlement is hardly short of extraordinary. It was impossible that Chinese reaction should have been favorable, for the settlement was primarily an instrument of revenge. Though the settlement was another example of the great powers' policy of dealing with the most reactionary forces in China, the reactionary groups were no better pleased with the outcome than the progressives were. The court was greatly relieved because the powers left the old regime essentially intact, but to have to expiate the deeds of the Boxers did not change the antiforeign attitude of the reactionary officials. The punishment inflicted upon China, if its purpose was to teach a lesson to the enemies of Western nations, failed to do so. The court continued to be reactionary. Antiforeign officials continued to be appointed. Peking showed no awe or repentance — a defiant attitude that, in the opinion of observers in Peking toward the end of 1901, increased in proportion to the troop withdrawals from China.[22] To appease the foreigners, a number of reform edicts were published, but they were not put into practice at the time.† The empress dowager remarked that she and the emperor had "slept on wormwood and eaten gall," meaning that they had nourished a desire for vengeance, and though the desire was without substantial consequence, it expressed the mood of many Chinese. Instead of trying to win the friendship of the Chinese people and to understand them, the Western nations antagonized them. A show of force and

* The *New York Daily Tribune*, August 15, 1900, thought that taking the viceroy into British "pay" was the beginning of China's break-up.

† One high official even suggested that the foreign powers should accept the promulgation of reforms in lieu of indemnities.

material superiority did not impress the Chinese as cultural equality, but (though there was an element of sour grapes in the feeling) only confirmed their disdain of the outer barbarians. Western policy worked in favor of those Chinese who favored seclusion, not in favor of those who had been most friendly toward the West.

The progressive groups in China felt that in the Boxer settlement they had been let down and rebuffed.[23] They had expected the Boxer settlement to provide an opportunity for the introduction of far-reaching reforms. The international conference at Peking seemed to them an ideal occasion for the inauguration of national progress "under the enlightened guidance and friendly pressure of the non-aggressive powers." They had interpreted the Open Door and integrity policies to mean that Britain and America were interested in maintaining and strengthening a free and independent China. They did not ask for radical or unfeasible changes. Indeed, they rejected the extreme demands of the revolutionary reformers under Sun Yat-sen's leadership, and requested the foreign nations not to lend their support to the extremists. But they were interested in the modernization of China for the benefit of the Chinese as well as foreigners. They believed they had a right to expect American and British cooperation in return for the protection they had given and because they had proved that the center of stability in China and the life-giving forces of the Chinese people were on the Yangtse and not in Peking.

The hopes of the southern viceroys and other forward-looking Chinese had grounds in the many vocal proclamations on the part of England and the United States of their good will. Both nations had repeatedly assured China during the rebellion that the country would not be divided up. Even during the negotiations preceding the settlement, the two nations kept encouraging the viceroys to hope for reforms. Balfour, in Parliament, assured a questioner that he would "gladly" support the viceroys in the promotion of measures for the development of China and the opening of trade. The American consul secretly urged Chang Chih-tung to press his views on a reduced indemnity through the official Chinese plenipotentiaries at the conference table and promised him American support. The United States, he was told, was interested, not in a high indemnity, but in administrative reforms and increased privileges to foreign trade. Chang gladly cooperated and asked for a list of the reforms that seemed desirable to the Americans. Such a list was drawn up by Minister Rockhill, Chang welcoming every suggestion that might lead to a mutually beneficial increase in trade. Among the things proposed were the abolition of likin (an internal trade tax); the opening of all China to foreign trade and residence; the improvement of regulations for navigation and mining; and China's strict adherence to the principle of equal opportunity to people of every nationality. But Chang and other progressive Chinese soon came to realize that these verbal assurances of sympathy and support meant nothing. To them, in their discouragement, it appeared that nations like the United States and Great Britain, while constantly proclaiming their sympathetic interest in China's fate, were "more occupied with the past than the future." [24] The final outcome of the settlement conference showed little evidence of any constructive influences at work. The complaint of the viceroys that there was a discrepancy between the "loud proclamations" of the nations and their actions was justified.[25] Foreign observers in China were as disappointed as the viceroys. The result, they anticipated, would not only be to affect China's progress disadvantageously but be detrimental, in the long run, to the interests of the foreign powers themselves.[26]

The progressive Chinese were willing to accept any reasonable demands of the foreign powers for indemnities and other reparations. But to eliminate the deeper causes of violent rebellions like the Boxer was the important thing to them, and the settlement was an unconstructive agreement that would do nothing to prevent the recurrence of similar outbreaks. In the payment of the big indemnities finally agreed upon, moreover, the share of the Yangtse Valley and the great southern cities was heavy. The central and south regions carried much of the burden that the settlement imposed upon the whole of China. Yet these were the regions that had been the most friendly and well disposed toward the foreigners. Throughout the Boxer troubles the foreign powers had maintained that the outbreak was local. But when the question of indemnities arose, the entire Chinese nation was made responsible. To be forced to pay for the mistakes of others was particularly repugnant to a people that had no feeling of national responsibility. The establishment of friendly international relations was not furthered by the indemnity provisions of the Boxer settlement.

Good Chinese government was not furthered, either, by its specific obligations. The suspension of the traditional civil service examination led to an increase in the sale of offices and to irregular appointments. The prohibition of the importation of arms resulted in the development of a flourishing arms industry, with much corruption.[27] Only the replacement of the Tsungli Yamen by a regular Foreign Ministry, the Wai-wu Pu (later the Wai-chiao Pu), could be considered a step forward.

In drawing up the Boxer settlement, the powers had chosen to make their peace with the most conservative and reactionary elements in Peking. They could have chosen to deal with the progressive viceroys instead, for the empress dowager could have been handled without too great difficulty. The formation of a strong, progressive government might have expedited the evolution of China and provided a solid foundation for the Open Door and integrity policies — assuming, of course, that these policies were what the foreign powers were really interested in at this time. Mgr. Favier provided a clue to the attitude of the foreign powers toward improvement in the government when he said that the nations found themselves "en face du gouvernement qui, depuis trente-cinq ans, nous donne concession sur concession, et que la rude leçon n'aura que rendre notre mission plus facile." [28] Obviously, grants for concessions and privileges were more easily obtainable from a government steeped in graft and corruption than they would have been from a progressive government which might have cleaned the Peking morass and might have cared more for the welfare of the people than for its own. So the settlement of the Boxer Rebellion, which might well have been a turning point in China's development, became only another of the episodes, typical of modern Chinese history, of how the foreign powers crushed the hopes of the more enlightened Chinese and antagonized the best friends they had in China. If the foreign powers had taken a different attitude, the moment might have been a decisive one in Chinese history. To say this is by no means to imply that foreign governments either should or did absolutely determine the fate of China. But the fact is that at that time, and at several others, the internal situation was so much in the balance that the weight of the foreign powers in the scale was crucial.

In spite of the fact that the settlement of the Boxer Rebellion favored the reactionary forces, China progressed. The rebellion itself, with all its horrors, contributed to that progress. More Chinese became concerned about the international fate of their country. Interest in the treatment of China at the hands of foreign governments increased among liberal forces abroad. The court itself seems to have considered the rebellion a last chance to undo the advances of the past few decades, and when the inevitability of substantial reforms became clear, finally surrendered to it, though not too gracefully or too quickly. The foreign governments alone appear to have missed learning any lesson. China found this out when she had to cope with the international after-effects of the rebellion.

70

6

Threatened Loss of Manchuria

WHILE the Chinese government was absorbed in dealing with the Boxer settlement, Russia presented a new problem in Manchuria. When the rebellion had moved into Manchuria, the Russians had moved into Manchuria too, for "precautionary measures." Using the Chinese Eastern Railway as a springboard, Russian troops had spread over large parts of Manchuria, occupying Newchwang and taking over the customs house there. They had acquired land concessions at Tientsin, laid hold of railroads from Tientsin to Peking, and seized another one, built by British capital, running from Tientsin to Shanhaikwan. Few people trusted the assurances of the Russians that their troops would be withdrawn as soon as the trouble was over. How well founded this distrust was appeared before the end of the year 1900, when it became known that the tartar-general and viceroy at Mukden, Tseng Chi, had reached an agreement with the Russian commander Alexieff,* ratification of which by Peking would have turned Manchuria into a Russian protectorate.[1]

The crisis precipitated by this Russian attempt to dominate Manchuria exhibited several features characteristic of Chinese diplomacy as well as some typical of the politics of the powers in China. In the efforts of the Chinese to get the Russians to evacuate Manchuria there was a mixture of fear and courage that reflected their varying estimates of foreign intentions and that remained characteristic until China was strong enough to devise a policy not necessarily adjusted to the policies of other nations. The crisis also brought to the fore again the differences between various groups in China regarding the right attitude for China to take when threatened by international developments, differences which had been somewhat obscured by the preoccupation of all groups with the primary problems posed by the Boxer Rebellion.

---

* There is some uncertainty regarding the exact date of the signing of the agreement. It seems that the agreement between the two officials was initialed on November 10 or 11, 1900, and signed at Port Arthur on January 30, 1901.

There was unanimity among all influential Chinese that the integrity of their country should be maintained and that territory should be surrendered only if absolutely necessary.[2] Beyond this point, however, ideas about a proper policy regarding Manchuria differed widely. A decision was difficult; what made it especially so was that it depended to a considerable degree on the attitude of foreign powers, as usual an unknown factor. For though the powers shared the Chinese apprehension regarding what Russia might do — an apprehension heightened rather than diminished by the fact that the terms of the Tseng-Alexieff agreement were only vaguely known — how they would act in an emergency could not be predicted. Statesmen and factions attempted to influence the empress dowager in so many different directions that she was at a loss to make any decision, and throughout the crisis, from 1900 to 1904, wavered between concluding and refusing an agreement concerning Manchuria.

To the outside observer this irresolution was unusual in the Chinese. Though disagreements regarding a desirable course of action existed on many occasions in the inner circles of the ruling groups, they were usually hidden from the outside world through the autocratic character of the government. The public merely learned the final result, in ignorance of how it was arrived at. Chinese policy now not only was but appeared indecisive. The novelty was not the indecision but its being public. Public knowledge was due to the unusual step of the government in consulting various groups outside the inner circles, including even the representatives of foreign powers. The step was almost unavoidable, for the Manchurian affair had stirred up not only all Chinese officials but the literati and other sections of the population, who flooded the government with petitions.[3]

In many instances the court undertook the consultations merely to appease the consulted, with no intention of following their advice. Nevertheless public opinion was heeded more, or more openly now, than ever before. What had brought this about? What had caused the broadening of public opinion? Some of the answers are uncertain, some can only be surmised.

A change of mind, if not of heart, had occurred in the empress dowager during her flight from the capital. The advice of Prince Tuan to support the Boxers was recognized as bad. She had probably accepted it because it was part of the antiforeign atmosphere in which she lived; because

Tuan seems to have had great influence with her; and because she had many personal resentments against foreigners: they had spoiled the magnificent plans for the celebration of her sixtieth birthday, they had prevented her from murdering the young emperor, and, above all, they had contributed to the weakening of the throne. The result of the rebellion seems to have sobered her thinking and made her realize the trend of history. While the rebellion had weakened the prestige of the dynasty, it had strengthened that of the Yangtse viceroys notwithstanding the fact that they had carried no weight in the Boxer settlement, and it was important for the court to win them over. Either to flatter them or to have their counsel or both, the court listened to them; sterile antiforeignism had rapidly been discredited, and the court could hardly get new inspiration from its own environment. The press, finally, had shown its great influence in the cities during the rebellion: it was on the whole anti-Boxer and effectively contained the movement wherever it was established. The court needed all possible popularity, and the press could evidently be most helpful. At any rate, it could not be ignored. The days when the court made autocratic decisions were gone. In realizing this, it at least showed a capacity for change and for adapting the pursuit of its interests to new conditions.

The growth of an aroused public opinion had several causes which became increasingly effective after 1900. The many civil and foreign wars enlarged the number of citizens aware of the emaciated condition of their country and anxious to do something about it. Natural catastrophes created unrest and dissatisfaction, which sought an outlet and led people to consider how floods might be prevented or droughts counteracted. Foreign contacts brought about a ferment affecting ever wider circles. The one thing, however, which probably aroused the masses more than anything else was taxes. Campaigns to oppose antidynastic revolts or foreign aggression, the building-up of armies, the expansion of public administration, technical innovations, and the payment of the many indemnities imposed upon the nation raised the expenses of the government enormously. The people had to pay, and resented it; the more so as the largest items of expense showed no visible returns to them. Since taxes were payable by every village, they were what made the masses eventually recognize the close relation between their individual lives and the foreigner in China.

Most Chinese might never have seen a foreigner, might never have

73

heard of the reformers, never have looked at a newspaper; but they all knew what taxes were. And as the government collected them and the foreigners benefited from them, resentment turned against both. Since the more progressive leaders had succeeded in getting control of the rising popular feeling, the court, regardless of its own convictions, but having to bow to the times, was forced to find a *modus vivendi* with the forward-looking Chinese. Yet it needed the good will also of the foreign powers. The fact is that almost immediately after the Boxer Rebellion, it attempted to conciliate the people as well as the foreigners, yet not to antagonize its own members too much.[4]

A conciliatory attitude in such circumstances required a compromise between the varied opinions of different factions, the public, and court officials, and this was the cause of the government's predicament in the Manchurian crisis.

The leadership of the anti-Russian forces was in the hands of Chang Chih-tung, Liu K'un-i, and other officials of the progressive type. Their objections to the Tseng-Alexieff agreement rested mainly on two bases. The first was that the agreement would threaten Chinese independence. The second was that China had placed herself in the hands of the concert of powers. She should therefore not conclude with an individual power, behind the backs of the other powers, secret separate agreements affecting important international treaties. The two viceroys went further and suggested the inclusion of a Manchurian agreement in the Boxer settlement.[5] These were clever arguments. China had more to hope for from multilateral than bilateral negotiations. Such a policy also corresponded exactly to the wishes of the powers (except Russia) and had every prospect of enlisting foreign sympathy and assistance. It would have forced Russia into the united front which the foreign powers were so anxious to create in the negotiations for the Boxer settlement, and China, instead of having to fight it out hopelessly with Russia, could have relied upon the powers to fight for China among themselves — and for themselves, of course, too.

The groups favoring agreement with Russia were led by Li Hung-chang, who also conducted the negotiations. True to Peking's long practice of calling in new statesmen to inaugurate a policy after disgracing the incumbents for a policy which had failed, Li had been ordered to the capital in June 1900 to conduct the nation's foreign policy in a more conciliatory spirit. He had concentrated immediately on the Russian problem as the most difficult one. He had the reputation of being a Russophile. The existence of a "Li Hung-chang fund" in St. Petersburg for buying the good will of Li and his assistants supported the common belief that he was completely in the pay of Russia. To say that he was exaggerates. Bribery in one form or another was an accepted means of diplomacy in China and elsewhere, and Li was true to type. The evidence seems to indicate that he did not betray his convictions for pay but merely accepted it when it was compatible with his convictions.

The premise of Li's policy was that Russia was China's greatest danger. On this point the anti-Russian factions agreed. But they wanted to oppose Russia, especially with Japanese help, while Li feared the Japanese long-range plans more than the Russian ones. He favored dealing with Russia on friendly terms.[6] His decision was not just appeasement. It was based on a judicious choice between evils, as his subsequent moves show. He was not deceived by the old trick of the Russians — used after the Sino-Japanese War and tried now again, during the Boxer negotiations — of secretly showing great friendship for the Chinese and then coming back for big rewards.*

Li was aware that Russia's friendliness covered aims detrimental to China. His chief adviser, Sheng, in an interview in September 1900, expressed his bewilderment at Russian friendliness, which aroused his suspicions. Sheng feared another Port Arthur coup, and was particularly afraid of the close Russo-German collaboration; this, he suspected, might again lead to territory-grabbing similar to that of 1898–1899. Russia, Sheng explained, should withdraw from Manchuria, Great Britain should come to an understanding with Japan, the United States should exert a moral influence upon all, and China should be opened to foreign intercourse.[7]

Li himself felt that, failing some agreement, Russia would stay in Manchuria forever and other nations would follow suit. Discounting effective outside help, he was convinced China had to come to terms with Russia, and this he endeavored to achieve. Even before reaching Peking, he began his work by offering a deal to Count Witte. Russia should renounce all ambitions in Manchuria, in return for which renunciation China would make concessions in Mongolia. But the Russians ignored

---

* For instance, the Russians kept Li informed about the progress of conversations among the foreign representatives regarding the Boxer settlement. — London *Times*, November 30, 1900.

the proposal.* They ignored Li as representing a weak central government and as having near to no personal influence. Instead, apparently unknown to Li, Alexieff proceeded to sign the agreement with Tseng Chi, in November 1900 or January 1901.[8]

Conversations between the Russian government and the Chinese minister in St. Petersburg regarding the ratification of the Manchurian agreement began on February 7, 1901. In the meantime enough information about Russian designs had leaked out to cause concern abroad.† Three weeks after the beginning of the conversations on ratification Peking called on the foreign powers for assistance in opposing Russian demands. The basis of this request was that the agreement would make equal treatment impossible and would exclude every other power from Manchuria. The Yangtse viceroys asked for "material assistance against the Russian encroachments." Peking asked for "mediation" and a postponement of the negotiations until after the completion of the Boxer negotiations — a difference between the requests which aroused comment in diplomatic circles.[9]

London, Berlin, Tokyo, and Washington were approached, but not Paris. Li knew that France was Russia's ally and had to acquiesce in St. Petersburg's Far Eastern policy as the price of support in Europe. So he used a more devious method. He visited the French minister in Peking to express his gratitude that the French government had not joined in the protest to China against the Manchurian agreement. This, Li asserted, had saved his country considerable embarrassment. The French minister replied that in view of the Russo-French alliance and Franco-Chinese friendship, France would never interfere in the relations between Russia and China.[10]

This reply supported the Russian view that the Manchurian affair concerned the two nations exclusively, and it was exactly what Li had not wanted to hear. He had hoped to establish a united front, including even Russia's ally. United resistance by all the great powers against the Manchurian agreement would have been an excellent excuse for

* Though not overmuch a Russophile, Chang Chih-tung, when he had the job of dealing with the Russians after Li's death, made a very similar proposal. See note 9.

† After the Russians felt sure of securing the agreement, Witte, Kuropatkin, and Lamsdorff devised a program for expansion in Manchuria through the exclusion of all non-Russian capital and the strengthening of the Chinese Eastern Railway. The plan received the tsar's approval on December 13, 1900. — J. J. Gapanovich, "Sino-Russian Relations in Manchuria, 1892–1906," *Chinese Social and Political Science Review,* XVIII (1933–1934), 459.

Li not to conclude it. But the idea was unrealizable, and later on Li had to be satisfied with using foreign pressure exclusive of the French as an excuse.

This call for help by the Chinese government was considered unusual. There was much speculation about the motives behind it. No one took it at face value. That China should simply invoke the principle of equal opportunity in Manchuria — to which all these powers had just adhered — that China should actively intervene in her own destiny at all — seemed unbelievable. The puzzle was the more mysterious as most foreign statesmen took it for granted that the Peking government was sold to Russia and not unwilling to let Russia expand in Manchuria. All sorts of devious schemes were ascribed to Peking, of which the one most persistently rumored was that Japan was behind it all in the hope of reinforcing the opposition to Russia.[11]

The response to China's appeal for help was poor. Japan was the only nation showing determined opposition to Russian ambitions. The Chinese government found itself in the perennially recurring dilemma of being squeezed between two or more power groups. The Western powers together with Japan demanded that it should not sign a Manchurian agreement; Russia demanded the opposite. China was too weak to give effect to decisions of her own. In a realistic fashion Chinese statesmen weighed carefully which might be the lesser evil. At most they could attempt to reach a compromise without antagonizing any party. They tried this, their usual first step. When they failed, there remained no choice but to give in to whoever was judged the stronger. Chinese policy was a policy of fear, and Li Hung-chang admitted so quite frankly in the Manchurian affair. He argued realistically that Russia's position in relation to China was different from that of any other nation. Russia had no commerce or missions in China, he explained, but was out for territorial aggrandizement and military expansion, and had the advantages of position and force to impose her wishes. For these reasons Li advised the throne to sign a Manchurian agreement.[12]

Li, like the Yangtse viceroys, would have preferred to deal collectively with the powers over the Manchurian question, but the Russians objected to this procedure. And as soon as China resisted Russian demands, so Li claimed, Russia became menacing. A reminder of Russia's obligations under the Open Door arrangement merely elicited the reply that the arrangement could be canceled and that it had been accepted only

77

conditionally in any case. In the face of such determination on the part of Russia, Li asked, what could China do? The fact that foreign powers chose to handle the problems arising out of China's international relations at Peking instead of at Moscow, the capital where the problems were created, was proof to Li that the foreign nations either were afraid of Russia and ought not blame China for also being afraid, or had little real interest in Chinese affairs and China could not count on their support. If Japan, the United States, and England would give a written pledge of assistance, Li was prepared not to sign the Manchurian agreement; otherwise he felt that China could only lose by irritating Russia on the very doubtful chance of support from other quarters.[13]

This reasoning impressed the empress dowager and the emperor. An edict was handed to the powers on February 28 in which the emperor announced that China could not incur Russia's displeasure by remaining firm in the refusal to sign an agreement. The question did not concern China alone but all powers with interests in the country, and these powers should therefore maintain a "balance of power."

As a proof of good will and in a supreme effort to reach an understanding, the emperor tried to persuade Russia, in April 1901, to refrain from bellicose action. He wrote to the tsar, expressing fear that ratification of the Manchurian agreement would destroy Chinese sovereignty and integrity, that other powers would be stimulated to make similar requests, and that Russia should therefore withdraw her demands.[14]

In the meantime, the delay in reaching a final decision permitted internal and external pressure against the agreement to build up to a point where, even without the guarantee of support from any one nation, Peking felt sufficiently encouraged to refuse to ratify it.* In its notification to St. Petersburg early in March 1901, the government explained that the memorials from the viceroys and the objections from friendly powers could not be disregarded. China wanted to be on friendly terms with all powers at this most perilous moment in her history. The government could not grant special privileges for the sake of acquiring the friendship of one nation at the expense of the friendship of the remaining ones.[15]

---

* This pressure, as well as differences of opinion within the Russian government, had also led to a softening of Russia's attitude. — See *Kobe Weekly Chronicle*, March 27, 1901, p. 278; April 3, 1901, pp. 300, 303; Gapanovich, "Sino-Russian Relations," p. 461; Edward H. Zabriskie, *American-Russian Rivalry in the Far East* (Philadelphia, 1946), p. 67.

This decision of the government appeared to be in accord with the expressed opinion of the Chinese people. The imminent ratification of the Manchurian agreement had awakened a new and unusual national consciousness and sense of dignity among the Chinese. A real outburst of popular feeling occurred. It is true that the number of those who made their voices heard so early in the century as this was still exceedingly small. The mass remained lethargic. The people in the Yangtse Valley and farther south ignored the significance of the Manchurian affair. Observers maintained that to them Manchuria was a foreign country and that they were indifferent to Chinese interests there.[16] But the Yangtse viceroys and most of the provincial governors in addition to a number of Peking officials opposed the ratification of the agreement or making any concessions at all to Russia in return for Russia's evacuation of Manchuria. They threatened to challenge the throne's authority if the Peking government acceded to Russian demands. To make their opposition more impressive, they even sent petitions to foreign powers to enlist their help. Unquestionably, anti-Russian feeling was strong.[17]

In many centers of the country the people were sufficiently aroused so that meetings were held; the emperor was petitioned; appeals went to Tokyo, and even to the tsar, asking for restraint and peace. Patriotic societies, literati, officials — all participated in these demonstrations. The main targets of attack were the Russians and Li Hung-chang and Prince Ch'ing, both accused of acting without due regard for the welfare of their people. Factions which had for a long time advocated a Japanese alliance became more popular. The activity, amounting almost to a movement among some sections of the people, seemed to represent a genuine uprising of progressive elements against old, established, reactionary groups and the Manchu ascendancy. This growing popular participation in the affairs of the country enabled the government more and more to speak with authority in foreign affairs. Foreign governments had to revise their impression that, in dealing with the Chinese, they were dealing with a group of individuals who would sell themselves to the highest bidder. The officials may have wanted to sell, and in many cases undoubtedly did, but the growth of public alertness proved to be an increasingly severe handicap.

The final result of all this agitation over Chinese policy was that in March 1901 the Russian government withdrew various suggested modifications of the Manchurian agreement, a diplomatic defeat for Russia. The withdrawal seemed like an encouraging beginning for a China with initiative. To be sure, Japan's determined stand is what had done the most to subdue the Russians, but China's spirited efforts had had a definite effect.[18] Pleasure over the temporary relaxation of international tension was widespread. But it was too early to count the chickens. Russia still insisted that a complete restitution of Manchuria could take place only after a normal state of affairs had been established, and it was clear to everybody what this condition could mean. "Tails I win, heads you lose," was a characteristic reaction at the time.[19]

Not a single Russian soldier was withdrawn from Manchuria. Only a breathing spell was provided during which China immediately attempted to balance Russia in Manchuria with other powers by offering them attractive possibilities for trade and residence in the area. But before the Chinese had time to exhale, Russia caused new anxieties by pressing on Tibet. Fearing the results if St. Petersburg were given the chance to exert pressure in too many places all at once, Peking urged a final solution to the Manchurian problem in August 1901. Russia was cool, maintaining that her conditions were known and all China had to do to settle the issue was to accept them. Li Hung-chang made clear that this would never happen and induced the Russians to submit another slightly modified agreement.[20]

After prolonged negotiations over the new agreement, Count Lamsdorff, the Russian foreign minister, finally drew up a plan for the withdrawal of Russian troops in stages. Foreign pressure more than Chinese diplomacy forced him into this concession. And, partly as a compensation, partly as a result of a dual policy in St. Petersburg, China was immediately presented with a draft agreement increasing the privileges of the Russo-Chinese Bank, the major Russian tool for the exploitation of Manchuria. After some unsuccessful haggling by Li, during which he indicated his willingness to sacrifice the Open Door for China's integrity, he agreed to sign the Bank agreement, but died before he could do so.[21]

At the end of November 1901 Prince Ch'ing resumed the conversations with the Russians. Again strong pressure developed from the anti-Russian factions against any concessions. The dilemma of six months ago repeated itself. The government, to be on the safe side and to attract help, instructed Ch'ing to consult with the foreign ministers in Peking before signing anything. Ch'ing inclined to ignore these instructions in the belief that China had nothing to hope for from the foreign powers. He so informed the diplomats, and this clever move was enough to stir them up sufficiently so that they implored their governments to show more interest in Sino-Russian negotiations. To the astonishment of the Chinese statesmen, assistance came from abroad.

Whereas during the March crisis, foreign protests had been sent to the Chinese government, much to its exasperation, they were now addressed to Russia directly in recognition of the fact that Russia was responsible for the difficulties.[22] The Peking diplomats encouraged Ch'ing to resist. Early in January 1902 the ministers of Great Britain, Japan, and the United States asked him to postpone signing the Bank agreement, and on January 29 he definitely declined to do so. On the following day the Anglo-Japanese alliance was announced.

The connection was obvious. To their own minds, the Chinese officials were justified by the alliance in adopting a stiffer attitude toward Russia without fear of evil consequences.[23] But the question was still open how much foreign support China could expect in an emergency. China was between the devil and the deep. Russia occupied Manchuria, and possession was nine points of the law; the Western powers still threatened to follow the Russian example if Russian demands were fulfilled.

The Chinese government therefore was given enough courage to resist, but not enough to refuse outright. It vacillated, carefully feeling its way through the maze of secrecy, jealousy, intrigue, and competition called Western diplomacy.

The alliance was appreciated as a help to China, but Chinese statesmen kept their heads clear about its possible results. Yuan Shih-k'ai, at that time viceroy of Chihli, sent a long and cynical memorial to the throne. He discounted the grandiloquent introduction to the alliance. The whole matter he considered from a coldly strategic and power-political standpoint. The Japanese land army combined with the British navy were all powerful, he argued. This power was a source of anxiety to other nations, and China also would have to be vigilant. The declared purpose of the alliance — Chinese and Korean integrity and the advancement of the interests of these two nations — was absurd. The real objectives of Great Britain and Japan were their own interests. The thing of greatest importance for China was to secure her own strength by armament, wealth, education, and administrative reform. No alliance could

be relied upon to replace China's own efforts, Yuan warned. At best
China could use the alliance for her own development. While he was
gratified by the alliance, he considered it a humiliation that China should
have fallen so low as to need such propping.[24]

The alliance had an undeniably favorable effect upon China's immediate problem. Negotiations for a Manchurian agreement now proceeded
more smoothly and swiftly. Prince Ch'ing was in permanent communication with the American minister, Conger, who did his best to encourage the prince without having anything concrete to offer. Ch'ing finally
confided in Conger that he found himself in a "most difficult" position.
He had, he said, secured some concessions, but Russia would not yield
beyond a point which was still unsatisfactory. He feared, however, that
if he held out any longer, he would never be able to obtain the same
terms again. Russia still insisted on the signing of the Manchurian and
Bank agreements. Nevertheless, Ch'ing complained, the occupation of
Manchuria was so annoying that China would have to accept the best
obtainable terms in order to terminate it. What the prince presumably
hoped for with this typical indirection was American assistance. He
was disappointed. Conger advised the prince to sign both agreements
provided that no American treaty rights were violated.[25]

On April 8 the Russians and Chinese signed the Manchuria Convention of Evacuation. Russia agreed to restore Chinese authority in the
area; China agreed to adhere strictly to the agreement of 1896 made
with the Russo-Chinese Bank and to protect the interests of Russia and
Russians in Manchuria. Russia agreed further to evacuate Manchuria in
three stages of six months each, beginning April 8, 1902, "providing that
no disturbances arise and that the action of other Powers should not prevent it." To make this escape clause watertight, China was forbidden to
increase her troops in Manchuria without previous Russian permission.
Chinese objections to this clause had long ago been overcome by contributions from the "Li Hung-chang fund."

The first stage of the evacuation proceeded according to plan, and
everybody breathed more easily. During the second stage Russia reoccu-
pied all the territory she had earlier evacuated, and more. Coupled
with this new aggression were demands upon China designed to keep
foreign powers out of Manchuria and guarantee special treatment to
Russians.[26] The foreign powers were shocked, but not sufficiently to
come to China's rescue. The French, always concerned about the effec-

tiveness of their alliance with Russia and Europe, advised Prince Ch'ing to be "more flexible" in regard to Manchuria. Conger warned him to protect American rights, and Great Britain and Japan sent a protest to Russia. Contrary to what Conger suspected, the Chinese were quite willing to oppose Russia, but not without help. The lukewarm attitude of the powers merely confirmed them in thinking that the powers not only were relatively uninterested in Manchuria but actually recognized Russia's special interests, if not predominance.[27]

Consequently Chinese policy toward Russia became increasingly conciliatory, to the point where Prince Ch'ing actually refused the token assistance finally offered by the United States and Japan and appeared willing to conclude some agreement with Russia. In doing so, he left no doubt that he was surrendering to superior force, and Chang Chih-tung as well as Yuan Shih-k'ai, both anti-Russian in principle, supported him. They advised against American and Japanese proposals that these countries should open new ports in Manchuria to counteract Russian pressure. The ports would be opened, they promised, as soon as Manchuria was free. The Chinese statesmen were unwilling to complicate a difficult situation by inaugurating a new policy at the request of powers which had themselves failed to obtain the restoration of their rights from Russia. There was a rare degree of unanimity among Chinese officials in the attitude that Russia should be antagonized as little as possible so that as much of Manchuria as possible might be saved. After much deliberation the Chinese government concluded that the best solution would be to leave Russia in *de facto* control of Manchuria rather than to accept the new Russian demands or become involved in war.[28]

Russia, however, was not satisfied with the *status quo*. She was out to establish exclusive control over Manchuria. This was her undoing. For as soon as this intention became unmistakably clear, the United States, Japan, and Great Britain stiffened their opposition, much to China's pleasure.

Taking immediate advantage of the new developments, Peking discarded the idea of leaving Russia in *de facto* control of Manchuria and looked for something more drastic. The change in Chinese foreign policy became noticeable after August 1903. Peking declined the Russian demands and informed the United States that China would insist upon Russian adherence to the Evacuation Convention. In treaties signed with the United States and Japan on October 8, 1903, several new places

83

were opened to foreign residence in Manchuria. The date was the one on which the evacuation of Manchuria was to be completed. The commercial community in China did not expect much from the treaties, but the political effect of the gesture upon Russia was obvious.[29]

She speeded up her activities in Manchuria, while the United States and Japan tried to hamper them by demanding immediate fulfillment of the obligation to open new ports. China's attitude was determined resistance short of war. Troops in Manchuria were increased and military defenses were established. But at the same time commanders were instructed to avoid a collision with the Russians. Anti-Russian feeling in the government, duly stimulated by the British and Japanese ministers, was high. The pro-Japanese party was in the saddle. But in spite of all the excitement, policy remained cautious. Japan and Russia were still negotiating about their respective spheres in Manchuria and Korea, and the outcome was uncertain. Inspired rumors sometimes frightened, sometimes encouraged Peking. Their net effect was to shake China's confidence in Japanese support and to put the statesmen on their guard more than ever.[30]

When it became clear that there was no chance of modifying Russian intentions in Manchuria, the United States and Japan acted fast. By agreement with China, the treaties of October 8 were ratified by telegram on January 13, 1904. This was a most unusual procedure, but it saved months. Within two or three days Secretary Hay was able to obtain funds from Congress for the consular positions in Manchuria and to appoint officials and so was able to get his consuls there before Russian control made it impossible. Russian threats against China were of no avail. Hay talked tough. The presence of American and other consuls in Manchuria, he said "will greatly tend to the establishment of order in this much disturbed border land of China and will powerfully contribute toward insuring the principles of the open door to which this country stands irrevocably committed, as well as aiding in insuring the integrity of China and its administrative control over its Manchurian provinces." [31]

For the time being, the Manchurian problem was settled, not altogether unfavorably for China. The major attempt of China to shape her international destiny had succeeded sufficiently well to encourage the Chinese to continue their policy. In this case its main features, typical ones, had been multilateralism, maintenance of the balance of power, hard bargaining, and complete adjustment to the finest nuances in the moods of the foreign powers. China had thus used all the means available to a nation whose physical weakness makes it dependent on the strong powers. She was to be in the same boat again and again. The consequence was, of course, that she could not pursue a policy completely her own but had to follow one reflecting the policies of the major powers. Since the main interest of these powers was concentrated on Europe, China's destiny was largely determined there.

7

Nurturing Nationalism

T HE Chinese government was gratified by the American and Japanese support given it in the Manchurian affair. Yet it did not over-look the possibility that war between Russia and Japan, which now seemed to be in the making, might wipe out all the advantages gained and more. To prepare a policy for such an eventuality was imperative. As past experience had taught, China was likely to suffer from any trouble arising in the Far East, and her territory might well become a battlefield. Several choices would be available, except the most desirable: that she enforce her integrity against all infractions. Since she lacked the power to do this, it would be open to her to join either contestant, thus influencing the outcome of the war; she might remain neutral; or she might call for the assistance of third parties. Sentimentally the majority of the officials and the people favored the Japanese; rationally they suspected Japanese aims even more than the Russian. The policy the government wanted, therefore, was one that would frustrate immediate Russian success and long-range Japanese planning.

A call for foreign assistance in the event of war remained unanswered. Neither France, the United States, nor Great Britain was willing to make advance commitments.[1] China stood alone. That she would not join with Russia was the only certain thing in the councils of the government. The question was whether to remain neutral, fight Russia alone, or fight as an ally of Japan. Every alternative had advocates. Only a few persons, for the most part "timid" souls, advised neutrality. Among them was the empress dowager, not because she was timid, but because she was sure Russia would win the war and China would have to foot the bill. Most officials and the military commanders in the north favored action against Russia. Their military preparations along the Manchurian border made it an "open secret" that China would join in the war against Russia. The war faction was convinced that here might be a unique op-

portunity to eliminate the Russian threat for a long time to come, perhaps long enough for China to become strong.[2]

Some circles seemed elated at the prospect of a victorious war. There
was a gratifying sense of importance when Japan, especially, but also
when Russia tried to enlist Chinese help. When the empress dowager
refused all advances from the Japanese, they approached Yuan Shih-k'ai
in Chihli province (now Hopei). They offered him complete equipment
for 16,000 men to act against Russian communication lines. But Yuan
promised help only if he received a written order from the empress
dowager personally. So the Japanese withdrew.

Yuan suspected Japanese motives. He wanted to act independently
in the hope that this would increase China's chances at the peace table.
He and his friends had long been known to favor independent action
against Russia, which could legally have been justified, they thought, as
enforcing neutrality. China, they argued, could not allow any power
to use Chinese territory as a base of operations. Consequently Russia
must be driven from Manchuria; otherwise Japan could rightly consider
Chinese inactivity as an unfriendly act and a breach of neutrality.[3]

When war broke out in 1904, China had no choice of policies at all.
Her role was determined by the foreign powers. As the final result of
pressure, counterpressure, intrigues, threats, and promises, the Chinese
government declared its neutrality on February 12, 1904 — neutrality
not in the positive sense Yuan Shih-k'ai had wished but in the sense
of complete inaction.

To the regret of many Chinese, China refrained from all military
activity, in spite of the fact that thousands of Chinese lives were lost
and heavy damage was done to Chinese property in the course of the
fighting. This forbearance, if that is what it was, earned her no appreciation abroad. An announcement by the Chinese government that the
belligerents would be asked for damages was greeted with hostility
by the Russians and Japanese. The Chinese government then quickly
withdrew its claim. The aim it concentrated on was bringing the war
to an early end. It discussed seriously the possibility of asking the United
States to arbitrate. As soon as Theodore Roosevelt's willingness to lend
his Good Offices to bring the parties together became known, the government expressed its hope to him that he would use his influence to
protect the sovereignty and territorial rights of China. The president
gave his promise, with the reservation that he would take no part in the

peace negotiations, and without mention, of course, of his hope that Manchuria would become an "area of friction" between Russia and Japan so that the United States would have a freer hand in the Far East.[4]

The Chinese took no stand during the negotiations, except to announce that they would not recognize any clause in the peace treaty which had not previously been discussed. They hoped by this announcement to prevent Japan from simply succeeding to the rights and privileges they had previously been forced to grant to the tsarist government. But the hope was short-lived. Neither then nor later could they prevent this step. The peace terms held out no very bright prospects for China. Japan's paramount interests in Korea were recognized. Russian rights in the Liaotung peninsula were transferred to Japan. The southern section of the Manchurian Railway was ceded to Japan, as was half of Sakhalin. Both parties had to withdraw troops but were permitted to leave railway guards (maximum 15 per kilometer). Both promised to maintain the Open Door in Manchuria and to use the Manchurian Railway for nonmilitary purposes, except in the Liaotung peninsula.

The hopeful mood of the Chinese and their guarded sympathy for Japan at the beginning of the war had by the time of the peace given way to a somewhat fatalistic resignation to the fate Russia and Japan might have in store for them. Russia was suspected, justly enough, of having designs on Mongolia and Turkestan. Japan was regarded with mixed emotions, felt toward her also by other nations. Her impressive victories were accepted with pleasure until a cool analysis of events led to the apprehension that Japanese predominance might turn into Japanese omnipotence. Of all the anticipated dangers, the Chinese feared most a Japanese demand for compensation from China for missed opportunities at the peace table. Peking launched various *ballons d'essai* to sound out Tokyo, but with little success. The government did not know where to turn for help. Sometimes leaning toward Japan, sometimes toward the Western powers, it arrived at no definite policy. "L'inertie est leur ligne de conduite et leur force," said a French observer. But inertia was not a policy deliberately chosen by Peking. It wished to steer the political future of the country, as its considerable diplomatic activity showed, but was frustrated in its attempts.[5]

Russia's defeat looked as though it might prove a good opportunity for China to recover administrative control over Manchuria and other outlying territories. The renewal of the Anglo-Japanese Alliance in

1905 was welcomed as facilitating this end and as making Japanese adventures more difficult as well. Russia's weakness looked promising and Chinese hopes were raised. The empress dowager, the emperor, Prince Ch'ing, Yuan Shih-k'ai, and other high officials anticipated a period during which China should be spared the incessant intrigues and aggressions of Russia, France, and Germany.[6] The territorial integrity and the rights of China seemed safe for the future.*

But in their optimism the Chinese leaders miscalculated the relation of Russia's weakness to that of China. Even in defeat Russia was strong enough to damage China. On second thought Peking could see new dangers threatening from St. Petersburg. Warnings reached China that Russia was about to restore her prestige by further expansion in the Far East, obviously at China's expense. Furthermore the blocs being formed among the major powers appeared to China as a threat rather than a blessing. Peking feared isolation and realized the need of attachment to some powerful nation as an ally. The only logical choice in Chinese minds was Japan. They laid plans for a Sino-Japanese alliance and for the recovery of control over Manchuria. On every occasion Chinese officials urged the Japanese to discuss the Manchurian question and other problems concerning the two countries. They appealed to Washington for a reduction in the number of Russian and Japanese railway guards and a shortening of the evacuation period, which was to last eighteen months. This last point was of particular importance to the Chinese, who remembered their previous sad experiences with the Russians. With the United States mediating, the Russians agreed to twelve months. But the number of railway guards was not changed.[7]

On October 17, 1905, the Portsmouth Treaty was first officially submitted by the Chinese Foreign Office to the empress dowager and the emperor for discussion. The empress warned the councilors that, no matter what the decision might be, Russia and Japan must be treated in such a way that no foreign criticism would be provoked. During another meeting on the following day it was determined to establish Chinese views on the three clauses affecting China most closely: the lease of the Liaotung peninsula, the evacuation period, and Chinese rights over the Chinese Eastern Railway. Settlement of these three prob-

* The Chinese minister in London stated that now, after the Russo-Japanese War, the Open Door would no longer be a diplomatic phrase but a reality. — London *Times*, January 26, 1906.

lems became the main object of Chinese diplomatic activity. But once again China had little opportunity to improve its international situation; the vital decisions were made by others.

Very soon after the ratification of the Portsmouth Treaty, Baron Komura went to Peking to settle the Manchurian problem, as affected by the treaty. By the time the conversations began, the Chinese had become disillusioned with Japan as the savior of the Far East. The Japanese talked about their wishes but ignored the Chinese. The question of an alliance or entente was apparently never brought up. The Chinese officials feared the worst. Animosity against Japan took on such proportions that the *Kokumin Shimbun* complained about the unfriendliness of the Chinese and pointed out that the Chinese cry for the "recovery of rights" was mainly directed against Japan. The diplomatic negotiations were kept secret. The Chinese plenipotentiaries apparently failed to maintain their stand. They had brought an impressive list of over fifty points into the conference and left with a treaty and protocols confirming Japan with more rights and privileges* than Russia had had.[8]

These agreements with Japan were a particularly hard blow to the Chinese, who were now pushed back into the role of pawn, from which they thought they had just escaped. But following the peace settlement, at least for a moment, outside pressure upon China relaxed. After the Russo-Japanese War the focus of international politics began its gradual shift from the Far East to Europe. The shift gave the Chinese a most welcome respite from the hectic days before 1905, which they used to evaluate the deeper meaning of the Japanese victory.

That an Oriental nation should have been able to defeat an Occidental power brought into relief once more the political and economic backwardness of China. As after the war of 1895 and the Boxer Rebellion, more Chinese now began to appreciate the need to modernize. A growing concern with material, technical things and with political and social institutions, an urge to stimulate the development of science, and concomitant changes in patterns of thought demonstrated how widely and deeply westernization had penetrated the leading minds of China. In many ways the reaction to the Russo-Japanese War was an accelera-

* Among others, new ports were opened to foreign residence, additional railway rights in Manchuria were granted, and Japanese capitalists obtained the right to exploit forests on the right bank of the Yalu River.

tion and strengthening of the trends set in motion earlier, especially by the Boxer Rebellion.

In 1900 the Chinese had been stirred by their inability to oppose the encroachments of militarily superior foreigners. The answer to the problem was then felt to lie in some method by which Western technological achievements could be superimposed upon Chinese culture without disturbing it. The doubts which had arisen in the course of searching for such a method were so increased by the Japanese victory that an investigation began of the deeper roots which might explain the phenomenon of an Oriental nation matching a Western antagonist, and a desire arose to emulate the example. Among a section of the Chinese willingness was shown even to surrender the Chinese "spirit," if surrender should be the price of respect as a nation. The reform movement now grew more radical. In the ideas it advocated, the type of leadership controlling it, and the methods it employed, it became a revolutionary movement. It inaugurated two major processes. One, the easier, was the introduction of Western physical achievements together with the corollary institutions. The other, much more difficult, was the creation of new modes of thought. The second of these alone could guarantee the first. The widespread awareness of this interdependence was in itself an indication of how much progress had been made.

Great plans were developed for the army. For several decades past a few individuals had paid special attention to the creation of a military force. But their efforts had been local and the armies, personal instruments of their creators. The idea now was to establish a national army under the centralized control of a Board of War and educated and equipped according to the most advanced Western standards. The plans were put into practice. By 1912 the army had not quite reached its anticipated size, nor was its efficiency up to expected levels. But, for better or worse, it had created enough respect for itself so that an army career was no longer disdained as the worst way to earn a living. Westernization had triumphed over an ancient Chinese antipathy.

Even more successful, temporarily at least, was the government's campaign against opium. Progress was made also in the field of education, especially of students abroad. Though the quality and the usefulness of the substance learned abroad may be debatable, a door was opened to the influx of Western ideas. Another was opened by the abolition of the traditional civil service examinations in 1905. But other innovations, particularly those requiring the immediate cooperation of large sections of the population, such as the modernization of the financial system, of the judiciary, of agriculture and forestry, remained mostly on paper. Their failure can easily enough be explained by the fact that they demanded sacrifices, or hurt vested interests, or required the abandonment of traditions.[9]

The second process, the changing of attitudes, had, of course, begun as soon as Western contacts intensified. The striking feature now was the attempt consciously to plan and control the change, an extremely difficult task. By comparing China with Japan, the Chinese soon found out that in Japan the latent forces in popular mass action had been awakened, concentrated, and exploited with an extraordinary single-ness of purpose for the aims of the whole national community. This essential dynamic in the life of modern nation-states had still not been utilized in China. The masses, including the educated among them, were politically indifferent, wasted their brain power on antiquated teachings, and failed to recognize a national center toward which their efforts could gravitate. The basic difficulty was the absence of public spirit.[10]

The ethical world-state of Confucius and the cultural unity of the Empire were not adequate concepts to substitute for the unifying force of nationalism, indispensable for national survival in an age of power politics and imperialism. They certainly could not rally the masses or supply the ideological impetus and emotional excitement which must back foreign policy in a world of nation-states and total wars. Chinese leaders became aware that organized nationalism in the West and in Japan was "the secret," was the background against which the great powers were conducting their foreign policy. The Chinese government set out, therefore, to create nationalism in the Empire.

The spectacular reform edict of September 1, 1906, explained the newly discovered cause of all Chinese evils to the people: "The lack of prosperity in the state is due to the separation between the officials and the people and the lack of cooperation between the capital and the provinces. The officials are ignorant of the needs of the people, and the people do not understand what is necessary for the safety of the state." The edict further pointed out that the strength of other nations lay in the fact that "the ruler and his people act as one body animated by one spirit."

This spirit of unity was thought to be the result of the constitutional form of government. The creation of a constitutional form of government was therefore promised in the edict, following the report of a commission which had been sent abroad in 1905 to study Western forms of government. An additional purpose of the commission had been to gain prestige for China by showing the world how modern the country was becoming. In fact, the number of European countries visited within a very short span of time by the commission, after the fashion of American tourists, permits the suspicion that publicity rather than study was the major function.

The commission was composed of members none of whom were radicals. They were not motivated by any desire to change the polity of China. Like their government, they sincerely hoped that the introduction of constitutional methods would strengthen the country and improve the government, while leaving its basic structure untouched. Their report to the court after their return showed clearly that their minds had hardly moved out of the traditional Chinese grooves. Most of the governmental institutions they had studied abroad were seen through conservative Chinese eyes and so misinterpreted to appear close to the Chinese government in basic features. The Chinese government, therefore, meant something entirely different by its promises of reform from what was read into these promises by the radical reformers, who were more familiar with the real meaning of Western constitutional government, and the seeds of conflict were sown right there. Nevertheless the commission had significance as a symbol of the new spirit which had entered the most conservative circles of China. A definite sign of the government's good will was the establishment of assemblies in the provinces to prepare the people for a future national assembly.[11]

The creation of assemblies as a preparation for constitutional government was, however, only a stimulus in the effort to develop nationalism. Assemblies could not in themselves create a national spirit. The very concept of the nation was strange to the Chinese, it had no place in their philosophy. The Confucian Chinese recognized no relations except personal ones, and it was within the framework of these that he was anxious to develop himself. Ties among family, kin, and friends were the closest and most concrete of all ties and so dominated all others. He could not abstract the community from the individuals who composed it and so could not develop a loyalty toward it. Loyalty could exist only toward actual people, living or dead; hence the almost complete absence of social consciousness or responsibility. Before the Chinese people could become nationalistic, the idea of a national community had to be made real to them. The attempt to make it so was undertaken first by the reformers, later by the Kuomintang Nationalists, and eventually by the Communists. For the last group the task was the easiest, because the strength of the family as a bidder for the primary loyalty of the Chinese citizen had been gradually weakened by urbanization, industrialization, and wars.[12]

In the meantime the government, on its own volition and prodded by the reformers, followed up the September 1906 reform edict with numerous other edicts, all designed to change the institutional pattern of China. Many of these edicts remained pieces of paper, others shook the foundations of the Empire. Some of the same changes which had produced the *coup d'état* of 1898, or changes even more revolutionary than these, were now resisted only passively or not at all. To be sure, the edicts setting forth the changes were made acceptable in various ways. Old institutions were used to disguise new procedures, and promises were given that vested interests would not be harmed. But no matter in what guise, the acceptance of far-reaching reforms amounted to a distinct break with venerable traditions. "China for the Chinese" as an expression of the newly discovered nationalism stopped being the slogan of a few advanced intellectuals and came to express the feeling of larger and larger groups in China. Not yet, however, groups large enough to constitute the mass of the people. The slogan was still not a mass slogan, nor were the reforms accepted by the masses. For this reason many did not endure, and their collapse left a dangerous void.

Under the new slogan "China for the Chinese" organized and deliberate resistance to all foreign influence developed among the Chinese elite. The reaction of the Western powers was naturally not one of approval. The almost unanimous report of contemporary Western observers was that the Chinese, in their exuberance over the newly found panacea, as they supposed nationalism to be, went straight into a chauvinism dangerous for their own good. Even discounting the prejudice and bias in such Western observations, there was probably much truth in them. The policy of handing out concessions in China had undergone changes ever since 1900. Now, beginning with about 1905, the Chinese government attempted to refuse concessions outright or attach to its grants conditions so burdensome as to make them useless. For instance, new mining rules were promulgated, putting such high royalties, export taxes, and likin on the minerals that the total charges on the output would have been prohibitive. Every minute violation of the terms of grants of concessions was used to declare the concessions forfeited. In many instances the attempt was made, though unsuccessfully, to buy back concessions. And only strong pressure from abroad prevented the government from absorbing private foreign interests in telegraph lines, steamship and railway companies, and other enterprises.[13]

These attempts by the Chinese government to hamper foreign operations were in the main merely symbolic declarations of independence rather than steps leading to concrete achievements. Of two other methods applied by the government in the hope of fortifying the country against foreign aggression and exploitation, the same may be said. The first was an improvement and centralization of the administration, including that of outlying territories. Innumerable rescripts changed the governmental organization, ranging from insignificant readjustments to such fundamental steps as the unification of Manchuria into one governmental unit and plans for the federation and Sinification of Mongolia.* The second method was to stimulate enterprise by Chinese. The establishment of industries was encouraged by promises of subsidies, and several other attempts were made to replace foreign economic activity by native.

Whether it was ever the intention of the Chinese government fully to apply these new prohibitive rules and regulations against foreigners, however, is questionable. To some extent the measures designed to eliminate foreign control and undue foreign influence over the economy were merely for the record — were a concession to the radical elements, especially the students, Young China, who clamored for outright confiscation of all concessions to foreigners and the revocation of all rights, privileges, and favors previously granted. These groups were loudly vocal and proved embarrassing to the Chinese statesmen who had to deal with foreigners. For the Chinese government realized how much

* The foreign political implications of these administrative reforms became particularly clear when the province in which Shanghai is situated was divided into two provinces. The likely reason was that foreign influence was strong in Shanghai and the neighborhood and that the Chinese hoped to contain it by erecting administrative barriers. — DSDD, January 30, 1905, No. 1804.

China needed foreign financial and technical help, and can hardly have wished to antagonize foreigners to the point where they would either overrun China or, more likely, withdraw their assistance. Economic nationalism was an obvious impossibility for a China eager to modernize. The Chinese Foreign Office judged it politic to dissociate itself from these radical elements and assured foreigners that only those concessions would be canceled on which the time limit set for the beginning of exploitation had expired. In the dilemma between speedy modernization with foreign assistance or slow modernization without it, only the most extreme Chinese chose the second alternative, ridding the country of foreign control being their obsession. But the urgent need to modernize was recognized by all factions alike. Even Young China's aim was not to prevent modern developments but instead to prevent foreigners from controlling them.

These efforts against foreign interests were quickly challenged. The powers had not worked "for China's good," so some foreigners maintained, to have the door shut in their faces. Various nations protested against the "high-handed" methods of the Chinese government. If the Chinese government was unable to check the agitation against foreign capital, the British minister threatened, he would notify his government to adopt remedial measures without consulting China. In answer to this and similar protests, the Chinese maintained that all recent decrees concerning the grant of concessions were China's internal affair and that there was no intention of violating existing obligations.[14]

There was indeed no reason for foreign complaint. China endeavored to exclude all foreigners alike from positions incompatible with treaty rights. Equality of treatment was maintained, even though China was bound only by the most-favored-nation clause, not the Open Door principle. The foreign objection to China's wanting to shut the door implied an interpretation of the Open Door doctrine which up to then had been mentioned once in a while by subordinate officials* but was not generally understood to be part of it, namely, that foreign powers had a right to economic opportunity in China. Normally the Open Door did not mean that China's door must be open. Mr. Alfred Sze pointed that out at the Washington Conference in 1921 when he said that "the

* For example, the French minister Beau, before his departure for China, said that no nation had a right to leave its resources untapped. If China would not exploit them, Europe had a right to do so. — Le Temps, April 8, 1901.

'open door' did not mean the opening of all parts of China to foreign trade, commerce, and industry." [15] It did mean that if China's door was open to any nation, it must be equally open to all.

The real controversy between foreigners and Chinese continued to be China's stress upon the territorial and administrative integrity of the Empire. To China this was an end in itself — the only one of any real concern; to foreigners it was only a means to an end, the end being the Open Door. The Open Door was occasionally mentioned in speeches by Chinese representatives abroad, but in all official and significant communications between Chinese and foreign officials emanating from China, mention was almost exclusively of the integrity and sovereignty of the Empire. China's policy after 1905 indicated clearer than ever before that equal treatment of foreign nations was a secondary consideration with her — or primary only in the sense that she did not want to hand out rights and privileges to anybody. In this different emphasis upon the priority of the Open Door policy or the integrity policy could be found much of China's disappointment even with "friends."

The Chinese overlooked the fact that certainly in the early years of the Open Door policy, the sponsors themselves had little hope of securing the territorial integrity of all of China. They also overlooked the fact that the notes of 1899 recognized the existence of spheres of interest, with all their implications, and that this recognition still had influence many years later in spite of the Hay circular of July 1900. It is legally correct that China did not become an actual party to an Open Door policy until 1922. But politically her involvement was much earlier. The Chinese government took a very long time to realize that forced treaties are binding according to international law. Peking argued frequently that all the concessions so obnoxious to China had been forced from her, that their granting had been due to the application of superior force, and that hence their revocation could not be an infraction of the principle of equal opportunity. But foreigners took a different view.

At any rate, the nation-wide agitation in China after 1905 for sovereignty, for a position of equality among nations, for self-determination, sounded somewhat hollow in the absence of all elements which could make such aspirations a reality. In the world of 1905 to 1910 China could not reasonably hope for complete autonomy until she could enforce and defend it with military strength. In the absence of such backing, there was danger in the aggressive, negative policy toward foreign nations into which she was now led. And paradoxically, the movement toward nationalism designed to unite the country against the outside involved measures threatening disunity within. Though the Chinese had probably correctly diagnosed one of the roots of their inferiority among nations, concretely they succeeded only in discrediting and abolishing the hangovers of times past without replacing them, for the most part, with more than paper edicts as far as the masses were concerned. The destruction of the traditional institutions on which Chinese society had rested unsettled things; what few new institutions were developed, such as the new provincial assemblies, were not capable of holding society together, let alone improving it. The short-run effect of the new developments was to split the people into a relatively small section of those accepting the innovations and a vastly larger section of those thrown into doubts and uncertainties.

Nevertheless, though social tension and disorganization existed internally in China after 1905 as the result of the new developments, and though, externally, powerful nations became exasperated with her new methods, little heed was paid to these new dangers in the exuberance of the incipient nationalism. The rebuffs China still had to endure now appeared to spur the Chinese to further action rather than drive them into withdrawal and isolation. Passive resistance disappeared from the methods of foreign policy. A new self-confidence seized the leaders, evoking a strong desire to shape actively the nation's destiny. The conviction was growing that with the introduction of Western methods and attitudes, China had wiped out the disadvantages which had caused her inferiority. The consequences of this belief became more strikingly evident than ever before in 1907 and 1908, when China was confronted with a policy of the powers which the government interpreted somewhat inaccurately* as a possible repetition of the dangerous days of 1900.

* China's major error was to overlook that the Far East no longer played so important a role in the policy of Western nations as it had played a decade earlier and that therefore moves having a certain similarity to those around 1900 might not have similar aims. China continued to consider herself the center of the universe, as most nations do.

8

Alignment with Germany and America

T HE event which aroused the Chinese and gave their new diplomacy a jolt was the Franco-Japanese agreement of June 10, 1907. It was a most shocking reminder that the sphere of interest concept was still alive. The official text was relatively harmless, though obnoxious enough to the Chinese. After confirming their adherence to the principles of the Open Door and the integrity of China, the two powers promised mutual support in assuring peace and security in the regions inside China bordering on territory in which they had rights of sovereignty, protection, or occupation. A letter supplemental to the formal agreement defined the sphere of interest of each power. France claimed Kwangtung, Kwangsi, and Yunnan; Japan claimed Fukien and certain regions of Manchuria and Mongolia. Japan's foreign minister, Count Hayashi, himself remarked that the treaty was not a contribution to the Open Door, as it purported to be, but was "something which very much resembles the significance of the sphere of influence." [1]

All soothing statements emanating from Japan and France that China should rejoice rather than be worried over a treaty guaranteeing its integrity, that there was no *arrière pensée* behind the agreement, failed to dispel Chinese suspicions; on the contrary, they heightened apprehensions.[2]

At Yuan Shih-k'ai's suggestion the government asked for the advice of the provincial officials, quite a novel procedure. Chang Chih-tung's typical proposal was to open more ports in Fukien and Kwangtung to international trade and to develop the resources of Yunnan and Chekiang with Chinese capital. He also advocated the strengthening of the Chinese navy and the frontier garrisons. Yuan implored the throne to study carefully the consequences of the agreement and to devise means for the safeguarding of the national interest.[3]

Then, as before and after, the Chinese resented the complete disregard with which their country was treated during the negotiations leading to the agreement. It hurt their pride and showed up the futility of all the measures taken to obtain equal status among the powers. In China's view foreigners had no right to guarantee peace and order inside Chinese territory. To the government such a guarantee appeared merely a disguise for the spheres of interest, and the Franco-Japanese agreement was therefore interpreted as the possible beginning of a new break-up of the Empire. "Whatever has been leased by the Chinese government is now almost invested with the rights of occupation, and whatever has not been leased but is bordering on leased territory, is in danger of being enclosed in the same," wrote a Chinese newspaper and added that Yunnan, Kwangsi, and Kwangtung, hitherto objects of vague ambitions, had now become in reality the reward of many years of French scheming.[4]

In August 1907 Peking protested to Paris and Tokyo. The replies were in a reassuring tone, and Peking had to declare itself satisfied.[5] But uneasiness remained, and subsequent events proved it to be well founded.

On July 30, 1907, the Franco-Japanese agreement was followed by a similar, French-instigated Russo-Japanese agreement; and on August 31 Russia and Great Britain settled their Far Eastern and South Asian differences in an agreement. A number of less publicized but more obnoxious treaties between Russia and China and between Japan and China completed this rush of treaty-making. In large part these agreements reflected European political conditions, particularly France's desire to have peace and understanding among its actual or potential allies in Europe. In part also they resulted from the need to reconcile imperialist ambitions in the Far East, especially those of Russia and Japan in Manchuria. Incidentally they had the effect, in the words of a Russian official, of preventing the United States from "outside interference" in Manchurian affairs.[6]

Manchuria once more became front-page news. Russia was reactivating her expansionism. Tokyo was reaping the fruits of the 1905 victory. Washington, or perhaps more correctly Consul General Willard Straight at Mukden and big businessman E. H. Harriman, had great ideas of dollar diplomacy, railway construction, and industrial development. Manchuria was again the focus of Far Eastern diplomacy. But the political settlements reached in the various treaties created the impression among outside observers, including the Chinese, that the renewed activities were taking place on the basis of broad, general understandings, as if the intense competition of former years had now been eliminated.

This trend of events appeared most ominous to Peking. The rivalry among the powers in China had always been a source of anxiety to the government, but its apparent diminution was feared even more. For international jealousies and suspicions had for decades been the best allies of China and had formed the basis, almost, of China's precarious existence, certainly of her foreign policy. Now a polarization had taken place on the basis of political understandings which reduced rival groups to two, each of which, the Chinese were convinced, had divided the spoils among its members. The need of immediate and decisive action to prevent complete encirclement seemed imperative to the Chinese government. It also realized that a balance-of-power policy had become difficult and that in view of changed circumstances new methods had to be employed.

Yuan Shih-k'ai, by this time the most prominent and active member of the Chinese government, had foreseen the situation and had hoped to prevent its arrival by an understanding with Japan. But Japanese aggressiveness in Manchuria and demands for special rights and privileges made friendly collaboration between the two Oriental powers once more impossible. Cultural affinity, or the much vaunted "Asian spirit," again proved incapable of overcoming national ambitions and interests. Instead, influenced by German propaganda, China feared Japan more than any other nation and turned for assistance to Germany and the United States, the two powers left out of the pattern established by the 1907 agreements. Peking decided upon a new balance-of-power policy, not one conducted, as hitherto, by playing a number of nations against each other inside China, but by attempting to create a Chinese-German-American entente. In addition, the more traditional method of attracting foreign, especially American, capital into Manchuria and China proper was also to be employed.

The entente scheme was a bold innovation. China now was to become an active partner in a rival group. The Chinese had been encouraged in this extraordinary step by the German emperor, who had actually suggested it.[7] The other scheme, the attracting of American capital, was the brain child of the Chinese and Americans, particularly Willard Straight. Once the plans had been worked out, the Chinese proceeded to realize them.

101

The Chinese minister in Germany was instructed to sound out Berlin on the possibility of an alliance. At the same time the German ambassador informed Theodore Roosevelt of Germany's willingness to join such a combination, the aim of which should be to guarantee China's integrity and to strengthen her backbone against encroachments by other powers.

The president showed no enthusiasm. He was experimenting with his Japanese policy and preferred to postpone any formal understanding at least until after the effect of the American fleet's visit to the Far East had become clear. He left the door open, though, and agreed with the Germans that the initiative would have to come from China.

It came in November 1907, when the Chinese brought up the topic of an understanding again. On this occasion the president made his only encouraging statement, just encouraging enough not to lose his opportunity with China in case the Japanese policy should fail. He said that in view of existing American ideas and principles a formal entente would be out of the question; however, an agreement with regard to common procedures among the three powers might be feasible.

Peking found the result of its investigations sufficiently attractive to continue deliberations on the entente. The Chinese statesmen agreed upon a number of points of extreme importance in the project. First, the discussions must lead to a positive result; failure, and therewith loss of face, was unacceptable. Second, the enterprise must be kept absolutely secret, since China could not afford to antagonize any power until the entente was a fact. Third, a discreet way had to be found of making the entente partners understand that China was unable to contribute military aid. Finally, there must be certainty that the entente would be strong enough to balance the Anglo-French-Russian-Japanese combination.[8] Toward the fall of 1908 the members of the cabinet agreed that all points could be settled satisfactorily.

The plan to lure American capital into Manchuria* was simpler because it was not so blatantly political in aim and because Willard Straight was more than eager to be helpful. After long discussions between T'ang Shao-yi and Straight and the hurdling of many obstacles in Peking, the government finally agreed to ask the United States for a loan to estab-

* The Chinese would have taken British capital as well, though for financial more than for political reasons. But the British Foreign Office, stressing the political significance of such loans, was unwilling to support them because of the possible annoyance of Japan.

lish a central Manchurian bank designed to encourage the development of the region, for funds to establish a uniform Chinese currency on the basis of the gold standard, and for permission to increase customs duties in exchange for the abolition of internal trade taxes (likin).[9]

T'ang Shao-yi was appointed special commissioner to visit the United States and to negotiate the entente and the loan. But since the real mission had to be kept secret, an excuse for T'ang's trip had to be found. Conveniently, Congress had just passed a law remitting part of the American indemnity for damages suffered in the Boxer Rebellion. So, to thank the United States for this magnanimity became the official purpose of T'ang's voyage. Apparently this ruse was effective. Only the very highest members of the various governments concerned seem to have been fully aware of the plans for an entente. Even Straight and Minister Rockhill appear to have been uninformed.*

Possibly the Russians, and certainly the Japanese, had at least an inkling of the entente plan. For when T'ang stopped in Tokyo on his trip to Washington in the fall of 1908, he was warned that Japan was China's best friend and that an alliance between China and any other power would be regarded by Japan as an indication of China's distrust. In January the *Hochi Shimbun* wrote editorially that T'ang's mission for the establishment of an American-Chinese-German entente had failed. It was Japan's knowledge or conjecture of the Chinese plans which prompted Tokyo to rush the State Department into the exchange of the Root-Takahira notes, in which through recognition of the *status quo* in the Far East the Chinese plan was to be frustrated. The Japanese would have preferred to sign the notes before T'ang's arrival in Washington, but the American officials decided to delay this final act, and then performed it on the very day T'ang entered the capital, November 30, 1908.[10]

T'ang's disappointment when he learned of the notes can be imagined. Straight and Ambassador O'Brien in Tokyo had warned the State Department of the bad effect the notes would have in China. Minister Rockhill had shown the notes to Yuan Shih-k'ai on November 22. A conversation

---

* Rockhill's ignorance may be concluded from his letters to the State Department. Straight wrote in his diary in February 1910, on thinking over T'ang's mission, "I am sure that T'ang had something big up his sleeve and that his reluctance to discuss the Loan and his apathy when he arrived were due to his feeling that he had been forestalled, that he had never been given a chance" (Croly, *Willard Straight*, p. 276). Since Straight knew about the financial plans, this leaves only the entente.

had ensued which indicated the unfamiliarity of Rockhill with the entente project and of Yuan with Roosevelt's policy of reaching an understanding with Japan. To Rockhill's "surprise," so he reported home, Yuan showed considerable disappointment and some irritation on seeing the contents of the notes. He asked whether the notes would be exchanged if China had objections to their terms. Rockhill replied that they would be exchanged and that he could see no reason for Chinese objections; rather he expected the Chinese to be pleased with this re-affirmation of America's beneficent policy. Yuan then expressed aston-ishment at the sudden decision to exchange such notes and remarked that if Washington had waited until T'ang's arrival "the United States' desire to strengthen the *status quo* in China could have been more effectively accomplished than by the present plan." Rockhill was some what bewildered as to what T'ang's mission might have to do with the notes; as far as he knew, he wrote, T'ang was on a thank-you mission. Yuan then lifted the veil of secrecy just a trace by hinting that Japan desired the notes only to forestall a similar American-Chinese agreement.

Yuan's undiplomatic emotions were explained away the next day as a "misunderstanding." Peking explained that Yuan thought the Root-Takahira notes were too much like some of the agreements of 1907, to which China had serious objections, but now it was fully realized that the notes would have a beneficial effect. On the next day, Rockhill was informed that the regent and the Council were very much pleased with the notes and asked to obtain a sympathetic hearing for T'ang in Wash-ington. Rockhill was informed that the emissary had no special in-structions but would merely like to make further arrangements for the strengthening of Chinese-American friendship if he found conditions favorable. All this was puzzling to Rockhill, who could not quite com-prehend what these remarks had to do with the Chinese desire for loans.[11]

Peking resigned itself to the chain of agreements and exchange of notes by rationalizing that one agreement more or less would make no difference and that if the new situation should provide a few years of peace to the country, there was no reason for complaint. Roosevelt justified his policy by pointing out that an understanding with China might have encouraged that nation to embark upon a Japanophobe policy, which might have resulted in a war in which neither the United States nor Germany could have given assistance.[12] The entente project was thus disposed of before T'ang had an opportunity to broach the subject. The financial part of his mission remained to be settled, and the State Department had well-prepared plans for T'ang's suggestions too.

During the summer of 1908 the State Department had learned from Rockhill that T'ang would try to obtain a loan for the development of Manchuria as a countermove to spreading Japanese influence. As a security for the loan the Chinese intended to use the remission of the Boxer indemnity. Rockhill advised the Department to frustrate this scheme, presumably because, first, the Chinese intended to refuse foreign control over the expenditure of the loan and because, second, he, more than Straight, favored the Department's policy of appeasing Japan by allowing her a free hand in Manchuria.

The Department heeded Rockhill's advice and the Far Eastern Division hatched out a plan by which T'ang's hand was to be forced. The origin of the plan was the Chinese note in which the government acknowledged Congressional action regarding the Boxer indemnity. Without formally connecting the topic with the remission, the last paragraph of the note referred to the possibility of sending Chinese students to the United States. Only in conversations with Rockhill had the Chinese mentioned casually the idea of using the remission for this purpose. The Far Eastern Division, however, took up the idea as excellently adapted for obligating the Chinese to a definite use of the funds. Just before T'ang's arrival, the Department published throughout the United States the exchange of notes in which reference was made to the vague educational project, thus creating the impression that the Chinese intended to use the remission of the indemnity for educational purposes. Before they knew it, the Chinese were thus committed, and the Manchurian loan plan was wrecked.[13]

The American officials were very much pleased with their cleverness, while T'ang, who saw through the scheme, resented it. He did not give up before making a last attempt to save the situation. He told the officials of the Far Eastern Division that "it would be unfortunate should an impression be created either in this country, in China, or abroad, that the remission had been made conditionally." China was grateful and would faithfully observe the promise to send students to America, but for the United States to insist that the remission should be used for educational purposes would be an obvious indication of America's doubt of "China's good-faith." He repeated this point to the secretary of state during his first interview. But the American officials were unimpressed. Apparently they judged their policy with Japan so successful that China could be ignored. For even the interview with the secretary was not granted freely to T'ang.

Huntington Wilson, chief of the Far Eastern Division, had to urge the secretary to give the "impatiently waiting" T'ang an appointment and to make him feel "that he is at any rate having a most complete and sympathetic hearing"; T'ang was "bursting" with matters of vital concern to China, and his aims were consistent with and beneficial to American interests. On December 9, 1908, T'ang finally got his interview, in which he reported the Japanese warning against an entente, explained Yuan Shih-k'ai's misunderstanding with Rockhill about the Root-Takahira notes, and then conversed at length about the financial plans of his government. The loan for Manchurian development was not mentioned.[14]

The State Department conveyed its decision to Willard Straight, who had returned to Washington. Chinese wishes accorded with American aims. Nevertheless the government did not want to be involved in the loans. However, Straight was authorized to introduce T'ang unofficially to New York financiers.[15] This reluctance to interfere actively with Japan's plans in Manchuria was merely a corollary of the administration's major aim in the Far East, the improvement of American-Japanese relations, even at the risk of antagonizing China.

T'ang's conversations in New York had a good beginning but soon came to nothing. On his way to the United States the empress dowager and the emperor had died. Yuan Shih-k'ai was ousted from the cabinet, and with him went the influence of his protégé T'ang, who could not make up for this loss by producing any diplomatic success abroad. Early in January 1909 he announced his sudden departure via Europe to China. His brief meetings with American and European financiers did not lead to concrete results. The hurry of his leave-taking stood in stark contrast to the pomp and circumstance of his arrival.[16]

From the standpoint of China's foreign policy the mission failed completely and was a rude reminder that China still was a pawn in the game of international politics. Notwithstanding "friendly" professions to the contrary, Peking had to learn that concern for the principles of the Open Door and Chinese integrity was not a primary one in the Far

Eastern policy of the Western powers. Placating Japan had priority. Theodore Roosevelt wrote to the German emperor that T'ang was completely upset by the events and that "the Chinese are so helpless in carrying out any fixed policy, whether home or foreign," that one could have only the most cautious dealings with them. This was a most remarkable illustration of failing to behold the beam in one's own eye while wishing to cast out the mote in another's. It was American, not Chinese, policy that was moving in circles. On the inevitable premise that China must adjust to the policies of foreign powers, Chinese policy was quite consistently directed toward obtaining any outside assistance available against foreign aggression. It was only reasonable, therefore, that after the Root-Takahira notes China should incline toward Germany to the exclusion of the other Western powers, including the United States. Germany was the only major power with interests in China remaining outside the ostensibly united front and hence was the only usable one to be played against the other nations in the financial and economic imperialism which reached its height between 1909 and 1914. Luckily for the Chinese, they underestimated the competitiveness among the foreign powers that was their most reliable ally. In the years ahead this spirit, more than Chinese efforts, succeeded in driving the nations apart, so that at last was ended the Chinese nightmare of encirclement and of extinction as an independent nation.

9

Strengthening the Empire

NEITHER the failure to create an American-German-Chinese entente nor the various agreements of the major powers in 1907 discouraged the Chinese government from pursuing its activities to cope with foreign demands. These demands now referred mostly to railroad concessions and loans. Only in Manchuria and other outlying territories did Russian and Japanese aggressiveness continue to represent a threat to the territorial integrity of China. The government, remembering the popular clamor of 1905 and 1906, and spurred by its own newly discovered courage, continued to integrate these areas more closely into the Chinese governmental organization. In Peking's estimation the greatest danger threatened in Manchuria, and this opinion seemed completely justified when international rivalry there, which had begun to be intense in 1907, reached a climax in 1909 and 1910. Consequently the Chinese government concentrated primarily upon the solution of that problem.

Internationally the government stood alone at first. The recent policies of the foreign powers appeared to have eliminated every prospect either of assistance from any one of them or of playing one against the other. Japan used her foothold on the mainland for all that it was worth. Innumerable conflicts arose with China — over railroad building, customs stations and payments, exploitation of natural resources, laying of telegraph lines — which China had to solve single-handed, hence most of the time in Japan's favor. Relations with Russia were little less obnoxious. No foreign help was forthcoming here either, merely warnings that whatever China did, she must interfere with no foreign rights. The biggest blow came when Great Britain seemed to surrender to Japan by disavowing British commercial interests in favor of the Anglo-Japanese alliance.* This was as revolutionary in British Far Eastern policy as it must have been depressing to the Chinese.

---

* The Hsinmintun-Fakumen railroad case.

Internally, too, Peking lacked support. Popular enthusiasm for an active policy of opposition did not extend, at this time, to Manchuria. Only the inhabitants of Manchuria itself were greatly upset over developments there, and they were unable to enlist the sympathy of the Chinese across the Great Wall.[1] The reason was partly that encroachment by economic and financial means is in its nature more subtle and less spectacular than overt aggression. But a more powerful reason was the absorption of the Chinese masses in the complex national and international developments south of the Great Wall that eventually led to the revolution of 1911.

The reform movement was getting more and more into the hands of the revolutionaries, and the Manchu dynasty was becoming the focus of the most diverse "anti" feelings. Inspired by the West and expecting Western support, the revolutionaries in their propaganda ascribed all responsibility for China's unfortunate position in world politics to the Manchu dynasty. They exonerated the foreign powers and, one sometimes feels, enjoyed the ammunition which foreign aggression provided them against the dynasty. This attitude was not due to a lack of patriotism (though it did facilitate Western aggression). It was, rather, a result of the revolutionaries' theory that China's instability was an inevitable consequence of its historical development — regardless of contemporary foreign activities — and that only the destruction of the old order, by any means, and the establishment of a revolutionary republic could remedy things. This resentment against the Manchus was bound to carry over to some degree into popular feeling about Manchuria. The end effect of the lack of support for the government's policy in Manchuria was the weakening of its position and the encouragement of Russian and Japanese expansion.

Peking was quite aware that it did not possess the substance of control over Manchuria, in spite of the withdrawal of Russian and Japanese troops, the restoration of Chinese civil administration there, and the administrative reorganization tying the area closer to Peking. The basic military superiority of Russia and Japan was decisive and could not be overcome at this time. To diminish the economic superiority of these two countries seemed to be the more feasible plan. Therefore Peking urged upon China's own nationals and upon other countries the further economic development of Manchuria and especially the building of railroads. Preferably China was to control these, but in the absence of

109

resources, the government was willing to share control with assisting foreign powers. And so, not daunted or disabused by recent happenings, Peking once more tried to stimulate the growth of economic interests that would be in competition with those of Russia and Japan.

Its tenacity was rewarded. Assistance came from abroad. The change in the American administration in 1909 brought a reversal of the American Far Eastern policy of reconciliation with Japan. Now the policy was to be a determined attempt at extending American interests in China. The aim was supposedly the strengthening of the principles of the Open Door and Chinese integrity, an aim from which China might have benefited if American policy had been forceful. Unfortunately it was not. With a helpless China as a disconcerted onlooker, the Taft administration weakened Peking's chance of stopping the trend toward the domination of Manchuria by one or two powers. For against the determined expansionism of Russia and Japan, the half-hearted and somewhat unsophisticated policy of the United States could not be very effective.

The foremost means of American policy was American dollars, which were to be spent in Manchuria to counteract Russian and Japanese influence. The State Department worked hand in hand with Straight and Harriman, who were still dreaming of a world-wide American network of communications. Their immediate goal was the acquisition of the Japanese-owned South Manchurian Railway. Since the Japanese refused to sell, the Americans planned to force the sale by their purchase of the Chinese Eastern Railway, or, failing this, by the construction of a new railway from Chinchow to Aigun, roughly parallel to and competing with the Japanese line. A concession for this line was still to be got from the Chinese, but lack of that was never considered a hindrance.

In order to get the concession, Straight went to China as the representative of a group of bankers, the American Consortium, and signed a preliminary agreement with the Manchurian authorities for the financing of the Chinchow-Aigun line by Americans and its building by a British firm. Neither the Manchurian officials nor Straight had authority from their superiors to sign such an agreement. But the American government came to the rescue and saved it. In a note to the British government in November 1909, Secretary of State Knox inaugurated his famous proposal for the complete commercial neutralization of Manchuria and suggested that, if the proposal proved unacceptable, the United

States and Great Britain should become the protagonists in the Chin-chow-Aigun project. Thus the project was to become the strongest lever in American hands to force Russia and Japan into acquiescence with American plans. In the words of Knox, "While it might not be necessary, if the larger (neutralization) plan is generally approved, to construct the Chinchow line, the possession of the right to build is in any case an essential part of the plan of the United States." [2]

Peking, rather than sign the agreement, would have preferred to revive the Manchurian bank plan and to build a railroad connecting Manchuria with the Trans-Siberian Railway. [3] This would have been in conformity with the secret protocols to the Sino-Japanese Treaty of December 22, 1905, which forbade a railroad parallel to the South Manchurian. It would have been altogether less antagonistic to Japan. And it would also have fulfilled the Chinese desire to introduce foreign capital into Manchuria. The Americans would not agree. Torn between two powers as usual, the Chinese broke off negotiations with Straight, who then signed the preliminary agreement with the Manchurian officials.

These officials were even more concerned about the fate of Manchuria than the government in Peking was, and they were much less reluctant to pursue an anti-Japanese policy. The viceroy foresaw annexations and demands for indemnity by Japan and provided against them by mobilizing his troops. He also requested permission in a memorial to the throne to invite foreigners to compete with Russia and Japan and to do everything else to compete with the South Manchurian Railway. The American consul general in Mukden noticed the change in attitude. He reported home that whereas formerly the officials at best complacently approved of his suggestions to attract foreign capital, the viceroy now "virtually begged" for investments from the United States as well as Great Britain and France. [4]

Once the United States government had taken over championship of the Chinchow-Aigun project, pressure upon Peking to sign the preliminary agreement increased. The Chinese delayed action and were vague as to whether or not an edict granting the concession had been approved by the regent. The tactic was the familiar one of deliberately bogging down in administrative formalities in order to avoid making a commitment. Straight believed that this vagueness was a game to subordinate the concession to the preferred Manchurian bank scheme and to keep the door open for the introduction also of British, French, and German capital to counteract American control. The situation was complicated, he added, by palace intrigues, jealousies among the different government departments involved, and "the fears which are very real to these high officials, of Japan and Russia on the one side and a growing public sentiment, as noisy as it is ignorant, on the other." [5] The situation contained almost all the aspects which perennially confronted Chinese officials. And they responded to it with their customary go-slow tactics.

The State Department resented Peking's delay in granting the concession. The delay weakened the neutralization proposal. Impatiently the American minister impressed the president of the Foreign Office, Liang Tun-yen, with the importance of the concession to "stand out as a certain, concrete, tangible fact, well started on its way to accomplishment." [6] But the Chinese were hesitant about assisting in the schemes of the State Department. They had good reason to be, and the fears Straight had detected behind their dilatoriness were justified.

Peking had found out, upon inquiry in Tokyo, that the Japanese reaction to the neutralization proposal was very sour indeed. The accomplishment of the neutralization scheme, so Peking was told, would engender a Russo-Japanese coalition. This was a nightmare of the Chinese. Such a possibility, Liang confessed to the American minister, was of great concern to him and very disturbing. But the minister was out to save the scheme and needed Chinese cooperation. "America assumes the full responsibility for the proposal," he assured Liang, and asked again for immediate ratification of the Chinchow-Aigun preliminary agreement. The assurance, as adventurous as it was meaningless, was nevertheless approved by Knox, who instructed the minister to remind Liang that American efforts "on behalf of China" needed Chinese cooperation and support in order to succeed. He also suggested forcing China's hand by an official American acknowledgment of China's impending approval of the preliminary agreement. [7]

American pressure upon Peking was paralleled by that of the Manchurian viceroy. In a memorial to the throne he pointed out that the Chinchow-Aigun line would have an excellent effect on the covetous Russians and Japanese and that it would intersect the Russian line at its most important point and be an invaluable counterpoise to the South Manchurian Railway.

In response to such urging, an imperial edict was issued in January

1910, but not published, apparently making the preliminary agreement valid. There was no certainty on this point, for the edict contained, it would seem, so many conditions and restrictions as to cause doubt whether the agreement had really been accepted by Peking.[8]

This effect was undoubtedly intended. Peking was still undecided. Pressure and counterpressure were strong; which side Peking's ultimate decision would favor was unpredictable. Early in February 1910 Russia and Japan notified Peking not to finalize the Chinchow-Aigun agreement without prior consultation. When Peking, typically, turned to Washington for "advice," Knox recommended that China should wait until the reaction of all the powers was known and in the meantime should be "firm and patient but not aggressive."[9] This suggestion was most welcome to the Peking government, for it permitted China to sit on the fence till the failure of the American scheme was complete and to avoid complications with both Japan and the United States.

During these international rivalries Japan and Russia were solidifying their own spheres in China. Russia forced upon China an agreement relating to the municipal administration of Harbin, which in the view of the foreign minister contained many bad features, but which he accepted in the expectation of "eventual objections of the Powers to get them eliminated." Tokyo pressed China for a number of similarly disadvantageous agreements.[10]

The Peking cabinet viewed these developments with the "greatest concern and anxiety," Liang told Rockhill. Russia "openly and brutally," Japan "indirectly and with many professions of friendship but none the less effectively," he said, encroached upon Chinese integrity. The same assistance the United States was giving in Manchuria should be granted south of the Great Wall, where conditions were even worse.[11]

The neutralization proposal, perhaps well intentioned, was a poor response to such appeals. For its most serious result was that it hastened between Russia and Japan an understanding which the State Department might have prevented altogether had it made use of the antagonism existing between the capitals of the two nations and within the cabinet of each.*

An agreement was signed between Russia and Japan on July 4, 1910,

---

* The American minister reported from China that the Russo-Japanese agreement was in its initial stages before the neutralization proposal was made. — DSDD, July 30, 1910, 794.611; cf. Zabriskie, *American-Russian Rivalry*, p. 155.

in which they promised each other assistance in the exploitation of their Manchurian railroads and in the maintenance of the *status quo* as established in existing treaties and agreements. In a secret protocol the mutual spheres of interest were extended and plans laid for the expansion of their railway systems.

The Chinese were perplexed. The officials were "visibly disconcerted." The Grand Council held many conferences, but none of the grand councilors had any observations to make. The minister of war advocated an alliance with Germany and the prince regent agreed. Yuan Shih-k'ai suggested an alliance with Germany and the United States, and the prince regent agreed. Peking asked the United States for "advice"; in other words, Peking wanted to know what the United States would do about it all.

The answer was that China should acknowledge the Russo-Japanese agreement with an air of optimism (as President Taft was doing), that China should restore order in Manchuria with the help of foreign officials, and, of all things, after what had just happened, that China should attract foreign capital into Manchuria. The only concrete evidence of American friendship for China was a letter autographed by the president and transmitted to Peking by the secretary of war himself. Ineffectual as may be thought such gestures, foreign diplomats in Peking noticed some diminution in the aggressiveness of Russia and Japan, which they ascribed to close American-Chinese cooperation.[12]

Mongolia was a second danger spot in the Chinese Empire. There too administrative reforms had been carried out in 1907, and the Chinese had proceeded to fill the new forms with the substance of sovereignty. The innovations amounted to a reversal of traditional Chinese policy. For almost two centuries Mongolia had been a no-man's-land and had served only as a buffer. Mongols had been forbidden to use the Chinese language. Mixed marriages were forbidden. There were no Chinese schools. Chinese could not enter Mongolia without a special permit. In short, the Chinese attempted to maintain the differences between themselves and the Mongols. Suddenly all these rules were abolished. Mongolia was to become a military base. Mongolian children were sent to newly constructed Chinese schools. Mixed marriages were encouraged. Chinese farmers were sent to Mongolia. Lamaism received government support. Mongolian princes were given high government positions in Peking. Mongolia was to become an integral part of China.[13]

The Mongol leaders, willing to recognize Chinese suzerainty but re-
senting integration into China, turned to Russia for help, not without
Russian encouragement. For Moscow watched Chinese activities in the
outlying territories with growing concern. The tsarist government prepared a military demonstration with the intention of halting the reorganization and "colonization" of Mongolia. Russian consuls were dispatched
into areas not open to them, and pressure was exerted upon Peking. Anticipating international complications, Russia sounded London on possible reactions and asked Tokyo outright for an opinion on Russian plans
in Mongolia. The Russian ambassador reminded Baron Komura that a
promise of Japanese support in Mongolia had been the *quid pro quo*
for Russia's agreement to the annexation of Korea in 1910 and that this
support was now needed.

Komura's answer is of special interest because it evidenced the success of Chinese policy. The baron, while not refusing Japanese assistance, warned Russia that after the Russo-Japanese understanding of
1910 China had become very suspicious. Russian pressure might drive
China into the arms of America and Germany. The very weakness of
China was the greatest danger. Komura doubted that China could conclude a political agreement with America or Germany, but the two
Western powers might obtain some valuable material advantages and
great influence over Peking. Japan too had plans for Manchuria, the
Russian was told, but before proceeding with them, Japan would wait
until Chinese suspicions had been allayed. Policy dealing with China
should be conducted with the greatest care and patience.

Russia accepted the advice. An ultimatum was sent to Peking which
contained no new demands but merely requested the fullest compliance
with concessions granted at an earlier time.[14] For the time being, Mongolia was saved for China.

In Tibet the Chinese government followed an almost identical policy
of Sinification. Subtly at first, then with increasing vigor, Peking attempted to realize the old ambition of turning Tibet into a regular
Chinese province by changing suzerainty into sovereignty.[15] This time
China antagonized Great Britain, which was willing to recognize Chinese suzerainty but not sovereignty over Tibet. Eventually in 1912 the
people of Tibet themselves put a stop to Chinese inroads upon their
independence by throwing Chinese troops out of the country.[16]

115

The enterprising spirit of the Chinese government showed itself in activities in China proper as well. Here the attempt was made to break the British quasi monopoly in the Yangtse Valley by the establishment of a better balance of foreign interests. The British had adhered to a sphere-of-interest concept and carefully tried to protect the Yangtse Valley from invasion by foreign interests. When the Chinese assaulted this position, they naturally had the help of Britain's competitors, especially Germany.[17]

Step by step, on the ground of equal treatment, China succeeded in granting concessions in the Valley to the nationals of other countries. The concession originally granted to certain Germans for a railroad from Hankow to Szechwan, for instance, was for the political purpose of breaking the British hold in the Valley. This concession was eventually included in the Hukuang Loan project of May 1911, in which France, Germany, and the United States participated with Great Britain. The loan was hailed as a Chinese success in establishing substantial non-British interests in the Yangtse Valley.[18] So many concessions were granted to various foreign powers in this region in the years following that a detailed study of the situation in 1914 not only indicated that Britain had lost her monopoly but even raised doubts as to her predominance. The situation became so serious from the British standpoint that there were rumors of British diplomatic action, and a member of Parliament complained that the Yangtse Valley seemed to be "open to anyone." [19]

These minor successes in foreign policy did not blind the Chinese government to the basic difficulties still confronting the nation. Especially after Japan's annexation of Korea in 1910, which occurred without resistance from any quarter, the Peking cabinet, harassed already by the events leading up to the revolution, was seized with a deep pessimism. The many meetings of statesmen in Peking always ended upon the same note : that the situation was most unfavorable. China had few true friends. France, as Russia's devoted ally, could not be trusted, and was even suspected of aggressive designs in the south. Great Britain was no longer accounted a friend because her Far Eastern policy looked completely dependent upon Russia and Japan. Furthermore, she was suspected of designs upon Tibet. These were aspects of the international situation which the American minister underestimated when he wrote home that the knowledge of the Chinese "of international politics is not sufficiently great to enable them to discern the varying degrees of danger which, in the latter two instances (i.e., French and British aggressiveness) is in my opinion at present imaginary, while their timidity dissuades them from taking efficacious measures where real peril exists." Facile judgments of this kind (and they were frequent) are what led foreigners into getting their superiority complex regarding China and into adopting the paternalistic attitude that helped China not one bit. No one at the time who had viewed the situation impartially and clear-sightedly could have denied that China was threatened from many sides and had every cause to be upset.[20]

In the view of the government, Germany and the United States were the only powers from which assistance could be expected. Yuan Shih-k'ai told the Regent's Council that collaboration with these two nations was the only means by which China could be strengthened sufficiently to resist further foreign demands. The press supported him. Some newspapers wrote that China's relations with the United States and Germany were so close that the conclusion of an entente would be a mere formality.[21] This, as the Chinese found out, was wishful thinking.

In August 1910 the American minister was called to the Foreign Office and told that in view of the dangerous situation, the regent felt the need of friendly counsel from powers "not directly or indirectly connected with either Russia or Japan." As such a friendly power, the regent was turning to the United States. He had decided to send Foreign Minister Liang Tun-yen to Germany and America on an important mission. In a subsequent conversation with Liang, the American minister was told that Peking realized an alliance was out of the question but thought that some announcement similar to the "Hay doctrine" might be feasible. To obtain this, Liang would go to Berlin and Washington. The American minister was told by another official that Liang also planned to negotiate about currency reform, the creation of the gold standard, and a large national loan from American bankers.[22]

By the time Liang arrived in Berlin in October 1910, he had changed his plans. Instead of asking for a guarantee of China's sovereignty and integrity, which might lead to complications, he would prefer an identically worded note to all powers as follows:

In the course of recent years several powers had agreed in treaties to maintain the status quo in the Far East and to defend the sovereignty, integrity, and Open Door of China. The Chinese government gratefully

117

recognized these agreements, as the viewpoints expressed therein are in complete harmony with the main line of its own policy. However, all these treaties were concluded without China's participation. The Chinese government considers it very desirable to receive corresponding direct assurances from the treaty powers. It declares therefore expressly that it will preserve its full sovereignty, will not cede any territory in favor of any power, and will keep the door open for the trade of all powers alike. China requests the named government to confirm this declaration and to give the assurance that it too will uphold these principles and support the Chinese government in the execution of this policy.[23]

Germany was pleased with the idea. But the United States again was disappointing. Secretary of State Knox opposed the project because "repetition might weaken earlier declarations" to the same effect. He was, however, prepared to sign a general arbitration treaty with China if all other powers would do the same. But to this Germany would not agree because of European political considerations. Liang's mission had been kept fairly secret, and no outsider had definite information about it. Chinese face was saved. In China Liang's trip was at first explained as an attempt to get capital for a bank, then simply as a departure from home "in disgust."[24]

Peking could now forget about the friendship of the United States as well. Knox's reaction indicated clearly that the attempt to reassert American interests in Manchuria and China generally was limited within very narrow confines. Knox and Taft — possibly under the influence of Roosevelt — still were willing to sacrifice much for Japanese friendship. The secretary confirmed that there had been "no serious thought of an alliance with China." He agreed with Roosevelt and Taft that the United States should not appear hostile to Japan in Manchuria and should insist only on the protection of American commercial rights.[25] The implication of these statements was the renunciation of the principle of territorial and administrative integrity, at least in regard to Manchuria, and a reverting to the principles expressed in the first set of Hay's notes. They were one more indication that Washington was resigned to writing off Manchuria as lost to China. It was unfortunate that this should have been American policy at a time when China was endeavoring to give the principles of the Open Door and integrity a more solid foundation.

That the Chinese government should have emphasized the one or

118

the other of these principles according to expediency is not surprising. And that in a dilemma it should have been willing to sacrifice the first for the second is natural too. The inability to defend both principles at all times was due, very simply, to the military weakness of the nation, not necessarily to incompetence, as many foreign critics liked to believe. Interestingly enough, such criticism did not come very often from the countries that understood power relations and took unscrupulous advantage of them, notably Russia and Japan. It came from those, like the United States, that had not yet learned to see politics as the art of the possible and power as an inevitable element in politics, or those, like Great Britain, that preferred to compromise and keep power in the background. Furthermore the complaints of Western nations about the nature of China's political behavior were largely rationalizations of their own diplomatic reverses and mistakes in strategy. They berated China for failing to do for them what they failed to do for themselves: oppose force with force.

The Chinese government's internal position was almost as weak as its international. The initial impetus for its active foreign policy and the attempted Sinification of the outlying territories had come from the reform movement. But by the time Peking fulfilled some of the popular demands, the reform movement had largely fallen into the hands of the revolutionaries and was far ahead of the government. The demands of the early 1900's had become almost antiquated. Unfortunately for the government, its relatively mild reforms both failed to satisfy the revolutionaries and began to antagonize vested interests. Natural catastrophes highlighted the prevailing misery of the masses. The government was increasingly isolated. Spectacular success in foreign policy might have somewhat strengthened its hand. But the trend toward revolution could hardly have been reversed even by that, and the failures in international relations, combined with inefficiency in internal affairs, now contributed to the final collapse of the dynasty.

10

Revolution and Foreign Money

THE administrative reforms in the Empire, the "coloniza-tion" of the outlying territories, and the missions of T'ang Shao-yi and Liang Tun-yen for closer collaboration with friendly powers were new aspects of Chinese foreign policy and were due to the initiative of the government. But they developed far away, undramatically, or even secretly, and remained mostly unnoticed by the interested and vocal sections of the people. The absence of any popular support for these enterprises was probably one reason why their results were minor. When known at all, they were rarely judged on their merits. The government hardly ever got any credit for its valiant efforts; its failures alone were played up and used as propaganda against the Peking regime. The people of the eighteen provinces who had any interest in state affairs were in general preoccupied with matters having an immediate bearing upon their own geographic areas and personal welfare. Between about 1908 and 1913 these had to do mostly with railway-building and loans, matters in which foreign governments retained the initiative. So, from the standpoint of the masses, relations with foreign nations during these years showed little change. Circumstances once more were combining to give foreigners an undue influence, and the shape foreign relations now took had a considerable share in bringing about the revolution which was already then in the making.

It was to be a revolution of minorities, taking place on the surface of Chinese society. Not only were the groups in the vanguard minorities; the followers and fighters — an unusual circumstance — were a minority as well. Both before and during the revolution, the people in general were rather unconcerned about the goings-on. The inhabitants of the cities and the farmers in the fields pursued their business, showing little excitement and frequently no interest. Their most prominent emotion was apprehension lest in the fighting they lose their livelihood and their few possessions. Even in large urban centers like Peking and Nanking

120

the masses did not show much comprehension. At most they were looking forward to the realization of the revolutionaries' promises of fewer
taxes and more wealth after victory. Occasionally, after the outbreak of
the revolution, there was some mass participation locally, but this was
due to special conditions rather than to revolutionary enthusiasm.
Though the people had many grievances, mostly economic, these did not
lead to concerted, rational political action. In fact, apart from scattered
uprisings, they did not lead to any activity at all and were of little rele-
vance. In China, writes E. R. Hughes, the psychology of a revolutionary
time is more passive than active. The majority is concerned with the
drama of judgment. So a minority must act and decide. The revolution
had no depth. It was an affair concerning essentially the upper strata of
Chinese society, leaving the masses and their problems unaffected.[1]

The fighting, of which there was relatively little, was done mostly by
professional soldiers, attached to one faction or another; these were
joined by bandits, destitute persons, occasional mobs, and idealistic
individuals who thought they knew what they were fighting for. There
was neither a great revolutionary ideal to inspire the masses nor a revolutionary army to fight for it. The results of the revolution were correspondingly superficial. The reason why the establishment of a republic looked at all like a unanimous goal was that the professional revolutionaries were noisy and quickly monopolized the leading positions,
either by forcing themselves into them or by obtaining them through
default of the more moderate elements. They behaved like spokesmen
for all factions joined in the struggle against Peking, but in reality were
only one of the groups making up the leadership. Among other important groups were military officers, the gentry, the merchants, and some
officials. They all had their own reasons for wanting a change in the
government, but with few did this desire go so far as to include a change
in the governmental system. Most of them, true to Chinese tradition,
would have been satisfied with a change in personalities. The consensus
in favor of change as such was not paralleled by any on the form the
change was to take. Such unity was lacking even within the composing
groups, different local conditions creating different special interests.
The antagonisms arising from this situation among the "revolutionaries"
were sometimes as strong as those uniting them against the dynasty, or
stronger.

This multiplicity of motives had a very obscuring effect upon China's foreign policy in the immediate pre- and postrevolutionary period, and foreign policy played an important part in the propaganda of both the imperial and revolutionary forces. The obscurity deepened as any strict dividing line between the imperial and republican parties disappeared. In a sense the revolution finally synthesized the two disintegrating processes at work within China: the internal deterioration of society and the foreign impact upon an ancient culture. These processes, of course, had been reciprocal in their effect. With the disappearance of their individuality disappeared the possibility of separating any longer the two major political fronts vaguely related to them: the imperialists identified with the crumbling old order, the republicans representing the Western spirit. The lines separating the various political groups became nebulous. The attitudes on foreign policy which had up to this time been the generally distinguishing mark of these groups melted together. There was no longer certainty as to where anyone stood. Expediency began to rule, and foreigners became objects of political maneuvers. Nobody in China wanted to expose himself to the accusation of having surrendered to foreign powers, yet everybody was vying for foreign sympathy in the knowledge that sooner or later he would need foreign help.

The imperial government's diplomacy as well as the stand taken by the revolutionary groups was therefore dominated by the vagaries of internal developments, especially the chances of each to defeat the other. As long as Peking was the recognized government, the opposition objected to any move designed to enlist foreign assistance and actively intervened with foreign governments to prevent it. Yet they betrayed their "principles" as soon as such assistance was coming their way. What looked to the outsider like a rather confused diplomacy on the part of the government and the revolutionaries made sense from the standpoint of each judged by the requirements of the internal politics of the moment. The one fortunate feature for the foreign powers was that few Chinese wanted to antagonize them, and the prevailing antiforeignism was therefore often sublimated in hatred of the Manchu dynasty in general.

Both sides being hamstrung by the lack of money, loans (with which railway construction was closely tied up) became a focus of revolutionary propaganda and an important factor in the revolution. In spite of considerable differences regarding their purposes and conditions, most of them became involved in Chinese politics in ways making them objectionable to one or the other political faction. This involvement was particularly a feature of the three main loan projects which reached an acute stage of negotiation between 1909 and 1913: the Currency Reform and Industrial Development Loan, the Hukuang Railways Loan, and the Reorganization Loan.

The revolutionaries objected to these loans because they hated to see Peking obtain any financial support at all. Since a popularly appealing reason for objecting to outside financial assistance had to be found, patriotism was used to disguise the revolutionaries' motive. The government was accused of selling out to foreign nations, of mortgaging China away, of subjecting China to foreign control and supervision. The accusation made effective propaganda and caused the government much trouble.

A second source of opposition to the loans was the various groups whose vested interests were endangered by the provisions governing their acceptance. Most of the loans would have required centralized control over expenditure of the funds granted, and hence centralized control over many incidental political operations. Provincial officials, small provincial bankers, loan sharks, and the relatives of all these stood to be hurt by the new financial transactions, and so they joined the revolutionaries against the imperial government.

There were, third, the genuine patriots among all groups who sincerely objected to some of the control conditions in the loan proposals. They had good reasons for believing that these conditions were, in many cases, not meant just as a security for the lenders or a protection for the Chinese people against their own corrupt officials, but were intended as a means to gain political control. They joined in the opposition to any government or faction willing to accept such conditions.

A fourth kind of objection to the loans, this one common to both the government and the opposition, sprang from the monopolistic character of the loan arrangements at this time. The major lending powers, Great Britain, Germany, France, and the United States, had after years of negotiations joined, in 1910, in the Consortium of Banks, which had the exclusive official backing of their respective governments. This Consortium assumed the handling of all foreign loans needed by China. When the Consortium was joined in 1912 by Russia and Japan — themselves borrowing, not lending nations — the Consortium took on an undeniably political tinge. The Chinese, both government and opposition, resented the arrangement, which mixed politics with business in a fashion detrimental to China. The monopoly robbed the country of the advantages of competition economically and gave her an inferior status politically. The tie-up between the banks and the governments backing them provided foreigners with an undue influence in Chinese politics through the unsound competition for foreign recognition it aroused between the groups struggling for political control.[2] Strong differences of opinion arose among the Chinese whether the need of money was sufficiently great to justify acquiescence in what all felt to be a degrading arrangement.

The Currency Reform and Industrial Development Loan was intended to fulfill two functions. A small part of the total sum was to be devoted to the economic development of Manchuria; the larger part was to help in the standardization and stabilization of the Chinese currency as the first step in bringing order into the chaos of Chinese finances, and, incidentally, in improving conditions for trade inside and with China. Most of the security for the loan was to come from Manchurian taxes.

The part of the loan intended for Manchurian development aroused only the Russians and the Japanese, who saw in it an attempt to frustrate their own ambitions. But the part intended for the Currency Reform created strong antagonism in the provinces, understandably enough. The fluctuations and uncertainties in the value of the different coins and notes circulating in China were an important source of income to many officials, to small bankers, to owners of cash shops, speculators, and numerous merchants. They naturally objected when they saw their livelihood threatened.

The indirect results of a successful currency reform threatened even wider circles. For there would be centralization and order in the whole financial organization. This would mean the undermining of the bureaucratic system, which rested largely on the local financial autonomy of the civil servants. The practice was that every official could squeeze from his underlings as much as he pleased as long as he handed the required sums to his superiors and kept peace in his area. In the strong words of H. B. Morse, the Chinese official "exists solely for his own maintenance and that of his fellow-officials, his superiors and his subordinates." Exacting money was therefore his major mission in life; the means were left up to him. No wonder he resented the idea of the Currency Reform Loan.[3]

Peking's need of money was so great, however, that it was willing to risk antagonism. The cabinet thought it could make the Currency Reform Loan less objectionable by concluding it with the American bankers alone as the best liked and least suspected foreigners. But such a step, though it might have reduced somewhat the protests from the patriotic revolutionaries, could not have changed the much more fundamental and less patriotic objections of the vested interests. They were concerned about the possible success of the enterprise, not where the money was coming from. Peking's plans, however, could not be realized anyway. Higher politics in Washington caused the full fury of all revolutionary groups to be loosed against Peking. The American government insisted on handling this loan (initiated by T'ang Shao-yi in the United States in 1908) through the four-power Consortium. The Peking government said it would reluctantly agree to this if the United States held the majority of the shares. But even on this point it was disappointed, and had to acquiesce in an equal distribution of the bonds among the four powers. On April 15, 1911, an agreement was signed. But a loan was never floated, thanks to Russian-Japanese objections and the interference of the revolution.[4]

The Hukuang Loan for the building of the great trunk lines from Canton to Hankow and from Hankow to Chengtu had a more turbulent history and was a more important agent in contributing to the revolution. Negotiations for this loan dated back to the beginning of the century between China, Germany, and Great Britain. Later a group of French bankers had joined the German-British combination. This three-power Consortium initialed an agreement with the Chinese on June 6, 1909. On the basis of an earlier concession, the United States government insisted upon having a share in the loan; a personal letter from President Taft to Regent Ch'un succeeded in getting the American bankers admitted in May 1910, and thus was established the four-power Consortium.

This new arrangement, which necessitated changes in the loan agreement initialed by China and the three-power Consortium in June 1909, opened the door for further long-drawn-out conversations between the lending powers themselves and for new objections by Peking. When the four-power Consortium submitted a new agreement to China on May

23, 1910, Peking rejected it, mostly out of fear of internal complications. The combined pressure of the four powers plus the needs of the government finally made it sign the Hukuang Loan in May 1911. The interval between the initialing of the agreement in 1909 and the final signature in 1911 gave the Chinese opposition an opportunity to crystallize.

The acceptance of the loan by Peking was part of a program designed to strengthen the country as well as the dynasty. The lack of transportation was a great handicap in creating centralized control over the country and in mobilizing the army in case of an antidynastic or international emergency. Hence Peking was less anxious that the Chinese should build the railroads than that the railroads should get built. It had nevertheless attempted to keep the enterprise in Chinese hands. After 1906 concessions had been handed out to provincial companies for the raising of local funds and the building of railways. This move, ran the argument, which was in the reform spirit of the times, would provide the needed transportation and make the country independent of foreign support. Appeals for money had gone out to the people, appeals based on patriotic and economic grounds. Sizable sums were forthcoming, and thousands of small shareholders bought an interest in the many provincial railway companies established for the purpose. But the enterprises were all condemned to abortion. There was evidence that the new enthusiasm was used by officials and members of the gentry as just another means of squeezing money out of the people. The subscriptions and taxes were never used to build railways.

Peking therefore took over the job of constructing the vital Hukuang Railways itself. The foreign loan was to serve the purpose. And around this loan the struggle between the provincial and central authority developed. Railroad associations were formed in the provinces to collect funds for the building of the Hukuang Railways and to protest Peking's policy. Delegations and telegrams flooded the capital. Patriotism was the leitmotif of the complaints. An ugly mood developed. Meanwhile the provincial bureaus did not improve their showing in either collecting funds or building railways.

The government was willing to come to terms with the provinces. It looked as if Chang Chih-tung might be able to make some mutually satisfactory arrangements. But he died in 1909, and his great prestige was lost to the cause of the dynasty. Peking finally became aggressive without really having the means or the prestige to support such a policy.

It accused the provincial leaders of inefficiency and corruption, a correct but useless accusation. Sheng Kung-pao was appointed successor to Chang as President of the Board of Communications and Posts in the hope that his good relations with the Hukuang gentry might help the government. But they were of no avail. Besides, his own record was not clean enough to inspire popular confidence.

In May 1911 the government announced its intention of nationalizing all trunk lines. Two high officials were sent to the provinces of Hupeh, Hunan, and Szechwan to explain the government's policy. They were accompanied by imperial troops. At the same moment the Hukuang Loan was signed. There was no doubt left in the minds of the provincial officials, gentry, and shareholders that the government, in collusion with foreign powers, was planning to subject them completely to central control. Peking tried to cool tempers by promising to repay investors for that part of the funds which had not been lost in outright speculation and embezzlement, but failed. Agitation, duly stimulated by revolutionaries, finally ended in uprisings in Szechwan, just at the time when the explosion of a bomb in Wuchang on October 10, 1911, signalled the beginning of the revolution. This event gave the upheavals in Szechwan a revolutionary flavor.

The Hukuang Loan had become one of the links in the chain of events which caused the revolution.* China never obtained any funds from this loan. But, here again, the agitation existed mainly among the wealthier classes. The masses remained untouched. The groups directly concerned in the provinces of Hunan and Hupeh behaved as upper classes are expected to behave: they protested in writing but did not go into the streets to fight. Only in Szechwan, where dissatisfaction was more widespread because funds had been raised by taxation as well as by voluntary subscription, did unrest finally turn into action.[5]

The Reorganization Loan also turned out to have vital political significance. But while the Currency Loan was primarily an issue between the imperialists and the republicans, and the Hukuang Loan one between the central and provincial forces, the Reorganization Loan became the focus of a struggle within the revolutionary groups, in fact helped to separate the true revolutionaries from those who had been opposed

* Two other results of the Hukuang Loan affair in China's foreign relations were, first, that China was driven deeper into the arms of foreign powers and, second, that the popular outcry against the loan led to a relaxation of the conditions originally insisted upon by the Consortium.

mostly to the Manchu dynasty or even only its policy. Though foreign powers became involved in Chinese internal politics through the loan, the loan was a football of national politics more than an issue of foreign policy.

The Reorganization Loan was to be used mainly for administrative reorganization, for the discharge of soldiers employed during the revolutionary period, and for other similar purposes. This function — organizational rather than economic — was its novel feature. Potentially it was therefore a wedge by which foreign powers might gain direct control over the Chinese government. This possibility made it obnoxious to many Chinese, independent of their political sympathies. Its timing in regard to the internal situation was even more important for the role it was destined to play.

Negotiations for the loan were begun with the four-power Consortium in November 1911. One month earlier the revolution had broken out under Sun Yat-sen's spiritual leadership. Yuan Shih-k'ai, the strong man, was recalled from his banishment in the hope that he and especially his well-trained and disciplined army might save the ruling house. Yuan failed in this task, probably not unintentionally. The emperor abdicated on February 12, 1912, transferring all power to Yuan, although before the abdication Sun Yat-sen had already been made Provisional President of the Republic of China by the victorious revolutionary forces in the center and south. Yuan was attractive to the majority of the groups which had participated in the revolution: the wealthy families, most of the generals, most of the merchants, many officials in the provinces. Because of their pressure, combined with Yuan's political strength and, perhaps, Sun Yat-sen's patriotic desire to see China united, Sun resigned the provisional presidency in favor of Yuan. This was two days after the Manchu abdication, and Yuan had suddenly discovered his sympathy for the Republic.[6]

An uneasy peace was established between Yuan and Sun, who retained the loyalty of the professional and ideological revolutionaries. On April 29, 1912, a national advisory council convened, and on April 8, 1913, Parliament opened. Both organs were controlled by Sun's followers. They immediately began to oppose Yuan. He on his part immediately began to consolidate his position by every legal and illegal means, including political murders. The outcome of this struggle between the conservative and reactionary forces behind Yuan and the more progressive elements supporting Sun became essentially a matter of money; and here arose the importance of the Reorganization Loan.

Both sides in this struggle lacked popular support. The inability to offer concrete advantages to the masses was one reason. The absence of ideals appealing to large sections of the people was another. In fact, the struggle between the two sides was not a contest between ideals. Only Sun's followers could be called idealists at all; there were no such on Yuan's side. In the end the physical ability to maintain themselves in power would decide the outcome of the struggle and here, money was vital. A way had to be found to obtain it without offending popular concern for China's integrity.

Money was needed to satisfy the demands for repayment by the merchants, bankers, and other rich Chinese who had backed the revolution financially. Their continued sympathy was particularly vital to Yuan.[7] Both sides needed funds to influence officials and representatives in the popular councils. Most important of all, money would decide who would have the armies. Thus the negotiations for the Reorganization Loan coincided with the height of the struggle for power between the two contending forces, and the granting of the loan became an important factor in determining the character of the Republic.

Neither faction objected to foreign money in principle, for obvious reasons. Objections were raised by one faction only against the other's obtaining it. Even the followers of Sun Yat-sen, most vociferous in their opposition, had no intention of refusing loans to themselves. At all times in the revolutionary struggle the radical leaders readily admitted that they would ask for foreign money in the future. All through January and February 1912 they made intensive and partially successful attempts to raise loans from the Japanese, Germans, and British. In September 1912 Sun Yat-sen recommended to an audience of high officials and influential citizens the policy of the Open Door, the utilization of foreign capital, and the employment of foreign advisers. Occasionally, "unusual opportunities" were offered to those who, "favorable to the Open Door," would assist China in maintaining her integrity. This was the core of a policy most ostentatiously friendly to foreign powers. The motivation, in addition to the need of help, was genuine sympathy among the revolutionary leaders for foreign nations.[8]

General opposition to the Reorganization Loan arose because of its extremely harsh terms. Special opposition from the Sun group arose because of its involvement in the internal politics of China. As the abyss between Yuan and Sun deepened, leading eventually to Sun's abortive revolt in 1913, Sun's opposition to the loan became absolute as the only way to prevent Yuan from getting it. Yuan was highly tempted to accept it. But he still had qualms about the strings attached to it, though whether for reasons of patriotism or fear of popular reaction is hard to tell. In any case, he refused the loan by informing the Consortium that the National Council and public opinion would not permit its acceptance.

By that time the Consortium powers had not only made up their minds that Yuan was to get the loan but that he ought to accept it. They wanted the "strong man" in power. Negotiations continued. In June 1912 Russia and Japan forced themselves into the Consortium, now composed of six powers. Arrangements for the admission of the new members delayed negotiations with China. Furthermore the participation of the new states made the Consortium even more political, hence more obnoxious to the Chinese. Simultaneously their need of funds was growing rapidly.

The American minister in Peking urged Washington to make a loan to Yuan for the sake of order — Yuan's order. He did not believe in the success of the revolution and felt that, unless Yuan received support, "nothing but anarchy is in sight." [9] The British were equally anxious to make a loan, partly because they were interested in business, partly because they feared competition from private finance groups if the Consortium should fail to make it. Both nations were satisfied with reasonable economic guarantees. But not so other members of the Consortium. Poincaré, speaking for France and prodded by Russia, considered the loan a matter of politics, not economics, and was determined that, regardless of the nominal form of the loan, the Chinese must be forced to give in. [10]

Eventually the loan agreement was signed by Yuan Shih-k'ai, but without the constitutionally necessary approval of Parliament. Some of the most stringent conditions had been eliminated, a concession by the Consortium to the widespread resistance to the original terms. Nevertheless there remained a sufficient degree of stringency for the new Administration of President Wilson to withdraw American membership from the Consortium in March 1913.

To this step, Chinese reaction was sour-sweet. They appreciated the president's feelings and expressed their thanks for them. But one fear arose, that this new complication might again lead to interminable discussions among the Consortium members and delay further the payment of the loan. Another fear was that if the loan was granted, it would lack the "moderating" influence of the United States. American participation was considered by the Chinese their best guarantee of fair treatment.[11]

Yuan received a few installment payments "on account" of the main loan (which was never paid), large enough to have a decisive influence upon the struggle for power in Yuan's favor. But the Consortium and its activities became increasingly repulsive to almost all Chinese. Sheer necessity had forced Yuan to deal with it. The foreign nations had bargained for a confirmation of their existing rights — which, as usual, they considered better preserved by a "strong man" than a popular parliament — in return for their recognition of Yuan's presidency of the Republic. Yuan's desire for power and the internal conditions of the country had driven him to accept the money, the prestige accruing from foreign recognition, and the security from political refugees abroad.[12] But he and his friends still feared the foreign nations. No amount of foreign support could prevent him from counteracting foreign influence. And since foreign activity in China was now typically represented in the Consortium, it became the main target of Chinese attack.

Politically the Consortium was considered a weapon of imperialism and a threat to China's integrity; economically it was judged a monopoly and an infraction of the Open Door through its elimination of competition among foreigners. And such competition was the most attractive feature for the Chinese of the Open Door principle. The most obvious recourse of China was therefore the traditional one of inciting rivalry among the foreigners for the nation's benefit, much to the annoyance of the foreign powers — most of them great believers in the benefits of competition. Angry outcries could be heard in many languages. The new regime was accused of being a change in name only and of continuing the old game of playing one power against the other — as if the revolution were supposed to have taken place for the benefit of foreigners. To the great disgust of the foreign powers, the Chinese policy was blessed with some success. China got some funds from individual firms (e.g., C. Birch Crisp), which negotiated with provincial governments, and from Japan. These occasional breaks of the Consortium monopoly, in addition to bringing funds to China, frightened some of the Consortium members into willingness to come to terms with the Chinese.[13]

Yuan found a most hopeful opportunity to break the monopoly when a former director of the French Banque de l'Indo-Chine created, early in 1913, the Banque Industrielle de la Chine with the help of a group of French and Chinese citizens. When approached for financial assistance, Yuan Shih-k'ai agreed to supply one third of the bank's capital of 45 million francs. He suggested to the French that the bank should be substituted for the American group which had just withdrawn from the Consortium. Such a step would have strengthened his position vis-à-vis the Chinese assembly. He could have countered their criticism of his playing with the Consortium with the argument that the newly introduced Chinese influence would safeguard national interests. As a further inducement to accept Yuan's idea, the French minister in Peking was given to understand that Yuan was badly in need of 8 million francs "pour fonds speciaux" and that the supplier could expect an attractive reward in the form of concessions.

The bank did not join the Consortium. But the required funds — called "contribution to the government" by the French and "bribes" by the London *Times* — were forthcoming and were reciprocated immediately with concessions for railways and public utilities. As a guarantee of the loans necessary for these concessions, the bank received a mortgage on the tobacco and alcohol tax.

These were the only taxes left to the Chinese government; all others had been mortgaged previously. Their estimated yield was considerably higher than the envisaged loans. A number of likely reasons can be found for so apparently strange a financial move. By this mortgage Yuan put the taxes out of reach of the Consortium. He also created a credit for future needs with this more accommodating bank. And by this "sound" position of the bank, French investors might be induced to subscribe to future loans, which could be used partly for Yuan's personal ambitions and partly for the speculative enterprises of the French bank partners.

While there was no definite proof of these considerations having motivated the founders of the bank, it was certain that the bank had a political character. The puzzle of the French government's approval of the bank, a competitor to the Consortium which also had the approval of the government, was solved when the bank went bankrupt in 1921. It was found that the Consortium's approval came from the Ministry of Finance, whereas the bank's approval came from a high official in the Foreign Office, who gained a personal advantage from the bank. But regardless of the scandals, the Chinese used the bank to good advantage. For in 1919, when the second Consortium was created to succeed the first, prewar one, the Peking government opposed the membership of the Banque Industrielle on the grounds that China had become a partner in order to escape from the Consortium. This attitude encouraged several other banks to stay outside the new Consortium. Thus, against strong pressure, the Chinese government succeeded in restoring at least a semblance of free competition in the field of Chinese international finance.[14]

Although this was considered a blessing by practically all Chinese, the fact is that the Consortium was not altogether disadvantageous to China, at least in the negative sense that it prevented China from getting unfavorable loans. But few Chinese would admit this at the time. The Consortium had members who seriously attempted to emphasize the business part of the enterprise. In view of the deep involvement of the participating governments, this desire to escape politics may have been naive, but the attempt nevertheless was made. With some encouragement from public opinion in China and elsewhere it might have led to beneficial results, all the more because it coincided with a trend toward the internationalization of economic problems throughout the world. The atmosphere might have become very favorable to an Open Door policy and the maintenance of the principle of integrity, even though via the hurdle of a monopoly vis-à-vis China.

Another advantage the Consortium might have had for China would have been to offset her lack of experience in handling foreign loans. In many cases where China obtained a loan under reasonable conditions or built railroads, management was poor, expenses were high, and money was squandered. The foreigners' argument that foreign supervision and advice were to China's advantage was not entirely a rationalization for the sake of exploiting the country. Since the Chinese were eager for loans and since repayment would be enforced anyhow, efficient operation, even if foreign-managed, might have kept the financial burden down and might even have taught the Chinese something of the art of finance.[15]

Unfortunately for China, and partly owing to her own policy, developments did not take such a favorable turn. The question of loans remained largely in the field of politics. On the part of the Consortium the friction between the members, each with its own particular suscepti-bilities, reflected the political tensions of the West. On the part of the Chinese negotiations were heavily colored by the internal political struggles. Such being the case, relations between the Consortium and China were unavoidably political. It seems remarkable that in spite of political and economic inferiority China was able to force any con-cessions from the foreigners at all. Credit for this must partly go to the world political situation. The focus of world politics had returned to Europe after 1905, with the result that tensions relaxed in other areas. The Chinese welcomed this comparative calm until they realized that the shift of international attention gave the Japanese a freer hand. Yet, looking at Russo-Japanese relations again, they grew a little easier, in the Pollyannish belief that the chain of secret agreements of 1907, 1910, and 1912 between these two nations, dealing with the delimitation of their respective spheres of interest in Mongolia and Manchuria, indi-cated an increase of foreign counterinfluence in those areas and of mutual mistrust. They learned better soon.

The treaties were far from being symptoms of rivalry. In substance they were sanctioned internationally when Japan's and Russia's condi-tions for joining the Consortium — that their special interests in Man-churia and Mongolia be safeguarded — were accepted.[16] Russia espe-cially now felt secure in intriguing in Mongolia. A favorable opportunity offered itself when the Mongols used the turmoil caused by the Chinese revolution to declare their independence in December 1911. The Rus-sians immediately lent their moral and material support to the Mongols in return for extremely favorable political and economic concessions. It appears, however, that the Russians were not ready at this moment to risk serious complications by going to extremes. The European situation did not permit that. They decided, therefore, to take advantage of the situation only so far as diplomatic action would permit, which meant that they were willing to compromise.

Yuan Shih-k'ai objected to Mongolian independence. He informed the Mongolian leaders that under the new republican regime Mongolia would become an integral part of China and be treated like the home provinces. But no number of concessions to local autonomy and other promises of lenient treatment could reduce Mongolian demands. The Mongols felt strong in the security of Russian backing, a misjudgment of Russian policy. Russia was not ready to support Mongolia's claim for independence. She was satisfied with autonomy for Mongolia. She was, however, prepared to sign a protocol to that effect with the Mongolian leaders, and news of even this rather moderate protocol caused an uproar in China.

Sun Yat-sen asked for military action. This was a rather transparent ruse to get Yuan's troops to faraway Mongolia and clear the field for the opposition to act in the south. But Yuan could not be fooled so easily. He actually began to suppress the "anti-Russian" agitation. To deal with the Mongolian problem he chose diplomatic negotiations. He began by asking certain foreign powers for "advice," a term which had become standard for assistance. He was told not to count on it and that there was no choice for him but to surrender.[17]

Extended negotiations with the Russians eventually led to an agreement on November 5, 1913, and a convention on July 7, 1915. In essence Outer Mongolia received autonomy under Chinese suzerainty. In other words, the *status quo* of about two centuries now became a matter of legal arrangement. Russia retained some of the concessions granted to her by the Mongols. And the Mongols obtained the right to participate in negotiations between Russia and China concerning their territory. Thus China did not succeed in keeping her relations with Mongolia an "internal affair," Mongolia failed to obtain independence, and Russia had to be satisfied with some commercial concessions. No party was content. Yet the principles established served as a basis for later agreements between Soviet Russia and China. From this fact perhaps the conclusion may be drawn that the principles were reasonable under prevailing conditions.[18]

These arrangements and the apparent moderation of Russia did not in any way put to rest Chinese fears about the international situation in general — quite apart from the fact that Yuan's government needed success in the field of foreign policy for strength and prestige. The government submitted a number of proposals to the American minister, Reinsch, designed to enlist American help and showing signs of having been inspired by Reinsch in the first place. Peking realized that an alliance was unfeasible, but hoped that close cooperation would be possible. American naval officers and technical experts might be lent to China to assist in the building of a fleet. Also, now that China was a republic, she would rely on American moral support as well as actual assistance in the making of a constitution and the reorganization of the administration. Greater American help in the development of Chinese resources would put the nation more on a par with other powers and give the United States more influence. "The Chinese Government is desirous of affording Americans unusual opportunities should they be ready to cooperate in this matter." Americans were promised far-reaching opportunities for the Huai River Conservancy scheme; they could obtain a contract for the development of the Shensi oil resources; they would be given the selling agency for the tobacco monopoly envisaged by the government.

Reinsch was very enthusiastic about these prospects. But nothing came of them. In fact, the financial records showing the economic interests of Americans in China beween 1908 and 1914 indicated a decline. To all the enticements offered by China the American businessman remained unresponsive. China's policy of sacrificing equal opportunity to the maintenance of integrity failed — in spite of the eager support given by the representatives of the nation whose basic policy in the Far East was the Open Door.[19]

11

"Theoretical" Ally in World War I

W<small>HEN</small> the war approached in 1914, Yuan Shih-k'ai's pre-dominant political leadership was no longer seriously threatened. He still had to contend with the revolutionary group, the "rebels" that had fled from Peking to Canton in the south. But thanks to his own abilities and the decisive support of the foreign powers, he was the supreme ruler of China.

Foreign policy was again conducted by a few individuals in Peking, except for some opposition groups who were willing to intrigue with foreign nations against the central government. In his struggle for power Yuan had emasculated or perverted every liberal institution conceived during the revolution. He had destroyed the last vestige of a progressive regime by the clever use of constitutional means. He even prevented the dissolution of some political parties, seemingly in compliment to the demand for constitutionalism, really for his own dictatorial ends. The influence of public opinion upon the government had waned. Since it could not be suppressed, it too was now directed from above and used to serve the ambitions — not always selfish — of the premier.

Notwithstanding the reactionary policies of the regime, China's progress toward modernization continued. The evidence was a clearer understanding of the modern world and a more enlightened approach to its problems, quite apart from improvements in the social institutions of the nation. Indeed, the manner in which the government itself pursued its reactionary policies was an advance over imperial days. Yuan had dreams of perpetuating the quasi-feudal system of the Manchus, but he was a citizen of the twentieth-century world.*

The Chinese reacted to the critical days of July 1914 by looking at

---

* Though he never left China, never even traveled much in his own country, he had an excellent knowledge of the Western world. — Hummel, *Eminent Chinese, sub* Yuan Shih-k'ai.

their country in perspective. Naturally they considered themselves very important. But they fully realized the global interdependence of international relations. They had no exaggerated conceptions of China's place in world politics. They no longer regarded their nation, or the Far East, as the center of the modern universe and did not determine policy as if it were. On the contrary, they carefully evaluated world affairs and China's modest role in them before they chose their course of action. Their political means remained unchanged. Their thinking was modern before their methods were.

In consequence of this heightened sensitivity to world affairs, the tense situation in Europe greatly affected Peking. Yuan and his ministers knew that war in Europe would mean war in Asia. They tried to prepare for the emergency, something they could do only with the cooperation of the foreign powers. The discouraging attitude of these forced the Chinese back into their unwanted role of, at best, spectator, at worst, pawn and victim. To the great disturbance of the government, when war broke out, nothing had been settled.

The international character of the foreign Settlements, the contiguity of the rights and concessions of the belligerents on Chinese soil, made things complicated enough. But the Chinese feared Japan above all else. Yuan knew and disliked the Japanese, had done so ever since his days as Imperial Resident in Korea.[*] "Japan is going to take advantage of this war to get control in China," he predicted, expressing the fears of all Chinese officials.[1] To recognize this danger, however, was easier than to contain it. The political constellation of the world in 1914 made useless China's foremost weapon, internationalization of her troubles. The United States was the only strong power with both interests in the Far East and relative freedom to protect them. No wonder that wishful thinking in China started the rumor that the American fleet was coming to the rescue of the nation. But a sense of reality was soon restored. The

---

[*] Sun Yat-sen and his followers were very naive about Japan's policy. They were so indebted to Japan for the help they had received ever since 1900 in promoting the revolution that probably they could not conceive of any duplicity in Japan's behavior. Japan seemed no threat to China. In 1914 Sun wrote a letter to Count Okuma pleading for aid and promising the most elaborate commercial benefits in return. — Marius B. Jansen, "The Japanese and the Chinese Revolution of 1911," Committee on International and Regional Studies, Harvard University, *Papers on China*, II (1948), 159. Compare Roger F. Hackett, "Chinese Students in Japan 1900–1910," *Papers on China*, III (1949), 134–169.

American minister declared unequivocally that the rumor was without foundation; the State Department considered it "quixotic in the extreme to allow the question of China's territorial integrity to entangle the United States in international difficulties."[2]

The Chinese, thrown upon their own resources, decided that neutrality would be their best policy. This needed the agreement of the powers. The United States as the most friendly nation and Japan as the most dreaded one were asked to obtain it. The United States went into action accordingly, but Japan disapproved, confirming Chinese fears about Japanese intentions. Indeed, from the beginning of the war, Japan used the preoccupation of the powers in Europe to realize her long-cherished desire for further expansion on the Asian mainland. With the application of that queer mixture of coercion and enticement which eventually led to the Greater East Asia Co-prosperity Sphere, the attack upon China began without delay.

On August 14, 1914, Japan dispatched an ultimatum to Germany and declared war on August 23. Japanese troops landed on the Chinese coast and began to move into Kiaochow and Shantung, the German spheres of interest. From there the Japanese armies spread further into territory having not the remotest connection with any German interest. Following their habitual method, the Japanese used the elements of surprise and speed to place before the world a *fait accompli.* They thus frustrated possible Chinese countermoves almost before the slower-working Chinese had time to think them out. They prevented a plan of transferring German-held territory to either China, Great Britain, or the United States for safekeeping during the war. They eliminated any possibility of allied participation in the conquest of Shantung as a restraining influence. They made futile all talk about the creation of a strictly delimited war zone. And they ignored China's declaration of neutrality. By their quick victory, they obviated Chinese assistance and were thus enabled to pose as sole victors with exclusive rights to the spoils.[3]

Some of China's suggestions of means to enforce her neutrality might have been realized had other powers been willing to assist. But they were not. On the contrary, they discouraged all Chinese plans. In their scale of values China was placed low. In their inability — more inability than unwillingness — to risk complications in the Far East, almost any price was worth paying to keep Japan pacified, and China's integrity was considered a cheap price.*

The first indication of independent Chinese action (China's attempt to regain full control over Shantung) was used by the Japanese as the pretext for a broadside attack upon China's independence. On January 18, 1915, Japan presented China with Twenty-One Demands, divided into five groups. Had these groups of demands, characterized as Japanese "wishes," been fulfilled, especially the fifth, China would have become the vassal of Japan. The Chinese were confronted with their severest crisis in modern times at the cleverly timed moment when other powers with Far Eastern interests were almost completely absorbed in Europe. Furthermore, the Japanese tried to counteract the likely Chinese reaction—publicity for their troubles and procrastination in their negotiations—by demanding absolute secrecy and an immediate decision. In being handed the Demands personally, Yuan Shih-k'ai was threatened with dire consequences in case of disobedience. The Japanese, he was told, would encourage the Chinese revolutionaries in their endeavor to overthrow the government; they might use force themselves; even Yuan's personal safety might be endangered; whereas, if he complied, they might support his monarchical ambitions.[4]

Japanese bullying was of no avail. The Chinese did not let themselves be robbed of their most effective weapons. They publicized their troubles and drew the Japanese into prolonged negotiations. It was a risky step, but the Chinese were desperate; and they were successful.

Within a very few days after the presentation of the Demands, news about them leaked out, in a rather devious manner, via the minister of finance, Wellington Koo of the Foreign Office, Reinsch, and William Henry Donald, "Donald of China."[5] The government argued quite rightly that the Demands touched upon the vital interests of other foreign powers, who could be expected to defend them and therewith China. But the leak could hardly be confined to the legations. Not in Peking. Very shortly after it was engineered, the existence of the Twenty-

* There was, however, some concern about Japan's penetration into China beyond the sphere controlled by Germany. The dean of the diplomatic corps in Peking turned to the United States, asking for American troops to take points along the Peking-Mukden railway line, hitherto held by Germany. Washington made immediate preparations for this purpose via the Philippines command. A high officer was sent to China to report on the situation. But by September 14 these points were occupied by Japan.—DSDD, September 9, 1914, 893.00/2171; September 10, 1914, 893.00/2173; September 10, 1914, 893.00/2175; September 16, 1914, 893.00/2177.

One Demands became common knowledge, and the remaining uncertainty regarding their exact nature served to heighten the general excitement. It is very doubtful whether Peking enjoyed the wide publicity given to the Japanese undertaking. Not only were prestige and "face" involved now on both sides, making negotiations more difficult, but it was still an open question whether the Japanese might not react to the breach of secrecy by making their threats real.[6]

However, the facts were known and could not be annulled. The Chinese public reacted in a remarkable manner. Throughout the country individuals and groups made their voices heard against acceptance of the Demands. The government and the press were flooded with letters, telegrams, and pamphlets demanding resistance to Japanese aggression. Soldiers demanded war and offered their services for the front lines. Students appealed for resistance regardless of governmental decisions. Merchants started unofficial boycotts against Japanese goods. Civic associations advocated higher taxes for defense purposes. The refugee revolutionaries in Tokyo, New York, London, and elsewhere edited manifestos professing their patriotism and assuring the nation that they would not embarrass the hated government of Yuan in the hour of China's crisis. "Who is there that would fight his own country by another country's strength, or who will invite one wolf to drive away another one?"

There suddenly was unity across the land. Provincial particularism seemed to have disappeared. National solidarity was at last, if temporarily, established. A sense of nationality emerged which aroused the wonderment of foreign observers. The people seemed to have been waiting for just such an opportunity to indicate their disgust with the prevailing factionalism (soon to deteriorate into tuchunism and civil war).

In temper these manifestations were different from those of earlier years. They were less impassioned and effervescent, more determined and mature. They abounded in the customary self-criticism, but also in an unusual willingness to sacrifice. A development "as novel as it is full of warning," as the *North China Herald* put it.[7]

While the popular reaction strengthened the hand of the government, it also proved embarrassing. Peking learned that public opinion can be detrimental as well as beneficial in the conduct of foreign affairs. The government fully realized the impossibility of resisting determined Japanese aggression. Enthusiastic demands for strong action were heroic rather than rational. Counsels of prudence were frequently brushed aside with the argument that surrender would mean sharing Korea's fate and that resistance, though hopeless, would at least guarantee to China the esteem Belgium had won for going down upholding a worthy cause.

Peking dampened public enthusiasm for self-sacrifice. More, it checked the expression of popular feeling. Open discussion of Sino-Japanese negotiations was prohibited as "injudicious" and "impolitic." In an order telegraphed to all provincial governments Peking requested the suppression of antiforeign agitation; prohibition of the formation of patriotic corps; censorship of all foreign telegrams, to frustrate any fishing by revolutionaries in troubled waters; and supervision of public meetings to prevent the formation of secret societies. Everything was to be avoided that might give the Japanese a pretext for expanding their demands or create the opportunity for an organized opposition to form against the Peking government. The government assured the provinces that it would assume full responsibility for the conduct of the negotiations and the safeguarding of Chinese sovereignty, independence, and territorial integrity. Police power was used abundantly and on the whole successfully to control agitation and to prevent undue incidents.[8]

Thus protecting itself against too much popular pressure, the government proceeded to deal with the crisis on a political level. The cabinet and the presidential advisers met in frequent and excited sessions. The situation looked hopeless. Japan seemed determined to force China into submission. The world was preoccupied with the European war. Western governments were extremely reluctant to do anything about the Twenty-One Demands. They did not even believe in their authenticity. The suspicion was widespread that all this was a German trick to divide the Allies. The Chinese were left to their own meager resources.

The question of resistance or surrender created a split in the government. Since a decision depended upon unknown Japanese intentions, either side of the argument could be supported by speculations only. The advocates of resistance maintained that surrender would be the end for China, as once it had been for Korea. Resistance would rally national feeling and create sufficient strength to harass the Japanese until the European war was finished and the Allies could help China. The opponents of resistance argued that the Japanese would not enforce their Demands or execute their threats. Even if they did, the Chinese people would suffer less by surrendering. The hand of those opposing resistance was strengthened by a slow awakening of the West to the realities of Japanese policy. Public opinion abroad began to support the Chinese. A few diplomatic protests to Japan improved China's chances. Time seemed to be on the side of the Chinese, and this encouraged them in the full use of their traditional procrastination.[9]

Fully aware of the need of giving in to some degree, the Chinese divided the Demands into those which infringed upon the treaty rights of other nations or upon Chinese sovereignty and those which might be conceded. They were prepared to discuss only this last group on the basis of a principle established several years earlier for the purpose of restraining foreign appetites, namely, "that concessions shall cover only specific enterprises or expressly delimited areas, which shall be commensurate with the scope of the respective undertaking, and that they will avoid all arrangements for a general preference or for options carrying contingent implications." [10]

The Japanese had no intention of permitting such fine distinctions. They were pressing for the acceptance of the Demands *in toto*, and they were pressing hard. They too realized that time was on China's side. After five months of negotiations resulting in nothing, they prepared an ultimatum. News of it caused a panic among Chinese officials. Those favoring acceptance of the Demands now split over the question whether concessions should quickly be made to prevent the ultimatum or whether the ultimatum should be awaited and acceptance of the Demands be excused to the Chinese public as surrender to the inevitable. Apparently the first opinion prevailed. The government declared its willingness to the Japanese legation to concede a number of important points. Luckily for the Chinese, it was too late, though they were furious for unnecessarily having shown their hand. The Japanese ultimatum, dated May 7, 1915, was on its way, and milder than expected. In particular Group V of the Demands was eliminated and reserved "for future negotiation." Even the advocates of resistance in the Peking government no longer insisted upon their view, and the ultimatum was accepted on May 9.* At least China's sovereignty was saved.[11]

* The American government gave China moral support in her negotiations with Japan. The British government was much more active. After first having exerted considerable pressure upon the Japanese to reduce their demands, they then strongly urged the Chinese to accept the ultimatum. — Fifield, *Woodrow Wilson and the Far East*, pp. 45–47; Li, *Woodrow Wilson's China Policy*, p. 125.

The Chinese public was less favorably impressed than the government with the final outcome of the affair, and not without reason. Had Peking given in more to popular demands for a very strong stand, the Japanese might conceivably have retreated still further. For while the government's tactics contributed to the moderation of the Japanese attitude, internal Japanese politics had the most to do with it, and better advantage could have been taken of disagreement there. Tokyo had come to the conclusion that there was no *casus belli*. The policy of the *fait accompli* had failed, thanks to Chinese tactics, and Premier Okuma was increasingly criticized by the press and in the Diet. Japan's financial position was weak, and had money been spent on adventures abroad, the nation's foreign credit would have suffered. The Genro was annoyed and dissatisfied with many details of Okuma's policy and behavior and urged a more conciliatory attitude.[12]

Japan's mildness was, however, merely temporary. The fundamental aim of expansion on the mainland and the domination of China remained. In its pursuit the Japanese spoiled systematically every chance of China to improve her international position during the war. In particular, Tokyo foiled Yuan Shih-k'ai's agreement in 1915 to become one of the Allies. China was not to have a voice at the peace table, at any rate not until Japan had secured her own spoils, to wit, succession to Germany's rights, privileges, and property in Shantung and the Pacific islands as a minimum. This succession was accomplished by secret understandings with Great Britain, France, Russia, and Italy and by a presumption that Secretary Bryan's note of March 13, 1915, tied the United States unwittingly to it. This note recognized Japan's "special and close relations, political as well as economic, with China," and was reinforced in November 1917 by the Lansing-Ishii notes. After the completion of these arrangements, Japan was no longer so adamantly opposed to China's entry into the war, and that country was confronted once more with the problem of joining the Allies. But the problem was no longer the same, because the China of 1917 was no longer the China of 1914 or 1915.

Yuan Shih-k'ai had died in 1916, before achieving his ambition of becoming emperor. With the "strong man" the last remains of a central government disappeared, though at first it seemed as if his death might lead to greater unity among the political factions. Vice President Li Yuan-hung succeeded to the presidency. The leaders in Peking accepted him, and so did the southern provinces and the provisional government in Canton which had been formed in opposition to Yuan's regime. Li reconvened Parliament, which Yuan had dissolved, on August 1, 1916, and the Provisional Constitution of 1912 was put into force again.

The real political power, however, was not in the hands of Li but of Premier Tuan Chi-jui. He was the man of the war lords, the tuchuns, who had no patience with Parliament. These were the military officers and civil governors whom Yuan had distributed across the country in good positions as a reward for their support. With Yuan's death they felt relieved of their loyalty to government or nation and deteriorated into robber barons.

For ten years the nation fell into complete anarchy. The war lords took over and became a law unto themselves. They recognized no higher authority, except as it suited their selfish purposes to do so. They lived in great style at the expense of the people. And yet, with all their evil qualities, they were better than the hired brigands upon whom they relied for their personal rule. China's "government" became an impenetrable jungle of local plots and counterplots, of alliances and counteralliances, of jealousies, intrigues, and constant strife among the tuchuns for power and position. The people had no part in this. They suffered. They were exploited by each successive set of war lords and their brigands that swept the country like locusts. The concept of public welfare had disappeared from Chinese government. There were no principles or ideals involved, except those of the robber. There were no issues struggling for recognition. An end to the situation could come only through the physical suppression of the war lords. China's sickness was not that political power had passed into the wrong hands but that it was absent at the center. Viewed from the standpoint of Chinese provincialism, warlordism could perhaps be interpreted as the last gasp of political regionalism. The war lord, as one observer stated, was sometimes the "effective agent spearheading a regional separatism that was supported by the populace." [13] But if warlordism was regionalism struggling to survive, the sooner, in the circumstances, death should come, the better for China.

From the standpoint of its idealistic conception, the complete failure of the revolution was now demonstrated. Its intellectual leaders, the selfless ones, had failed to create, hence to obtain, political power. Their influence disappeared as an immediately effective force. They existed by the grace of the war lords, to whom they oftentimes attached themselves to maintain any standing at all. The militarists, for their part, frequently tolerated the trappings of a constitutional regime either as a front or as a convenient tool. The poor intellectuals who were writing constitutions apparently failed to realize the pitiful role they were permitted to play as they were sitting in "parliaments" either in Peking or more often in the south and "opposing" some group claiming to be the central government. Their activities created the impression, especially in the south, that there was a progressive democratic government in Canton desperately fighting the north of China, ruled over by a reactionary, selfish clique. These intellectuals as represented in the Kuomintang were little superior to the war lords. They were an odd conglomeration of individuals with diverse beliefs and motivations. Intrigue and strife within the party were almost as ripe as among the militarists. There was as yet little hope that from this party might emerge the salvation of China.

The country was torn to pieces, each under the autocratic rule of a war lord whose power reached as far as he could maintain the loyalty of his bandit outposts. Some form of cohesion between the pieces remained in the north and south respectively. But it was no more than was tolerated by the tuchuns, and it was tolerated only to the degree that it did not interfere with their pursuit of self-enrichment or actually furthered it. The difference between the north and south at this time remained what it had traditionally been: the north had the prerogative and experience of government, the south was more advanced and represented the opposition. Even the chaos could not quite wipe out this hangover of centuries past, and the war lords paid their respect to it.

The tuchuns of the north and south granted something like *de facto* recognition to the claim of the faction and the Military Government controlling Peking that they were the central government. In Canton, the situation was more confused, though equally unrealistic. There existed the southern Military Government, the refugee Parliament, and a Provincial Assembly which had been dissolved from above years ago but which refused to recognize this dissolution.

The members of the Military Government failed to attend meetings. They sent nobodies as substitutes. Sun Yat-sen and T'ang Shao-yi were among those not attending; so was Wu Ting-fang, who had been appointed a member because of his good reputation abroad. His appointment was expected to bring foreign dividends. The Parliament did not recognize the Military Government. And neither of the two was recognized by the Provincial Assembly, whose delegates, split into two groups, were subservient to two rival tuchuns. This was not a unique situation; it was typical of the whole country. In these circumstances a Chinese foreign policy could hardly exist. Questions of international significance were primarily objects of internal political controversy. They were judged from the standpoint of factional interest before the national interest was considered.

The foreign powers, confronted with this bedlam, had to decide how to deal with China. They chose two ways. A subversive one was to fall in with Chinese intrigues and to strengthen their own positions by supporting the faction which happened to control the area of their special interests. Occasionally they would support all factions, just to be on the safe side. The Japanese were particularly clever in this practice. The other way was to deal officially with the clique which happened to control Peking. This was justified on the formal grounds that Peking was the capital. Beyond this, any northern clique was likely to be more reliably reactionary than any southern, hence more acceptable to foreign governments. Recognition of Peking also saved the powers the inconvenience of having to move headquarters about the country. In a few cases there existed an honest conviction among some foreigners that the advanced ideas of some Canton intellectuals were undesirable for China and that Canton therefore should not be accorded the prestige of foreign recognition.

When President Wilson appealed to the neutral countries in 1917 to break off diplomatic relations with Germany, this issue became the focus of a struggle between individuals, cliques, factions, parties, Parliament, and the executive in China. But the struggle, not the issue, was the important thing. For here was a situation which lent itself well to political maneuvering, which promised great benefits to the winning group, and which, to a remaining few patriotic Chinese, held out the hope of an improved position for their country in world politics at the end of the war. To be sure, the many opinions and arguments offered in the controversy were all dressed up in the coat of patriotism. But for the most part purely selfish, personal, and expedient motives prevailed. Any progress China had made in the past toward developing an independent and national foreign policy seemed to be wiped out, and foreign

147

powers were once more wielding an undue influence over her international fate.

Once the Japanese had secured themselves against unwanted eventualities at the peace conference by the secret treaties and the Bryan note of 1915, and once the British had replaced the German sales organization for their Lancashire and other goods with an organization of their own, objections to China's becoming an ally were eliminated. The Russians and the French had always been in favor of it. Agitation to that effect now began under the enthusiastic leadership of American Minister Reinsch and his unofficial henchmen, William Henry Donald, Dr. George Morrison of the London *Times*, Samuel G. Blythe of the *Saturday Evening Post*, and two American writers, Dr. John C. Ferguson and Charles Stevenson Smith. In view of broken-down cable communications with the United States, Reinsch took it upon himself "to prevail upon China to associate herself with the American action," and he did so with all the energy and influence at his command — to the great embarrassment of the State Department and President Wilson. There had been no intention in Washington of leading China into the war. In fact, such a step was considered dangerous and there was every desire at the highest levels to avoid it.* But Reinsch had started the ball rolling, and the best the State Department could do was to slow down its pace.[14]

The day after President Wilson's proclamation, on February 4, 1917, appealing for the diplomatic break with Germany, Reinsch had a long talk with President Li and Premier Tuan, urging them to join the American action. Li expressed great doubts and many objections, while Tuan remained unconvinced — anxious, as later events showed, to use his assent as a bargaining point. But Li, too, wanted to have certain guarantees, though these were more for the benefit of his country than himself. Japan was used as the lever to raise the price to the Americans. The Chinese had, since the beginning of the year, played upon American fears of Japanese intentions in order to obtain American support. They wished to prevent any developments during the war or at the future

* There were, however, officials in the Far Eastern Division of the State Department who felt, like many Chinese, that China's entry into the war might decrease Japan's influence in the Far East. Arguments that China's entry into the war might delay the development of democratic, parliamentary rule were brushed aside by these officials as "inaccurate" or as influenced by "personal grievances." — Memorandum Far Eastern Division, February 14, 1917, Papers Breckinridge Long; Memoranda, China, Military Loan, and Memorandum of the Division of Far Eastern Affairs, June 11, 1917, DSDD 893.00/2585.

peace conference which might make of China a field of "compensations" or lead to restorations or expansions of spheres of interest.[15] The disclosure of Reinsch's anxiety to have China break diplomatic relations with Germany seemed the perfect moment to press the Chinese demands.

The Chinese statesmen wanted to be assured that they would retain full control over their arsenals and military forces and have full membership in the peace conference. They demanded an American loan of $10 million for the improvement of arsenals, the funding of the American portion of the Boxer indemnity in long-term bonds, and the promise that America would urge the Allies to do likewise. Reinsch, still incommunicado with the State Department, on February 8 gave the required assurances regarding the loan and the Boxer indemnity and much vaguer assurances on the other Chinese terms, pointing out, though, that specific commitments would be subject to confirmation from Washington. On the next day the Chinese protested to Germany and threatened her with a breach of diplomatic relations if the submarine warfare were not stopped. Confidentially they assured Reinsch that if the United States went to war with Germany, China would at least break off diplomatic relations.

Things were moving in accordance with the wishes of Reinsch, but not with those of the State Department. While Washington increasingly discouraged any Chinese participation in the war, the Chinese premier himself encouraged Reinsch in his activities by constantly raising the bogey of Japan. In the meantime the Chinese government requested financial benefits also from the allied powers before it should agree to taking any further steps in the direction of war with Germany. But before the answers were known, and before Washington's refusal to support the assurances by Reinsch reached Peking, the Chinese cabinet, on March 3, decided to break diplomatic relations with Germany and made the official announcement on March 14.

After the government knew, or thought it knew, the line-up of the major powers, fundamentally its course of action was determined by the internal Chinese struggle for power. Tuan Chi-jui, representative of the reactionaries in the cabinet, opponent of parliamentarianism, friend of the tuchuns, and ambitious politician, proved a willing collaborator of the Allies. He did not need much persuasion. The power and prestige that would redound to him and his friends through cooperation with

149

the Allies overruled all other considerations. And precisely because cooperation would strengthen Tuan's position, but partly also out of patriotic considerations for China's welfare, opposition developed to Tuan's decision.

President Li Yuan-hung was the most prominent spokesman for the opposition. He was a decent, kindly man, who believed in the republic and parliamentarianism. He also believed Germany was going to win the war and he wanted to stay friendly with her. He was opposed to war. His support came mostly from the Kuomintang-dominated Parliament, though its members were much more motivated by considerations of political power. But from the beginning the opposition hardly had a chance. The foreign powers did not support it and it had no army at its disposal. Li's cooperation with Parliament had no influence because Parliament itself had no power. It could not very well be ignored, but it could be manipulated.

The internal struggle for power came to a head when the question of declaring war against Germany arose. The tuchuns, the real power in China, were feted by the diplomats of the nations engaged in a war for democracy, and told to ignore parliamentary opposition. By threats, intimidation, promises, intrigues, and financial contributions Tuan and his friends were encouraged and strengthened. Considering the behavior of these diplomats, the Chinese could hardly be blamed for refusing to enter the war just in order to defend democratic principles. They insisted on very material rewards — beyond and above those accruing merely through association with the Allies.

After lengthy negotiations about the nature of the reward and some vague assurances that Chinese participation would result in far-reaching benefits, three specific promises were set down on paper. A moratorium on the Boxer indemnity was declared, the tariff rate was increased to an effective 5 per cent, and Chinese troops were allowed to enter the demilitarized zone around Tientsin.

Why did Tuan insist on any rewards at all? The easiest answer is that they benefited his regime. Possibly there may have been a vestige of patriotism in him and his supporters. And very definitely they weakened the arguments of the opposition. One of the strongest points Tuan used to swing public opinion in his favor was his holding out the chance that China would sit as an equal partner with the victorious nations at the peace table. He had no certainty that this would be so, but his use of the argument shows that the national feeling which had developed by 1917 had not been crushed by tuchunism.

Tuan's cabinet decided upon war against Germany on May 1. Parliament was asked to approve the measure on May 8. The cabinet's message started long and heated debates on the merits of the measure, quite contrary to Tuan's expectations. The situation became incredibly complicated; not only were there numerous Chinese factions struggling against each other, but foreign powers, particularly Japan, were intriguing in Peking. Tuan's methods to frighten Parliament were ineffective. Neither his invitation to all the war lords to assemble in Peking nor his organization of a mob outside Parliament moved the delegates to pass the desired resolution. President Li, sticking bravely to the Provisional Constitution in the midst of all this tumult, dismissed Tuan on June 11 and, in the face of a threatened military move by the tuchuns against Peking, dissolved Parliament on June 13. The parliamentarians left town en masse. They settled once more in Canton and established the Government of the South — one of whose first acts was a declaration of war against Germany! In Peking one of the worst war lords called in by Li to mediate the dispute engineered the restoration of the Manchus. This step, however, did not please the other war lords, who now marched on Peking and by July 13 ended the monarchy. Tuan was restored to the premiership, and Vice President Feng Kuo-chang became president.[16]

The road was now clear for a declaration of war, and this was decreed on August 14, 1917. The move was, however, not a complete surrender to the allied powers, especially not to Japan, who, as soon as she had realized the inevitability of China's participation in the war, had switched her line and tried to get China under her wings as an ally. The Chinese were clever enough to realize her motives. Following America's precedent, they gave their declaration of war the character of an independent action which would not tie them to the Allies. "In the case of declaring war upon Germany," President Feng said, "we can do so at our own perfect will, but if we go to war on the side of the Entente, we should not be as free as we should like to be." [17]

The Allies soon began to realize what China's "independent" war action meant for them. The major purposes of France and Great Britain in getting China into the war had been the elimination of German interests and competition in China. Their own welfare, not China's, was their motive. China was to confiscate all German property, intern German nationals, eradicate every trace of German influence. Extraterritoriality was to be ended for Germans, but not for other nationals in German concessions. German vessels were to remain nominally in China's possession, but had to be "subleased" to the Allies.

To the Chinese government participation in the war was a matter of prestige and getting material aid. From its standpoint the elimination of German interests was largely detrimental, for any benefits possible from such action would go to the Allies (just as the Allies, not China, benefited from the collapse of Russian domination in Manchuria). The Chinese were therefore most negligent in fulfilling their duties as an associate of the Allies against Germany. They had to be pushed and edged. They felt very friendly toward the Germans and saw no reason to fight them, at least no more than to fight any of the other nations exploiting China. They definitely preferred the Germans to the Japanese. From their standpoint breaking off relations with Germany meant losing a friend. "There is one province in which the people pray for a German victory," said the governor of Shantung, the German sphere of interest; "that is Shantung!" [18]

The mass of the people were largely unaware of China's participation in the war. They certainly did not realize the implications of belligerent status, nor had they much knowledge of the war aims. No wonder China's war effort was limited. The government reluctantly contributed what meager resources were left after internal affairs had been taken care of. Its major attention and that of the public were absorbed by the civil war. To the Chinese people foreign affairs were about equivalent to Japanese aggression against China.

This aggression proceeded apace after 1917. Japan had little to fear from the European powers. The Lansing-Ishii notes of November 1917, confirming Japan's "special interests in China," were interpreted by the Japanese as giving them practically a free hand for their maneuvers, in which they began to engage with extraordinary energy. By innumerable loans to the Peking government, by supplying money and arms to all factions to keep the civil war alive, by an agreement in 1918 for "cooperative" participation in the war, by military agreements also in 1918, by all sorts of secret treaties and intrigues, they succeeded in obtaining increased control over Chinese politics, economics, and territories. Between 1918 and 1920 Japan thus obtained a position in China,

152

especially in Shantung, which she did not occupy again until her invasion of Manchuria in 1931. Since almost all Chinese factions intrigued with the Japanese, the few patriotic Chinese who objected were powerless to do anything about the situation. They were hoping that the peace conference would solve their national problem.

Their first disappointment came when for some time no invitation to participate in the peace conference reached China. The Chinese became so worried that they planned to send a delegation in the hope of forcing the hand of the Allies: once a delegation was in Paris, it could not very well be refused admission. Their worries were not unjustified. Some voices were heard among the Allies opposing representation of the "theoretical" belligerent. Eventually, however, China was permitted the limited representation granted to "belligerent powers with special interests," on a level with Greece, Poland, Portugal, and some others.[19]

For the purpose of sending a delegation to Paris, the Peking and Canton governments were able to agree sufficiently so that the five-man group had three representatives from the north and two from the south. But the group was far from united. Mutual suspicions, criticism, and personal idiosyncrasies had a divisive and weakening influence. The humiliating role the delegation was destined to play further added to its unhappiness. It was treated by the Allies as a negligible quantity, if not a nuisance.

In part, its exaggerated hopes were to blame for this treatment. It had gone to Paris with the expectation of getting satisfaction for all Chinese grievances. Minister Reinsch had warned the Chinese to confine themselves to questions and problems directly related to the war. But the Chinese, under the influence, presumably, of Wilson's ideals, were under the impression that a solid foundation for world peace was to be laid at Paris. Surely the protection of China's integrity and independence, the restoration of her sovereignty, the equality of 400 million human beings among the peoples of the world would be an indispensable part of that foundation. So, in addition to asking for the return to China of all former German rights in Shantung, the liquidation of German and Austro-Hungarian economic interests in China, and the abrogation of the treaties and notes originating in the Twenty-One Demands of Japan in 1915, the Chinese planned the submission of a list of requests called Questions for Readjustment, which dealt primarily with the broad issues of the unequal treaties.

During the first and only appearance of the Chinese delegates before the Council of Ten on January 28, 1919, Wellington Koo dealt only with the Shantung problem. He did it very brilliantly, although until two days before his presentation he did not even know that for 20 million yen the Japanese had bought a secret agreement from the Peking government in September 1918 by which Japan's position was secured in Shantung. The delegates congratulated him. Groups all over China were jubilant. The Chinese delegation was flooded with congratulatory telegrams. For a short while fratricide in China gave way to common joy, and, as the machinations of Japan became more widely known, to common hatred of the Japanese and their henchmen in the Peking government. Tokyo's pressure upon Peking to take a more conciliatory stand at the peace conference aroused the Chinese public.[20] The delegation, encouraged by the backing at home, took an increasingly stiff attitude in Paris and expanded its demands against Japan to include Manchuria and Mongolia.

The situation seemed very hopeful to the Chinese delegation. Their first appearance was successful. The Japanese were embarrassed by international demands into producing at least some of the various secret treaties they had forced upon or bought from China. The American delegation was most sympathetic to the Chinese cause and practically considered China its ward. Though the United States government had discouraged the appointment of official American advisers, the Chinese had them unofficially, and besides the closest possible relations existed between the Chinese and the American delegation in Paris.*

But the Chinese were to learn very soon that sympathy and friendship are not enough to guarantee the victory of a just cause. From their standpoint the situation began to deteriorate very rapidly. They were given only a few moments to present their case to the all-important Council of Four and had to restrict themselves to the matter of Shantung.

The Americans, more specifically President Wilson, took up their case. Wilson started out valiantly with the proposal that German interests in Shantung should be restored directly to China. He based the proposal partly on moral, partly on legal grounds, as the Chinese had done earlier

* It was reported at the time that the Japanese offered 1 million yen, the Americans, through the International Banking Corporation, $600,000, for the privilege of being advisers. — New York Times, December 10, 1918; North China Herald, December 14, 1918; Patrick Gallagher, America's Aims and Asia's Aspirations (New York, 1920), p. 185.

before the Council of Ten. The Japanese were quite willing to recognize Wilson's sincerity and agreed with the general principles governing his ideas on international relations. Perhaps for that reason, however, they stood adamant on their legal case. So did the British and French delegates. Since the legality of Japan's position was recognized by the non-American delegations to the Council of Four, China's case could be won only on political grounds. Yet on political grounds Wilson had been maneuvered into such a difficult position by the time the Shantung question was discussed — in April and May 1919 — that his defeat was practically certain. In the end the choice was, or so he thought, either to grant Japan's requests for succession to Germany's position or to lose Japan as a participant in the peace conference. This Wilson was unwilling to risk. And so, fighting a lonely battle all along, he was forced gradually to recede from his original position. The final arrangement reached in the Treaty of Versailles gave to Japan all former German rights, privileges, and properties in Shantung.

The Chinese had had no other advocates in the Council of Four. To criticize them for relying too much on the American delegation and not enough on the British and French is therefore pointless.[21] These powers sided with Japan throughout the conference. Wilson tried to console the Chinese, and perhaps himself, with the thought that by sacrificing Chinese interests, he had saved the creation of the League of Nations, in which China's grievances could be taken up and settled. The Chinese delegates, however, found Articles 156 to 158 of the Versailles Treaty so unacceptable, even temporarily, that, not allowed to sign the treaty with reservations, they refused to sign it altogether and proclaimed peace with Germany in September 1919.[22]

Popular reaction in China to the betrayal of the country at Paris was strong but, at first, confused. There was no concerted action against the guilty ones. Guilt was diffused among too many. Resentment was directed against the Japanese, against foreigners in general, and against traitors in Peking. Unrest increased throughout the country. But soon public indignation began to crystallize and focus on the Japanese and on the officials who had sold out to them. The engineers of this process were the students, Young China. Quite spontaneously on May 4, 1919, when definite news of the results in Paris reached Peking, a group of three to five thousand students marched in protest to the Legation Quarter and from there to the house of Tsao Ju-lin, the chief negotiator with the Japanese of the traitorous September 1918 treaties. The demonstrators ranged in age from thirteen to twenty-five. They were quiet and well behaved until they reached Tsao's house. This they destroyed, beat up the Chinese minister to Japan who happened to be there, but failed to catch Tsao. He had slipped out through a window. The episode nevertheless ended Tsao's career. By a group of schoolboys thus was ousted a dictator who had a personal army of several hundred thousand men — a feat that had been attempted in vain by the press, many foreigners, and clever politicians of both the south and north.

The event created an impression all over China. It scared the friends of Tsao and encouraged the patriots. The idea spread like wildfire. In all major cities students began to assemble, to demonstrate, to propagandize. Their activities aroused popular curiosity, then interest. The public began to learn more about China's government and foreign relations. A great part of the press took the students' side. Newly organized labor unions struck in sympathy. Merchants joined in the boycott against Japanese goods, partly out of fear of retaliation if they refused, but partly out of conviction. The student movement created a remarkably strong and united expression of public opinion.

Tsao, in a forgiving mood, labeled the May 4 movement a pacemaker for bolshevism. This was not altogether wrong as a prediction, but for reasons which Tsao could not foresee. For by default this movement and its potentialities came under the influence of Soviet Russia. The Western powers found it too "radical" and were antagonistic to it. They thus deprived themselves of an important ally for the future, whereas the Russians established contact with the movement in the early 'twenties and have derived some benefit from it ever since. The Japanese laughed the whole thing off as the usual Chinese "five-minute patriotism," a correct evaluation for the short but not for the long run. The effervescence of the movement subsided before the new disappointment of the Washington Conference arrived in 1922. But the fundamental educational effect of the movement persisted.* The enlightenment of the public through formal and informal education continued, and the foundation was laid for the nationalist revolution which was to come in the middle 'twenties.[23]

* In view of this result it is irrelevant whether the movement was begun by *agents provocateurs* working against Peking and whether it reached the masses (which it probably did not).

For the time being, however, all this agitation could not alter the fact that Shantung and other international questions remained answered unfavorably for China. Shantung's fate was sealed in Article 156 of the peace treaty in an almost studiedly inconsiderate manner toward China. The clause contained nothing regarding the rights and privileges of China in her own territory. China was mentioned only in connection with the infamous treaty of 1898, which began the break-up of the nation. Thus the very evil was reanimated for the eradication of which the war had presumably been fought. Besides, for decades the avowed policy of the powers had been to abolish special privileges and spheres of interest in China. These were now solemnly confirmed. All the other territory-grabbing sanctified in the treaty was disguised in some form, such as by being called an "adjustment of wrongs" or a "mandate." The only quasi annexation for which no excuse was provided was Shantung, the territory of an ally.[24]

The fate of China at the peace conference was part of the general unwillingness of the powers to lay an adequate foundation for peace. The material benefits China derived from participation in the war were practically nil. That she lost nothing, on the other hand, may perhaps be considered something won, in view of her past experience. And she made imponderable gains. To the surprise of the representatives of the powers assembled in Paris, and to the embarrassment of some, the esteem in which she was held was augmented greatly by her refusal to sign the Versailles Treaty. She took part in the conference on an equal footing and did set her signature to some of the treaties. The most important result was the enormous, world-wide publicity obtained not only for the Shantung problem but for China's ignominious position generally. Even before the conference the Allies had owed a debt of honor to China. The weight of this obligation was now made more onerous by the fact that the Allies' lack of good faith became known everywhere and that one of the war aims had been to adjust the very wrongs from which China was suffering. To all those in the world who had honestly believed in the cause in whose name the war was fought, it was obvious that the settlement of the Shantung question could not be the final one.[25]

The Chinese used this conviction in their appeals to the world for justice. But they overestimated the interest in their cause among foreign peoples and the influence of liberals abroad. They acted under the misconception that there was such a thing as a world public-opinion which might work in their favor. They also forgot that headlines rarely make lasting impressions. Their enlightenment and final disappointment came at the Washington Conference. In the end they were brought to a reorientation of their whole foreign policy.

12

The Washington Conference, 1921

THE Washington Conference of 1921 came at a most inopportune time for China. Internal conditions were chaotic. The central government had, in the words of the American minister, "virtually ceased to function." The American consul in Canton, on the other hand, sent the State Department enthusiastic accounts of the southern government under Sun Yat-sen. No inferences were drawn from these reports. The United States and other governments continued to deal with the corrupt and reactionary Peking government.

There was great doubt whether the situation could continue very much longer. The central government was about to suffer a financial collapse. There were defaults on some foreign loans. But instead of leading foreign governments to a reappraisal of the diplomatic ledger, the imminence of a debacle merely spoiled the atmosphere for the Chinese delegation at Washington. The Chinese government made desperate attempts to delay the final break-down until after the conference in the hope that a miracle might happen at Washington.

Foreign governments were once more in a dilemma, since granting or withholding financial assistance would equally be regarded as an interference in internal Chinese affairs and as taking sides in the civil war. Some foreign observers did not consider financial collapse an unmixed evil. It would force a realistic approach to the problems of China and do away with the pretense that all was as well there as it could be. Possibly the Chinese delegates shared this opinion. Such a disaster would relieve them of their obligations to Peking and enable them to speak freely about facts.[1]

Naturally neither Peking nor Canton wished for collapse. Both were anxious for power, and both wooed foreign governments, Peking to retain recognition, Canton to obtain it. Knowing very well what the foreign powers liked best to hear, they both said it. Peking spokesmen constantly painted rosy pictures of the great potentialities in China that awaited foreign exploitation under an Open Door regime. When the Washington Conference brought disappointment to China, however, the Chinese chargé d'affaires in London no longer hesitated to call much of the talk about the Open Door "unctuous humbug." [2]

Canton, frantically striving for recognition and for permission to send a delegate to the Washington Conference, published a manifesto over Sun Yat-sen's signature which pointed out that the mobilization of China's vast resources needed foreign capital and expert knowledge, both of which would be welcome "in pursuance of the open door policy." In a personal letter to President Harding Sun wrote: "The John Hay Doctrine is to China what the Monroe Doctrine is to America. The violation of this Hay Doctrine would mean the loss of our national integrity and the subsequent partition of China. Just as America would do her utmost to keep intact the spirit as well as the letter of the Monroe Doctrine, so we in China are striving to uphold this spirit of the John Hay Doctrine." [3] They were striving, of course, for no such thing. Territorial integrity rather than equal opportunity for foreigners remained the preoccupation of the Chinese. The fact became obvious once more in the Chinese approach to the Washington Conference.

The Chinese suspected the motives behind the conference. They feared in particular that the problems of China were not uppermost in the minds of those who had organized it. The combination of disarmament and Far Eastern problems on the agenda proved puzzling. Highly propaganda-minded, they welcomed the combination as bringing the greatest possible number of participants to the conference table. But they wanted some elucidation. Was the conference the result of a British suggestion to settle the question of the Anglo-Japanese alliance that the recent Imperial Conference had failed to settle? Was it to be merely a funeral for that alliance (in which case the Chinese would gladly be pallbearers), or was it to be an occasion for the discussion of broader Far Eastern problems? Only if it was to be the latter did the conference appear promising to the Chinese. They felt that its success would be more certain, in fact, if the British would commit themselves not to renew the alliance under any circumstances. [*]

The conference appeared desirable to China only if it should result in

* Their agitation found an echo in several dominions which were equally antagonistic to the Anglo-Japanese alliance. See J. Bartlet Brebner, "Canada, the Anglo-Japanese Alliance, and the Washington Conference," *Political Science Quarterly*, L (1935), 45–58.

a guarantee of sovereignty and territory in the Far East in general and, in regard to China in particular, in a commitment on the principles to be applied and the methods to be used in connection with administrative integrity, tariff autonomy, the Open Door, special privileges and concessions, equality of treatment in railways, and the status of existing commitments.[4] Peking carefully worked out a dossier of grievances showing thirty major issues. Unfortunately for China, the other participants in the conference were far less conscientious. They appeared little prepared, if at all, for the Far Eastern section of the agenda.

One evening, four days after the opening of the Washington Conference, the Chinese delegation was given ten hours' notice to present its case. These four days had been sufficient to indicate that the mood of the conference was not very favorable to an elaborate discussion of China's problems. So all through the night the delegates worked to reduce their program to ten points. They further decided not to present specific details but instead to begin by stating "certain general principles" which should "guide the Conference in the determination which it is to make." This proved to be a great blunder, as the Chinese should have known; for any international conference likes to evade specific issues by taking refuge in "general principles."

Dr. Alfred Sze read the ten-point program. The powers should respect China's territorial integrity and political and administrative independence, in return for which China would not alienate any of her territory to a foreign power. China would apply the Open Door principle. The powers should not conclude between themselves any agreement directly affecting China or the general peace in the Far East without giving China a chance to participate. All special concessions by China to any one power should be declared null and void, while all general concessions should be re-examined and, when found valid, should be harmonized with one another and with the general principles to be declared by the conference. Existing limitations upon China's freedom of political, jurisdictional, or administrative action should be removed. Definite terms should be set to Chinese commitments originally granted without time limit. Instruments granting special rights or privileges should be narrowly interpreted in favor of the grantor. China's rights as a neutral should be strictly observed in future wars. Provision should be made for the peaceful settlement of international disputes in the Pacific and Far East. Conferences should be held from time to time to discuss problems of the Pacific and Far East with a view to determining common policies among the interested powers.

This catalogue of China's grievances was meant to be a starter and to provide a basis for discussion. Acquiescence on all points could hardly have been hoped for by the Chinese themselves. The presentation had mostly propagandistic value, largely reduced, however, by China's failure to insist that the program be announced in a public session. The response was even cooler than might reasonably have been expected. The long list of Chinese demands produced a feeling of tiredness and impatience among the delegates. If these principles were to be discussed point by point and all the details taken up, no end to the conference could be foreseen. If the Chinese had at least dramatized their points, they might have provoked a lively and stimulating debate. But the legalistic approach which they chose facilitated long quibbles and the evasion of real issues. The Japanese delegates found a sympathetic echo when they weakened the Chinese position with the remark that the conference could not last forever to discuss all these "innumerable minor matters."

Elihu Root, of the United States, seized upon the opportunity provided by the Chinese catalogue of principles to advance an expanded reformulation of the Open Door and integrity principles, which was accepted on November 21. The powers attending the conference expressed their firm intention

1. To respect the sovereignty, the independence, and the territorial and administrative integrity of China;
2. To provide the fullest and most unembarrassed opportunity to China to develop and maintain for herself an effective and stable government;
3. To use their influence for the purpose of effectually establishing and maintaining the principle of equal opportunity for the commerce and industry of all nations throughout the territory of China;
4. To refrain from taking advantage of the present conditions in order to seek special rights or privileges which would abridge the rights of subjects or citizens of friendly States and from countenancing action inimical to the security of such States.

Subsequent meetings were filled with discussions of this resolution and other matters of general interest to China. In China most of the attention was focused on the Chinese negotiations with Japan regarding Shantung, which proceeded parallel with the Washington Conference.

The impression left by the conference in general was not favorable. The comments of the Chinese press were critical. The discussion of principles was watched with coolness. China was waiting for their interpretation and application. There was enough realism not to expect a reversal of Western policy. But there was hope that the injustices would be eliminated which China had suffered during and after the World War, especially from Japan.

As the weeks passed without any of China's concrete problems being discussed, disappointment grew. Newspapers suspected bad faith on the part of the Western powers. Why else would they engage in high-sounding platitudes instead of seeking a solution to Far Eastern problems? If there was good will, nothing would be simpler than to point out specific actions violating China's sovereignty and to condemn them.

Most of this criticism was provoked by the abstractness of the conversations at Washington. Specific Chinese grievances were at first scarcely mentioned, and though eventually some of them were dealt with, it was mostly in a rather evasive manner. Anarchy in China was ignored. The Peking government was treated as if it had real power.* The conference seemed to think, as one observer put it, that "such sleeping dogs were better left undisturbed." Yet the conference had been called for the express purpose of finding "a solution of Pacific and Far Eastern Problems of unquestioned importance at this time." And what greater problem was there than China's chaos? Before the conference opened, the widely held assumption had been that international assistance in the establishment of a stable government and sound finances in China would be the foremost task at Washington. On this assumption many foreign ministers in Peking impressed upon their governments the need of doing a number of things. But they had no success.

In spite of these shortcomings the conference was of some benefit to China. These were the results: The resolution of November 21 was incorporated into the Nine-Power Treaty as part of the Open Door definition. In addition the Treaty specified that it would be incompatible with the Open Door principle for a nation or its nationals to seek a general superiority of rights in the economic development of China or

---

* The attempts of the southern government in Canton and of its very active sympathizers in the United States to get recognition for it and permission to send a delegation remained fruitless. The United States was known to be anxious to have a delegation composed of both factions but could do nothing about it. See *North China Herald*, October 29, 1921, p. 292; November 5, 1921, p. 363; November 19, 1921, p. 490.

a monopoly in private or public enterprise. The creation of spheres of influence was prohibited. In a further article equal treatment with regard to railways was specifically stipulated for the foreign powers and China. Foreign post offices were withdrawn from Chinese territory (except in leased areas), foreign radio stations came under Chinese control (except in leased areas), foreign troops were to be withdrawn from Chinese soil under certain conditions, and some leased territory was to be returned by Great Britain. Extraterritoriality remained, but with a view to its eventual abolition an investigation of China's judicial system was to be undertaken. The tariff was raised immediately, and a commission was to investigate the possibility of making concessions toward China's tariff autonomy.

These direct results were not particularly impressive. The indirect ones were perhaps slightly more so. The breach in the formerly solid wall of resistance to any change in the tariff or in the extraterritorial system was an admission on the part of the foreign powers of their bad conscience. These issues were brought alive and kept so until settled in China's favor. The conference widely advertised China's grievances again, and it increased sympathy for her abroad. The Nine-Power Treaty, though paternalistic in its attitude toward China and without any guarantees of fulfillment, created a détente providing China with an opportunity to reorient her foreign policy. The Chinese finally learned that no matter what the powers professed, they would proceed only very slowly in their actions, much too slowly for Chinese taste.

The final results of the conference received only scant public attention in China. The regretful and apologetic tone of the official Peking communiqué announcing them indicated disappointment. Some nonofficial comments were more outspoken. Not a single concession in favor of China had been made, one paper pointed out, with even a semblance of good grace or without some condition attached to it — quite apart from the fact that often the concessions made referred to privileges which China had never been willing to grant in the first place. Perhaps the Chinese reaction was overpessimistic. But a detached appraisal could hardly have been expected in the Chinese atmosphere of 1922. Partisanship colored everything.

The Chinese themselves were not entirely without blame for the vagueness and generality of the agreements. Foremost among their mistakes was the tactical one of presenting principles rather than issues, permitting the powers an escape from specific commitments. General principles and policies had been agreed upon in the past in abundance. In 1921 specific Chinese complaints were sufficiently concrete and well known to have permitted their discussion before the eyes of the whole world. An American adviser to the delegation commented correctly that "unfortunately" the Chinese ten-point program "defined China's position in language so mystifying to the general public and so consolatory to the bureaucracy (as only general principles were involved) that there was an almost audible sigh of relief from the delegation which had greatly feared that China at one blow would mobilize the immense force of American public opinion and sweep the field." [5]

On the one issue which was made specific and dramatic and on which American public opinion was aroused almost as much as Chinese, some satisfactory conclusions were reached. That was Shantung, or perhaps, more broadly, Sino-Japanese relations. This issue had never been permitted to rest since the Paris peace conference. The American government had pressed the Japanese to make some statement on their future Shantung policy. Instead of giving in, the Japanese initiated exchanges of notes with the Chinese, which led to no rapprochement at all. In January 1920 the Japanese asked for bilateral negotiations, which the Chinese government refused, mostly owing to pressure from the public. The public knew that the country's only hope lay in an international treatment of the dispute. The rulers of Peking might have been willing to come to terms with the Japanese for a consideration.[6] Finally a compromise was reached to the effect that while the Washington Conference was in progress China and Japan would "converse" about Shantung under the Good Offices of the foreign ministers of Great Britain and the United States; the conference would be informed of the results. After two months of "conversations," from December 21, 1921, to January 31, 1922, an agreement was reached upon terms generally satisfactory to the Chinese. Its result was, in the main, to leave only private Japanese interests in Shantung.[7]

The direct and indirect results of the Washington Conference, taken together, were therefore of some advantage to China. Though their small scale greatly disappointed the Chinese, the Peking government proceeded to make the best of things. It took the agreements seriously and used them as the basis of future plans. It put constant pressure upon the foreign powers to live up to their own principles. It protested against action incompatible with the Washington agreements. It implemented by rules and regulations the general principles evolved or reaffirmed at Washington. Much to the annoyance of foreigners, it threatened to promulgate numerous edicts like the following, which was considered in 1922 to meet the eventuality that all of China might be opened to foreigners:

I. Mixed Residence in the Interior. At first only provincial capitals and important commercial ports and other places accessible by steamships and railroads, limited to a radius of 30 li (10 miles) in all directions, should be thrown open for mixed residence. This is to be carried out in one year during which time an investigation commission should be appointed to study the question and complete preparations.

II. Land Ownership. Alien residents in the interior should have no right to own land; those who possess leasehold rights may exercise them within certain prescribed periods.

III. Prior to the abolition of extraterritoriality, foreign companies already established in China should register themselves in accordance with Chinese laws.

IV. Foreign companies whose head offices are situated in foreign countries and who have only appointed agencies in China should register with the Chinese government the names of their agencies together with their articles of association.

V. In the manufacture of raw materials with a view to their improvement, and in all companies, mills, and factories which undertake the manufacturing of improved products, foreign capital, if any, must not exceed 50%.

VI. Foreign subjects should have no right to own any forest or woodland. They may, however, invest capital in this industry and its accessory side-lines, to the amount limited in the preceding article.

VII. The present Mining Regulations have already permitted Sino-foreign capitalization and cooperation but foreign shares must not exceed 50% in value of the whole capital. This restriction is identical with that imposed in the two preceding articles. Since foreigners are already obeying these regulations, I suggest that they should remain in force after the abolition of extraterritoriality in order to protect our interests.

VIII. In all special rights assigned to Chinese subjects alone by Chinese laws and mandates in agricultural, industrial, and commercial pursuits, foreign subjects should be precluded from participation.[8]

These efforts remained mostly fruitless. China had to take what the foreigners were willing to grant. Nothing else could be expected in view of the internal conditions of the country. This type of edict had therefore an air of unreality about it. But it had the effect of keeping the

166

issues before the public eye, at home and abroad, and of maintaining agitation for their settlement. Furthermore, the failure to achieve any settlement helped to convince the Chinese that the generalities of the Washington Conference were indeed meant to be generalities. It was therefore one of the determinants in their turning away from the Western powers and toward the Soviet Union, in the general redirection of their policy which was now to take place.

13

Turning from the West to Russia

MUCH more important for China than the results of the Paris and Washington conferences were less conspicuous developments inside the country between 1918 and 1922. What attracted the attention of most observers was the political chaos of the period and its dramatic consequences, which overshadowed the changes taking place more quietly. But these last determined the nature of China's position in the world more deeply and lastingly than the spectacular struggles of the tuchuns which, though significant and detrimental, were nevertheless an episode whose consequences could be and were overcome.

Unless it be by the vague term "cultural revolution," these developments can hardly be designated by any one descriptive title. Though having common roots, they became manifest in the most diverse forms. They made their appearance in all spheres of Chinese culture, and they affected all sections of the population, though they were most pronounced among the intellectuals, the workers, and the school youths. They were a logical outcome of Chinese history during the preceding hundred years.

In the intellectual realm a complete reversal of traditional trends took place under the leadership of Hu Shih and Ch'en Tu-hsiu. In form the change occurred through the abandonment of classical Chinese as the medium of scholarly expression and the substitution of the daily spoken language. This broke a long tradition. The works of scholars now became accessible to greater numbers of people, and new avenues for creative work, closer to life and reality, were opened up. In substance a change took place under the influence of Western thinkers. The scientific method, accepted by the Chinese for some time in the natural sciences, was now introduced in social thought as well. An air of down-to-earth realism entered the writings and discussions of Chinese intellectuals. Their research related to the contemporary social problems of China.

168

The whole of Chinese culture was subjected to severe criticism from the standpoint of its social utility.

Intellectual activity ceased being the monopoly of any ruling class. It was no longer separated in form and substance from the masses by a deep gulf. Large sections of the people could now participate in it, actively or passively. The new interest which the intellectuals and the masses found in each other stimulated and benefited them both. The political significance of this new relation became clear very soon. Policies advocated by the intellectuals had good prospects of obtaining mass support. An affinity was created the absence of which in earlier days had been a contributing factor to the failure of reform attempts. Some of the leaders, Sun Yat-sen among them, were steeped deeply in traditional thinking. They still had to be convinced of the importance of mass action. But this was a relatively easy task after the basic relation between the intellectuals and the mass had been established. The danger that mass action might remain merely outbursts without direction or political effectiveness was avoided by the simultaneous growth of a labor and student movement which provided an organization for coordinated action.[1]

Speaking absolutely and not relatively to the West, industrial development in China had made good progress during the war. A working class had developed with it. In 1916 the number of industrial workers was estimated at one million, in 1922 at two million. A number of unions were formed during this interval which were aggressive and political-minded from the very beginning. The frequent strikes in this early period, motivated often by a desire for the improvement of working conditions but also by political considerations, were usually successful and led to rapid further unionization. The politics of labor were of particular importance for international relations because they almost exclusively dealt with foreign policy and were antiforeign. This deviation from usual labor politics in other nations can be explained by conditions peculiar to China.

Under the guild system and in factories owned by Chinese, special social relationships prevented labor-management conflicts from ever really turning into an intense struggle. In the foreign-owned factories these relationships were absent. The Chinese worker was imbued also with the growing nationalism and felt that he was helping his country economically and politically by opposing the foreigner. This attitude was greatly stimulated by the organizers, who with almost unfailing success used nationalism as an argument to create unions and instigate strikes. Much of the industry was either located in the foreign section of the major cities or owned by or connected with foreigners. The friction normally arising from union activity and labor disputes therefore had an international flavor in China even before communism made inroads into the labor movement and used it for its own international purposes. The Chinese labor movement because of this characteristic was of special interest to the nationalist student movement and vice versa. The two established a close relation, to the benefit of both, and labor often looked to the students to represent it in political matters.[2]

The student movement had already proved its effectiveness after the Paris Conference. It had appeared spontaneously throughout much of China's history. But now, with more widespread education and improved communications, the movement grew to considerable proportions and promised to be of more continuous influence. Politically this influence had several bases. Education is at a high premium in China and commands respect, and students have always been an important group there.* From them have come many of her leaders, and they seem to have been conscious not only of their own prestige and importance, but of their social responsibility and their obligation to use their knowledge for leadership. In the years of tuchunism the students were untainted by the politics tearing the nation apart, and to many Chinese disgusted, for altruistic or personal reasons, with the state of the nation, their trustworthy idealism was attractive. Organized in local and national unions, they were a nation-wide force, cutting across the artificial barriers erected by the tuchuns. Thus they reinforced the bonds of national unity created by other organizations, especially professional ones, existing in the shadow of the tuchuns' struggles.

Young China became a rallying point around which all those groups desiring a new, united nation could gather. It embodied the spirit of nationalism that had been in the making at least since the Russo-Japanese War and that was brought to fruition by the behavior of the foreign powers, particularly at Paris. The watchword of this nationalism was antimilitarism in internal politics and anti-imperialism in foreign policy. Its major aims therefore became the elimination of the

* In 1922 there were about 100,000 students in the middle schools; in 1920 about 2,000 were in institutions of higher learning, and in 1924, 3,500.

tuchuns, the abolition of unequal treaties, and the restoration of China's sovereignty. These were aims well suited to the times, for support of a common program by diverse groups is always facilitated by an "anti" platform. Hostility against the tuchuns was widespread, and a program of action against them attracted many followers. The same was true of foreigners. The recovery of Chinese sovereignty seemed to offer a positive, inspiring goal which was badly needed in the spiritual vacuum created by the political deterioration and intellectual skepticism of the postwar years.[3] Nationalism suited many merchants and manufacturers as a weapon against foreign competition, and it was a platform upon which labor and students could unite. Altogether it was a program covering up nicely the disagreements among the members, the followers, and the fellow-travelers of Young China regarding the reconstruction of the country after victory. It succeeded in giving the nationalist movement strength for the coming battle.

It was to be expected that the labor and student movements, melting into one, would not long be satisfied with simply exerting diffuse pressure, that instead they would look for a power-center to give their programs direct political expression. Neither among intellectuals, workers, or students was there any thought of forming a government themselves. The tuchuns were obviously unsuitable for translating the new tendencies into reality. This left the Kuomintang.

The party, if such it could be called at that time, was vegetating, by grace of the generals in Canton. Sun Yat-sen was frantically trying to keep it alive by currying the favor, soliciting the help, or showing his appreciation for the tolerance of any and all groups or individuals willing not to oppose him in his endeavors. This strategy forced him to keep his program rather vague, even ambiguous, and at any rate away from extremes. Though on the whole the students and the workers were more radical than Sun, he turned to them as soon as he realized the political potentialities of their movements. They responded. Inadequate as the political ideas of the Kuomintang may have appeared to them, here was at least a party which offered ideas in addition to the customary intrigues and internal struggles, ideas not too far removed from their own to be adjusted to them. Again, nationalism was the strongest uniting element.

Close relations were established between the students, the workers, and the party; the party contributed a sprinkling of merchants and manufacturers, but practically no peasants.[4] Each group stimulated and invigorated the others. Since most of the groups had a membership distributed across the nation, the Kuomintang, though maintaining a most precarious control even in its home province of Kwangtung, extended its influence throughout China. It gained no international standing until toward the end of the 'twenties, but it nevertheless influenced the nature of China's foreign policy from 1919 on.

The intellectual renaissance, the student and labor movements with the changes they produced, were evidence of a considerable vitality. The civil wars had apparently been unable to affect seriously the cultural development of the nation. Underneath the spectacular chaos in Chinese politics something was working that few observers seemed able to discern. Paul Painlevé of France was one of the few that were able. He recognized that Chinese military operations were of superficial importance and paralyzed only to a "faint degree" the working activity of the nation. China was not stagnating. The evolution of ideas, customs, industries was quickening in a striking fashion. "The twentieth century will be China's century," was Painlevé's pronouncement. It may yet come true![5]

This quickening of the national life had its inspiration in the West and could be traced back to the early reformers. But now, not only had the West antagonized the Chinese, it did little to make this inspiration productive in political action. Help here came from Russia, both in the spiritual and material sense. A mutual attraction arose between Russian communism and the new Chinese nationalism soon after the First World War. The attachment could be accounted for in large measure by pure expediency, especially on the Russian side. But it rested on more than that: it rested on that promise of a better world which the Russian revolution in its initial stages seemed to hold out to many peoples everywhere.

The Chinese had observed the Russian revolution with great interest and much good will. In their perennial search for the "secret" of Western success, many now thought they had found it in communism. What attracted these Western-influenced Chinese particularly was the apparent dynamic quality, the virility, and the unashamed utilitarianism and materialism of Communist doctrine, which seemed to compare favorably with the apathy, femininity, and antiutilitarianism of Chinese society, patterned after Confucian teachings. To many, especially to young

Chinese, communism incorporated all the modernism and progressivism they were seeking in Western civilization.[6] Most of them admired the revolution as a successful blow against monarchism and imperialism also, not only in Russia but everywhere. The Russian experiment seemed to teach a lesson in how to get rid of oppression, internal and external. Communism, even before it congealed into organized form, therefore aroused sympathy in China not as a foreign system to be taken over, but as a weapon to achieve the major goals of the Chinese nationalists. They became convinced that the new Russian regime, in means and methods, had a good deal to offer that would be useful to the Chinese nationalist revolution.

The Russians, for their part, had many good reasons for wanting to work with China. Here was an ally in anti-Western, especially anti-British agitation. Since Russia was too weak for direct action against the West, indirect stabbing at Western interests in the weak spots — the colonies and "quasi colonies" — was a good substitute. China was also a valuable object to gain for her own sake. According to Leninist theory, the chances of conquering the country looked promising. Lenin prescribed that the first objective of the revolution in colonial and semi-colonial countries was the elimination of imperialism and feudalism. If this could be achieved with the help of a "bourgeois-democratic revolution," such as in Communist eyes the Kuomintang was planning, it could be participated in by Communists, provided always that the identity of the proletarian movement was completely preserved and the right retained to educate and organize the masses in the Communist revolutionary spirit. Collaboration must cease, prescribed Lenin, when inherent class antagonisms came to the fore in the course of the "bourgeois-democratic revolution" and the bourgeoisie again allied itself with imperialism against the proletariat. According to the theory, then, it was advisable for Moscow to cooperate with the Kuomintang, both because the party appeared about to instigate the "bourgeois-democratic revolution" and because it had already attracted organized groups useful for the success of the eventual "proletarian revolution."

Communism and the Kuomintang thus got together on opportunistic grounds,* each intending to use the other for its own ends. Moscow hoped to enliven the revolutionary movement and to gain control over it once the proper moment for the switch to the Communist revolution

* In the left wing of the Kuomintang there was sympathy for communism.

had arrived (and, incidentally, China's friendship was immediately useful against Japan and the White Russians in the Far East). Canton hoped to make use of Russian support, to play Russia against the West, to profit from Russian revolutionary experience and organizing talent, and, above all, to keep the Communist ally under control. Once more nationalism was the convenient tool through which was to be achieved what the Russians considered the first stage of the revolution, but what the Kuomintang considered an end in itself.[7]

Sun Yat-sen, the leader of the Kuomintang, was won over to the idea of cooperation by the successful methods of the Russian revolution much more than by its philosophy. His own political philosophy had certain basic points in common with Communist doctrine; some aspects of it, like anti-imperialism, he emphasized more strongly after the disappointments with the Western powers; but he retained enough of his own fundamental views to make his outlook distinctly different from that of the Communists. The difference did not prevent him, however, from admiring Russian internal achievements and from wishing the same for his own country. The Russian revolution, he said, "is really a complete success. This is so because their methods are good." On innumerable occasions he compared the success of the revolution in Russia with the failure of it in China and concluded that the reason lay in the "inferiority of our revolutionary methods and spirit as compared with those of the Russians."[8]

Soon after the Paris Conference the first contacts with Russia were established. Sun Yat-sen sent a number of his young followers to Moscow to study the techniques of revolution. Moscow sent a large number of agents to China, always carefully using the Comintern as the front. The Russian government maintained "correct" diplomatic contacts with the official Chinese government throughout the period of collaboration. Among the more prominent agents were Pavlov, Maring, Joffe, Karakhan, and especially Borodin and Galen. The last two were responsible for the major political and military work within the Kuomintang, though the others also used every possible means of influencing Sun Yat-sen and his party.*

After 1924 Chinese Communists were directed by Moscow to join

---

* Moscow also worked with Feng Yü-hsiang, the powerful northern tuchun, supporting him with military personnel and materials. For details see American Consulate General, Hongkong, *Current Background* (mimeographed), No. 194, July 24, 1952.

the Kuomintang as individuals, though under retention of their loyalty to the Communist party as well. This move met with considerable opposition in both camps. Some of the newly fledged Chinese Communists opposed joining the Kuomintang, and the more conservative factions within the party objected to receiving them. Sun Yat-sen's mind, however, could not be changed by any argument. To him the advantages of the policy far outweighed the disadvantages. He felt strong enough to control the Communists, and he disregarded possible reactions in the Western world because "the Chinese Revolution has never been liked by the foreign Powers, and some of them even assisted our opponents, hoping to crush our party. It is clear that no capitalist country will show us any sympathy. We can only hope for sympathy from Russia and from aggrieved countries and peoples." [9] Sun did not live long enough (he died in 1925) to learn that his policy permitted the Communists to come very close to subverting the Kuomintang.

Before they were near success, however, they rendered the party a signal service. They made a true and effective political organization out of the Kuomintang. They gave it life and verve. They made it stand on its own feet, instead of as an appendage to some personage. They formulated a concrete program. They established discipline and obedience. They supplied money and arms for a military striking force. They built a structure feigning democracy (democratic centralism!) and establishing strict control from the top. They taught the members the art of revolution and, above all, of propaganda. In short, they made a dynamic, totalitarian instrument of the Kuomintang and used it to obtain mass support from the students, workers, and peasants.

For a while concentration upon this building process and upon the immediate goal each side had in mind kept together this odd combination of Russian Bolsheviks and Chinese Nationalists. However, tension and distrust between them were perennial and threatened to break up the union. Only the usefulness each found in the other kept the parties together. The conservatives in the Kuomintang, under the leadership of Chiang K'ai-shek, were as frank about the expediency of cooperation as the Communists were. "We will be pro any country which helps us to put China on her feet," stated the generalissimo. And even after the cooperation had ended, a man like T. V. Soong had in retrospect no regrets about the policy of cooperation. He felt that Russia had provided the impetus to the movement which had made the Nationalist revolution successful and that without this the National Government would never have secured what it gained in 1926 and 1927.[10]

There were others in the party who did not take such an optimistic view, who were less confident that the Communists could be kept under control, and who therefore favored an end to cooperation. They could not agree with the argument, frequently heard, that flirting with Russia and accepting Russian aid would assist unification within the country and protect against imperialism from without. Developments within the Kuomintang-Communist coalition as well as in Sino-Soviet relations strengthened the hand of these more cautious elements. By 1926 doubt was widespread regarding the three most important reasons which had served as the justification for cooperation. The expansionist policy of the Soviet Union in Manchuria, especially as it related to the Chinese Eastern Railway, contradicted her professions of disinterested good will toward China. The Russian support of several mutually antagonistic Chinese factions squashed expectations that Russian assistance might bring order out of Chinese chaos. And, finally, the intensity and partial success of Communist propaganda seemed to make the control of Russian influence increasingly difficult.[11]

By 1926 the end of the Nationalist-Communist coalition was foreseeable. The decision in that year to send the Nationalist armies north to put an end to political chaos and unify the country under the Canton regime was largely determined by the desire to utilize the coalition for this last, supreme effort.

The campaign was surprisingly successful. Russian training and leadership proved their usefulness. The small Nationalist force was well trained, disciplined, and full of fighting spirit. The enterprise was backed enthusiastically by the party's members and supporters.

Treachery and intrigue among local political leaders everywhere worked in favor of the advancing Nationalists. Their antituchun and antiforeign slogans struck a responsive chord among the Chinese people. Above all, however, the excellent propaganda activity on both sides of the front contributed to Nationalist victory. The Nationalists knew what was troubling the people, and the corps of 20,000 propagandists preceding the army used the knowledge to advantage.[12] The novelty in the campaign was that the masses were no longer objects of exploitation,* but became participants in the enterprise. Thus their opposition

---

* Some atrocities by the armies, however, were committed against Chinese citizens as well as foreigners.

or at least apathy was turned into cooperation and a great asset to "the cause." (Forgetting this lesson in the struggle against the Communists after World War II was, by admission of the Nationalist leaders themselves, a major cause of their defeat.)

The very success of the campaign precipitated the break-up of the Communist-Nationalist union. The unifying bond of antagonism to the tuchuns weakened as they were being defeated and as the need of constructive policies arose. The inevitable split between the Communists, under the tutelage of Russian advisers, and the conservatives, under the leadership of Chiang K'ai-shek, occurred when the armies had reached the half-way mark in their unification campaign. It ended in the elimination of the Communists from the Kuomintang and in their weakening, though not in their defeat.* For the time being, however, the Nationalists had the upper hand, and they completed the Nationalist revolution by the nominal conquest of all of China in 1928.

In the process of fighting the extremists on the left, the Kuomintang had become extreme on the right. It had become a conservative party. Chiang K'ai-shek had stopped the revolution in time to prevent its turning into a "proletarian" one. The marriage of convenience with the Communists had lasted just long enough for the Kuomintang to get the benefit of their experience, without which it would probably never have been successful. Chiang had been able to control the revolutionary process because he had become strong enough to finish the formal unification of the nation, the foreign powers had become frightened enough to be ready for concessions, and Chiang had proved himself enough of a conservative to win the favor of the foreign powers (in addition to retaining that of the Shanghai merchants and bankers).

There was an additional deeper, though perhaps more imponderable reason why the revolution turned Nationalist rather than Communist. Considering its mass basis, it had to be a Chinese revolution. No matter how Westernized some of its intellectual leaders may have been, even if they had wanted to they could not have imposed a Western system upon China. This time the movement had roots in the masses, and the masses inevitably influenced its nature. To be sure, even the masses had reached a point by 1928 which was far removed from the traditions which had dominated the Chinese people for so many centuries. But

---

* The life of the Chinese Communist party was saved, thanks largely to Mao Tse-tung's unorthodox (from the Leninist standpoint) activity among the peasants of Honan, where he established a strong foothold for the party.

they were not ready for Russian communism or Western democracy. Even the Comintern admitted this. Whatever evolved from the revolution, this time it had to have ties with the Chinese spirit. And it did.

The new Chinese spirit, developed over a period of about fifty years, had become translatable into political reality through the formulation given it by Sun Yat-sen in his Three Principles of the People. Though they were principles related in their translated name to Western concepts — democracy, nationalism, and socialism, or the people's livelihood — they grew out of Chinese traditions. The history of the development of European states into nation-states did not repeat itself in China, notwithstanding superficial similarities. The Chinese nation-state still was to be based on the traditional primary social unit, the family. Chinese democracy, the leaders determined, was to be neither rugged individualism nor a constant interference of the electorate in the process of government. Rather it was to be the expression of groups and a periodical check upon the government's job of running the country. The people's livelihood was not to be a struggle for power and wealth between classes but rather a cooperative effort to increase the people's welfare.[13]

The consummation of the Nationalist revolution was not achieved with the defeat of the tuchuns. The problem of the foreigners had yet to be solved. Of the two "anti" promises with which the unification campaign had been conducted, the one relating to foreign powers remained to be fulfilled. To this difficult task the Nationalist government devoted most of its energies after it was established at Nanking. While still an opposition group at Canton, it had begun its strong antiforeign agitation. The result by the end of the 'twenties was some diplomatic successes that materially improved China's international position.

14

Diplomatic Successes

ANTI-IMPERIALISM, equal treaties, and the restoration of sovereignty had from the start been the war cries of the new nationalism. Understandably most foreigners did not look upon the movement with great favor, and most of them refused to recognize their own role in bringing it about. Their respect for it was as little as their liking. They usually wrote Sun Yat-sen off as a naive dreamer not to be taken seriously. The students were considered a bunch of misguided schoolboys who had better get back to school instead of causing trouble in the streets. The labor unions, as indeed the whole nationalist movement, were decried as a Communist-inspired conspiracy.

There were exceptions. The missionaries and foreign educators in China tended to side with the nationalists, presumably because they had fewer tangible interests in China than the commercial community and because, not incorrectly, they saw in the movement some results of their inspiration. A number of journalists also could see the real situation.

The antagonism of foreigners in general toward the revolution served to confirm the Chinese in their conviction that the revolution was vitally necessary for the salvation of the country. The narrow outlook of those who could discover nothing but red in the nationalist movement aggravated rather than improved the situation about which they complained. For by antagonizing the liberal elements they drove them into the arms of the Communists and gave the movement a redder tinge than it originally had. They ignored or pretended to ignore its deeper causes and failed to see that the solution of their own problems lay not in labeling the movement as a whole but in differentiating its composite class structure and motivation. Their tactics gave a Chinese no choice but to join up either with the "imperialists" or with the reds. What this choice had to be, considering the temper of the times, was obvious.*

* "As long as anti-Communism was, in any way, identified with pro-foreignism, there was little hope of the better elements among the Chinese really opposing the Communists," wrote the *China Year Book, 1926*, p. 1011. George E. Sokolsky ob-

The outlook of the diplomats, unfortunately, was frequently not very different from that of the merchants.[1] These two influential bodies naturally colored governmental attitudes toward developments in China. Friction between China and the foreign powers increased before a change took place at last after the middle of the 'twenties. Only Chinese relations with Soviet Russia took an inverse course. They were fair shortly after the war, but deteriorated as the true face of the new Russia became visible.

In the confusion of the Russian revolution the Peking government succeeded in recovering some of the positions once surrendered to Imperial Russia. Much of Russia's influence in Manchuria was replaced by Chinese influence. In Mongolia Peking reasserted some control at the expense of Russia. Some influence was regained over the Chinese Eastern Railway; that it was not regained in toto was thanks to the interference of the Allied Powers.[2] All these issues were negotiated with Russia on a de facto and ad hoc basis, since Peking had not yet recognized the new Russian government.

Then, in 1919 and 1920, Russia began to make use of her weakness to recover her strength. The government began a high-pressure propaganda and organizing campaign all over Asia against Western imperialism.[3] It picked China as the scene of action because little physical resistance was to be expected and because propaganda would find the best response there. In a widely advertised announcement it renounced the "predatory and violent" policy of the tsars and all rights flowing therefrom and promised to support the Chinese people in their struggle for freedom. For the moment the effect was purely propagandistic. Peking was suspicious of Communist subversion, was being high-pressured by the foreign powers not to make agreements with Russia, and had still hopes of assistance from abroad. But these promises sounded convincing. They were in line with the ideology of the revolution and bound to impress many Chinese. They undoubtedly created much sympathy for Russia, which was all Russia intended to achieve by them. As became clear later, she was quite unwilling to surrender any substantial advantages. The great Russian "sacrifices" to China referred to privileges which Russia had never possessed legally and/or could not enforce factually,

served in the *North China Herald*, February 20, 1926, p. 359, that it was "almost childish" to call even the left wing of the Kuomintang Bolshevist. The *Herald* always called the Canton regime "Red" and Chiang K'ai-shek the "Red General."

or which were given up not for China's but for Soviet Russia's sake — for instance, extraterritoriality, which was designed to damage the White Russians.

Only after the Washington Conference was Peking in a more responsive mood. With the change in the ruling clique there, and in the atmosphere of disappointment with the Washington Conference, Russia was able to take advantage of her growing influence in the Kuomintang and the fund of good will built up by clever propaganda to improve her own position. Her policy was a rather aggressive and expansionist one, from which attention was deflected by a spectacular anti-imperialist propaganda campaign. Moscow's means did not differ basically from those of the tsars: "friendship" for the Chinese people, which had to be reciprocated; open or secret threats; intriguing between Chinese factions; playing China against Japan. This policy was reconciled with the magnanimous declarations of 1919 and 1920 by a differentiation between the "legal" and the "political" aspects of Russia's position in China. When the Russians renounced the "predatory and violent" policy and its results (so they now clarified their meaning), they were not saying that all "legitimate" claims and interests in China were abandoned. The net result of their activities was that Russia was restored, not to the identical position in China that she had enjoyed under the tsars, but, in fact, to an even stronger one.

Diplomatic relations were established in 1924. Russia won considerable influence in Outer Mongolia, which in practice became a part of the Soviet Union. She regained a strong position in the Chinese Eastern Railway, which meant restoration of full influence in northern Manchuria. Communism was well established in Canton. Notwithstanding the divorce of the Kuomintang and the Communists in 1927 and attempts by the National Government to eliminate Russian influence from northern Manchuria, this Russian position remained intact until the Japanese invasion of Manchuria in 1931. The major agreements which settled this Russian position were greeted by some Chinese, rather Pollyannish in outlook, with satisfaction that they had been concluded on an equal basis and that they eliminated extraterritoriality.[4] This rather mild reaction, or, at times, absence of any reaction at all, to what was a very aggressive Russian policy — a policy amounting in some cases to the *de facto* loss of territory by China — contrasted strangely with the enormous agitation against the Western powers. These, compared to Russia and their own earlier selves, were now actually on the defensive.

China's relations with the Western powers passed through some very disturbed periods before they began to improve again. The signatories of the Washington Treaty were dilatory in fulfilling their modest obligations. The insistence of the Chinese that the promises be translated into reality had little effect. A number of Western statesmen began to wonder whether even the small concessions of the Washington Conference had not gone too far, whether, perhaps, in Sir Austen Chamberlain's words, "the representatives of the assembled nations took a too rosy view of what was possible."[5]

A few minor promises were fulfilled. But antiforeign feeling was heightened by the failure to tackle the important points, by the controversy developing out of French insistence that the Boxer indemnity be paid in prewar gold francs, by the ridiculous demands of foreigners following a bandit raid on the "Blue Express" in 1923, and by a number of other incidents. The feeling reached an apex on May 30, 1925, when the Shanghai police under foreign command fired into a crowd of student demonstrators, and on June 23, 1925, when in Canton foreign troops fired into a Chinese crowd protesting against the Shanghai incident.

These events were just what the Nationalist and Communist propagandists needed, and possibly engineered. They were blown up into tremendous proportions,* and their settlement occupied much of the time and attention of foreign diplomats. Even without propagandistic exaggerations, the events were enough to arouse the Chinese, who refused coolly to examine the legal side; instead they demanded a change in the basic conditions which made such events possible.

Pressure for the abolition of unequal treaties was steadily building up and obviously would relax only after concrete concessions had been made. The demands brought about by the nationalism now prevailing among all sections of Chinese were further intensified by the political competition which obliged each faction to outdo its rivals. The spearhead in the drive was the Canton government, the Nationalist-Communist combination, which was adamant in its refusal to discuss any-

* After the May 30 movement gained impetus, the membership of the Communist party jumped from about 900 to about 20,000. — Chao Kuo-chun, *Thirty Years of the Communist Movement in China, A Chronology of Major Developments 1920–1950* (Russian Research Center, Harvard University, mimeographed, 1950), p. 6.

thing but complete equality and which advocated a policy which, from the Chinese standpoint, was almost reckless. Canton's enthusiasm began to reverse the traditional pattern of China's international relations: now the foreigners were procrastinating and the Chinese were pushing; things could not go fast enough for them.

Canton was not merely bluffing or trying to embarrass the government in Peking. It acted. Disgusted with the delay of the powers in regulating details for the customs surtax granted in principle by the Washington treaties, it began to levy the tax without regulation. Here was a test case on the unilateral repudiation of unequal treaties, and it was successful. The foreign powers split over the issue, and Canton's prestige grew. The successful precedent made it inevitable that the Peking government should follow it. For inner political reasons alone a conciliatory spirit could not be expected from the officially recognized government.

Canton's agitation reflected fairly accurately the temper of the people. It did not permit either appeasement or temporizing. Peking had to put up a bold front. Besides, Peking and Canton were in genuine agreement over the need to abolish unequal treaties. They differed on the methods. Canton chose outright, one-sided cancellation, Peking diplomatic means (with the people everywhere using demonstrations, strikes, and some amazingly effective boycotts).[6]

Peking, in its way, seized the initiative by proceedings which eventually led to a modification, and, in part, even abolition, of the unequal treaties. It presented a memorandum, on June 24, 1925, to the representatives of the Washington Treaty powers in China. In the interest of consolidating the friendly relations between China and the foreign powers, the memorandum said, the subject of readjusting China's treaty relations with the nations should be tackled. Even some foreign statesmen shared the feeling that these relations should be more in line with the generally accepted conceptions of international justice and equity. After recalling the circumstances under which most of these treaties had been concluded, the memorandum pointed out that the situation had greatly changed and that these treaties had become anachronistic. Circumstances hardly warranted the further continuance of the extraordinary political and economic privileges conferred in these treaties. As long as these privileges and inequalities continued to exist, they would be a source of friction with foreign powers. China was encouraged to enter the war, the memorandum recalled, by the promise that her international status would be changed to that of a great power. Not only had this hope remained unfulfilled, but she was in a position inferior to that of the defeated powers. In Paris and again in Washington she had made an effort to adjust treaty relations. While a sympathetic hearing was given, very few substantial results had been accomplished. The Chinese government was convinced that foreign rights and interests could be better preserved without, rather than with, the enjoyment of extraterritorial privileges and immunities. It hoped therefore that the governments addressed would give an encouraging response to the request for an adjustment of China's treaty relations on an equitable basis, in satisfaction of the legitimate national aspirations of the Chinese people.[7]

This memorandum was prompted to some degree by the desire of the Peking regime to placate radicals demanding the immediate and one-sided abolition of unequal treaties. But it also represented the views generally held in China and became the leitmotif of China's international activities. The diplomatic representatives in Peking suggested unanimously to their governments that the replies to the memorandum should contain certain things: a reminder that the conference for tariff revision would meet soon; a promise that the sending of the commission to investigate extraterritoriality would be hastened, though the abolition of extraterritoriality would depend upon equality of rights between Chinese and foreigners; and a statement that the re-establishment of order in China would be an indispensable preliminary to the consideration of Chinese grievances.

The diplomatic reaction was distinctly conciliatory. Its remarkable unanimity indicated a change in the atmosphere. The diplomats, though not yet necessarily their governments, were beginning to understand what was happening in China. The fact that the Communists, much to their advantage, had comprehended it a few years earlier helped bring about in others a more realistic attitude.* "Except by good fortune and unless the foreign powers are able to devise some defensive action in the circumstances," the American minister had already cabled home in 1924, "the chances seem to be that the radical wing of the Kuomintang party and the Soviets are to have their day in Peking." The British min-

* It has been a frequent and unfortunate fact in Western policy in Asia that concessions to Asian demands have been made not to satisfy the Asians but to counteract Communist propaganda. Many Asians therefore feel that they have the Communists to thank for many improvements.

ister was more fearful still and suggested a conference of the Washington Treaty powers in which a statement should be issued expressing sympathy for China's international aspirations and containing at the same time a warning that the powers would not recognize any Chinese government composed of leaders known to be antiforeign.

The American minister approved of this suggestion as a good antidote to the reds. He had also asked C. T. Wang, a high official, how Communist influence might be counteracted and the conservatives be strengthened. Wang's answer was that the powers should announce their agreement to treaty revision as soon as a strong Chinese government could enforce international obligations; otherwise the Communists would monopolize the popular cry against unequal treaties and gain the people's sympathy. He disapproved of the proposal that, in order to make resistance to Russian ambition more effective, China should be unified by foreign mediation; such mediation would prove too embarrassing.[8]

The antiforeign uprisings following the May 30 incident in Shanghai, the effective boycott against the British, and the determination shown by the Nationalists in particular but by many other Chinese as well, helped to soften the foreign attitude toward China. Notwithstanding political and economic chaos in China, there could be no doubt that a fair degree of unanimity prevailed concerning the absolute necessity of obtaining a rectification of the unequal treaties. It was this strong conviction in all quarters which overcame rivalries among the politicians sufficiently to give the government of Tuan Chi-jui enough backbone and standing to obtain some foreign political successes. The fact that the climate of opinion in Western countries was favorable to Chinese aspirations may also have contributed something to the lessening of foreign intransigence.

The American government was the most sympathetic to Chinese demands. It favored the general request for treaty revision. The Japanese were more reluctant, but were willing to go along with the United States. The British, before the Chinese had given signs of strength and determination in these various instances, were the least willing to meet the Chinese. They argued that anarchy in China made concessions unfeasible and that these would merely be interpreted as weakness. Washington did not share this view. It pointed out that conditions in China had not changed since the various promises had been made at the

185

Washington Conference and that "a policy which consists in carrying out agreements undertaken in good faith and already overdue can [not] be interpreted as a sign of weakness."

This point of view won out. In September 1925 an answer to the Chinese memorandum was sent to Peking indicating the willingness of the governments to send delegates to a tariff conference and an extraterritoriality commission. China's hopes were further raised by the "warning" that a modification of the unequal treaties would depend in a large measure on the willingness and ability of the Chinese government to fulfill its obligations and to protect foreign rights and interests now safeguarded by the "exceptional" provisions of the unequal treaties.[9]

Internal chaos was therefore proving to be no absolute impediment to an improvement of the international atmosphere from China's standpoint. Even the Nationalist revolution, which ended in 1928 in victory for Chiang K'ai-shek and the Kuomintang, did not interfere with the trend; on the contrary, it helped it along. The change in regimes did not affect the continuity of China's foreign policy. A split between the extreme right and the extreme left of the Kuomintang in 1927 during the march of the Nationalist troops north provided the opportunity for the foreigners to regain some initiative in Chinese affairs, which they used to strengthen the conservative wing by making concessions in the field of foreign relations.

The lead came from the British government, which badly needed an improvement of its position. In an attempt to achieve that, in December 1926 it transmitted to the diplomatic corps in Peking a note outlining a set of principles which should in the future guide the policy of the powers in China. The principles pointed in the general direction of appeasement of Chinese nationalism. The reason why the British more than other nationals felt the urge to initiate such a move may be that they had been under successful special attack by the Communists and the left wing of the Kuomintang. The note was followed by some concrete steps by the British to ameliorate certain abuses of which the Nationalists complained.

The British policy of appeasement reached an apex when the break within the Kuomintang occurred, following the disclosure in China and London of the Communist conspiracy to turn China into a soviet state. Great Britain was thus enabled to restore her own prestige by discrediting anti-British propaganda and to resume her leadership among foreign nations in China. The Chinese gained in their campaign for equality. The British government very distinctly favored the conservatives in the Kuomintang, including Chiang K'ai-shek as soon as he succeeded in exiling the Communist leaders, crushing the labor and farmer organizations, and establishing his own government. The American government kept out of internal Chinese politics at this time. It was preoccupied with the settling of the Nanking incident, in which foreigners had been killed by the victorious Nationalist armies moving into the city on their march north. But the House of Representatives discussed a resolution in January 1927 which was very sympathetic to Chinese Nationalist aspirations and which forced Secretary of State Kellogg to make, on January 27, a statement similar in essence to the British note of the previous month.[10]

This change in atmosphere was accompanied by changes in the legal relations between China and the foreign powers. In 1926 Peking, following the precedent in methods set by the Canton regime, gave notice to Belgium that their unequal treaty would not be renewed, but that China was prepared to negotiate a new, equal one. In the eyes of the foreign powers this was an unjustified measure. But Peking proceeded with it and succeeded. Japan's treaty was the next to expire. A repetition of the method failed miserably. But it succeeded later with Spain and, partially, with France. By testing the opponents' willingness to support their claims by force, the Chinese discovered their weak spots, which were then exploited to the greatest possible degree.

The Special Conference on the Chinese Customs Tariff opened at Peking on October 26, 1925. It was called in fulfillment of the Washington Customs Treaty of 1922. According to the terms of this treaty the powers were pledged to raise the duty on China's imports by a surtax not exceeding 5 per cent ad valorem on luxuries and 2½ per cent on other articles. A further increase in the tariff to 12½ per cent was foreseen if the Chinese would abolish the likin, the internal tax system. Beyond this, the American government had indicated a willingness to consider an increase above 12½ per cent for certain kinds of goods and the question of tariff autonomy.

Opinions were divided among the Chinese on the advisability of such a conference. One group felt that the conference should be made the occasion for discussing the broader question of Chinese tariff autonomy. They urged an expansion of the agenda and advocated meeting with the foreign delegates only if the delegates would commit themselves

187

from the beginning to the granting of tariff autonomy. Another, more radical group, with its center in Canton, objected to the whole conference on the grounds that tariff autonomy was no subject for discussion in the first place, that not any individual issues, but all the issues known as "the Chinese question," needed discussing. One useful consequence of these debates was that there could be no mistake, at any rate, about the temper of the Chinese regarding the tariff question, and the course of the conference indicated that the foreign delegates paid proper respect to it.

The paradoxical result of the calling of the conference was that instead of leading to general satisfaction among the Chinese, it fanned the flames of civil war. The reason was simple. The government of Tuan Chi-jui was just another faction. A successful conference would have meant filling the coffers of Tuan, something that naturally none of the other factions would tolerate. What had been foreseen happened: before the conference opened, the civil war broke out with renewed vigor. While the conference was in session, Tuan's government was overthrown. Largely as a result of this, the Washington Customs Treaty terms were not carried out; no formal treaty was ever signed and no resolution was ratified by any of the participating nations. Nevertheless the conference had not been in vain, and in the end China gained by it.

The advantages that accrued to China from the conference showed that when political and moral pressures are great enough, legal obligations are not needed. All the advantages were granted in response to Chinese demands. The resolution to return tariff autonomy to China by January 1, 1929, was essentially fulfilled. The abolition of likin was forever after kept as a problem separate from tariff autonomy, on the basis of the Chinese argument that this was an internal affair. On the same ground the powers refrained from discussing the measures by which the Chinese would dispose of the increased income from raised tariffs. The technical work done by experts at the conference served the Chinese well when they came to draw up their first national tariff in 1929. Above all, the discussions of the delegates indicated quite clearly their realization that the days of unilateral dealings with China were gone, even though their manners still showed traces of the past. When the Chinese Nationalists seized power toward the end of 1926, the encouragement the conference had given them was evident in their policy.[11]

On January 12, 1926, the Commission on Extraterritoriality convened in Peking, also in fulfillment of an agreement reached at the Washington Conference in 1922. The task of the commission was to gather the facts on the structure and operation of the Chinese judicial system and to make recommendations for the improvement of existing conditions as well as for reforms to enable the foreign powers to give up their rights of extraterritoriality.

The commission spent many months investigating conditions and gathering facts as conscientiously as circumstances in China permitted. The Chinese cooperated willingly, smoothing out the roads of travel and whitewashing the walls of prisons so that the commissioners might get a favorable impression. But there was not enough whitewash available to cover up the chaos existing all over the country. That chaos alone made the exercise of any reasonable judicial activity impossible. It was mostly responsible for the negative report which the commission produced in September 1926.

The first part of the report dealt with the history and practice of extraterritoriality; the second, with the laws and the judicial system of China; the third, with the administration of justice. The Chinese member of the commission refused to sign these three parts because he could not agree to all details, although he failed to point out any inexactitude. The three parts in general were not very complimentary to China and particularly to the various regimes in control, and the Chinese delegate was obviously giving in to political pressure. He signed the fourth part, which consisted of recommendations. In going even so far he risked his head. The essence of the recommendations was that if all the shortcomings pointed out in the preceding parts of the report were rectified, the powers would consider the gradual abolition of extraterritoriality. This was tantamount to saying that extraterritoriality should not be abolished, for all members of the commission were perfectly aware that the suggested reforms were unfeasible in the foreseeable future.

Although the contemporary situation was such as fully to explain the results of the meeting of the commission, the deeper reasons for the reluctance of the foreign powers to abolish extraterritoriality were two: First, extraterritoriality was a very favorable arrangement for foreigners on economic grounds because it exempted them from many financial burdens. Second, the way of life foreigners were accustomed to did not fit into the judicial system of the Chinese — the gap was too great. Concerning the second differences of opinion were legitimate on both sides; to settle them would have required a degree of acculturation not even yet attained. The meeting of the Commission of Extraterritoriality left the situation unchanged.[12] But the foreign powers were not given any respite. The Nanking government continued to press for the abolition of extraterritoriality and was encouraged in this activity by some minor concessions made in the International Settlement in Shanghai. It was encouraged also by the sympathy shown at least to the principle in the notes of foreign governments, in which the surrender of extraterritoriality was denied only until changes in China's judicial system should have taken place.

In 1928 and after, the government began to use very strong language. A number of officials threatened that the unequal treaties would be declared "null and void." [13] Then late in December the Central Political Council of the Kuomintang passed a resolution to the effect that extraterritoriality should be abolished and the National Government issued a mandate correspondingly: extraterritoriality was to end on January 1, 1930. This absolute decision was apparently largely for internal consumption. The foreign minister immediately made a statement in which he pointed out that a plan was now "under preparation" to abolish extraterritoriality and that he was anxious to hear representations from the foreign representatives against it.[14] Exchange of notes between the Chinese and the foreign governments continued, as did public pressure. Finally the government's hand was forced again, and in May 1931 "Provisional Regulations Governing Jurisdiction over Foreigners Residing in China" were promulgated, to become effective January 1, 1932. The second article read, "Foreigners shall be under the jurisdiction of Chinese courts." [15] Again the tough language was softened by the willingness of the Chinese to continue negotiations and by Article 12, which stated that "The date when this law shall come into force shall be announced by the National Government." However, all the pressure and all the toughness did not bring success. Extraterritoriality remained a foreign privilege at this time.

In addition to these more noteworthy events between 1921 and 1931, other improvements in China's international position took place. Ten states concluded treaties omitting stipulations of extraterritoriality. Weihaiwei was eventually returned to China. Some foreign concessions

190

were given back. The Chinese were granted representation in the administration of the Shanghai Settlement. Several nations declared their willingness to renounce extraterritoriality if others would do so. The Chinese had reason to congratulate themselves upon such progress.

It was true, of course, that this progress was made at a time when the mood of many European peoples and especially of the American people was very sympathetic to Chinese aspirations, duly advertised by widespread Nationalist propaganda. Furthermore Sino-Japanese relations were growing tense, and Western friendliness to China might have been intended as a warning to Japan. Nevertheless the Nationalists deserve credit for the diplomatic victories. The Peking cliques agreed with the aims of the Nationalists, but it was the latter group that actually brought the changes about, mostly by their impetuous and insistent methods and by their propaganda (in the use of which the Communists had trained them). Secretary Kellogg summed up the situation when he wrote that the developments conformed to "the trend of modern events in relation to all self-governing countries where extraterritorial privileges have existed. It is reasonable to suppose that a great nation like China will not long permit foreign control of its domestic affairs." [16]

The powers felt that China's demands for concessions were irresistible. They could have taken their chance and resisted, but only, so they were convinced, at the risk of losing the Chinese to Soviet Russia, and that was considered the greater evil. The foreign representatives in China were extremely sensitive to any cooling of Chinese feelings toward their nations. They were remarkably quick to prevent any deterioration by the granting of favors. They were clearly on the defensive. They were almost wooing China. Exploiting the situation, the Chinese diplomats maintained their barrage of demands so that foreign representatives admitted they might have to go "rather more than half way" in meeting the Chinese. [17]

Actually the Chinese were not so much concerned about what the foreigners surrendered as that they should surrender something. The movement which had engulfed the Chinese people (or, more correctly, its politically active section) was psychological rather than material. Imponderable emotional elements were involved which could not be measured according to any table of definite claims or grievances. The First World War had stimulated national self-consciousness and had convinced the Chinese that the Westerners were barbarians after all —

that, at any rate, they were not superior, and morally were possibly inferior, to themselves. Hence there was no basis at all for the overbearing attitude of the West. The inability of the Chinese to unite internally only stimulated their ardor to obtain recognition as a great power. Their zeal was the compensation of an inferiority complex which had seized many of them personally. Some Chinese leaders expressed privately their anxiety to have some avowal of respect from foreign powers for China's dignity as a nation, whether in the form of material concessions or otherwise.[18] This psychological pressure within themselves was to a considerable degree what gave the Chinese the courage to press their claims politically, so that they succeeded in adding a diplomatic to their nationalist revolution.

15

"Incident" with Japan and Reconstruction

THE nature of China's nationalism contributed to the ill fate that befell the nation early in the 1930's. The new nationalism was not intensive, or perhaps not genuine, enough to overcome factional strife and bring about unity. Yet its antiforeign bias aroused among foreign powers a concern that could be prevented from turning into aggressiveness only by unified resistance. China was not given the chance to develop that.

The campaign of the Nationalists had superficially united the country. The National Government was established in Nanking and recognized as the central government of China. But vast areas had remained under the control of groups opposed to Chiang K'ai-shek's regime. In the south, north, and northwest war lords had yet to be eliminated at considerable cost to the central government. In Canton a leftist, non-Communist group, the "reorganizationists," established a rival government because they suspected Chiang of being nothing better than a successor of the tuchuns. The Communists, strongest in south-central China, presented the most difficult problem; indeed, as it turned out, an insoluble problem.

The expulsion of the Communist leaders from the Kuomintang, the destruction of the labor unions, the establishment of strict controls by the central government had stunned, but not killed, the Communist movement. Sections of the revolutionary army had remained loyal to communism. Many leaders, Mao Tse-tung and Chu Teh among them, retained their enthusiasm for the cause. And Moscow remained a helpful source of inspiration and support. Instead of disappearing, the Communist movement grew, especially in the hinterland. Mao's "unorthodox" practice of working with peasants instead of the urban proletariat, as Leninism prescribed, was paying dividends. All endeavors to eradicate the movement merely seemed to strengthen its hold over large sections of the population. The reasons were not difficult to find.[1]

193

The ferment of new ideas flowing into China had provoked skepticism and doubt about the viability of traditional values. Great hopes were raised during the World War and the Nationalist revolution. The people were ready for changes, reforms, reconstruction. They were ready for action and were groping for a master plan. Communism pretended to provide it. What is more, the early policies of the National Government held out little hope to either workers or peasants that their sacrifices had been for a purpose, that their expectations would ever be fulfilled. By contrast, therefore, the Communist movement appeared doubly attractive. It seemed to realize its plans wherever it was in control. Putting matters in the simplest terms, a local observer stated to the *North China Herald* in 1930, "Since the government has failed so far as these poor folks can see to make good their promise, the people must now take it into their own hands and secure the money from the wealthy just as was promised them during the revolution."

In each district under Communist control, soviets were established. The gentry and well-to-do farmers, or at least what passed for such in poor China, were spectacularly robbed of all power and influence. The population was given the illusion of self-determination. Agrarian reforms were introduced as the first act of the soviet governments. Land was redistributed, food-growing replaced poppy cultivation, irrigation projects were begun, a proportional land tax was introduced, cooperative banking and credit systems were established, working hours were shortened. In the process much human suffering and destruction were caused, though many of the acts of violence ascribed to Communists were committed by bandits or brought about by officials for their own benefit. But it is also true that the Communist movement contained a very considerable number of people in the leadership who, to quote a Catholic priest, were "really Communists in the simplicity of their lives and their personal disinterestedness in riches" [2] — in itself something that must have been a novel attraction to the exploited Chinese masses.

In the end, so it appears, the welfare of the individual under the Communist regime was not any better than before. An opposition group, the Anti-Bolshevik League, functioned for a while in Communist territory. But, composed as it was mostly of the deposed gentry, its opposition was no indication of popular feeling. There is no doubt that in the initial stages of the Communist regime, when only the potential benefits were apparent, the masses were sympathetic. Although in the course of time many may have come to dislike having to support the Red army as much as they did supporting any other, in general there was no evidence of any widespread antagonism to the Communists. On the contrary, by and large the people seem to have welcomed them. The enthusiasm of many followers, the hardships they suffered for the cause, and the voluntary accessions to the movement indicated that it was attractive.* In other words, by propaganda and indoctrination as well as by action, the Communists had succeeded in the vital undertaking of making the movement psychologically acceptable to large sections of the people. From the standpoint of their struggle for power it is therefore of subordinate interest whether or not they succeeded in actually improving the material welfare of their followers.

By contrast, the policies of the National Government had little to inspire the masses, and their projected reforms were slight. The Nationalist revolution had been a "bourgeois" revolution, and the "bourgeoisie" — in China the small wealthy class of landowners, industrialists, and merchants — now demanded their pound of flesh. No matter how serious Chiang K'ai-shek and his advisers might be about economic and social reforms to help the masses, they could not ignore their main supporters. Their influence with provincial authorities, moreover, was often negligible, so that reforms decreed from the center never were put into practice. Problems seemed to crop up constantly which demanded the government's attention before the more basic national question could be tackled. Whether because of unwillingness or inability, the fact is that the National Government did very little indeed to convince the masses that their lot was the primary consideration of the statesmen in Nanking.[3]

Even the blueprints for the future contained little to arouse mass support. Modernization of the legal system and prison reform, development of railway communications and road construction, research on public-health programs, currency reform, spread of education were all laudable but long-run enterprises. There was nothing in them which the masses could directly relate to the alleviation of their misery, let alone which could lead to any immediate improvements.

In contrast to the Communists, who acted, the National Government talked. It talked in grandiose terms, while the Communists did the little

* For example, probably more than 30 per cent of the Red army's equipment came from Nationalist army detachments which joined in and after 1927; defections from the Nationalist army in favor of the Communist reached into the highest ranks and occurred as late as 1933.

things which convinced the people. It talked in terms of tomorrow, and tomorrow never came, not for the masses.* The National Government apparently hoped to be able to defeat communism by military action alone. Such action was undoubtedly necessary, but it was not sufficient. By its failure to supplement military policy with a progressive social and economic policy, the government of Chiang K'ai-shek, even in the hour of victory, contributed to developments which eventually led to its own destruction. As a refugee on Formosa, Chiang recognized this fatal mistake.

The need to defeat the Communist movement handicapped the conduct of foreign affairs just at the moment when the nation needed all its strength to consolidate its gains from the "diplomatic revolution" of the 'twenties and deter potential enemies who looked askance at the improvement of China's international position and the consolidation of the central government.

Soviet Russia and Japan were two such enemies. Both disliked the existence of a strong China because both had expansionist ambitions at Chinese expense. The conflict with Russia over the Chinese Eastern Railway between 1929 and 1931 and the numerous incidents with Japan during that period, the many arguments back and forth based on this or that treaty, were symptoms of the fundamental conflict between Russian and Japanese imperialism on the one hand and China's aspirations for full sovereignty on the other.

When Japan struck on September 18, 1931, the National Government was faced with the outright opposition of the Communists, the passive disobedience of the war lords, and the uncertainties of an uneasy occasional coalition with the opposition government in Canton. Nanking lacked money and troops to cope with all these antagonistic groups.

Because of the world depression, internal political developments, floods and famines, the fluctuating value of silver (China's currency standard), and above all the enormous amounts needed for the support of armies and campaigns, China's finances were in a desperate state. This, at least, was the judgment of those who tried to untangle the

---

* Even the most sympathetic reports on progress in Nationalist China show only very slow progress, but they all paint rosy pictures of the future. T'yau's and T'ang Leang-li's books may serve as examples. The same is true of the innumerable speeches of government members — for example, H. H. Kung's in the *North China Herald*, February 3, 1931, p. 148. Professor Gideon Chen pointed out hopefully that the government's "exercise in economic dreaming is a better thing than the old practice in 'eight legged' essay writing" (*Chinese Government Economic Planning and Reconstruction Since 1927* [Tientsin, 1933], p. 26).

chaotic financial situation. For a moment, in 1932, T. V. Soong as finance minister seems to have achieved something that was called a balanced budget. But even that was temporary, and balance did not mean that there was money in the coffers. There was not, certainly, enough to maintain and equip armies able to fight in all directions and against such a well-prepared enemy as Japan.

In fact, the Chinese military machine was in a state of reorganization when the Japanese attacked. Chiang had hired a German military mission after the break with the Russians. The plan was to create a relatively small but well-disciplined force, with emphasis on political as well as military training and on loyalty to the nation rather than to a commanding general. The experience of former times, not to be repeated, had been that a large army not only was unwieldy but lacked organization, spirit, and efficiency. Before this plan could be fully realized, some problems had to be overcome. The first was to find a minister of military affairs loyal to the government. Between 1928 and 1930 all those appointed to the post had organized rebellions or joined opposition groups. This made any constructive work impossible. The second problem was to get rid of the armies which had accumulated in the course of the Nationalist revolution. Not only were they inadequate from a military standpoint, but consumed all the public money there was. In February 1929, therefore, a Troop Disbandment Conference was held at Nanking. The decision was to be to limit military expenditure to $192 million, representing 41 per cent of the estimated revenue or 36 per cent of the gross expenditure for the year. If, however, from the revenue were deducted sinking-fund charges and tax-collection expenses, which were first charges on revenue, military expenses amounted to 78 per cent of the net revenue. Obviously, practically nothing would be left for other expenses at a time when the government poured out blueprints for reconstruction projects [4] (and the communists had no military or foreign responsibilities!). The generals at the conference showed little interest in disbandment. They were only concerned with rewards for themselves. The conference had few results. When the Japanese struck, the problem was unsolved, though the new army was in process of formation. It never succeeded in defeating the ill-equipped Communist armies in the south, and to have exposed it to the Japanese to be slaughtered would have been almost criminal.*

* Though the main body of the new army never did face the Japanese, some of the best sections of it were killed in the defense of Shanghai in 1932.

In the face of these realities Nanking had to decide, first, how to handle its internal enemies and, second, how to deal with the enemy from without. A decision was reached fairly quickly on the internal situation. There was good prospect of a compromise with Canton. At the worst, severe criticism was to be expected from that quarter, but no military action. The Canton group was split within itself, and Nanking was confident it could handle the situation by political maneuvering. The Communists were an altogether different proposition. They were disciplined and united (though occasional purges took place). They knew their objective. They were determined to oust the central government from power by physical force. A reconciliation with them was out of the question. Nanking considered them the major threat and their elimination worth every effort. The decision therefore was to leave the government troops in the south to control the Communists rather than to withdraw them for use against the Japanese. The government's reasoning, as explained by Finance Minister T. V. Soong, was that "military concentration in the North would leave the South a prey to chaos and communism and is therefore impossible for this, if for no other reason." [5] The Nanking government felt, very typically, that a Communist victory would be definitive for a very long time, with no outside help to be expected to reverse the situation. A complete Japanese victory, however, would not be tolerated for long by the foreign powers. Sooner or later they would interfere and provide the opposition which Nanking now felt unable to marshall. The only force Nanking decided to employ against Japanese aggression was local Manchurian troops, remnants of personal armies of the tuchuns. They were to be a buffer so that the well-trained troops of Nanking would not be involved, and they were to save the government's face by showing some resistance. Nanking's real intention regarding Japan was to bring about international action.

The government considered this vital not merely to the fate of the nation but its own fate. Primarily out of fear for its own survival, it regarded the internal and external threat as one. The danger from the Communists was direct. The danger from the rest of the population could develop out of an "appeasement policy" toward Japan. Nanking was acutely aware that the temper of the people demanded action against Japan,* if not first and foremost, at least with an urgency equal to that of any demand for action against the Communists. The urgent

* It was not easy for the government to control this temper; the students especially were eager for action. The Kuomintang appealed to them, urging "obedience to a

pleas of Chinese statesmen for international action against Japan were therefore motivated by fear of internal reactions as much as by fear of what the Japanese might do.[6] Once more, then, the internal political consequences of international events rather than the consequences of these events upon China's international position had first place in the government's interests.

Presumably the Nanking government was convinced that its own welfare was identical with that of the country. But the Canton opposition took no such benevolent view. It was convinced that Chiang K'ai-shek, with his "medieval conceptions," was selfishly ruling the country for his own and his "so-called" family's profit.[7] They weighed the threat from within and without quite differently and advocated a stronger stand against Japan. Upon this difference turned the politics between the two groups and their evaluation of China's international position.

Nanking had a number of alternatives through which to start international action: the League of Nations, the Kellogg-Briand Pact, the Washington Nine-Power and Four-Power treaties, and, of course, bilateral negotiations with various nations. It used them all.

Probably the result most surprising to it was the outcome of its negotiations with Russia. Early in the conflict with Japan the Chinese government had hinted on several occasions that, failing support from the Western powers or the collective security agreements, it might find itself obliged to turn to Russia for help. This was generally interpreted as an empty threat, but wrongly so. The Chinese did turn to Russia for help, but found no response. Moscow declared Japan an aggressor and that was the end of Russian action. Notwithstanding the credit certain writers now wish to give the Soviet Union for resisting Japanese aggression, the Soviet government was most scrupulously neutral and had no wish whatsoever to get involved in the Manchurian "incident" from the moment it started. It did nothing to assist the Chinese. Maxim Litvinov confirmed later that Russia had no intention of getting into war with Japan.[*] This was known to the Chinese, but they tried nevertheless to

unified and single command and persistence in the attitude of calmness and restraint which has been enjoined upon the nation at large by the National Government" and exhorting them "to apply themselves close to their studies" and to refrain from "irresponsible and ill-advised acts" which would harm rather than help. — *Chinese Affairs*, September 30, 1931, Nos. 146–147, pp. 472–473.

[*] This was true of all other nations. Litvinov had therefore no right to suspect the sincerity of their protests on the ground that they were not followed by action. For the Communist interpretation of the Manchurian affair as of 1951, see *Soviet Press Translations*, VII (1952) 131–151.

enlist Russian aid as their disappointment with the Western powers grew. They appear to have tried even an alliance. The net result of this diplomacy was the resumption in 1932 of diplomatic relations interrupted since 1928. The resumption, Nanking felt, was useful first as a good-neighbor policy, second as an appeasement of radical elements in the internal opposition, third as a demonstration that the government had success in foreign policy, fourth as a political victory against Japan, and fifth as something to play on the fears of the Western powers of communism in the Far East. But the success was too small and too late to reverse the trend of Japan's policy in Manchuria.[8]

A policy of direct negotiations with Japan was a very delicate enterprise from an internal political standpoint. The students were clamoring for action against Japan. A very effective boycott against Japanese goods had been established. Under such conditions negotiations could not be conducted openly and officially. But this did not prevent the Nanking government from hinting that under certain circumstances conversations could be held and a compromise reached. The conditions of this would be minimum concessions to China's "dignity," such as withdrawal of Japanese troops to their original positions or participation of neutral observers in the conversations. At one point, in its eagerness to regain a free hand in internal politics, the government asked the United States minister what he would think if China should "yield to Japan control over railways, built or being built, in Manchuria, plus a dominant economic position, on condition that all Japanese troops now in Manchuria be removed."

This extreme plan was perhaps a *ballon d'essai* to gauge American feelings. But in its willingness to appease, the possibility that Nanking may have been prepared actually to make all these concessions to Japan cannot be excluded. Even Eugene Chen, a member of the Canton opposition group, when he became foreign minister in December 1931 during a temporary strategic withdrawal of Chiang and his cabinet, was willing to negotiate with the Japanese if some "dignified way" to do so could be found. It never was.[9]

Nanking put the greatest effort into evoking one of the treaties of collective security: the League Covenant, the Nine-Power Treaty, the Four-Power Pacific Treaty, or the Kellogg-Briand Pact. To obtain international action proved difficult. The Japanese had chosen a most opportune moment for their aggression. For many reasons most nations were unwilling to be bothered by the troubles in the Far East. The first spontaneous thing most of them did, even before they knew the details of the events in Manchuria, was to attempt to push the incident onto a level where their principles and obligations might not apply. Henry Stimson in Washington announced that as far as the State Department knew, the Manchurian matter did not affect the two governments and therefore there were no grounds for invoking the Kellogg-Briand Pact. At the League, the Council of which was in session, several powers had informally decided to prevent the case from being brought up. All through the first few months Sir Eric Drummond, the secretary general, privately made statements indicating that he was loath to see the Chinese bother the League with this unpleasant affair. He expressed the hope to the American consul in Geneva that he might "avoid being placed in a position where he is continually being approached by the Chinese with protests and threats of action on their part . . . The Chinese now should undertake to do their share with as much independence as possible during the adjustment period lying immediately ahead." [10]

That China succeeded in getting her case before the League and keeping it there was considered by many a great diplomatic victory. All through the proceedings the Chinese did indeed show a considerable skill in their maneuvers to keep the issue alive. They always went just as far as they could to obtain a hearing while avoiding the accusation of unreasonableness. They were powerless, however, to change the basic attitude of the powers, because this might have meant willingness to wage war. The whole issue was put succinctly in a telephone conversation between Ambassador Charles G. Dawes and Secretary Stimson. The secretary told Dawes that the most the United States could do would be to deny recognition to any treaty which Japan might force upon China by the pressure of military occupation; that the United States would not enforce an embargo against Japan but would not interfere with one established by others. An embargo would lead to war, he said. "That is what Sze [the Chinese representative in Geneva] wants to do," answered Dawes. "Yes," replied Stimson, "Sze would like very much to get all of the nations of the world in war with Japan." Dawes: "Exactly." Stimson: "We have no sympathy with that and we do not intend to get into war with Japan." [11]

Here was the crux of the whole situation, the crux of any collective security system. And since many other nations felt like the United States,

China could not get satisfaction from the League. The fact also that the United States was not a member of the League gave Japan a stronger position and permitted it to use unhampered its European relations as a bargaining point in the Council. Nanking put a major share of the blame for the failure of the League upon the United States. The impression was widespread in China that Washington "tempered what might otherwise have been unsparing condemnation by the League of Nations of Japan's military invasion of Manchuria, and that the United States has failed to take, with respect to Japan's military measures, those steps which were to be expected of a sponsor of the Nine-Power Treaty and the Pact against War." [12] The nonrecognition doctrine was received by the Chinese as a token of American friendship, but with no expectation that it would stop aggression.[13]

Chinese disappointment with American policy was extreme. Hopes for American support had been so great that Nanking had hesitated for a moment at the beginning of the incident to turn to the League at all, of which the United States was not a member. In order not to prejudice any American action by prior League action, the Chinese postponed making an appeal to the League until they had made certain that the United States would not act under any collective security agreement to which it was a party. The Chinese would have preferred the Four-Power Pacific Treaty to the Kellogg-Briand Pact because under the latter they would have had to admit the existence of a state of war, as they were reluctant to do.[14] With the now available hindsight, it may be said that it would not have made any difference under which treaty the Chinese appealed to the powers. Japanese aggression would have been permitted to proceed in any case.

The Lytton Report, the meager result of all the League's activity, was generally considered a fair summing up of the facts. But its conclusions were mostly condemned. The failure of the League to do anything for China did not surprise many Chinese. They had expressed skepticism about the potentialities of the League from the very beginning, and the weak and dilatory policy at Geneva throughout the incident had convinced them that China had nothing to hope for there. China, they maintained, merely experienced once more the old principle, still valid in the days of collective security, that militarily weak nations adhering scrupulously to treaties and agreements were bound to lose out against nations supporting their violations of the law with force. Their main

202

criticism was leveled at Great Britain, France, and the United States. Their final conclusion (which produced no permanent consequence upon their foreign policy) was that no one could help China but the Chinese themselves.[15] Manchuria became the Japanese puppet state Manchukuo and the base for further Japanese aggression against China during the years ahead.

The disunity within China lasted through the whole incident. In this disunity the Nanking government had a good excuse for not organizing effective resistance against the Japanese.* To bolster its own unwillingness to fight them, it could always claim inability. But the internal disunity, it is true, would have prevented a determined stand against the aggressor no matter who had been in the government. When at a most difficult political moment Chiang and his cabinet resigned† — most cleverly to let the Canton opposition bear the burden of the failure to solve the almost insoluble problem — the Canton people too found that their radical program of war and resistance against Japan could not be realized. They blamed Chiang's obstructiveness for their inability to get tough with the Japanese, but they were perfectly aware that China could not risk a war with Japan, that an attempt to negotiate — as the Kuomintang chiefs decided formally to do on January 26, 1932, when, having permitted the opposition to learn its lesson, they had returned to power — was the only realistic policy.[16]

As on so many similar occasions previously, the whole responsibility for the situation was put on the foreign powers, who were accused of betraying China in her hour of need. This perpetual scapegoat policy relieved China of self-criticism and prevented improvements. The misfortune that had befallen the nation in the present case was at least partly owing not only to her long-run failure to strengthen herself but to the conduct of an aggressive policy with nothing to back it up. The early success of the Nationalist policy had been intoxicating. The brusque tone of the Nationalists' statements was as provocative as it was hollow. In many cases the tough front was put up for internal consumption, but the foreign powers could not be blamed for taking it seriously in

* Nanking had the larger part of its army in Kiangsi fighting the Communists at the time of the Tangku Truce, and only 70,000 to 80,000 men in the north. Of these, according to the Chinese vice-minister for foreign affairs, only four to five divisions could be counted upon to fight the Japanese. — U.S. Foreign Relations, 1933, III, 269, 453.

† C. C. Wu called the resignation "reculer pour mieux sauter" (North China Herald, December 22, 1931, p. 402).

view of the trouble it caused them. Luckily, for a while there was no need to support the statements by force. Most nations were conciliatory, though as much for reasons of their own as because they were cowed by the Chinese. Japan's characterization of the Nationalist demands as "outrageous" and the clashes with Russia should have warned the Chinese instead of encouraging them to continue on the path of a "strong" policy. Without a strong army the brave spirit was insufficient to withstand Russian and Japanese aggressiveness, and besides it made the traditional balance-of-power game in Manchuria much more difficult and costly.[17]

Until the renewal of the war with Japan in 1937, internal affairs continued to preoccupy the government. Nanking's relations with Canton remained uneasy, though not outright inimical until 1936. Then, when Canton in cooperation with some southern generals moved an army north, they were defeated, and their movement was liquidated by Chiang. The Communists were a tougher nut to crack. Chiang never succeeded in defeating them, yet the attempt to do so absorbed most of the government's strength. He dislocated them from the south and southwest, driving them on the "long march" to the northwest. This brought them closer to Russia, though it extended Chiang's jurisdiction into the areas vacated by them. Unfortunately for China and the world, Chiang's success was based on methods some of which were hardly distinguishable from the totalitarianism of the Communists. He thus got the Chinese accustomed to a regime into which the Communists could fit with relative ease in 1949.

The endeavor to strengthen the regime and the lesson learned from the failure of international arrangements for collective security spurred Nanking — as it had spurred its predecessors on similar occasions — into building up the country's political and economic strength. Accordingly the watchword "internal reconstruction" replaced the previous one of "equality in the society of nations." The shift did not by any means stop persistent agitation for complete equality and full sovereignty; there was no let-up in China's propaganda barrage for the achievement of these goals. But the order of importance was reversed. Nanking and its followers now gave priority to internal reconstruction and technical and economic revival. This concern with internal matters colored Chinese attitudes toward foreign policy and can in part explain the eagerness of Nanking to come to terms with the Japanese.

In 1931 a National Economic Council was set up and a three-year and a ten-year plan announced. Across the country appeals were made to the effect that "to preserve our national independence, we must reconstruct our country." Newspapers and journals carried "Reconstruction" columns. The faculties of the natural sciences at the universities were developed. The national life of China was geared to "Reconstruction." The response was promising. Practical problems of reconstruction became the topic of discussion everywhere; they were no longer the preserve of the central government. But there were some serious difficulties, quite apart from the shortage of resources, to be overcome before Reconstruction could get into full swing. The Chinese economy, especially agriculture, was so closely interwoven with cultural concepts and social traditions that any change was bound to be revolutionary.

The rationalization of the economic process, the introduction of labor-saving devices, immediately raised the serious problem of what to do with the saved manpower. An answer also had to be found to the question of how human beings could be prevented from becoming the servants of machines, for such an eventuality was repulsive to the Chinese and greatly feared. Above all, before these points could be settled, there was the difficulty of getting the trained manpower. In the past, under the influence of Confucianism, not only had it been beneath the dignity of the educated Chinese actually to do anything practical, as distinct from planning or theorizing about it, but he had refused to become a specialist. The mission of man was by self-perfection to become an integrated, harmonious individual who would fit into the cosmic order. A gentleman would not descend to becoming a tool, a means to an end, a one-sided, unharmonious specialist. The hangover of this philosophy still hampered the reconstruction program. Nevertheless the younger generation stopped talking in the old complacent, theoretical way about the "secrets" of Western success and searching for panaceas. Instead, quietly and stubbornly many young people began to act, to work, to contribute. The new spirit even penetrated the masses, and, though progress among them was slower, there was some readiness to respond to the appeals for reconstruction.[18]

Observers were astonished to find that the Chinese peasant was not completely hidebound and tradition-ridden, but willing to accept innovations if they could be shown to be practicable and profitable. Such acceptance was now made easier by the adaptation of the new methods

205

to Chinese conditions. There were no more attempts to impose foreign, ready-made methods in order to bring about modernization overnight. Instead, proper respect was paid to local conditions and customs, and the aim was organic growth, not revolution. China began to count upon herself, upon her own spiritual and material resources. "Reliance upon China's own resources" became a standard phrase in Chinese political and diplomatic terminology. This reliance did not prevent the government from calling upon the League of Nations for expert assistance, though the call was very carefully worded to indicate that the initiative must in every case come from China and be granted only within the limits set by the government. The League responded favorably and enthusiastically, with the express blessing of the Japanese. Thus by combined effort, and despite internal disunity, natural disasters, and an economic depression of the first magnitude, China made some slight progress.[19]

In addition to technical help from the League and funds from Chinese bankers, some foreign loans for building railroads and for other purposes were again forthcoming. Foreign interest in such loans had been dormant since the Chinese had refused to deal with the New Consortium shortly after the World War. Now that the country seemed to be quieting down politically and devoting itself to constructive purposes, foreign confidence and money were returning. A number of commercial missions from several countries and a mission from the League testified to the growing trust in China's economy. China seemed to be starting on the road to strength and unity — though it was a unity which some observers found increasingly synonymous with regimentation.[20]

Foreign powers were eager to participate in the reconstruction program. They concentrated their activity now on direct business investments and trade rather than loans. Heavy industry was especially well represented in China. Numerous transactions were concluded involving armament, railroad stock, and machinery for nascent industries and the building of industrial plants. These deals were made more quietly than earlier loans. But competition among foreign nationals was no less keen, and "equal treatment" was closely watched. Occasionally complaints about infractions of the Open Door could be heard or about illegal methods. But faults were usually due to poor organization or the shortcomings of individual officials, not to bad faith on the part of the Chinese government.[21]

Complaints about the program or actual resistance to it from within

206

gave the government more difficulty. To the more radical reconstruc-tionists foreign aid was repugnant and a threat to the whole purpose of the program. It seemed an invitation to intervention and a return to the evils of former years. But the government assured its critics that it would not tolerate intervention or political pressure by foreign powers. It pointed to the regulations governing the utilization of foreign experts and resources. All foreign participation in China's reconstruction was carefully surrounded by the most detailed precautions, and the evidence is that an attempt was made to enforce these regulations.[22] Accusations that the government was considering military alliances with foreign powers to obtain economic help were refuted equally convincingly. "Unless we possess a certain degree of national power, no nation would be so imbecile as to ally itself with us for the purpose of checking others," said Wang Ching-wei as president of the Executive Yuan.[23] This remark, however, did not exclude such an alliance for the future, and it contained some hint of an ulterior purpose behind the reconstruction program.

The reconstruction was meant to have significance beyond the sphere of mere economics. An improvement in communications, an important aspect of the program, would help the National Government concen-trate power internally and put up a better resistance against enemies from without. The international implications were frankly admitted: the program was conceived with the idea of making China an inde-pendent, sovereign state. For this reason many nations looked askance at the possible success of the undertaking. Political stability and inde-pendence and economic competitiveness would cut across the plans of one or the other foreign power. But what exactly these plans were was difficult to determine in the early 'thirties. Most nations were preoccu-pied with their own economic problems. Soviet Russia's intentions around 1934 were a matter of speculation. France was suspected of harboring old-fashioned imperialistic ambitions with regard to south China. Japan was the only nation that made a straightforward announce-ment of plans in China — and they were plans that kept China pre-occupied for the decade to follow.

In April 1934 Eiji Amau, spokesman for the Japanese Foreign Office, made his famous statement pointing out that Japan was responsible for the maintenance of peace in the Far East. This responsibility did not permit other nations to interfere in the affairs of China. Financial and economic help could be one form of interference, but there were others. The League commission and its report on technical assistance to China were singled out for attack by Amau. Japan objected because the "fundamental premises of the proposals do not coincide with Japanese opinion." Self-awakening, not foreign assistance, was the only help China needed. Financial assistance coming from the League would eventually take on a political tinge and affect China's affairs adversely.

Japan's objection against even strictly nonpolitical assistance was a practical demonstration of the inseparability of political and economic matters in the age of total war. Objectively speaking, the Japanese were right, and the whole premise of the League's approach to "neutral" assistance was wrong. Anything improving conditions in China was improving the military position of the country.

Two days after the Amau statement, China protested. She affirmed that she would permit no one, nation or League, to infringe upon her sovereignty. She refuted the idea that Japan alone or in combination with her was to maintain peace in the Far East; instead she reaffirmed trust in the global collective-security system represented by the League. Other foreign capitals were disturbed, too, by the Japanese plans. The Japanese felt constrained to make a number of declarations intended to soften the shock, none of which, however, repudiated the Amau statement, so that Chinese fears were increased rather than alleviated. The government announced that it continued to hold the Japanese government "wholly responsible" for Amau's statement.[24]

This announcement contributed little to discourage the Japanese. Foreign reactions were so weak that in effect they were rather encouraging to Japan. For many different reasons there was a general tendency in the West not to antagonize Japan. China's suspicions of Western policy in the Far East, aroused by the failure to get help in the Manchurian incident, now became certainty. China could expect nothing from that direction. Even before the Amau statement the Nanking Foreign Office and the Chinese press were greatly perturbed by the *rapprochement* between the United States and Japan. The exchange of notes between Secretary of State Hull and Foreign Minister Hirota, confirming collaboration and friendship between their two nations, was interpreted by the Chinese as a first step toward American recognition of Manchukuo. The semiofficial Chinese Institute of International Relations even sent a telegram of protest to Hull, accusing him of tacitly recognizing Japan's activities of conquest in northern China. Perturbation changed into "profound disappointment and perplexity" when Presidential Secretary Stephen Early implied that the American government favored a Monroe Doctrine for Europe and Asia also.[25]

The first impulse of the Chinese after the Amau statement was to invoke the Nine-Power Treaty, more to confirm their pessimism than in the hope of getting action. Confirmation was duly forthcoming. They did not succeed in invoking the treaty either through diplomatic channels or through the League. The United States and Great Britain, the two powers China would have liked to see assume leadership against Japanese aggression, failed to respond and were satisfied with note-sending. China realized that the foreign powers were unwilling to act, and so did Japan.

The Amau statement turned out to be a fairly accurate prediction of Japanese policy. Between 1934 and 1937 the Japanese expanded their physical, political, and economic control over north China, either directly — through military action or through the provocation of "autonomy" movements, for which they could find Chinese puppets easily enough — or through economic measures which were not always either legal or moral. They also succeeded in reducing the scope of the League's technical assistance. All this expansion took place under the slogan of "cooperation" with China. It was interspersed with policy statements in Tokyo, such as Foreign Minister Hirota's Three Principles of January 1936 * and Foreign Minister Sato's speech to the Diet in March 1937,† which created the impression that Japan was willing to compromise and come to terms with China. But upon close examination and as afterward proved by the facts, these statements never really did imply a deviation from the policy of expansion which Japan in fact pursued. They were presumably meant to pacify foreign and especially home opinion (there were many Japanese who did not relish the idea of further complications with China).[26] It is barely possible also that they sincerely expressed the government consensus in Tokyo, but failed to influence the Japanese military on the mainland, who pursued a policy of their own.

The Chinese government and a section of the public, though not fooled by the conciliatory statements coming from Japan, nevertheless seized

---

* "Active and effective collaboration with Japan," "recognize Manchoukuo," "suppression of the communist activities."

† "China demands treatment on an equal footing. This wish should be respected and past differences forgotten."

upon them, not having any other choice.[27] The government negotiated endlessly without ever succeeding in getting the Japanese to modify any of their unacceptable demands. Even the Tokyo *Oriental Economist* admitted that the initiative for better Sino-Japanese relations came from China and that the Chinese government had turned to a "pro-Japanese" policy.[28] But any *rapprochement* that might have been noticeable during this period was due to unilateral concessions which the Chinese eventually felt forced to grant in view of the continued absence of assistance from Western powers.[29]

The government's policy faced some internal opposition. There was strong agitation among the students, the merchant guilds, and the labor unions, especially against the "autonomy" movement in the northeast provinces, and there was pressure upon the government to take a stronger stand.[30] They were joined in their criticism of the government by the Communists, Chinese and otherwise, until Moscow switched the party line to the United Front in 1936. Up to that moment Chiang had been accused of being pro-Japanese and of accepting "imperialist" America's weapons and military advisers. As far as the Communists were concerned, Chiang was playing Japan's game. His government and the Canton regime were both "counterrevolutionary" and were engaged "in a competition of backsliding, trying to surpass each other in their reactionary activities." [31] Not one of these critics had any concrete proposals on how China might overcome her weakness rapidly enough to resist the determined and strong aggression from Japan. Chiang K'ai-shek was trying to gain time in the hope that Reconstruction might prove successful enough to deter further Japanese attacks. The prospect that this hope might be fulfilled made the Japanese decide to crush it. They resumed their war against China with the Lukou-chiao incident of July 7, 1937.

16

Renewed Aggression and Internal Discord

WHEN Japan attacked in the summer of 1937, though China was still disunited, the situation was not quite so confused as several years earlier. Chaos was giving way to relative order.[1] A few influential war lords survived, mostly in the south, whose cooperation was bought by Chiang K'ai-shek with the grant of considerable autonomy in their areas. Basically only two antagonistic groups remained: the Nationalists, controlling by far the largest part of the country, and the Communists, concentrated in the northwest province of Shensi and relatively insignificant in numbers. There was another change. The lines between the opposing groups were more sharply drawn. Each group had become more cohesive. In addition to loyalty to the leader, they had developed a loyalty to an ideology. Absorption of one group by the other had become virtually impossible. The split inside China had, so to speak, been reduced to the absolute minimum.

The attack by the Japanese resulted in the temporary union of these two opposite groups, or at least in cooperation and the temporary cessation of active hostility between them. The cooperation for common action against the Japanese was never anything like a real fusion. The fundamental antagonism between them never disappeared. The Communists refused to abandon their identity or their final goals, the Nationalists never trusted the Communists and never ceased to contain them in the northwest by a large number of troops.[2] Cooperation usually meant the publication of parallel manifestoes and announcements of policy — hardly ever joint ones — and of party decisions by both sides for public consumption. As the war progressed, periods of good relations alternated with periods of bad ones, each side blaming the other for the deterioration of relations and for not keeping to its bargain — and both were right. But in the years 1937 and 1938, when the war was still new, the two groups achieved a fair degree of cooperation, and a number of concrete steps which seemed at last to provide a solid foundation for unity were taken by both sides.

From the pattern of events in World War II it is now clear that the foreign policy of the Chinese Communists was determined in Russia. But in the early years of Japanese aggression it was possible to disguise this Russian-determined policy in the cloak of Chinese nationalism, a disguise facilitated by the fact that Soviet Russia pursued the dual course of neutrality with Japan and material support to the Chinese. Since the Communists shared with the Nationalists the objective of ridding China of Japanese domination, they were able to play the role of Chinese patriots (which some of them undoubtedly thought they were) and to enlist sympathy far beyond the circle of their immediate followers. Their declaration of war against Japan in 1932 had brought them much popular approval. Their widely advertised guerrilla activities against the Japanese gave them the halo of heroes. Following the conclusion of the German-Japanese Anti-Comintern Pact of 1936, they inaugurated their United Front policy and went all-out for cooperation with the central government. For the sake of national unity they even pleaded with Chang Hsueh-liang in Sian in 1936 for Chiang's life and freedom, after he had kidnapped the generalissimo to force more national cooperation and a stronger stand against the Japanese. This spectacular bid for unity was successful because the Communist demand expressed a widespread popular feeling. In that sense the Sian affair could well be called a Chinese-type General Election! [3]

This appeal by the Communists for cooperation forced the hand of the National Government and prevented it from continuing with full force its campaign of extermination against them. In the long run, perhaps, the Nationalists might have eliminated the Communists by sheer force, though the latter represented ideas that were bound to find expression in one way or another. In fact, the Communists represented many ideas which the Nationalists had represented earlier but had neglected, as they themselves confessed on Formosa, to keep alive. At any rate, the war stopped any attempt to wipe the Communists out. It was their life-saver. As a concession to popular feeling at home and the demands for unity from abroad, Chiang was obliged, or perhaps he wanted, to take seriously the overtures the Communists made proposing common action. A certain anxiety among the members of the National Government regarding the meaning of the Anti-Comintern Pact for China may also have made them more receptive to the Communist call for unity. It took a good deal of argument on the part of German Ambassador Trautmann to quiet the fears of Chiang and his cabinet and to convince them that the Pact was directed against Russia, that Germany did not intend to fight communism in China and had not joined Japan for the purpose of doing so.[4]

By their attack the Japanese therefore achieved the very opposite of what they had aimed at in China. Far from nipping in the bud, as they thought, the growth of a movement toward unified resistance against themselves, they accelerated it.

Nevertheless the best that could be hoped for in the way of union between two such diverse groups as the Nationalists and the Communists was a truce or an uneasy coalition in the face of the danger that confronted the country from without. And even this minimum solution could not be held for long in equilibrium. The trouble was that the two groups did not fear the Japanese danger with the same intensity at all times. On occasion each feared the opponent more than it feared the Japanese. Hence, after the period of relative quiet and cooperation in the initial years of the war, there was frequent fighting between them, at the expense of a united war effort. The psychological effect of the internal situation upon foreign nations was to increase their apathy toward China in the years before 1941 and to make them refuse to take her seriously as a major power in the years succeeding.

The attitude of the Nationalists was fairly consistent. They were afraid of the Japanese as well as of the Communists. The victory of either would have meant their end. Chiang felt justified in doing everything to maintain his government in power, for its own sake and the good of the country. This meant splitting the war effort between two fronts. To do so, the government argued, and many foreign observers agreed, was inevitable. Disappearance of the central government, whether caused by the Japanese or the Communists, would have meant a relapse into chaos and certain victory for the Japanese. Furthermore, the Nationalist troops which were adequate to contain the Communists would have been impotent against the superior Japanese. Against them, space, time, and mass were the most effective weapons.

The Communists' attitude was far less consistent, at least from a Chinese standpoint, though perhaps not from a Russian. The Communist outlook on foreign affairs was determined by the Soviet Union. The Communist leaders faithfully followed the party line. They turned cooperation with the Nationalists on or off as suited their tortuous politics.

213

Depending therefore upon the degree of tension prevailing between the Soviet Union and the Japanese and other powers, the Communists would tend to cooperate or fight with the central government, regardless of the continuing Japanese aggression. They were thus much more concerned with the vicissitudes of international life than the National Government, which had at least the national survival as one fixed point from which to evaluate world politics. The several astonishing shifts in the policies of some major powers between 1936 and 1941 highlighted the variability of Chinese Communist foreign policy and its dependence upon Moscow.

A Communist reversal of the United Front policy inaugurated in 1936 occurred in September 1939, following the conclusion of the German-Russian nonaggression treaty. The "fascist dogs" — the Germans who had associated themselves with the Japanese in the Anti-Comintern Pact of '36 — suddenly became fighters for the world's freedom, and Chiang K'ai-shek became the fascist dog. Posters went up in Communist China saying, "England and America are our enemies, Soviet Russia is the Fatherland." Mao Tse-tung assured his friends that not Germany but Great Britain was China's bitter enemy in the West, as Japan was in the East, and that the Communist task was to turn the "imperialist" war into a civil war within each nation, no matter on what side it fought.

The next major turn in the crooked party line came in April 1941 with the conclusion of the Russian-Japanese Neutrality Pact, to which was attached a Frontier Declaration, in which Japan pledged the inviolability of the Mongolian People's Republic and Russia that of Manchukuo. The treaty was greeted by the Communists as a contribution by Russia to peace, which would permit the continuation of Soviet socialist construction for the benefit of the working people everywhere and the oppressed nations of the world. The implied recognition of Manchukuo in the Frontier Declaration was harder to swallow. The Communist explanation (speaking of Manchuria and only once referring to "so-called Manchoukuo") did not explain. Instead, it berated as "craven tricksters" those who criticized Russia for behaving "incorrectly." It failed to mention Molotov's excuse that "Manchukuo" was used for "lack of a satisfactory substitute name" and that it was put in quotation marks in the official text.

The final turn of the Communists came when the Soviet Union was attacked by Germany. That changed the struggle between the "fascist

214

imperialists" and the Germans into a "great patriotic war for democracy." [5]

This pattern in Chinese Communist foreign policy is clear in retrospect. It was harder to recognize as it developed. The difficulty of doing so may in part explain the very good press the Communists had abroad throughout World War II. The distrust of the National Government toward the Communists seemed unjustified to many observers, and the absence of national unity was largely blamed upon the obstinacy, or qualities even worse, of Chiang K'ai-shek.[6] The task of the central government, however reluctantly undertaken, of organizing resistance to the Japanese and of developing a foreign policy in support of that primary aim was made very much more difficult not only by the strife and distrust within China but by the sometimes inaccurate appraisal of that situation by powers friendly to her. The task would have been difficult enough without these extra complications.

At the time the Japanese attacked, the government's reconstruction plans were still largely on paper. A few pilot projects in agricultural and industrial improvement had been undertaken. A good many research and organizational changes were in progress. But China was not much better prepared in 1937 than she had been in 1931 actively to combat an enemy like Japan. Given time, the situation might have changed. But neither the Japanese nor Chinese public opinion tolerated delaying tactics. China used up her essential military resources in the first few months of active resistance. Thereafter passive resistance, with occasional stabs at the enemy, had to be the Chinese strategy.

The incompleteness of China's preparation was particularly disadvantageous, of course, as it affected the army. Reorganization there had just begun. The government's basic plan had been to form a small model army as the core of a larger force later on. But the need prematurely to call upon sections of the new force and to maintain parts of the old, inefficient revolutionary armies for use against the Japanese, the Communists, or some war lord ruined the plan. The foundation of the army had to be broadened and its standards lowered. The employment of foreign military missions, especially German, could not offset the handicap. Moreover these missions were prevented from contributing in the fullest possible measure by the resentment of Chinese officers over the meddling of foreigners in their affairs. The government was obliged to use the advisers mainly in the military schools and academies and forgo the benefit of their advice in the field. The traditional preference of Chinese officers for obtaining their training academically and for fighting their battles on maps made this lack of field training all the more regrettable.

The unsolved problem presented by the existence of the old nationalist, revolutionary troops, still undispersed, was the greatest handicap to the creation of an effective new striking force. Dismissal of the men might have been one solution. But a greater evil would have resulted — an increase in the ranks of the unemployed, the Communists, or the bandits. What to do with the officers created an even greater difficulty. They had a right to expect rewards for their loyalty to the nationalist cause. Occasionally they were given jobs in the civil service, to the detriment of Chinese public administration. Or they were put in command of some formation of the new crack troops, to the loss of many a battle. By and large the problem remained unsolved. The officers retained their troops and positions. It was better to have them as cooperating henchmen than as dangerous war lords.

When the war started in 1937, the government was burdened with a great number of these useless divisions. Lacking training and spirit, provided with insufficient and odd equipment, they proved a hindrance rather than a benefit to the war effort. The only good feature was that they were subordinated to the command of the central government. In the course of years, they even became used to taking orders from the government instead of their individual generals. Replacements and better training eventually made them more valuable. But quantity rather than quality remained their principal distinction. There were about two million men in these provincial divisions, which formed one part of the armies confronting the Japanese.

Another part was Chiang's "own" divisions — those that had been trained by the Germans. They were the only modern, well-equipped, and well-trained soldiers in China.* A large percentage of their 300,000 men were killed in heroic fighting and under not so heroic leadership around Shanghai during the first year of the war.

The third main part of the Chinese armies was the Communist troops in China's northwest area. Nominally these troops too had been subordinated to the central government under the name of the Eighth Route

* The only exception to this statement is the division created by T. V. Soong to police the Salt Administration. This was equal in quality to Chiang's troops.

Army, with Chu Teh and Chou En-lai as the highest leaders. Actually there was no coordination of any kind between this army and other troops (leaving aside some financial and material contributions from the central government). The Communists carefully refrained from ever merging their army with the Nationalist forces. On the contrary, they kept its identity intact for the day when China was to be conquered for communism. In 1937 it had probably about 50,000 men. In the course of the war, partisans were added so that eventually the Communists controlled about 500,000 men.*

The Communist armies were poorly paid and poorly equipped. Yet apparently their enthusiasm compensated for lack of funds. Here seems to have been achieved a complete break with Chinese traditions. Idealism rather than the quest for a living drove the men into soldiering. The intense political and ethical indoctrination of the organizers must have been effective; also the democratic nature of the organization. The "leaders" and "fighters" (in normal language the officers and men) led about the same life. Advancement was based on merit and the chance of it was equal for all. In any case, advancement was but a small step forward. The comforts of the "leaders" did not differ greatly from those of the "fighters." Kuomintang officials and other observers not inclined toward sympathy with the Communist cause agree that the morale of the Communist army was extraordinarily high, by absolute, not only by Chinese standards.[7]

The most astonishing development in China at this time was the growing friendliness between the armies and the people. At the beginning of the war the soldiers were, as usual, suspect; they suffered from the traditional onus. All too often, of course, these feelings were justified. After disasters, when the soldiers retreated in disorder, they marched pillaging through the villages. But the practice was becoming rarer. The soldiers were disciplined and met with sympathy from the people. At least the mass of them did, because they came from the peasants and workers themselves. Of the officers (in the non-Communist armies), this was not quite so true. They were still largely recruited from the wealthiest classes, and their bearing was at times most antagonistic.

Cooperation and mutual assistance between the army and the general

* The New Fourth Army was created in 1938 in eastern Kiangsi and southern Anhwei, also as a Communist force. It fought hard against Nationalist troops early in 1941; part of it survived the defeat and continued guerrilla activity behind Japanese lines.

217

population developed rapidly, in both the Communist and the Nationalist areas, although more in the former. The soldiers understood the suffering of the people, and the people appreciated the sacrifices of the
soldiers. The armies were not resented like a plague of locusts but
became part of the people. When, about 1939, the United Front began
to crumble, even Moscow had to admit that the Chinese people had
fully supported their government and its armies in the national war of
liberation against the Japanese and that these good relations were what
had made possible the brave fighting of the troops on all fronts.[8]

This growth in the cordiality of relations between soldiers and civilians occurred more slowly in the interior than in the cities. In the interim
it was necessary sometimes to corral healthy-looking young men and
drive them to the recruiting station, tied together and under military
guard. But as the war proceeded, there were more volunteers for service.
To be a soldier was considered almost an honor. The older generation
was puzzled indeed at the ways of modern youths!

Fundamentally the improved relations were only one token of a
changed mentality. A strong and widespread feeling of resistance was
another. Few thought of surrender. To some extent this attitude was
probably an adjustment to conditions poorly understood and an unavoidable reaction to the bullying tactics of the Japanese. Resistance became
a way of life, taken for granted.[9] But among large sections of the people
there prevailed a positive and conscious will to hold out against aggression for the sake of national survival. This determination kept the people
going for many years under extreme hardships, made impossible appeasement of Japan, and led to the failure of Japan's puppet regime
of Wang Ching-wei.

Unity of resistance was an outstanding characteristic of China at this
time. The Japanese had seen this coming. Their renewed attack was
timed to frustrate it, but was too late. The strategy of "divide and rule"
was no longer applicable to China. Its failure had been demonstrated
in north China between 1933 and 1937, when the Japanese attempted
to create "autonomous" regions.[10] Now this very strategy itself strengthened unity. The Japanese hastened the consummation of the very thing
they were trying to prevent.

Resistance increased everywhere in China during the war. In some
areas it was stronger than in others, but no province ever went over to
the enemy. The Japanese, comparing their experiences of 1931 with

those of 1937, admitted that the Chinese had become much harder "to deal with," that the close cooperation between soldiers and civilians made victory difficult.[11] The changes met with in China were so considerable that the more rational members of the Japanese government were concerned over the prospect of a long-drawn-out war in China. But the army was determined to go through with the adventure, and the army had the last word.

The factors which had been effective in bringing about the national revolution were again effective: the awakening of the masses, the increasing political and economic influence of the small bourgeoisie,* the political leadership of the Nationalist intelligentsia; the mass activities of the peasants and workers. Anti-Japanism served as the immediate outlet for nationalist emotions. But nationalism, from being merely a compound of "anti" feelings — antiforeignism, antiwarlordism, etc. — had matured into a more fruitful, lasting, and positive loyalty to China — just in time to fortify the people for their sufferings during the years to come.[12]

The government took some time to catch up with the changed mentality and turn it to good advantage for the Chinese cause. During the first few weeks of the war, its appeals for help rather unimaginatively used the vocabulary that had become standard at Geneva. "Enlightened people the world over now realize that China is fighting not merely for her own survival, but also for world peace and for international faith and justice," exclaimed Chiang K'ai-shek in a pep talk.[13] But, as he found out pretty soon, the world was quite willing to let China continue the fight, all by herself. To the Chinese people appeals to international faith and justice must have sounded particularly hollow. Presently the tune was changed, not to be taken up again until the outbreak of war in Europe, and then it was for foreign, not Chinese consumption. References to the outside world now ceased. The emphasis shifted to the Chinese nature of the war, to the Chinese cause involved. "Ours is a war for the very existence of our nation. It is for the completion of our national revolution." Or again, "We must realize that China is in a revolutionary stage and our War of Resistance is really aimed at the fulfillment of the San Min Chu I and the completion of the Nationalist Revolution."[14] This became the major theme in public speeches.

Such appeals struck home. They revived the hopes and aspirations

* A small part of the bourgoisie, however, were collaborators with the Japanese.

which once had inspired the Nationalist revolution. Its ideals became the "war aims." For them, not merely for the expulsion of the Japanese, the Chinese were called upon to fight and to die. And they responded. Because the war was being fought on this basis, morale was little affected by the refusal of friendly powers to lend assistance to China's struggle.

Such assistance was eagerly sought by the government, notwithstanding the nature of the war as a Chinese one par excellence. At the end of August 1937 the League of Nations was informed of recent events. China avoided the term war and did not declare war until December 1941.* One reason was that the government was anxious to keep open all avenues of peace. It shared the widely held view that the Japanese army was acting on its own in China and that strengthening the hand of the civilian officials in Tokyo might yet prevent a general conflagration.[15] China's appeal on the basis of Articles 10, 11, and 17 of the Covenant remained without result. The appeal was renewed in 1938 and the issue kept alive before the League for another year. The unmagnificent result of all these efforts† was a pat on China's shoulder for resisting so bravely and the gift of three ambulances to assist in the fight against epidemics.[16]

The calling of the Brussels Conference by the signatories of the Nine-Power Treaty in 1937 to discuss the treaty's violation was more spectacular but even less consequential. Every government seemed annoyed that the signatories had to meet. Why call a conference which promised nothing but embarrassment to all concerned? None of the great powers was willing to assume responsibility for the conference. Poor little Belgium was prevailed upon to do so. Before the nations assembled, the smaller nations made it clear that they wanted the conference to do little and end quickly. They all indicated that they wanted no measures exerting pressure — that, in fact, they wanted no measures at all. Moral condemnation was acceptable. But what good could that do when an aggressor by definition has no morals? Even the Chinese had no illu-

---

* The Chinese in Geneva were hoping that the League would declare Japan an aggressor. Such a declaration would have prevented nations from proclaiming themselves neutral and withholding the shipment of strategic materials to both parties, a move which would have hit China much harder than Japan. — *Peiping Chronicle*, September 11, 1937.

† There was a story that, anticipating these results in the League, Great Britain, France, and Russia agreed on January 28, 1938, to assist China secretly if in return China would desist from bringing the issue before the League. — *China Weekly Review*, LXXXIII (February 5, 1938), 271.

sions about the usefulness of the conference. The signatories nevertheless met (with the exception of Japan, and with Russia added). They
talked for about two weeks, knowing all the while that in the end they
would merely reaffirm lofty principles which everybody would refuse
to apply.[17]

One other attempt was made, shortly before the Japanese attack in
1937, when the threat to peace had become clear, and continuing for
a few weeks thereafter, to obtain something like collective action. A
hangover from olden days, the balance of power game inside China
was applied. Once more commercial opportunities in China were described in glowing colors. Whoever would assist China could expect
special rewards. The Japanese, if successful, would never apply the
Open Door principle. It was up to the foreign friends of China to insist
upon their rights, to expand and to defend them.

When the exodus of Chinese mercantile and industrial interest to the
west started, the parallel movement of foreign interests into the interior
was solicited. China was rediscovering its west and tempting foreigners
with its unlimited possibilities. "Now is the opportune moment to respond to the invitation of the Chinese people who in spite of their sad
past experience, still believe in the open door policy as the best means
for the preservation of self-existence and the promotion of international
peace." But this bait caught nobody. The facts were, first, that foreigners
expected little interference with their rights from the Japanese, and,
second, that business with Japan boomed every time she went to war
with China.[18]

The Chinese government expected greater success from individual
negotiations with select nations. The situation in the world had turned
increasingly tense. Nations distrusted each other more than ever. In
last minute efforts to secure themselves, many nations maneuvered
frantically on the international scene. They had to make up for the time
lost in dreaming about collective security and indulging in pacifist luxuries. They rushed back penitently to the old-fashioned standbys which
had served selfish national interests, though not peace, so well: secret
diplomacy, dual policies, ententes, alliances, counteralliances. Few
nations knew quite where they stood or who their friends and enemies
were. The international scene was bewildering. China, unable to influence developments and forced to make the best of unpredictable situations, was faced with a very confusing picture. The government con-

cluded that in the cross currents of international politics, the most realistic policy was to count upon nobody and accept whatever help was forthcoming from whatever quarter, "friendships," "ideological affinities," or any other sentimentalities notwithstanding since they were rapidly proving false fronts. "Meeting kaleidoscopic changes with an unchanging attitude" was Chiang's description of the policy.[19]

The basic nature of China's wartime policy was announced as early as December 1937. "Appraising the outcome of hostilities," Chiang stated, "we are convinced that the present situation is favorable to China. The basis of China's future success in prolonged resistance is not found in Nanking, nor in the big cities, but in villages all over China and in the fixed determination of the people. The time must come when Japan's military strength will be completely exhausted, thus giving us ultimate victory." What Chiang was relying on, that is, was the weapons of time, mass, and space. This policy fitted nicely into the idea that the war was being fought for the completion of the revolution. It was based upon self-reliance, on Chinese means for a Chinese cause. It made the best of the difficulty of getting outside help and at the same time aroused the people so that mass and space did become effective. Foreign aid was therefore a secondary consideration. If it could be obtained — good; and no stone was left unturned to obtain it; but its absence would not break the will to resist.

One of Chiang's first steps was an attempt to restore peace through mediation. He approached the United States and got a sympathetic response. Owing to Japan's unwillingness to submit to mediation, however, the matter had to be dropped. From then on until December 1941 the idea of mediation was kept alive, more in foreign than in Chinese or Japanese minds. All nations had their own reasons for wanting peace in the Far East. Since these reasons were dependent on national considerations, the intensity with which the foreign powers desired peace changed with the world situation.

Germany and Italy were almost resentful at Japan's adventures. They felt that Japan's action was driving China straight into the arms of Soviet Russia. Worse, the more the Japanese committed themselves in China, the poorer they would be as allies in a conflict between the Axis and the Soviet Union. The Germans also resented Japan's interference with their commercial interests. The Chinese did their best to play upon this fact to prevent a unified Axis policy. Early in the war the Germans, with Italian acquiescence, were the most eager to offer Good Offices and bring about a settlement, pleasing themselves greatly in the role of the benevolent neutral. With the appointment of Ribbentrop to the Foreign Office and the increasing recklessness of German foreign policy, further attempts at mediation ceased. Only once more, in November 1940, did the Germans as spokesmen for the Japanese rather than as friendly neutrals warn China that the last chance to make peace before the end of the European war was approaching. This step did not come as a great shock to the Chinese, preceded as it was by the establishment of a still closer tie to Japan in the form of the German-Italian-Japanese Alliance of September 1940. Neither had the alliance itself been very much of a shock. The Chinese deplored the loss of German sympathy. But they calculated that Germany would be unable to lend any concrete assistance to Japan. In fact, they argued, the alliance might turn out to be a blessing in disguise if it showed the British where Japan really stood and ended British appeasement of Japan. Furthermore they felt encouraged by the American agreement to "study" a proposal by Chiang K'ai-shek suggesting that quick American economic aid and aircraft manned by American volunteers might prevent China's collapse and enable the Chinese to prevent the Japanese from seizing Singapore or cutting the Burma Road.[20]

The Soviet Union never took a hand in mediation. In fact, it appears that Moscow disapproved of the idea unless peace could be obtained on the obviously impossible condition of a complete Japanese troop withdrawal from China. The Chinese did too good a job fighting Russia's battle.[21]

In the United States the possibility of mediation was discussed several times. But every time, for one reason or another, the moment seemed inopportune for action. Great Britain, most anxious to avoid complications in the Far East, seemed inclined to buy peace at China's expense rather than obtain it through mediation. Only later, after Churchill had succeeded Chamberlain as prime minister and the political picture had changed greatly, did efforts at appeasement stop. Japan was then showing ambitions in the direction of Southeast Asia, and her involvement in China therefore became important to Great Britain.[22]

For the Chinese government the pursuit of peace was a very delicate matter. All its enterprises in this direction had to be undertaken in extreme secrecy. The popular temper would not have permitted a peace in which there was the slightest suggestion of a Japanese victory. The only possible terms from the popular point of view were those which would have proved unacceptable to the Japanese. This was the situation which frustrated all attempts to establish peace. There was no choice but to continue the war, and in its pursuit the government negotiated for assistance with a number of nations.

The Soviet Union was China's most fruitful source of supply. There were many clashes between Russian and Japanese troops in the border region of Mongolia and Manchuria. Relations between Russia and Japan varied between ice-cold and lukewarm. War was an ever present possibility. Self-interest motivated Russia's aid to China. In the League, Russia talked tougher than anybody else; also at the Brussels Conference. From the beginning of the conflict until December 1941 Russia supplied more material to China than all other nations combined. The Chinese had no illusions regarding the cause of this benevolence. "Russia realizes we are fighting her battle as well as ours and does not stint her support," said the Chinese ambassador in London.[23] But motives were irrelevant to the Chinese government as long as help was forthcoming (though they paid for it in the popular sympathy the help created for Russia).

The good relations between China and Russia found expression in the conclusion of a Non-Aggression Pact in August 1937. The pact was the result of lengthy negotiations which might never have had any result but for Japanese aggressions. That made the pact a political gesture against Japan, though such intent was denied, as is diplomatic custom. Before the shooting started, the Russians had made three proposals to China: China should call a Pacific peace conference; Russia and China should sign a non-aggression pact; and they should sign a mutual assistance pact. China had refused the first proposal as useless, since Japan would not participate. The third proposal was no longer discussed after the Japanese attack. The major purpose of such a pact to act as a deterrent upon aggression had become an anachronism, explained Sun Fo, president of the Legislative Yuan. Japan, so to speak, had called the bluff before it was perpetrated.*

The Non-Aggression Pact caused a stir in Tokyo. But quite needlessly so, for it was harmless. It was a gesture on the part of the Chinese prima-

* Wu (China and the Soviet Union, p. 264) explains that China did not want a mutual assistance pact because it wanted to remain at peace with Japan.

rily toward Russia rather than against Japan. The Chinese hoped to keep Russia at peace and on good terms and thereby to keep the Chinese Communists in line; they also hoped to guarantee a continued flow of Russian aid. The anti-Japanese implication was incidental.[24] The Chinese announced that the pact was the first step in the creation of a regional security system in the Far East, and they offered to sign a similar pact with the Japanese! They hastened to explain, especially to the Germans, still on excellent terms with China, that the rapprochement with Russia was on purely utilitarian grounds. China could not refuse Russian assistance. Accepting help did not mean accepting communism, nor did friendliness to Russia mean friendliness to bolshevism. Trautmann, the German ambassador, seemed convinced. He reported home that China was just buying where she could. Chiang's mistrust of Moscow was much too great to permit any true sympathy between the two nations. All the stories about China or the National Government's going Communist were an old Japanese propaganda cliché "which no one in the Far East believes"; it was true, however, that Japanese policy was driving China directly into Moscow's arms and that the Japanese should be warned to change their policy before it was too late.[25]

Subsequent events proved the ambassador correct as far as Chiang K'ai-shek was concerned. There were times of *rapprochement* and times of estrangement. In general, Moscow's relations with the central government remained diplomatically "correct." The flow of Russian goods and advisers continued until Russia herself was attacked. Then it diminished to a trickle. Moscow interfered only occasionally in China's internal affairs, namely, when Chiang seemed to crack down too hard on Communists. On the other hand, Chiang was never friendlier than he had to be in order to get the most out of the Russians. He never compromised with the Chinese Communists for Russia's sake. Even the conclusion of the Russian-Japanese Neutrality Pact of April 1941 did not affect relations. The astonishing Russian move caused bewilderment in China rather than anger. The continuation of Russian aid quickly laid to rest any Chinese fears. Furthermore, by that time the Chinese could watch the warped policies of Russia with slightly greater detachment. The amount of Russian aid had greatly diminished while the United States and, to some degree Great Britain, had inaugurated a policy which held out some promise for China.

British policy had aimed at the avoidance of complications as long as possible, which was about the spring and summer of 1941. The greater the threat to Britain's security grew in Europe, the more determined became that policy. It reached its apex in 1939 and 1940. Attempts at an understanding with Japan, going as far as attempts at an alliance, failed, though London seemed willing to pay almost any price to make them successful. In 1940 Great Britain felt obliged to close the Burma Road for three months, one of China's main routes of supply of nylons, perfumes, and war materials. In the face of Japanese demands and German successes, Britain had no practical alternative to this step.*

The Chinese, impressed by their own courage, did not quite see it in this way. They were highly critical of Britain's soft policy toward the aggressor (they themselves had not been any tougher, though, against the aggressor in Abyssinia in 1935). Chamberlain was despised as the appeaser who would go to any length to satisfy Japan at China's expense. When Churchill took office in May 1940, they were wondering how far he would be willing to compromise with Japan. They hoped he would recognize who were Britain's friends and who her enemies in the Far East. They appreciated Britain's position sufficiently not to expect a defiant anti-Japanese stand. But they thought there was nothing to prevent Britain from being more helpful to China.

The fact was that Britain had granted financial assistance to China in December 1938, several times in 1939, in December 1940, and in April 1941. Churchill promised the Chinese that he would not press Chiang for terms or negotiations with Japan against his will. That was the best Britain could do for China. She had ceded the initiative in Far Eastern policy to the United States. Without American backing she had to appease; with American backing she would be as tough as America dared to be. The Chinese were aware of this position. They watched United States (together with Russian) policy as the key to Far Eastern politics, to their future. That future was to be a rosier one, but mostly because of Japanese blunders.

* When Great Britain asked the United States point-blank whether Japan was to be appeased or resisted and declared she would be willing to follow the lead of the United States either way, the United States said neither yes nor no (Feis, *Road to Pearl Harbor*, pp. 70–71). Although called China's "lifeline," the Burma Road was a most inefficient means of communication, partly for technical reasons, partly because of widespread corruption and graft (which the generalissimo tried to stop without success) (Charles F. Romanus and Riley Sunderland, *Stilwell's Mission to China, United States Army in World War II, China-Burma-India Theater*, Washington, D.C., 1953, pp. 44–47, 60).

Initial American policy regarding the Sino-Japanese War brought disappointment to China. The policy was firm in the convictions expressed, but did not contribute to the defeat of Japan. The United States would not be moved to more than moral condemnation of the aggressor and ineffective diplomatic protests. Chiang, full of disappointment and resentment, told an American official that the world would long remember the British refusal to cooperate with the United States in 1931 and the United States refusal in 1937 to cooperate with Great Britain in the League of Nations. He did not indicate what the beneficent result for China could possibly have been from cooperation in doing nothing.

The lukewarm support of the United States and the appeasement by Great Britain in the first period of the war were the despair of many Chinese statesmen. They strengthened the hand of those advocating closer ties with the Soviet Union. Some of them, Sun Fo and many young intellectuals among them, wanted to parallel Russian policy even to the degree of collaborating with the Axis powers (other than Japan!).[26] But Chiang remained firm. In spite of disappointments, in spite of the fall of France, in spite of the closing of the Burma Road, and in spite of perennial uncertainty about American policy, he remained confident of eventual support — beyond loans — by the United States and Great Britain. His reward was long in coming.

It appeared that China's territorial integrity was not of vital concern to the United States, if "vital" be defined as "worth fighting for." Concerning Manchuria the fact was beyond doubt. The years 1933 to 1940 proved it true concerning China in general. The conversations between Japanese and American statesmen, the American protests to Japan, the speeches of officials from the president down, show concern only over American interests in China. These were to be protected. For the record, the desirability of maintaining China's integrity and the undesirability of illegal methods in international relations were mentioned. The Japanese were quite justified in assuming that they would have a free hand in China as long as they took care of American individuals and treaty rights.

The character of American messages and actions changed rather suddenly when Japanese ambitions turned unmistakably toward Southeast Asia. Until that moment, as President Roosevelt pointed out, "the Government of the United States consistently endeavored to persuade the

227

Government of Japan" that friendly relations with other powers were Japan's best policy. But with Japan's move toward Indochina American "persuasion" gave way to something much stronger.

Sporadically the United States had shown some interest in Southeast Asia before. In the Taft-Katsura agreement of 1905, for instance, the United States recognized Japanese suzerainty over Korea in return for a promise that the Philippines would not be attacked. The Manchurian incident of 1931, Henry Stimson reported, seemed a danger to the American government mainly because an attack might also be launched southward against Hongkong, Indochina, and the Philippines. This same concern came to the fore again after 1937, this time with increased force because of European complications.

For a while no action was taken. The reluctance to impose an embargo on certain war materials for Japan was explained officially as springing from a desire to prevent Japan from feeling obliged to obtain these materials forcibly from alternative sources, especially the Netherlands East Indies. But the Japanese, as they were warned in February 1941, "must clearly understand that the forbearance of the United States in this respect springs from a desire not to impel Japan to create a situation which could lead only to the most serious consequences." [27] This was strong language. It was the language which had become standard in official conversations by this time and which had never been heard in regard to Japanese action in China. More important still, talk was accompanied at last by action which hurt Japan. Before this the stiffening of American policy had been indicated by such gestures as the abrogation of the United States–Japanese commercial treaty and by moral and legal embargoes on exporting goods which Japan did not need much anyway. Now steps were taken which impeded Japan's war preparation and which strengthened the Chinese war effort (e.g., Lend-Lease supplies and an American military mission were sent).[28] The potency of these steps was in direct proportion to the determination of Japan to move south.

The United States clearly considered an attack upon Southeast Asia of greater importance to her vital interests than aggression in China. Several factors contributed, of course, to her reluctance to take a firm stand and act in the Far East: internal politics, the pacifist mood, the possibility of a two-ocean war with a one-ocean navy, the preservation of Japan against communism. But the basic outline of American foreign policy in the Far East as involved in global policy is clear; fundamentally the policy was unaffected by those factors because its historic origin dates back at least fifty years. The basis of it was the belief that a strong Great Britain was a vital necessity for the security of the United States. Great Britain to be strong must have undisturbed access to British resources in Southeast Asia, South Asia, and the Anzac powers, but not in China. As President Roosevelt put it, the American strategy of giving the British "assistance toward ensuring our own security must envisage both sending of supplies to England and helping prevent the closing of channels of communication to and from various parts of the world, so that important sources of supply will not be denied the British and be added to the assets of the other side." [29] Japan threatened this access, and the United States felt obliged to act.

These American considerations were no secret. By way of warning, the Japanese were told of them on many occasions, officially and by the highest officers of the government.

China had not much to hope for from this policy. She was, once more, expendable. The efforts of the Chinese government to obtain support could be successful only by accident, when they happened to fit the policies of other powers. This was the case when Japan moved south. Chinese resistance against Japan then became an important part of the effort to stop the Japanese movement. Suddenly China became a factor, though still not a very important one, in the strategy of the Western powers. The fate of the Far East remained in the hands of Japan and the United States. The United States clearly defined her position to Japan: Japan had the choice of falling into line with the very broad-minded American concepts of a general Far Eastern settlement or of striking.

The possibility of the first choice greatly worried the Chinese. They had never been sure of American policy. Fears that the United States might buy security in the Pacific at China's expense did not die down until the day of Pearl Harbor. There were always those in Chiang's entourage who advocated reliance upon the Soviet Union alone or foremost, perhaps partly because of ideological affinities but certainly also because of the belief that Japanese aggression in China would always be considered a greater threat by Russia than by the United States. Even the use of such trite diplomatic jargon by the United States as that she had no territorial interests in the Far East began to be interpreted in China as meaning giving a free hand to those that had such an interest.[30]

229

The United States was ignoring too many appeals from Chiang K'ai-shek to suit the Chinese, was putting too much emphasis on the European war, was trying too hard to arrange a settlement with the Japanese.

November 1941 brought a climax. The United States was considering a modus vivendi with Japan. A truce was to be arranged, granting Japan considerable, though perhaps temporary, concessions on the Asian mainland and a relaxation in American action. This was unacceptable to the Chinese. They set in motion the full force of their considerable propaganda machine in the United States and Great Britain against the proposal. The president and secretary of state were irked at this Chinese expression of distrust (supported by the coolness of other powers to the proposal) in American policy and motives. But they gave in and abandoned the plan.[31]

To the Chinese the outbreak of war in the Far East seemed the lesser evil. It could hardly increase their hardships and might even bring some relief. They were pulling for a stronger stand of the powers, not appeasement. They found it difficult to understand the powers' benevolent interpretation (as they saw it) of Japan's policy, though they tactfully and prudently withheld outspoken comment. But the moment they realized the change in the attitude of Great Britain and the United States, they began to argue for the creation of a united front in the Pacific, consisting of the United States, Great Britain and the Empire, and the Netherlands East Indies. They were convinced that nothing else would deter the Japanese from aggression.[32] They may have been right.

17

The Alliance in World War II

THE outbreak of general war in the Far East had its pleasant aspects for the Chinese. It brought powerful allies into the struggle against Japan. The Chinese had high expectations of outside assistance and the position they were to be assigned in the Allied councils. Having been the first victims in World War II — a fact they liked to rub in — they claimed some sort of seniority right to special consideration.

Pearl Harbor was a great morale-booster. Talk in Chungking about the desperate situation and the possible need of suing for peace gave way to renewed hopes and increased effort.[1] The Chinese gladly subscribed to the humanitarian and political war aims of the Atlantic Charter and similar proclamations. The government promised full support in the war effort. A General Mobilization Act was promulgated, governmental organization was strengthened, one pep talk chased the other. The nation was to be streamlined for the most effective prosecution of the war. But where was all the extra effort to come from? Had not the Chinese themselves maintained that for seven long years they had prosecuted the war with Japan to the utmost? Chiang K'ai-shek disarmed all potential critics by frankly admitting that action in the past had been "partial and fragmentary and insufficiently thoroughgoing and widespread." He stated that "a searching review of the situation reveals that the spiritual and material strength of the nation remains at least fifty per cent and possibly as much as eighty or ninety per cent undeveloped. Now that we find ourselves allied to other friendly countries in a common cause, it is inconceivable that we should continue in such slackness."[2] This admission appeared all the more courageous because it confirmed the accusations of the government's opponents. Now, with the help of hindsight, one cannot help feeling that much of the spectacular ado was for foreign consumption, presumably to qualify for assistance and especially for equal, if not preferential, treatment.

On this last point the Chinese were extremely sensitive. Prestige as an ally was a prime consideration. Reaction to any suspicion of neglect was immediate and violent. Superficially China was rarely given cause for complaint. She was treated as a first-class power. Chiang was appointed supreme commander over all allied land and air forces in the Chinese theater. China became a member of the Pacific War Council, though not – to the generalissimo's great fury – of the Combined Chiefs of Staff.[3] She participated in the peace preparations at Moscow, Cairo, and Dumbarton Oaks. In 1943 Great Britain and the United States, with other powers following, relinquished extraterritoriality. The step was greeted by Chiang as a "beautiful and touching gesture." Japan, however, had stolen the Allies' thunder by relinquishing extraterritoriality just a little earlier.[*] Chiang's book *China's Destiny* showed that several more substantial remains of the unequal treaties would have to be abolished before China could be satisfied and her trustful friendship gained.

In a generally optimistic mood the Chinese indulged in postwar planning, the fashionable pastime of the period. They resented Churchill's failure, after the Quebec Conference in August 1943, to include them in his invitation of the United States, Great Britain, and the Soviet Union to another conference to make plans for a brighter future,[4] but this did not prevent them from making their own plans. The War for the Completion of the Revolution was to be expanded into a war for the recovery of all lost rights. Realistically the Chinese restricted themselves to this modest achievement rather than making a blueprint of the brave new world. Officially they demanded the return of all territories lost since 1895 and freedom for all the "submerged nations of Asia" – the diplomatic way the Asian nations have for putting their aspirations for leadership on the continent. Unofficially more specific discussions took place. Japan was to be disarmed and economically reconstructed so that she might rebuild China. Korea was to be independent, either in close cooperation with China or under United Nations tutelage, or at any rate there was to be some guarantee that she would not fall under the control of a wrong power. The Atlantic Charter was to be adapted to Far Eastern conditions. Thailand might have to come under a protectorate in view of her collaboration with Japan. The return of all Chinese territories and equality of international status were taken for granted. But nothing

[*] The *Oriental Economist*, IX (1942), 515, wrote, "Britain and the United States claim to have abandoned what they no longer held in any shape or form."

was said regarding Mongolia. Apparently ally Russia was not to be offended.[5]

The Chinese government lost no time in putting these plans into practice. It wanted to make the most of the favorable situation created by the entry of the Western world into the Pacific war. Taking given assurances at face value, it tried to draw the Allies into an immediate extreme effort against the Japanese, on a global basis. The Allies "must act on the principle of one for all and all for one," said Foreign Minister Quo Tai-chi in December 1941. "In other words, Germany and Italy should not be considered only as enemies of Great Britain and Russia, and similarly, Japan should not be treated only as the enemy of China, the United States, Great Britain, and the other members of the British Commonwealth. Consequently China has decided to declare war on Japan, Germany, and Italy."

At the same time, on December 8, 1941, Chiang K'ai-shek proposed a plan for the conduct of the war in the Pacific and Far East. There should be an alliance between the United States, Russia, China, and the British Commonwealth against Japan. The United States should propose a plan for joint war action by her, Britain, Russia, China, and the Netherlands East Indies. Even before Russia joined, the other powers should begin immediate action in the western Pacific according to a plan to be worked out in Chungking. Eventually there should be a mutual assistance pact among all the Allies. The Far Eastern war theater should have pre-eminence.

The initial Soviet reaction was sympathetic, but on December 12, Stalin informed Chiang that he could not consider the project for the time being. He assured the generalissimo that the Soviet Union would eventually fight Japan but that the war against Germany had overriding priority. The American reply to the proposal suggested conferences at Chungking, Singapore, and Moscow to work out preliminary details and expressed the hope that a permanent organization might be established.[6] Chiang, apparently anxious to have the Soviet Union join in the Far Eastern war, then addressed an almost open invitation to Moscow to join the war against Japan: "I strongly believe the spiritual affinity between our two armies is bound to become practical collaboration in action." To make the meaning quite clear, the official *Central Daily News* added, February 22, 1942, an appeal to Russia to take the initiative and strike first against Japan before waiting to be attacked. On a trip to India, also in 1942, Chiang espoused the cause of Indian freedom, but at the same time urged Indian leaders to join in the war.

Every effort was made to change the Allied plan of concentrating upon the defeat of Germany before Japan was tackled. Chiang's enthusiasm for fighting Japan suddenly reached unprecedented heights. Though he had been unable for years seriously to affect military action by Japan — for whatever reasons — the defeat of that nation was now presented as practically child's play. The Chinese, who should have known better, shared, or pretended to share, the widespread belief that Japanese tanks and ships were made of cardboard. Again and again Chungking assured the Allies that Japan could be eliminated in a matter of months.*

All kinds of arguments, moral, military, economic, were used to make "Japan first" the master plan of the Allies. The question of which was stronger, Germany or Japan, became the central argument in the controversy. But in China the conclusion was always the same — Japan first — either because she was weaker than Germany and could be defeated quickly or because she was stronger and the major effort should be concentrated on the Far East.[7]

The priority given the struggle against Germany and Italy strengthened China's suspicions that she was being neglected, and it was greatly resented. The defeat of Britain in Malaya and Burma, the initial weakness of the United States in the Pacific, created bitterness and disillusionment among the Chinese, even doubt as to the statesmanship of the Allies. If the United States and Britain allowed Japan free rein while finishing off Hitler, threatened Sun Fo, Chungking would question the wisdom of China's continuing the fight. Chiang also hinted again in June 1942 at a separate peace with Japan if his demands for American manpower and supplies were not met.[8]

To some degree the Chinese government itself contributed to the low esteem in which China was held by the Allies, at least from a military standpoint. Hardly had the war broken out when cries of desperation began to emanate from China, creating the impression that she was in her last gasps — unless Allied help forthcame immediately. These calls for help continued throughout the war. Chiang obviously aimed at preserving his forces for the foreseeable struggle with the Communists,

---

* One motive behind this campaign was to convince the Allies that they did not have to buy Russian support at China's expense. — T. F. Tsiang, in the *New York Herald Tribune*, January 21, 1949.

whom he feared most, leaving the major battles with the Japanese to the Allies.[9] At the first opportunity the Chinese had thus returned to their habit of playing upon sympathy rather than relying on respect for China, in spite of the fact that this practice had never produced good results and that resistance against Japan had created a good deal of respect abroad. It was the old diplomatic game of "poor old China," too weak to defend herself against her predatory neighbors and needing somebody to fight her battles.*

In 1942 the isolation of China led indeed to the worst position she found herself in during the war with Japan. But the unending and often unreasonable calls for help created the impression that either a major effort was needed or that she had to be written off. With the prevailing shortage of materials in the West, the second alternative seemed the more logical. China became the victim of her own propaganda.

Quite apart from the tactical errors in Chinese propaganda, the actual or potential contributions China could make to the war effort were not valued very highly by American statesmen and by Churchill were considered almost worthless.[10] They could hardly have been very valuable considering the state of industrial development, the years of war with Japan, and the political chaos. The Chinese did not possess the wherewithal to fight a modern war, and their military achievements were correspondingly negligible. The best that can be said for them — perhaps it is all that can be said — is that they tied down a Japanese army of considerable size. A number of Chinese were trained for the air force and the infantry in China and India by American instructors. They fought bravely and proved once more that given the proper training and equipment, the Chinese make good soldiers.[11] But neither they nor the trickle of American assistance could make any fundamental difference in the war situation. How much the restoration of internal unity or the improvement of government might have improved the military showing of China can only be speculated upon. There can be no denying that the immobilization of large numbers of troops on both the government and the Communist side for the purpose of keeping each other under control hampered the war effort. But the chances are that the use of these troops would not have affected fundamentally the fighting against the Japanese.

* This sardonic observation was made by the *North China Herald* on October 22, 1921, p. 211, on the occasion of the Washington Conference. It was still true in 1942.

From this standpoint the heated discussion whether the Nationalists or the Communists did more of the fighting or whether the fratricide prevented China from defeating Japan is rather irrelevant, except for American politicians. Both sides fought the Japanese and each other. Neither of the two groups nor both together would presumably have been able to beat the Japanese before or after 1941. The equipment to do so would have had to come from the outside. To get such equipment to them would have necessitated defeating Japan first and breaking her blockade — after which, of course, there would have been no further need for China to fight her. Chiang K'ai-shek never doubted that the defeat of Japan — as distinguished from resistance to Japan — could only come from the outside.[12]

Judged by these criteria, the inclusion of China in the ranks of the first-class powers — a step formalized at the Cairo Conference in November 1943 — was quite unrealistic. The artificiality of this position affected China's relations with the Allied powers, leading to annoyances and friction which were, of course, never permitted to come into the open. The pleasant picture of friendship in arms and the promise of an agreeable common future were not spoiled until almost the end of the war. They were needed as a prop to Allied and especially Asian morale, and for a while the American government appears to have accepted them as the real thing.[13] But when, behind the scenes, the jockeying for postwar positions began among the Allies, the inferior position of China in fact was very well taken into consideration in the policy of the powers. Before that happened, however, dissatisfaction, even tension, among the Allies developed over questions of much more immediate significance than China's postwar status.

For China, politically and socially, the period of the war from 1941 to 1945 was characterized by a steady deterioration of the internal situation. Innumerable causes were responsible. Some, like the corruption, the profiteering, the politicking, the intriguing, the disregard of public welfare and the resulting injury to Chinese society, could be blamed upon the men and the traditions involved. There were too many men in the government from the tuchun regimes, and their influence could not be overcome by the new officials who joined the administration during the war.[14] Other causes, like the absence of material resources and the isolation from the world, could be blamed upon circumstances beyond the government's control. The most fundamental causes were the social cleavages rooted in the transformation of China during the past hundred years. The mass of the people, little inclined to analyze and differentiate the reasons for their misery, tended to make the government responsible for all their ills, with the consequence that its standing grew constantly worse. This played directly into the hands of the Communists.

The Communists, however, were not docilely waiting for people to come over to their side. With considerable diplomatic support from the Soviet Union, they pursued a policy of moderation. In the name of the United Front, they demanded material support from the government and abroad, the better to be able to fight the Japanese. In fact, even while they fought the Japanese, they were eagerly engaged in fortifying their positions in their own and in Japanese-held territory, against the day when Japan should be defeated and their campaign against the Kuomintang government might be resumed fully and openly. They never relaxed their propaganda against the Nationalists, and throughout the war they continued their sporadic fighting against them. In the areas under their control they created conditions which led the Chinese living elsewhere to believe that the Communist regime had more to offer than the Kuomintang. Communist propaganda saw to it that this impression was strengthened. The rapidly increasing area and population under Communist control can be taken as evidence that Communist methods were successful.[15]

This fact made the split between the Communists and the National Government increasingly significant and definitive. For the stronger the Communists became, the more difficult would be conciliation between the antagonists and the more devastating the civil war, which had never died down completely and which constantly threatened to resume in full strength.[16] Considering the nature and tactics of the Communist party, unification became increasingly unlikely. Nevertheless many governments did not give up hope. In the early years of World War II Chinese disunity was accepted by them as a *fait accompli* which would prevent any considerable Chinese contributions to the war effort, but which, on the other hand, was not vitally harmful to the conduct of the war. When, however, the Japanese felt obliged to resume their campaign in China in 1944 and penetrated with great ease deeper into China, the United States government in particular became greatly concerned with the advanced stage of deterioration in China, partly for military reasons and partly for political reasons having to do with postwar relations between the Soviet Union and the United States. Washington asked Chiang for permission to take a hand in the internal conflict.

In 1944 Henry Wallace led the line of United States representatives who, until 1947, tried to mediate between the Nationalists and Communists and until 1949 tried to influence the course of events in China. They all failed either to strengthen the National Government or to bring about a compromise, just as American aid failed to prevent an economic collapse, though it sustained the economic welfare of a few individual Chinese!

On both sides and at all times the acceptance of America as a go-between was at best half-hearted. It was based on expediency, with a view to gaining time or obtaining American aid, never on an enthusiastic approval of American efforts. The so-called liberals, the small group squeezed between the Kuomintang and the Communists, heartily disliked the attention paid abroad to Chinese politics. They feared foreign intervention and China's becoming a second Spain. Any kind of intervention seemed undesirable to them. China should be let alone to work out her destiny. American activity, especially after American troops entered China, would hamper rather than promote civil peace.[17] The Kuomintang was the party the most willing to accept American mediation, though suspicion and criticism could be found within its ranks too. Only two or three very minor political groups fully welcomed American mediation. On the other hand a number of those who counted themselves among the liberals, such as Mme. Sun Yat-sen or Lo Lung-chi of the Democratic League, were so antagonistic to the Kuomintang government that they did not hesitate to cooperate with the Communists. As a result it was never quite clear whether these liberals genuinely expected a compromise between the two antagonists, whether their first concern was to prevent an artificial prolongation of the Kuomintang regime on the basis of American assistance, or whether they cared less about which party would emerge victorious than that there should be no foreign intervention in China.

The Communists throughout the efforts at mediation were critical of American policy, though until the middle of 1946 General Marshall was personally exempted from their customary vilifications and praised as a fair-minded and impartial man. The only compliment paid to American "imperialism," as compared to the Japanese brand, was that it was stronger and appeared more legal and civilized on the surface. The party line as it emerged from the Chinese and Russian papers was that there should be no interference in internal Chinese affairs, that the Big Three Moscow agreement of 1945 to this effect should be strictly adhered to. When during 1946 this line was supported by increasingly vicious attacks upon the United States and upon General Marshall personally, it was evident that the Communists found it inopportune to participate even formally any longer in the attempt to settle the civil strife through mediation.[18]

The basic reason for the failure of American efforts was that neither side wanted a compromise. Each was struggling for exclusive control over the nation. There was no willingness to surrender that fundamental objective. The occasional restraint which both sides imposed upon themselves was caused either by tactical considerations or the need to oppose Japan. It is clear that the Communists never, and it is doubtful whether the Nationalists ever, restrained themselves because they honestly desired a coalition government. Their struggle had never ended since 1927, and the war against Japan could not seriously affect it. The prize was absolute control of China. The result was that no important constructive enterprises could be embarked upon, hence the perpetuation of the country's material and political weakness. Sun Fo, as prime minister, put it this way in his New Year's message of 1949: "Unfortunately, all the parties concerned could not completely abandon their own selfish ends." And Li Tsung-jen, as acting president of China, confirmed the same view in a letter to President Truman, dated May 5, 1949, when he spoke of General Marshall's efforts as mediator: "All this work was unfortunately rendered fruitless by the lack of sincerity on the part of both the then Government and the Chinese Communists."[19] This is the situation which explains, though it does not condone, the inferior role China was assigned in the Second World War by the Allies; it is what made possible the Yalta Agreement of February 11, 1945, which inaugurated — but by no means caused — the tragic chain of events in the Far East during the postwar period.

18

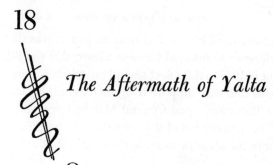

The Aftermath of Yalta

ON FEBRUARY 11, 1945, a secret agreement was signed at Yalta between Roosevelt, Churchill, and Stalin, with which Russia's entry into the war against Japan was bought. The price was the preservation of the status quo in Outer Mongolia; the restoration of former Russian rights "violated by the treacherous attack of Japan in 1904" — namely, the return of the southern portion of Sakhalin, the internationalization of Dairen, with the safeguarding of Russian "pre-eminent interests," the lease of Port Arthur as a Russian naval base, joint operation by China and Russia of the Chinese Eastern and South Manchurian railways, with the safeguarding of Russian "pre-eminent interests," and Chinese sovereignty over Manchuria; finally, Russian possession of the Kurile Islands.

President Roosevelt was to obtain Chiang K'ai-shek's agreement to the arrangement. The generalissimo had already agreed at Cairo in 1943 to make Dairen a free port, with the proviso that the Soviet Union should cooperate with China in the Far East and that there should be no impairment of Chinese sovereignty.[1] The rest of the stipulations were complete news to the Chinese government when it was apprised of the secret agreement in June 1945.* President Truman tried to break the news gently. He told T. V. Soong of Stalin's assurance that Russia had no territorial claims against China and would work with the Kuomintang government because, Stalin had said, Chiang was the "only Chinese leader capable of bringing about the unification of China." He also mentioned Stalin's willingness to have Kuomintang administrators come to Manchuria or China, wherever Russian armies might be, to set up a Chinese administration in the liberated areas. Soong was worried about the lease of Port Arthur to the Russians because this was closely reminiscent of the old system of leased ports. He also told Admiral Leahy that

* It is possible, however, that the Russians informed the Chinese government of the Yalta Agreement before the United States did.

240

China could not accept the intended degree of control over Manchuria promised the Russians in the Yalta Agreement. China, he said, would prefer to settle the controversy by military action during the "next five hundred years." [2]

These American-Chinese conversations were purely academic, since the Yalta Agreement provided that the Russian claims should be "unquestionably fulfilled." China was faced by a *fait accompli* of the worst kind. Here was a reverting to the practice of the big powers, which China had fought for decades, of making deals at China's expense without consulting China; worse, all the great powers seemed united in conspiring against her. This blow was all the harder as the Chinese had convinced themselves that their contribution to the war effort had definitely raised them to the status of a great power. But there was little they could do now. Action on China's part was prejudged.

When T. V. Soong and later his successor Foreign Minister Wang Shih-chieh went to Moscow in July and August 1945 to negotiate the pact of friendship and alliance foreseen in the Yalta Agreement, the basic outlines of the treaty were set. Only within narrow limits could the Chinese hope to ease some of the conditions agreed upon by the Big Three, while the Russians were quite determined to make the most of them. Because of the American share in the Yalta Agreement, the United States government insisted on being currently kept informed of Sino-Soviet conversations and consulted before the signing of the treaty.

From the very beginning of the conversations the United States felt concern regarding Soviet intentions. The government therefore made clear its position that the Yalta Agreement should be complied with, "no more, no less." Ambassador Harriman in Moscow kept in close touch with the Chinese. At the Potsdam Conference in July 1945 President Truman told Stalin that the United States insisted that Dairen should remain an open port, to which Stalin agreed, while Stalin hinted that the United States should urge Chiang to accept promptly the Russian proposals. Feeling the need further to strengthen the backbone of the Chinese negotiators, the American government sent a note specifically advising against concessions going beyond the Yalta Agreement. The total effect of the American effort to counteract Soviet pressure was to reduce Russian demands somewhat, but the final version of the Sino-Soviet treaty was still as favorable to the Soviet Union as the framework constructed at Yalta would permit. Russia obtained a much stronger position, and obtained it legally, than the United States thought she had bargained for. Belated American efforts to regain some of the lost ground by inducing Russia and China, for instance, to guarantee the Open Door in Manchuria, were in vain.[3]

In their Treaty of Friendship and Alliance, Russia and China undertook to fight Japan and not to enter into any negotiations with Japan without mutual consent. They agreed jointly to take all measures after the war to render impossible a repetition of Japanese aggression. If one of the two parties was attacked by Japan, the other would render every possible assistance. Neither of the two parties would participate in an alliance or coalition directed against the other. Both agreed to cooperate for the sake of security and economic development in the postwar period, with scrupulous regard for each other's sovereignty. In a supplementary note the Soviet Union promised to render all moral aid and material supplies "to the National Government as the central government of China," to recognize China's sovereignty over Manchuria, and not to interfere in the internal affairs of China as they related to Sinkiang.

In addition to the treaty, a set of notes were exchanged, referring to further agreements. After the defeat of Japan, a plebiscite was to be taken in Outer Mongolia to find out whether the population desired independence. This plebiscite took place in October 1945 and, to nobody's surprise, went in favor of "independence" * — in practice meaning that the status of Outer Mongolia as a Soviet Russian satellite continued as established in 1924.[4]

Regarding Dairen it was agreed that China should lease one half of the wharves and warehouses to Russia free of charge; that the administration should belong to China but the harbor-master should be a Russian; and that during a state of war with Japan, Russia should have military control of Dairen. In regard to Port Arthur an agreement was reached which made the port a naval base for joint Sino-Soviet use and put it practically under complete military Russian control. Another agreement provided for the joint operation, but with Russian influence prevalent, of the Chinese Eastern and the South Manchurian railways, now called the Chinese Changchun Railway. All these agreements were signed for a term of thirty years.

* On February 13, 1946, in a Treaty of Friendship between China and Outer Mongolia, diplomatic relations were established. But diplomatic envoys were exchanged only after the Communists seized power in China, and until that time no Chinese were admitted into Outer Mongolia. — Far Eastern Economic Review, XIII (1952), 291.

The Chinese officials who had to conclude the treaty and the accompanying agreements, but could not disclose to their people why, put up a bold front and announced that the arrangements were in the best interest of China, a guarantee of peace in the Far East, and in accordance with Sun Yat-sen's principles and ideals. These were phrases taken from the Chinese diplomatic textbook. But they were not altogether devoid of some conviction. Chiang K'ai-shek had told various American officials — Henry Wallace among them — that he desired a friendly understanding with the Soviet Union and that he would go "more than halfway" to reach such an understanding. The reasons for his desire were simple enough. The Chinese hoped that by satisfying Soviet demands they might induce the Soviet government to honor the promise of recognizing the central government as the only Chinese government. They also argued that obligating the Soviet Union to something by a treaty was better than leaving her a free hand. Finally, and most important of all, the National Government expected that if its policy satisfied the Soviet government, there would be no need for Moscow to support the Chinese Communists.

T. F. Tsiang, chairman of the Chinese delegation to the United Nations, explained in 1952 that "the Chinese Government and people were not blind to the meaning of the Yalta Agreement." But, in their opinion, "even if positive assistance from Soviet Russia might be too much to expect, at least the Government of the Soviet Union could not and would not pursue towards China a positive hostile policy in view of this treaty. Although the price China had to pay for the Soviet absence of ill-will was indeed high, it was felt that the price was not without compensation. It was under such psychological conditions that my Government yielded to the pressure of the Government of the United States in accepting the substance of the Yalta Agreement. Today," Tsiang concluded sadly, "we must pronounce the Yalta Agreement a great mistake, a disastrous mistake." [5]

The Chinese people, overwhelmed by official speeches and politically uninfluential, took the treaty and the agreements in their stride.* But the

---

* The initial reaction to the treaty and the agreements in the United States, official and private, was also favorable. For instance, Alfred Kohlberg wrote in the *China Monthly*, VI (1945), 14–17, that the treaty and the agreements were "the tangible results of the efforts of President Truman and his advisers at Potsdam to induce the Russians to greatly reduce their original demands on China . . . The success of our Administration officials is deserving every possible praise." Disillusionment set in by the fall of 1945, when it became clear how the Soviet Union

inevitable explosion was merely postponed. It came when the secret Yalta Agreement was published in February 1946. The Chinese Foreign Office tried to cushion the shock by announcing that as China was not a party to the secret Yalta Agreement, she was not bound by it, but that the Sino-Soviet treaty would have to be kept. The people could not be deceived by this legalistic subterfuge. They realized the meaning of the treaty and showed their utter disgust by attacking the Communists, demonstrating against the government, and protesting to the Soviet Union.

Chiang's government became the target of bitter attacks. It had to accept criticism of a position which presumably it had taken unwillingly but which political reasons forced it to praise highly. Besides, the government was genuinely afraid of Russian imperialism and saw no other chance of opposing it at that moment than by limiting its effects through the treaty. Privately, Chinese officials made it known that they considered the Yalta Agreement another despicable deal at China's expense and that only China's delicate position vis-à-vis the United States and Russia prevented open criticism. The Soviet Union was the main target of Chinese complaints. But the prestige of the United States also sank to a low ebb, and American attempts to bring internal peace to China were hampered by Kuomintang accusations that the United States herself was pushing China into the arms of Russia and the Communists.[6] How strongly the Yalta Agreement rankled under the surface in official circles became evident as time went on. More and more the Kuomintang press pointed out how the agreement had damaged the Chinese people. Eventually officials demanded American support as an atonement for the betrayal at Yalta.

Only the Communists did not consider the agreement a betrayal. They welcomed it and the Sino-Soviet treaty as most fortunate events for China. The Russian privileges, they explained, were necessary to keep Japan under control, to ward off the United States, and to prevent Chiang from getting into Manchuria. In reality, they commented, Russia's policy was anti-American and anti-Chiang, not anti-Chinese, because preventing the Kuomintang from gaining full control in Manchuria was equivalent to assisting the Chinese people.

The international situation of China at the opening of the postwar era was sadly reminiscent of many preceding ones which she had been un-

would implement its promises. Cf. Kohlberg's article in the *China Monthly*, VII (1946), 193–195, and the American Embassy report from Moscow, Department of State, *U.S. Relations with China*, pp. 122–123.

able to handle for her own benefit. Russian imperialism, determined and aggressive, was once again threatening from the north. Opposition could hardly come from an emaciated China. Yet the foreign powers that might have aided her were the very ones that had allowed Russian imperialism its head start in Manchuria. China herself was split. Foreign policy, instead of being an attempt at preserving the nation's welfare, became the football of the political game. The situation this time was aggravated in two ways. First, the reduction in the number of nations vying for position and influence in China and the growing polarization of power between the United States and the Soviet Union seriously limited the Chinese in their traditional political maneuvering; now there were only two rivals that could be played against one another. Second, one of the two leading factions within the country, the Communists, considered the defense of the Soviet Union of at least equal importance to the defense of their own country. In other words, there was not even the minimum agreement among all Chinese that foreign intervention should be resisted as a matter of principle or, if resistance was impossible, should be used as a means, never to become an end.

Faced by what seemed momentarily a front united against China, there was no risk in Foreign Minister Wang Shih-chieh's statement in March 1946 — for the diplomatic record — that the old Chinese balance-of-power game was ended, that China would stand for what was right and oppose what was wrong in any circumstances. Sun Fo, more frankly and honestly though less moralistically, stated that in the struggle between the powers China must adapt herself to the situation most advantageous immediately or in the long run and that there could be no alliances for sentimental reasons, but only for the national interest.[7]

In the search for a solution to China's foreign problems, the government's fundamental preoccupation was its own survival. Survival required primarily the defeat of the Communists, which could be promoted by enlisting the aid of the United States and at least preventing the Soviet Union from giving the Communists support. If the Chinese government wanted to get aid from the United States, it could never swing very far away from American policy. If it wanted to keep the Communists under control, it could never tie itself seriously to Soviet policy, since a condition of Russian aid would have been a coalition government with the Communists, which was not desired. In effect, then, China's policy amounted to siding with the United States, though not so openly as to make peaceful relations with the Soviet Union impossible. Neither could it be so fully as to expose any threat of closer ties with Russia as a blatant bluff for the purpose of blackmailing the United States or to eliminate any criticism of the United States on such questions as American policy in Japan.

Within the framework of this policy the art consisted in finding the right shades of closeness to one or the other side. Since this was a matter of reaction to American-Russian relations — in other words, a matter of subjective evaluation — the door was opened to much difference of opinion both within and without the Chinese government. During these years the greatest variety of counsels could be heard in China. Greater friendship with the United States and closer cooperation with the Soviet Union were both advocated. Sometimes the same people would advocate first the one, then the other, not necessarily always to play one power against the other, but out of a genuine repugnance to the policies of both. The right wing of the Kuomintang and its followers severely criticized the government for its "weak-kneed and impotent policy" toward the Russians. The government defended the policy as best it could on the grounds of realism. Russia was a big neighbor; not only could she herself interfere forcibly in Chinese affairs at any moment, but she had at her disposal a fifth column whose use had to be prevented. Another group felt that the government was not doing enough to establish friendly relations with the Soviet Union. Such relations, it was thought, were needed as a counterweight to American policy, against which many Chinese had a number of complaints. To this group the government catered by its occasional criticisms of United States actions in the Far East and by the frequent threats of closer cooperation with the Soviet Union if the United States should fail to grant China what she wanted. In addition to these groups, who subscribed in principle to a balance-of-power policy, there were, of course, those who favored a more independent Chinese course altogether. They wanted less opportunism in China's friendship with either the United States or Russia and branded the foreign minister's as a "kow-towing policy" which would gain China nothing.

The consistently antagonistic policy of the Soviet Union and the expectation of help from the United States always guaranteed a modicum of sympathy for American policy. The fact remains, however, that at no time between 1945 and 1949 was a pro-American policy announced unconditionally. Chinese spokesmen qualified their avowals of friendly relations with the United States. There were hints that "unless" American help was forthcoming quickly enough, or "if" that help was inadequate, China might have to turn to the Soviet Union. Lest their threats be taken too seriously in the United States, it seemed that, whenever the Chinese government had supposedly decided to veer toward the Soviet Union, carefully prepared leaks let out this news together with the comment that such a dire eventuality could be prevented by more help from the United States.[8]

The finality of the split between the American and the Russian camp and the increasingly desperate internal situation of the National Government put an end to this policy early in 1949. Thereafter the Chinese Nationalists definitely and irrevocably had to choose sides. They were then in the position in which the Communists had found themselves all along. The Communists could hardly threaten the Soviet Union, even as a bluff, with the possibility that they would side with the United States. They did succeed for a while, with the cooperation of the Kremlin and by United Front tactics, in creating the impression that they were no real Stalinist Communists at all, but merely agrarian reformers. And they did pay their respects, perhaps honestly meant, to the integrity and reliability of individual Americans, such as General Marshall when he was in China. But these are weak points to support the thesis that they once tried to come to terms with the United States.* All the documentary evidence indicates that at no time did they ever forget their primary aim of gaining exclusive control of China, their basic affinity with the Russian Communists, and their fundamental distrust of the United States. And while there were differences of opinion between the Chinese and Russian Communists on doctrine, strategy, and tactics during the early phases of the Chinese struggle for power, they never seem to have disapproved of Russian foreign policy.[9]

For the Nationalists, who were responsible, of course, for the conduct of their country's foreign relations until the fall of 1949, international problems were not solved merely by the development of the long-range policy just described. The difficult task of applying it to specific situations had to be achieved from day to day.

* In Mao Tse-tung's report to the Seventh National Congress of the Chinese Communist Party in April 1945, the vague statement that Great Britain and the United States deserved China's thanks for fighting the Japanese and that the Chinese Communists desired friendship with all nations might conceivably be taken to indicate a desire for an understanding with the United States. But against this statement stand innumerable and very specific statements from the Communists attacking the United States on many grounds. Cf. van der Sprenkel, *New China*, pp. 140–141.

19

The Loss of Manchuria and Sinkiang

T HE long-term postwar policy of the Chinese government was to gain American aid in forcing the Soviet government into "correct" behavior. The methods employed were traditional. The Nationalists, pretending faith in Russia's agreements, tried to be as friendly with this worst aggressor as possible and were willing to appease her. Simultaneously they tried to frustrate her intentions by enlisting the help of nations greatly antagonized by Russian aggression.

The Chinese government considered the restoration of sovereignty over Manchuria its most urgent problem. The problem, as so often before, was not a straight foreign-political one. It had serious internal-political implications on account of the position of the Chinese Communists in northern China and their close relations with the Russians. In the eyes of Chungking, the restoration of sovereignty over Manchuria was more important as a move against the Communists than as a goal of foreign policy. The Communists were considered a more immediate threat to China's welfare than was foreign aggression. This had been the interpretation of the National Government during the war; that it continued to be the interpretation was indicated by the government's postwar actions.

Unofficially the opinion was expressed in Chungking in 1945 that to give the Russians a share in the control of Manchuria would be preferable to letting it fall completely into Chinese Communist hands.[1] The Sino-Soviet treaties of August 1945 were justified by the Chinese government on those very grounds. Making a virtue of necessity, the government had hopes that in return for the high price paid, the Soviet government might fulfill its commitment to give all aid "entirely to the National Government as the central government."

Such hopes had been nurtured by the Chinese Communists when they held out the prospect of compromise during the summer of 1945 and even more by the Russians, when Premier Stalin and Foreign Minister

Molotov denied any affinity with the Chinese Communists and assured the highest American officials repeatedly that the Chinese Communists were not really Communists at all.[2]

The Nationalists were hardly deceived by such assurances. They had a deep distrust of the Russians.[3] But trying to make the best of an inevitable situation, they calculated that by giving the Russians what they wanted, they could quickly execute their part of the treaty and have their hands free to deal with the Communists. At any rate, they would regain formal possession of Manchuria, which was vital for a number of reasons. First, Manchuria in the hands of the Communists would have provided these with a valuable base and a first-class arsenal for their operations in north China. Second, Manchuria was assigned an important role in the economic reconstruction plans of the government. Finally, the reconquest of Manchuria had been a major war aim and to achieve it was an absolute political necessity for the Nationalists. The task was twofold: political, in arriving at an arrangement with the Russians, and military, in redistributing the Soviet, Communist, and Nationalist armies.

When the Japanese surrendered in August 1945, Manchuria was in the hands of the Russians. Only a few Chinese Communist guerrillas were scattered across the southern sections. South of the Great Wall Nationalist and Communist troops competed for the occupation of areas hitherto held by the Japanese. In this race the Communists had geographic advantages. As guerrillas they had infiltrated into these areas while the Nationalists were concentrated in central and south China, facing the Japanese. Consequently the Communists quickly established strong positions in north and central China, the region the Nationalists had to traverse in order to reach Manchuria. Whether the Communists would get there first depended upon the Russians; the Nationalists were unable to stop them.

The Nationalists' position was improved by the aid that as the legitimate government of China they received from the United States. An American program, begun before V-J Day and continued for some time thereafter, supplied the Nationalists with enough equipment to make their armies far superior to those of the Communists. Furthermore, to help the Nationalists accept the surrender of the Japanese troops, American ships and planes transported Nationalist troops to key sectors of eastern and northern China, directly into territory occupied by the Communists.

By September 10, Nationalist troops had occupied Shanghai, Nanking, Canton, Kukong, and Changsha. By the end of September they were in Peking and Tientsin. At the same time 50,000 United States marines entered Tientsin, and a little later, in October, entered Communist-occupied Tangku, Chinwangtao, and Tsingtao, to hold these places for the Nationalist armies. These arrived in Chinwangtao late in October 1945, reaching their closest station to the Manchurian border.

As was to be expected, wherever Nationalist and Communist troops met, friction and eventually fighting developed, often under the eyes of American soldiers. Before the year was over, civil war raged in eleven provinces south of the Great Wall. It kept important parts of the Nationalist armies engaged, without improving their position in regard to the occupation of Manchuria. The Communists prevented them from opening up any of the major north-south rail or water lines of communication and thus created problems of supply. The Nationalists, however, did not allow this serious impediment to interfere with their absolute determination to recover Manchuria.[4]

Lieutenant General Wedemeyer, commanding general of the China theater, looking at the situation in the cold light of military possibilities, was greatly worried. He found the Nationalists completely unprepared for action in Manchuria and warned Chiang K'ai-shek accordingly. He suggested to the generalissimo that all areas south of the Great Wall and north of the Yangtse should be consolidated and the overland lines of communications secured before the entry into Manchuria. These ends, he pointed out, should be achieved through political and official reforms, especially through the removal of corrupt practices in the government and the elimination of prohibitive taxes, evils which were already losing the government the vitally needed sympathy of the people. To save Manchuria for the legitimate government of China, he suggested to Washington the creation of an American, British, Russian trusteeship over Manchuria* until the Nationalists should be ready to take over.[5]

But by the time Wedemeyer gave his warnings, November 14 and 20, 1945, Chiang was already deeply engaged in preparations for taking over Manchuria. Before a military move could be made in Manchuria — preceding the creation of a civilian administration — the situation had

---

* Carsun Chang points out that Chiang might have accepted the trusteeship idea if it had been presented to him in 1945. The possibility seems unlikely in view of Chiang's great anxiety to take over Manchuria. — *The Third Force in China* (New York, 1952), pp. 251–252.

to be clarified with the Russians. In the course of the lengthy bargaining process which began in the early fall of 1945 regarding the military, political, and economic situation in Manchuria, it became evident that the Russians intended to interpret very broadly the rights given them in the 1945 Treaty of Friendship and Alliance and the accompanying agreements. They were much more eager to assure to themselves all possible benefits from the agreements than they were conscientious about fulfilling such less attractive conditions as the restoration of the territory to Chinese sovereignty or the withdrawal of their army by December 2, 1945. Moreover they used the dragged-out negotiations as a screen behind which to consolidate their own position. They closely coordinated their moves with the parleying, to the reciprocal advantage of each activity. All through the period of negotiations, which lasted until about May 1946 on most points and on some never ended — not, that is until the Chinese Communists took over on the mainland — their occupation of Manchuria gave the Russians a bargaining advantage which the Chinese could hardly countervail.

Some of the negotiations took place at the capital. Others took place at the generalissimo's headquarters in Changchun. The Russian representative in Manchuria was Marshal Malinovsky, the commander-in-chief. The Chinese delegates were Hsiung Shih-hui, director of the headquarters in Manchuria, assisted by Chiang's elder son, Chiang Ching-kuo, and Chang Kia-ngau, chairman of the economic commission.

One point of discussion was the joint control of the Chinese Changchun Railway. Negotiations proceeded smoothly, at times even in friendly fashion. When it came to putting agreements into practice, however, arrangements for joint operation broke down. Essentially what occurred was a division of the railroad administration into a Nationalist section in the cities and areas under Nationalist control and a Russian and Communist section in areas under Communist control.[6]

Another point of discussion was the transfer of Dairen from the Russians to the Chinese. A much less pleasant situation developed here. Russia had continued her occupation of the port on the grounds that the 1945 agreement stipulated military jurisdiction of the Soviet authorities at Port Arthur during times of war with Japan. Since no peace treaty had been signed, the Russians argued, they could stay in Dairen. When they finally agreed to let Nationalist civil administrators into the city, the Chinese Communists had surrounded it and were running its administration under the Russian aegis. The Chinese government therefore demanded that Nationalist troops should accompany the civilian officers. This the Russian occupation force forbade. In fact, regardless of the negotiations, it prevented either Chinese or foreigners from entering the city. American protests and requests to settle the question according to the 1945 agreement remained without effect. So did unending Chinese protests. The Chinese stated frankly that they were in no position to enforce their rights, which greatly encouraged the Russians to maintain their position. Continuing negotiations in Dairen were futile. They bogged down in legalistic quibbling. The Russians remained in the city, as they have even since the Communists took over the government of the Chinese mainland.[7]

A third point of discussion was the economic status of Russia and China in Manchuria, particularly the disposal of Japanese assets. Friction and difficulties over this point developed rapidly. According to the treaty and the agreements of August 1945 the Russians had no particular rights at all, but were, instead, under an obligation "to render to China moral support and aid in military supplies and other material resources." In regard to the Japanese assets, the Chinese government, fearing the worst, had already claimed at the London Conference in September 1945 "a liberal amount of and a high priority in respect to the total amount of reparations to be paid to the Allied Powers by Japan," and insisted that the Japanese public and private properties and enterprises in Chinese territory should be regarded as part of the reparations to be paid to China. The United States had fully endorsed this view, and the Soviet government had taken no exception to it.[8]

Yet by October 1945 it became known that the Russians were stripping Manchurian industries of equipment and machinery and carrying it away as "war booty." In complete disregard of the negotiations in progress, they took an estimated $858 million worth of goods, not including kitchen sinks and toilet bowls, which were smashed as symbols of capitalism.[9] The Russians did not deny their action, though they insisted that the value of the "booty" was only $95 million. They argued in a note to the Chinese government on January 21, 1946, that all Japanese enterprises in the Chinese Northeastern Provinces (Manchuria) which had rendered service to the Japanese army had to be regarded as Russian "war booty." Even if there had been any justification for this claim,[10] the amount seized was in no proportion to Russia's war contribution, for

252

the war in the Far East had lasted only a few days for the Russians. The American and British governments, supporting the Chinese, made known their view that the disposal of external Japanese assets was a matter for collective agreement among the Allies having claims to Japanese reparations. But they too failed to influence Soviet policy.

The only group that heartily approved of this plundering was the Chinese Communists, though the leaders experienced some difficulty in imposing their enthusiasm upon the rank and file. They found the procedure legitimate. The equipment was not taken from the Chinese people, they argued, but from the Kuomintang.* The Chinese people should not get excited. "National emotion" should not lead China into being victimized by anti-Russian propaganda.[11]

Russian economic ambitions in Manchuria went far beyond "war booty." Although Economic Commissioner Chang Kia-ngau announced at the end of November 1945 that negotiations were proceeding satisfactorily and that the taking over of Manchuria by the Chinese would "proceed smoothly," [12] it became known at that time that the Russians had submitted a list of demands for the "joint operation" of 80 per cent of all Manchurian industries. Chinese acceptance would have made of Manchuria a Sino-Soviet country instead of part of sovereign China.[13] The Chinese refused to give in, at least not without a bargain. Chang suggested to Malinovsky that in order to avoid any suspicion of negotiations under duress, the Soviet army should be withdrawn from Manchuria before these demands were discussed. But duress was what the Russians wanted. Malinovsky made it plain many times between November 1945 and January 1946 that the "joint" management of Manchurian industries was a matter of Russian "national security" and that until the problem of economic "cooperation" was solved, no schedule for the withdrawal of the Red army could be drawn up.† To frighten the Nationalists into

* However, this explanation does not seem to have been fully convincing. In due course the Communists rewrote history and explained in 1950 that the chief difficulty in the reconstruction of Manchuria was "the heavy damage which its industrial installations suffered at the hands of the Japanese invaders and their puppets."

† The withdrawal of the Russian army from Manchuria was originally scheduled for December 2, 1945. On that day it was announced officially that the National Government had asked for a one month's delay in the evacuation because Chinese Communist troops had made it difficult to introduce the Nationalist troops and administration into Manchuria. The exact background of this episode is not quite clear. It is reasonably certain, however, that the Russians were the originators of the idea. According to Carsun Chang, the Nationalists threatened to withdraw their

agreement, he hinted in addition at an independent Communist government in Manchuria.

However, the Chinese remained firm. Rather than give in to the economic demands of the Russians, they broke off discussions on this point. These were resumed in January 1946, and in February 1946 the backbone of the Chinese was strengthened by an American protest against the Russian economic demands on the ground that they violated the Open Door principle. In prolonged discussions Russia receded. She dropped all demands for any exclusive ownership of enterprises as "war booty" (though she did buy many private Japanese enterprises with worthless occupation money), and in the summer of 1946 she also dropped, "for the time being," her demands for partnerships.[14]

The Russian army in Manchuria partly failed to fulfill its function as a tool of pressure for economic concessions. But that had not been its only function. It had the second function of permitting the infiltration of Chinese Communists into Manchuria — an alternative way of the Russians of reaching their goals there. The Chinese government discovered this during its negotiations over the entry of its troops into Manchuria and the establishment of its civil administration. Of all the points under discussion between the two powers, this was the most important, for it involved, in effect, the restoration of Chinese sovereignty over Manchuria.

At first the situation looked promising to the Chinese. After two appeals by Chiang K'ai-shek to facilitate the taking over of Manchuria, the Soviet government promised toward the end of November 1945 that it would not interfere in the Chinese civil war, would not object to the advance of the Nationalist armies into Manchuria, and would honor its commitment of supporting only the central government.[15] Had it lived up to these engagements, the recovery of Manchuria by the Nationalists would have been an easy matter, for there were very few Communists to oppose it. Their threat existed in northern China. But in a number of

headquarters from Changchun. The Russians disliked that idea because such a withdrawal would have put them in an awkward position internationally, and they did not approve of a Communist government in Manchuria at that moment. If this explanation is correct, the Russians postponed the evacuation because they actually wanted to negotiate with the Nationalists. But it is also clear from later Russian policy that they wanted to keep their army in Manchuria as a means of pressure against the Nationalists and as a screen behind which the Communists could infiltrate into Manchuria. Manchuria was not evacuated until the end of May 1946. Cf. Chang, *Third Force in China*, pp. 164–165; David Dallin, *Soviet Russia and the Far East* (New Haven, 1948), p. 247.

254

oblique and devious ways the Russians circumvented or perverted every one of their engagements.

Their first and most important step was to allow Chinese Communist armies to infiltrate. Not as armies. That would have been contrary to the letter of the law, and they were conspicuously "legal." They let it be known that in August 1945 they had refused permission to Communist General Chu Teh to let Communist troops join the Soviet army in the liberation of Manchuria.[16] But they did not object to the infiltration of Communist soldiers as civilians, who, once in Manchuria, were permitted to help themselves to the arsenals left behind by the Japanese. By November 1945 a Communist army of several hundred thousand men had been formed in Manchuria, by this means and through accretion. It was referred to by the Russians as "nongovernmental troops" and called itself the Democratic Unity Army. It was a heterogenous force, composed of infiltrated Communists, local resistance groups, Chinese refugees returning from Russia, some Japanese, and some Mongolians. It spread all over Manchuria and especially along the southern border and the sea coast where the Nationalist armies would move in.[17] The Russians could now appear conciliatory at the negotiations and could even pretend to live up to their engagements, knowing full well that the Chinese Communists would take over the job of trying to nullify them in fact.*

There were reports in China in October 1945 that the Russians had permitted the landing of Chinese Nationalist troops in three Manchurian ports.[18] The facts turned out to be different. The landing in Dairen was forbidden by the Russians because the port was to be used for strictly commercial purposes. An American convoy bringing troops to Hulutao turned away because it was fired on by Communists who had taken over from the Russians. This left Yingkow. Malinovsky had agreed to permit troop landings there after the Russians should have evacuated the port on November 10. However, they evacuated before that day and let the Communists take over. A landing was prevented there too.† The Chinese troops were finally landed at American-held Chinwangtao.[19]

* There is sufficient evidence to prove that, with a view to expanding the power of the Chinese Communists, at the Political Consultative Conference in 1945, the Russians in their negotiations with the Chinese government were in collusion with the Communists in their negotiations with the government. — Chang, *Third Force in China*, p. 170.

† Early in 1946 Malinovsky ordered the Chinese Communists to permit Nationalist landings in Yingkow. There were no incidents. — Chang, *Third Force*, p. 165.

Only the land and air routes into Manchuria were now left at the disposal of the Nationalists. During the second week of November 1945 they started their march from Chinwangtao, presumably to be on the spot when the announced Russian withdrawal from the Great Wall should begin on November 10.[20] When they reached the Shanhaikwan pass, they found that the Russians had allowed the Communists to block the road from there into the interior. Frontal resistance was overcome, but the Nationalists were constantly harassed by raids upon their rail communications. By the end of November, they had taken Hulutao and were moving on to Mukden. Simultaneously, Chiang was negotiating with the Russians for flying troops into Manchuria, mostly to circumvent Communist blocks and raids.[21] After some very hard bargaining, during which the Chinese negotiators seem to have threatened to withdraw, the Russians finally allowed the air transport of a limited number of Nationalist troops and administrators into Changchun and Mukden, though not enough to be of real military value.[22] The Russians also turned somewhat more liberal in regard to moving troops into Mukden and other cities of southern Manchuria. It is a revealing fact that whenever the Russians permitted Nationalist troops to be landed at an airport or to enter a city, these troops were unmolested by the Communists, although the Communists were always nearby. The Nationalist troops had no opportunity of reaching northern Manchuria. Malinovsky told Nationalist headquarters at Changchun that as regards areas north of Changchun the Soviet army could not wait for the arrival of Nationalist troops and that therefore "local forces," meaning Communists, had to take over where the Russians left.[23]

By the time the Russian army evacuated Manchuria, the Nationalists were in control of the major cities and railways of the south. The Communists were firmly established in the rural areas and all of northern Manchuria, except the Barga region, which was in the hands of the Mongols. For some time the Nationalists do not seem to have realized their dangerous position. The Communists by their political measures were gaining the sympathy of the population, were not committed to any fixed military position, and lived off the land, whereas the Nationalists had to rely on unsafe communication lines to obtain their supplies from thousands of miles away and had no contacts with the masses in the country. They could not draw upon the resources of the land and actually had to supply the cities they held. They lacked the military and administrative personnel adequately to garrison and administer their holdings. Under such conditions, as the American White Paper on China suggests, their occupation "meant a loss rather than a gain." [24] This situation eventually was the beginning of their doom. Inner political necessity, their ambition, and the Russians' diplomatic and military maneuvering had conspired to bring it about.

The Russians emerged from the negotiations over Manchuria better off than when they went in. Indirectly they benefited by every advantage they had permitted the Chinese Communists to obtain. Their direct advantages were no less striking. They were in control of Dairen and Port Arthur and of the greater part of the vital Chinese Changchun Railway. They had established considerable economic interests. They did not have the form but they had much of the substance of power in Manchuria, and they used it to reinforce their position further as time moved on. In 1947 they created an "independent" Kwantung Administration in Dairen. In July 1949 they signed a trade pact with the Manchurian People's Democratic Authorities. The pattern of Soviet control became quite clear. Manchuria was destined to become a part of the Russian "safety belt," as Outer Mongolia had been for many years. Sinkiang was the only gap in the "belt" left, and the Soviet Union set out to turn it also into a satellite.

This goal could not be achieved, however, through an "interpretation" of the treaty of 1945, which had served the purpose for Manchuria. The Russians had committed themselves in 1945 to noninterference in China's internal affairs and therefore to staying out of Sinkiang and its involved politics. The treaty provided no opening through which the Russians could enter. They had to use indirect and subversive methods, which had already been employed both before and during World War II in the attempt to prepare Sinkiang for its satellite role.

In the recent past, generally speaking, the loyalty of Sinkiang to China or the Soviet Union has depended largely upon the person who happened to be governor of the province. From about 1932 to 1942 this was Sheng Shin-ts'ai. He had gained control under Soviet guidance and maintained a regime of virtual autonomy oriented toward the Soviet Union. But times were bad in 1942, when Germany invaded Russia, and few supplies came to Sheng from across the border. The voice of the Chinese government began to sound persuasive and, apparently, became irresistible when Mme. Chiang K'ai-shek in person flew to Urumchi to change Sheng's loyalty. Sheng reaffirmed his loyalty to the Chinese government. Russian advisers, trade agencies, and troops were withdrawn from the province. Relations with the Soviet Union were interrupted. In 1944 Sheng was recalled to Chungking, upon Russian demand, it was said, and promoted to a nominally high position. Chinese national troops were reinforced in Sinkiang, Soviet sympathizers were purged, and the central government regained control.[25]

But the government's success was not to last very long. Also in 1944 the Soviet Union resumed interest in Sinkiang and — perhaps by coincidence, more probably not — at the same time a revolt broke out in the Ili area against the Chinese government. Within one year the rebels conquered the country down to the Manas River and declared the three northwestern districts of Kulja, Chuguchak, and Altai the independent "Eastern Turkestan People's Republic." The remaining two-thirds of the province stayed under central Chinese control. The rebels had justified grievances, but without the moral and perhaps other support of the Soviet Union it is not likely that they would have gone so far.[26]

General Chang Chih-chung was sent to negotiate with the rebels. He did so, the Russian consuls at Kulja and Urumchi serving as intermediaries, a circumstance which lent credibility to Chinese claims that the revolt was Russian-engineered. In 1946 an agreement was reached in which some slight concessions toward autonomy of the Ili group were made. This was followed from the central government by a few mild attempts at improvements in the administration and occasional conciliatory gestures. But the after-effects of the corrupt, despotic, and mismanaged administration of Sheng remained too pronounced, and the number of Chinese and pro-Chinese officials too great to please the rebels. The Chinese reforms under the slogan "Peace, Unity, Democracy" carried no conviction. The rebels demanded independence and engaged in strong anti-Chinese propaganda.*

The rebel-controlled and the Chinese-controlled parts of the province remained divided into watertight compartments. There were no direct relations between the rebel territory and China. On the other hand, the rebel area had close relations with the Soviet Union. Sinkiang minerals

---

* A few years after Sinkiang had become Communist-controlled, this line was changed. The people were then told that their struggle had formed "part of the general movement of the revolution of the Chinese people" and that nationalism was "unjustified" under a Communist regime.

flowed freely to the west. All communications with the outside world went through Russian channels.

By the spring of 1949 a pro-Russian trend developed in the Chinese-controlled area as well. The Ili group used it immediately by pretending to veer toward the Chinese government and suggesting closer cooperation with the provincial government. The approach that took place between the rebels and the Chinese turned out to favor the Communists. For a few months later, in September, Sinkiang went over to them.

This was only one of several developments which permitted the gradual expansion of Russian influence and control over the province. There were also international complications which arose from numerous border incidents between Sinkiang and Outer Mongolia. In every incident the Chinese government considered the Russians involved and sent its protests to them as well as to the government of Outer Mongolia. Naturally the Russians never admitted any part, though they confirmed that the Outer Mongolians had Russian-trained pilots and Russian-made planes with markings "very similar" to those of the Russians.

The Russian explanations of the incidents varied. Sometimes they claimed the territory involved was not Chinese at all; or they claimed that the incidents had been provoked by the American consul; or they maintained that the Chinese had provoked them because they "liked what was going on in Greece" and wanted American aid. No settlement was ever reached, and until Sinkiang became Communist, the incidents continued, all, somehow, tending to favor the Soviet Union.

The Chinese government had been aware of this trend and tried to stop it. Simultaneously with its protests and angry outbursts, it tried to reach an agreement with the Soviet Union by which the Russians might be satisfied in return for withholding their support from the Chinese Communists or other groups friendly to Russia. Taking up a suggestion by the Soviet Union of early 1947, the Chinese early in 1949 began to negotiate treaties for trade, mining rights, and air communications. They hoped to kill two birds with one stone: by increasing but specifying Russian rights, they hoped to limit Russian penetration into Sinkiang and to strengthen their own hand against the Chinese Communists.

The reported Chinese plan was to give Russia a three-way monopoly: a monopoly on trade in Sinkiang's raw materials, in return for the supply of finished goods; a monopoly on mining rights, to be exploited by enterprises run jointly by Russians and Chinese; and a monopoly on civil aviation in the province. These proposals were not as radically new as might appear. In many respects they merely confirmed and legalized a situation which already existed in fact.

Since 1939 the Russians had had a monopoly on air traffic in Sinkiang (with the exception of a direct line, Urumchi-Shanghai), and their planes landed in several places controlled by the Ili rebel group. The Chinese National Assembly, in an attempt to put pressure on the Soviet Union, had called upon the government to cancel the 1939 agreement. The government announced its intention of doing so. But when the negotiations were terminated, an agreement emerged in which Russian privileges were extended for another five years, instead of the twenty-four asked for by the Russians. The government had not even succeeded in making the Hami-Ata line a less Russian and more Chinese affair.

In mining and trading the Russians already had a monopoly in the "Eastern Turkestan People's Republic" and wanted to extend it to all of Sinkiang. The Chinese objected on general principles. At the same time they wavered and were considering what concessions ought to be made to reach their political purpose of satisfying the Russians. The indecision reflected the split within the cabinet over the insoluble problem of how far Russia ought to be satisfied in order that it might stop supporting the Chinese Communists. No treaty was ever signed with the National Government. The Communist government later concluded agreements with the Soviet Union through which the Russians obtained in Sinkiang what they wanted.[27]

The Chinese government's position was indeed an unenviable one. Its attempt to stop the double-barreled attack by the Soviet Union and the Chinese Communists by appeasing the one in the hope of weakening the other was obviously a choice among evils. The policy had its opponents inside the cabinet and failed to find favor with large sections of the public. Yet with occasional rescues by Chiang K'ai-shek, Foreign Minister Wang Shih-chieh succeeded in maintaining himself and his policy in power against all attacks until early 1949. It was a policy in which the Chinese government relied on good relations with the United States to counteract bad relations with the Soviet Union. Depending upon the response from Moscow and Washington at any given moment, of course, relations with both had their ups and downs. The basic theme of this policy, as Wang described it, was close cooperation "forever" with the United States and "moderation" and strict enforcement of treaties with the Soviet Union.[28]

20

The Collapse of the National Government

THE "forever" cooperative policy toward the United States had one simple aim: getting as much aid as possible. The means were as traditional as they were unsentimental: direct requests, lobbying, and playing upon American fears of a Communist victory. The policy was successful to the amount of hundreds of millions of dollars between 1945 and 1949, in addition to military services and diplomatic support. Exactly how many dollars in money and worth of goods were supplied and how useful they were are matters of debate. The State Department thought about two, useful billions; the Chinese Embassy in Washington thought a billion and a half, not altogether useful; and the American China Policy Association thought one billion, mostly useless.[1]

For this material, military, and moral aid on various occasions the United States did not receive unadulterated gratitude from those Chinese who were to benefit by it. The Communists would obviously be opposed to any kind of aid from America. They were often joined by the Democratic League, which parallels Communist attitudes on many political questions. But frequently independent liberals and sometimes Kuomintang members were heard to be dissatisfied with American policy in China and the Far East generally. In all the craving for American assistance there could frequently be discerned a note of unhappiness at the same time. The necessity of relying upon the United States seemed to hurt Chinese self-respect, and feelings of frustration and indignation found expression in very severe criticism — sometimes justified, sometimes unjustified — of specific American actions.

There were, of course, other than psychological dissatisfactions at the bottom of Chinese criticism. A main object of Chinese displeasure was the status given Japan in the postwar world as a result of American policy.

Like most countries interested in Japan, the Chinese had a mission in Tokyo attached to the Supreme Commander for the Allied Powers. Its functions were practically nonexistent. It could not deal with the Japanese government directly and had no influence upon the supreme commander. The Chinese also were members of the Far Eastern Commission in Washington, which was to formulate policies for Japan, and of the Allied Council in Tokyo, which was to be the watchdog of the commission. The United States had reluctantly agreed to the creation of these two organs, considering them largely an unwarranted interference in what she regarded as her primary right to rule Japan. The functions of the two organs became rapidly insignificant because of the treatment they suffered from United States authorities. The mutual distrust of the American and Russian delegates further contributed to their unworkability. Attempts by the Chinese, as well as other delegates, to facilitate and expand the work of the organs were completely frustrated. The Chinese finally resigned themselves to their unimportant role.[2] But there was bad feeling, which increased as American policy toward Japan became more and more displeasing to them.

The American support given to many reactionaries in Japan, the development of Japan as a military base, the rumored restoration of the big, monopolistic enterprises aroused Chinese suspicions as early as 1946. The Chinese feared that Japan might again become the greatest manufacturing and trading center of the Far East, thus assuming the position that they intended to occupy themselves. They watched Japan being turned into the "stabilizing factor" of the Far East, which they themselves, as the victorious nation, wished to be. Japan was suspected of superficially bowing to every American wish so that in case of war with Russia she might emerge victorious on the side of the United States and have her empire restored as a reward. The Chinese were also worried over various aspects of American policy regarding reparations and territorial adjustments. While they were in this state of mind, their views on a peace treaty with Japan underwent a metamorphosis.[3]

Immediately after the war the Chinese had been willing to grant Japan a "soft" peace. Now they felt that they had to press for hard conditions, if only to counteract the increasingly criticized American "leniency." The strong and widespread dissatisfaction with American policy in Japan became evident in discussions provoked by the American invitation to the members of the Far Eastern Commission in July 1947 to hold a conference for the drafting of the preliminary terms of a Japanese peace treaty. Some rather radical demands by the Legislative and Control Yuans and similar organs of the Chinese government [4] could be restrained only with some difficulty by the cabinet. The desire to maintain friendly relations with the United States as well as not to antagonize the Soviet Union entered very largely into the formulation of Chinese policy. But it was quite clear from the statements made by responsible officials that they shared in some of the popular criticisms.

They still insisted that China had a "deep sympathy" with the new-born Japan and did not wish for a "peace of revenge." But at the same time they insisted that the reconstruction of Japan should not advance to the point where her rearmament or interference with plans for the development of Chinese industries would become possible. They seemed inclined to set this limit fairly low. In doing so, they occasionally found themselves in far-reaching agreement with Russian policy and at opposite ends from American plans. [5]

Resentment also came to the fore when the United States concluded a Treaty of Friendship, Commerce, and Navigation with China in 1946. Though the feeling was expressed primarily by the Communists, it was shared by many non-Communists. The most-favored-nation clause was opposed as reminiscent of the Open Door — a similarity for which "we cannot but express regret." It was pointed out that formal equality did not mean substantial equality when two greatly unequal nations were partners to the treaty. Conservative Chinese trade journals envisaged the possibility of the dumping of cheap American goods in China and of American imports to the detriment of the development of Chinese industries. [6]

To these grievances may be added the more imponderable ones stemming from the presence of American troops in China and from the general suspiciousness toward Westerners. The resulting dissatisfactions were, however, never permitted seriously to interfere with the direct pursuit of the fundamental policy.

As matters became worse within China, the need of American help became greater. Threats to turn to Russia could be heard more often, and simultaneously appeals to the United States became more fervent. Arrivals of Chinese propagandists and officials in Washington to start "drives around town" for help, to use Secretary Forrestal's words, [7] became routine. The inauguration of the Truman Doctrine gave them a special impetus. For when the Chinese government realized that the United States was willing to spend untold sums abroad to defeat communism, it began to appreciate the cash value of its Communist problem. Confident that few nations could boast of a better case, and to highlight it, the Chinese government now began to berate the Soviet Union at the risk of diplomatic complications.

Russia was openly accused of violating the treaties of 1945 and of assisting the Chinese Communists. The accusations were well justified. But hitherto, pursuing its policy of friendship, the government had been more discreet. At the same time, Chen Chi-tien, the minister for economic affairs, warned that the Communists might take over unless American aid was forthcoming. Two or three billion dollars was needed, he pointed out. Half of this amount would be needed to pay the armies fighting the Communists, the other half for political and military purposes. Since as a democratic nation the United States could not supply arms direct, the minister suggested, it would have to supply cash "to get around public opinion."

These addresses to the United States were accompanied by official self-criticism and resolutions to improve internal conditions and redouble the fight against the Communists, presumably to prove China a worthy recipient of American aid. In innumerable speeches Chiang K'ai-shek decried the corruption, defeatism, apathy, and spiritual deterioration of the government, the party, and the leaders of China. He held up to his followers the organization and the propaganda of the Communists as examples to be emulated.[8] He had good reason to be concerned. The general mobilization order against the Communists, promulgated in the early summer of 1947 as the beginning of a supreme effort, had met with very little enthusiasm among the peasants and lower classes.* Perhaps, as one observer put it, because they were already "half convinced that the Reds are their friends and not their enemies."[9]

The government's flurry of activity reached a height when General Wedemeyer went to China in the summer of 1947. His visit was hailed by the Kuomintang as the beginning of new, all-out American aid to the National Government. Only a few members failed to share this hope, some of them having very mixed feelings about an extension of the Truman Doctrine to China: they were afraid of unsympathetic public reactions if there was too much American "intervention." When the expectations of increased aid were not fulfilled, the disappointment in

* Some Kuomintang officials in southern Hopei advised halting conscription because most young men there had "Red ideas."

264

Kuomintang circles was tremendous. General Wedemeyer's conclusions seemed to add insult to injury. The general advocated in his reports to President Truman that all funds be withheld until the Chinese stopped blaming everybody but themselves for their ills and until a housecleaning had taken place in Nanking. His remarks in Nanking, on his departure, that "considerable time and effort has been spent in blaming outside influences" were interpreted by the Chinese to mean that he did not recognize the alleged Russian cause of China's difficulties.[10]

The general's mission evoked from the Chinese exactly the type of response he had criticized them for — namely, the blaming of everyone but themselves. They began to heap all kinds of reproaches upon the United States. They recalled that the root of all their international troubles was the American policy of bringing Russia into the Far Eastern war, against which the Chinese had warned Washington. They pointed out that the Yalta Agreement was the direct foundation of the country's present difficulties. They discredited General Wedemeyer's report,* although Chiang K'ai-shek had made very similar criticisms immediately preceding the general's arrival.[11]

The effect of General Wedemeyer's visit was to strain Sino-American relations.[12] The government promptly resumed the practice of threatening closer ties with the Soviet Union. These threats continued until the middle of 1948, at which time the internal political situation made its continuance patently absurd. By November 1948 the government's position had greatly worsened. Chiang K'ai-shek sent a letter to President Truman in which he blamed the deterioration of the military situation primarily upon the nonobservance of the Sino-Soviet treaty of 1945, which "the Chinese Government signed as a result of the well-intentioned advice from the United States Government." He then requested speedy and increased military aid and a firm statement of the American government's policy "in support of the cause for which my Government is fighting." [13]

This is the argument the Nationalists have used ever since in their demand for American aid.[14] It had multiple political usefulness: it lessened political criticism at home; it put moral responsibility for aid upon the United States; and it favored China in what came to be called the Great Debate in the United States. As the situation of the Nationalists

---

* The general's report was not published at this time, mostly because it again suggested trusteeship for Manchuria. The Chinese reaction to his informal remarks may well have been an attempt to discredit the report in advance of its publication.

became desperate, the theme was expanded and elaborated upon. Not only was the United States criticized for withholding adequate help, but by many Chinese and their American fellow-travelers Washington was blamed for almost all of China's ills.

This practice of first relying on outsiders and then putting upon them the responsibility for failures* was severely criticized by the highest government and party officers. Yet at the same time they often indulged in it themselves; it was too useful to be abandoned. Many Chinese Nationalists, like many Americans, seemed to suffer from delusions about the ability of the United States to direct the fate of China. Most responsible Chinese, however, regardless of what they were saying in public, knew very well the complex reasons for the decline of the National Government. This fact became evident when the reasons were being discussed in retirement on Formosa. But it would have been impolitic to talk about them before, the more so as the officials were either unwilling or unable to do much about them.

It was the recognition of these reasons which cooled the ardor of the American government to rescue the National Government and which also led to the failure of Chiang K'ai-shek to enlist the aid of other Asian nations. He made this attempt by participating in a plan to create an alliance or some form of union among nations of the Far East. In April 1948 the Foreign Affairs Committee of the Chinese National Assembly suggested the idea. The main initiative came, however, from Syngman Rhee of Korea and Elpidio Quirino of the Philippines. Chiang K'ai-shek cooperated eagerly. In May 1949 Ambassador Wellington Koo suggested to the American secretary of state an Asian alliance similar to the Atlantic Alliance. At the same time Syngman Rhee made a proposal very much like Koo's, with strong emphasis upon the military aspects of such an alliance.

In the West the idea was unpopular, and it was not very attractive to many Asian nations. In the face of such opposition the military features of a union were discarded. When Chiang visited Quirino in July 1949 it was therefore announced that he went to discuss the formation of a "nonmilitary" Pacific front. This variation still did not appeal to the United States government. The two statesmen proceeded nevertheless to invite Asian nations to form a Pacific union in the hope that the United

* There is a Chinese story the moral of which is that when one saves a man from drowning, one becomes responsible for his and his family's support forever.

States would eventually join it. But the response was poor, partly because the National Government was envisaged as a partner in the union. Chiang was losing his following at home. He was unpopular in many Asian nations, such as India, whose membership in the union was considered important. His support in the United States was unenthusiastic. He was quickly turning into a liability as a union member. His friend Quirino properly evaluated the situation and quietly dropped Chiang, suggesting a Pacific union without him to make it more palatable to other potential members.[15]

Quirino's move was typical of the policy of most free Asian nations. As long as Chiang continued on the mainland, they maintained proper but cool relations. But there was no willingness for close cooperation. The National Government's policy in Asia during its better days after World War II had not been such as to arouse Asian sympathies. The Asian peoples resented a number of things. There had been some indications of Chinese expansionist ambitions, and China was feared by its smaller neighbors in Southeast Asia. The reliance of the government upon Western, especially American help, made it suspect in Asian eyes. Its policy toward Chinese residents in Asian countries provoked in particular a good deal of ill will, for in its solicitude for the wealthier Chinese merchants, it could not wholeheartedly support the freedom movements and was sometimes even forced to oppose them. As such support was in postwar Asia the criterion by which friend and foe were distinguished, the National Government did not emerge very well from the test. Neutrality was considered tantamount to opposition to the freedom movements, and by pursuing a neutral policy the Chinese government removed itself into the camp of the opposition.* The rapid recognition of Communist China by a large number of free Asian nations may be taken as an indication of their feelings.

On December 8, 1949, the Chinese National government abandoned

* In February 1947 Sun Fo stated that China would support any "reasonable" claims of the Vietnamese against France. If France used force, the move would make France imperialistic and would create ill will in Asia, including China. China so far had been neutral but would welcome a Vietnam offer for diplomatic relations as soon as the state was capable of handling foreign affairs. This was about as far as the government ever went (apart from agreeable, abstract phrases) in encouraging freedom movements, and even this statement may have been meant merely as a threat to France. For the French had just landed on one of the Paracel Islands over which the Chinese claimed sovereignty, and negotiations were under way to settle the incident. — For Sun's statement see the *North China Daily News*, February 9, 1947; for the incident, January 26, March 5, 1947.

the mainland and moved the capital to Formosa. The collapse of the regime was owing to a complex of causes. It was closely tied in with foreign policy. Whether it could have been avoided if the government's calls for help had had a greater response from abroad, particularly on the part of the United States, is, however, by no means certain. The question has since become an internal political football in America, where only a few scholars have made an attempt to find an answer on the merits of the case. The Chinese Nationalists themselves have indicated on many occasions, during and especially after their struggle for survival on the mainland, what they consider to be the reasons for their defeat. As the inside experts on the case, it may therefore be useful to approach the subject from their point of view.

In evaluating the reasons the Nationalists have given for their own defeat, one must keep in mind, of course, that some of the statements made were not intended as historical analysis but as inspiration and encouragement to further effort. One must remember also that for obvious reasons criticism of American policy had to be restrained in tone. Nevertheless a pattern develops from the statements which is an outline of the picture as the Nationalists see it. Since many foreign observers have drawn a very similar picture, it may be accepted as containing a very large measure of truth.

One of the causes of defeat mentioned is inefficiency in government and corruption in the highest places. In numerous speeches Chiang K'ai-shek complained about the "individual selfishness" of the leaders, and in his inaugural address on May 20, 1948, he stated that "the principal task of the new Government is to purge itself of corrupt officials." In 1947 the Control Yuan, the investigating branch of the government, submitted a report which claimed that "privileged corporations" had received undue and extraordinary financial advantages and which singled out T. V. Soong and David Kung, son of H. H. Kung, for special criticism. Similar criticisms were made by the right-wing C. C. Clique and "Christian Marshal" Feng Yu-hsiang, Li Tsung-jen, one-time president of the Formosa government, and many other high personages.*

Another apparent cause was disunity and unrest, as well as constant intriguing between cliques within the Kuomintang. It seemed that personal power counted for much more than the welfare of the country.

* Newspapers in China during 1946, 1947, 1948 were full of scandals concerning deals in rice, currency, luxury goods, and many other commodities — deals usually involving high officials.

And the stronger the Communists became, the worse was the political struggle within the party. Chiang pointed out in the fall of 1947 that the great problem was how to organize and reform the spirit of the party "in the midst of chaos and confusion." In the spring of 1948, in order to stem the unrest in the party, he pledged to fight the Communists even at the cost of his own life. But his perennial appeals for unity in the face of danger were of little avail. There was too much doubt whether his anti-communism sprang from a concern for China or for himself and his friends. Splits within the party grew deeper and deeper, until by the time the Communists gained control of the mainland all semblance of unity had disappeared. This condition in the leadership naturally affected the people. Apathy, demoralization, and defeatism spread — yet another reason for the decline of the National Government.

On many occasions Chiang complained bitterly about the lack of enthusiasm and the inactivity of the public. "The campaign against the rebels has not had the benefit of coordinated efforts on the part of the army and the people, and we have suffered many setbacks. This is the main reason for our reverses," Chiang stated late in 1948. And in an apology at about the same time for failing to drive out the Communists, he explained that he had miscalculated the people's reaction to the introduction of constitutional government, that he had expected them to shoulder more political responsibility and lend better support to the army. This failure, he again said, was "the main reason for our defeat." The defense minister, Pai Chung-hsi, had an explanation for this situation. In view of low pay and short supplies, he said, the "army takes from the people indiscriminately, thus alienating the masses." The Communists won their mass support not by some "magic formula" but by organizing the populace, systematically making use of all available manpower and delegating duties to everyone. The people who escaped from the Communists, he complained, were "privileged persons" who became a liability to the Nationalists because they had to be housed and fed though they refused to work, whereas those who remained in the Communist areas helped the Communist war effort; this made a vast difference in the comparative strength of the Nationalist and Communist troops. He blamed American efforts at mediation as in fact having helped the Communists by preventing their defeat when they were weak. The government should not rely upon foreign loans, which alone could not solve the problem. It should adopt "revolutionary methods," improve the administration, arouse the people to cooperate, and manufacture its own arms and ammunition as the Communists did.

He was not alone in criticizing reliance upon foreign assistance. Many other officials did, among them Chiang himself. He felt that past reliance upon outside help had deprived the party of the "courage to reform within ourselves." Such an attitude was the cause of the prevailing apathy and weakness. "As the situation stands today," he stated in September 1947, "even without foreign help, we shall be able to sustain ourselves for another two years" (which turned out to be a pretty good prediction!). The trouble was not lack of foreign help. The heavy losses of the government forces were "entirely due to the negligence of high commanding officers and to miscalculations of their own . . . Once our strategy is set and fighting is done in earnest by the field commanders," he maintained, the Communists would not have a chance.

This remark pointed to still another major factor in the defeat. Not only was the strategy poor, but many of the officers were corrupt and more interested in graft than fighting. Periodically news items appeared in the press telling about the execution of generals for "avoiding battle" or for similar offenses. Later on many officers escaped execution by simply going over to the Communists. Fu Tso-yi, general of the armies in north China, stated bluntly shortly before he joined the Communists that the government forces in Manchuria were beaten by corruption and inefficiency. To a very considerable extent, wrote the *Free China* (January 16, 1950) on Formosa, the Nationalist army was never beaten, it simply disintegrated.

Summing up this Nationalist analysis of defeat, Chiang Ching-kuo, Chiang K'ai-shek's son and a high officer, ascribed it to the corruption of officers, spiritual disintegration, and, in many cases, Communist infiltration, rather than to inferior fire power; while Chen Cheng, prime minister on Formosa, stated more concisely that the Chiang government did not have the people's confidence and did not deserve it.[16]

The lack of confidence, the low morale, the deadening apathy, had many other causes about which the Nationalists have not said very much. Some of them were the inevitable results of the years of war into which China had been forced by her foreign enemies. Some, more fundamental, originated in the nature of Chinese society and the character of the land. But many were brought about by the government's action or failure to act. The middle class was ruined by the tremendous inflation which the government never attempted to stop with the full means at its disposal. The peasants were overworked, in debt, and miserable. The government did very little to ameliorate the feudalistic structure of land ownership and to protect the peasant against exploitation by the landowner or the moneylender. Laborers in the cities never enjoyed modern working conditions, and their inadequate wages could not compete for the purchase of consumer goods in the speculative and black market prevailing.

The economy of the country fell more and more into the hands of politicians of the Kuomintang. In the name of economic reconstruction and development, the government had announced a plan to nationalize certain heavy industries and certain activities of a normally governmental and monopolistic character (so-called bureaucratic capitalism). What actually happened toward the end and after the war was that not only those types of enterprises were nationalized, but a large number of other enterprises became government monopolies and functioned for the benefit of the cliques which controlled the government. This antagonized Chinese capitalists and merchants, who therefore often sided with the Communists in opposition to the National Government and in any case became unable to contribute to the welfare of the country. These monopolies even extended to supplies shipped into China by the United Nations Relief and Rehabilitation Administration in the first years after the war. The National Government insisted that the Chinese National Relief and Rehabilitation Administration handle all policies and distribution in China, even when UNRRA had the facilities to guarantee the functioning of the program and CNRRA did not.* The monopoly was then used in several instances to obtain special benefits for small cliques.[17]

Large sections of the population were also antagonized by the failure of the government to democratize the regime. The period of political "tutelage" by the Kuomintang never in fact ended to make room for the final stage of democracy. Numerous liberal groups were driven by resentment to the side of the Communists.[18]

The incessant appeals to the masses to rally around the government, the exhortations to officials to become honest, the pleas to the army to fight for the country were bound to remain ineffective without a better-

---

* An eternal source of friction between UNRRA and CNRRA was nondiscriminatory distribution between Nationalist-held and Communist-held territory. The Communist-held areas received disproportionately small quantities of relief supplies.

ment in living standards, or at least without a serious show of effort on the part of the government to improve the conditions of the people.

On Formosa the Nationalists seem to have become aware of their shortcomings or to have grown willing to discuss them. Chiang K'ai-shek promised that upon his return to the mainland, his government would pay "fundamental attention" to the principle of the People's Livelihood. He also announced that the Communist redistribution of land according to the principle of "the land to the tiller" would be recognized, with the difference that the disowned landowners would be reimbursed.[19]

These are important admissions. They appear to imply that the Nationalists ascribe their defeat to their own faults rather than to any positive attraction the Communists have exercised,* and they are not far wrong. The Communists could appeal to many internal and external political and economic grievances to fan the dissatisfaction of the Chinese people and present themselves as saviors. It is likely, however, that, above and beyond material considerations, the Communists could also attract Chinese intellectuals by offering them a new, universalistic view of man and history that may have come as a relief to the intellectual confusion prevalent since the downfall of Confucianism. Communist doctrine in form or substance is not altogether "un-Chinese." China has had regimes in the past not dissimilar to the present Communist one, and Communist propagandists have formulated some fundamental aspects of the doctrine in a way that is compatible with Chinese cultural traditions. — Communist leaders are seeing to it that those traditions which are incompatible with that doctrine are ended ruthlessly.[20]

---

* The "arguments" of the Great Debate on American China policy are not considered here in detail. The debate had little to do with the facts. It belongs, not to Chinese history, but rather to the sad history of American party politics.

21

The Theory of Communist Foreign Policy

On October 1, 1949, the Communists officially claimed assumption of the government of China. The capital was established at Peking. Chiang on Formosa claimed his as the only legitimate Chinese government. In the process of his flight from the mainland, he lost many of his followers, prominent and otherwise. Some of those who went with him were motivated less by loyalty than by a desire to save themselves. The Formosa government began as a miniature edition of its former self, with all the shortcomings and all the difficulties. Slowly, with considerable American aid, it has improved — so much that several foreign observers, formerly highly critical, are now impressed.[1]

The Communist government requested recognition from all governments "willing to observe the principles of equality, mutual benefit and mutual respect of territorial integrity and sovereignty." When offers of recognition were forthcoming, the Communists laid down certain conditions for some countries before they would accept the offers. They demanded, for instance, a complete break with the Chinese "reactionaries," and the renunciation of privileges acquired in an "imperialistic" manner. Occasionally they would make specific conditions for specific countries. They had never left any doubt that most nations would have to expect a complete change in their relations with a Communist China. They had announced on various occasions that many of the treaties entered into with the National Government would not be recognized. And in their fundamental law, the Common Program of September 29, 1949, they embodied the clause that "the Central People's Government of the People's Republic of China shall examine all treaties and agreements concluded between the Kuomintang and foreign Governments, and recognize, abrogate, revise or renew them according to their respective contents."[2]

Recognition by numerous non-Communist countries was the occasion for hard bargaining. For the People's Democracies the pattern was set by the Soviet Union, which offered recognition on October 2; the offer was accepted on the same day with a great display of mutual friendship and affection. Yugoslavia's offer of recognition was completely ignored.

The delay by the non-Communist governments in granting recognition was used by the Nationalists on Formosa to prevent their own disappearance from the international scene. Although in better days they had insisted that their feud with the Communists was an internal affair and, for the sake of "friendship," had pretended that the Soviet government was acting "correctly," they now brought their grievances before an international forum. They appealed to the United Nations on the grounds that the Soviet Union had threatened the political independence and territorial integrity of China as well as the peace of the Far East by violating the Charter and the Sino-Soviet treaty of August 1945. Specifically the accusation was that the Soviet government had persistently obstructed the National Government's effort to re-establish authority in Manchuria and had given military and financial aid to the Communists.

The United Nations Assembly seemed in no mood to become involved in the controversy. It passed a colorless resolution on December 8, 1949 — in the reluctance of its tone reminiscent of the Washington Nine-Power Treaty — in which the nations were requested to preserve China's political independence, to honor its right to choose its own political institutions, to respect existing treaties, and to avoid spheres of interest. At the same time the question of threats to the political independence and territorial integrity of China was referred to the Interim Committee of the United Nations for continuous study and examination and for a report to the Assembly's next meeting.

When this meeting took place, the Interim Committee announced that it had not considered the question because many of its important aspects were on the Assembly's current agenda anyway and because a debate "in the context of the present political situation" would serve no useful purpose. The ensuing discussion indicated again a considerable aversion, especially among the Western European nations, to the Nationalists' request for further investigations and recommendations for action by a special commission. With much bitterness the Formosa government withdrew its request, and the Assembly resolved on December 1, 1950, that the Interim Committee continue its enquiry.

In the meantime the worsening of the Cold War in the Far East worked in favor of the Chinese Nationalists. On January 29, 1952, the

General Assembly accepted a resolution, by a vote of 25 to 9, with 24 abstentions, stating that the Soviet Union in its relations with China since the surrender of Japan had failed to carry out the Treaty of Friendship with China.[3] Thus the Chinese on Formosa finally obtained moral satisfaction and an indication that some nations were now more willing to take up their cause. The trend seemed favorable to them. It was the first really encouraging sign since the dark and gloomy days of the winter of 1949–1950, when many supporters of Chiang K'ai-shek feared that there was nothing left for them but to wait for a third world war which might liberate them, this time from the Soviet Union. To add to the dejection of the Nationalists, the appeal of the Communist regime for recognition had been getting results.

A considerable number of free nations recognized the government of the People's Republic of China; among them Burma, India, Ceylon, Pakistan, Great Britain, Holland, Switzerland, and the Scandinavian states. But those nations labeled "imperialist" by Communist China gained little by their action, and in some cases recognition was not followed by the establishment of diplomatic contacts through representatives. Great Britain in particular has had to suffer rather humiliating treatment, reminiscent sometimes of her experience in the early nineteenth century. The British chargé d'affaires has never been received by the highest Chinese officials, and no Chinese Communist diplomat has been sent to London or to any British colony. The main official reasons originally given for this treatment were the British abstention on several votes on the admission of Communist China to the United Nations; alleged border incidents around Hongkong and complaints about the treatment of Chinese Communists in the colony (but no requests for a return of the colony); and questions of Chinese property, particularly airplanes, on British soil.[4] Many of these questions have been settled, yet Sino-British relations have failed to improve. The British government has used every possible avenue to create regular contacts, particularly in trade, with the Communist Chinese. To the British government this approach is not only a matter of realistic policy but a necessity for the welfare of Hongkong and Malaya.* However, Great Britain has con-

* Hongkong depends upon the mainland for its supply of fresh foods and water. Its livelihood and Malaya's depend to a considerable extent upon trade with the mainland. However, British trade with China is relatively insignificant to Great Britain (it is much more important to China) and is not the major motivation in British policy toward Communist China. This must be sought, rather, in the British

sistently met with rebuffs from the Communist government. Only occasionally does she receive friendlier treatment from China, namely, when Chinese propaganda is attempting to disturb American-British friendship.[5]

Several other nations have had similar experiences. The Chinese Communists obviously intend to lower the Iron Curtain and cannot tolerate representatives of free countries in their midst. This treatment of nations and foreigners in China has not been conducive to persuading other nations to recognize the Communist regime. Even India, more anxious than most important powers to establish friendly relations with the Communists, has periodically had difficulties and has had to be satisfied with a fickle friendship.

The rationale of those nations that recognized Communist China varied. Some hoped to maintain their trade, some to prevent China's isolation from the free world, some, perhaps most, to have observers in China. On the last point they have been disappointed, and on the two others, expectations remain to be fulfilled. The rationale rests on the assumptions of traditional international politics. But the Chinese Communists have long since made it known that their concepts of international law, diplomacy, and relations do not necessarily fall into the customary patterns — though whether they will always be able to act according to their ideology and whether their ideology can serve as a guide to specific action remain to be seen.

Being Marxists, the Communists have theorized a good deal about foreign policy and international relations.[6] According to the Communist Chinese writer Huan Hsin-yi, "the foreign policy of the People's Republic of China is founded on the scientific principles of Marx, Engels, Lenin, and Stalin, and on a scientific knowledge of the laws of social development. These four great masters of social science have formulated the laws governing capitalist economy and politics, as well as the salient characteristics of two simultaneously existing social systems; and they have scientifically postulated the tasks and methods of foreign policy for socialist nations. Chairman Mao — the most outstanding student of Marx, Engels, Lenin, and Stalin — uses this knowledge in shaping the national policies of the People's Republic of China."[7]

view that China is not irrevocably tied to the Soviet Union, that an expansion of war in the Far East would threaten Britain's vital interest in South and Southeast Asia, and that a third world war would be the end of Britain's existence. Cf. *World Today*, VII (1951), 537–543; VIII (1952), 495–498.

According to these "scientific principles" foreign policy is an instrument in the world-wide struggle of communism for power. Its purpose is to create revolution everywhere, to unite the proletariat of the world, and lead it to victory over the "imperialists." The Chinese Communists underemphasize, for obvious reasons, that the protection of the Soviet Union as the Fatherland of the Socialist Revolution and the citadel of communism is the foremost task of Communists everywhere and a major goal of any Communist foreign policy.

During the struggle for power, Communist doctrine permits relations, coalitions, or alliances with "bourgeois" and "capitalist" nations in certain circumstances, provided that these further the Communist cause and that the identity of the Communists can be preserved. But regardless of the nature of the temporary compromise, the final goal must forever be kept in mind: policy must always tend toward the preservation of the Soviet Union, a united front must be established against the "imperialists," and the struggle against "imperialism" must be an aggressive one. With "imperialism" itself there can, for a Communist, never be compromise, for it is the immutable enemy of communism and, indeed, represents everything that Communists must fight. On this point the law has been laid down very distinctly by Mao Tse-tung in his *On the People's Democratic Dictatorship*, written in 1949.[8]

Mao stresses the necessity of China's allying herself with the Soviet Union, the People's Democracies of Europe, and the proletariat and the masses of the people everywhere, to form a united front. To the criticism that this is to "lean to one side," Mao answers, "That is right. The forty years' experience of Sun Yat-sen and the twenty-eight years' experience of the Chinese Communist party have convinced us that in order to attain victory and consolidate it we must incline to one side. According to these experiences the Chinese people must either incline toward the side of imperialism or toward that of socialism. There can be no exception to this rule. It is impossible to sit on the fence; there is no third road. . . . Neutrality is merely a camouflage; a third road does not exist."

In the attempt to enlist the tremendous force of nationalism in the service of communism, the struggle against "imperialism" is identified with the liberation movements of the colonial peoples. This identification, however, creates a difficulty. The discrepancy between the encouragement of nationalism on the one hand and, on the other hand, the

277

constant call for a world-wide united front to support liberation movements everywhere and for loyalty, above all, to the Soviet Union is something the Communists have to explain. They do so by a dogmatic distinction between good "proletarian patriotism" and bad "bourgeois nationalism" or good proletarian internationalism and bad bourgeois cosmopolitanism.[9] Actually the distinction rests on no other foundation than the Communists' faith that Good in the world is represented by communism and Evil by capitalism, so that even when a Communist and a capitalist nation behave alike, their actions are nevertheless classified differently. Communist doctrine, however, provides a more elaborate, theoretical foundation for this distinction.

"Bourgeois nationalism," so the doctrine explains, is the vehicle by which the bourgeoisie, the ruling class of the nation, attempts to enlist the participation of the people in the subjugation and exploitation of another nation. Its motivation is the search for "profits and more profits," and the people are its dupes and tools. The offer of military and economic aid by a capitalist nation to another nation is merely a variation of nationalism's methods, merely another form of oppressing the receiving nation. "No imperialist country can be expected to extend genuine help to the cause of real independence and liberation," says the dogma, but help from a "socialist" country cannot but be genuine since the motivations of profit and exploitation are nonexistent there.

There is one situation, the doctrine further explains, in which the proletariat can cooperate with the bourgeoisie, namely, when a national movement led by the bourgeoisie, such as the Chinese under Sun Yat-sen, has "as its objective the struggle against oppression by other nations and the creation of a national state." In such a case the movement is "historically progressive" and the proletariat supports it. But support must end as soon as the liberation has been achieved and "bourgeois nationalism" begins itself to oppress other peoples. Then the Communists must fight it; for in their "liberating" qualities lies the merit of "proletarian patriotism and internationalism," two "perfectly compatible concepts."

"The proletarian-internationalist approach to the national question," Liu Shao-ch'i points out, "and its basic principles for dealing with the national question throughout the world proceed from the basic interest of the masses of the given nation, and at the same time, from the common interests of the masses of the people of every nation, which are the

278

common basic interests of all mankind." "Proletarian patriotism" can never deteriorate into oppression or exploitation of others because "the proletariat cannot countenance in society any system of oppression of man by man for otherwise it could not achieve its own emancipation." For the same reason the proletariat has an obligation to assist in the overthrow of "imperialism" everywhere else, as well as fight any "imperialism" of its own nation. The proletariat can thus be patriotic and internationalist at the same time because its internationalism leads to liberation, never to suppression of other peoples. "The genuine patriotism of the masses of the people in all countries," concludes Liu, "is not in contradiction to proletarian internationalism, but is, rather, intimately connected with it."

This seemingly so logical and clear-cut theory appears to organize neatly the complex matter of international relations, reduce it to simple black-and-white propositions, and prescribe the exact course of Communist foreign policy. In practical application it turns out to be fairly flexible, to provide few rules for the day-to-day conduct of foreign policy, and to prove Marx's own idea that ideology is nothing but a superstructure (*Überbau*). The reorientations and reversals in the Chinese Communist party's policy since its birth would in themselves be testimony that almost any practice can be justified in the name of Communist doctrine and made to consist with it. There are a number of reasons why the doctrine is such a conveniently adjustable tool and why almost any and all, often mutually exclusive, actions of the Communists seem to fit it.

Quite apart from the general nature of social doctrines and ideologies, which, in practice, always allow a wide choice of not necessarily compatible actions,[10] there are specific reasons why Communist doctrine is so flexible. Stalin himself provided a perfect escape from any rigidity in application by his pronouncement in July 1950 that "Marxism does not recognize immutable conclusions and formulae, binding all epochs and periods. Marxism is the immutable enemy of all dogmatism." Mao has echoed this idea by introducing the qualification into his statements that they are true "in China" and "under present conditions." Furthermore, as Liu Shao-ch'i stresses, "Marxism-Leninism considers all questions in their historical settings." The nature of a given "historical setting" and hence the answer to a specific question depend entirely upon subjective interpretation, and so the door is opened wide to expediency.

279

Furthermore, the language used by Communist doctrine is vague and ambiguous. Basic terms are left undefined. A concrete situation classified as Communist, hence acceptable today, may be rejected tomorrow as "imperialist." The perennial rewriting of history in Communist countries to make it fit contemporary purposes rests on this technique. The political expediency which determines the classification is hidden behind the doctrinaire smoke-screen by emphasizing some and underemphasizing other aspects of the doctrine or by forcing the facts to fit the pat phrases of the doctrine.[11]

Finally, tactics as distinct from basic goals are largely undetermined, so that in their name many compromises with supposedly fundamental principles can be made. Such compromises occur particularly often in foreign policy as that branch of governmental activity over which the government has the least control, partly because national survival is given as its foremost objective and partly because it has to dovetail with the policy of many other nations.

Through the application of all these devices of their doctrine, the Communists are able to give diametrically opposed interpretations to similar phenomena. They are never satisfied with judging actions as such. They always evaluate them as manifestations of the system from which they spring. Depending therefore on whether the system is considered good or bad, the manifestations are good or bad. Thus, in the eyes of the Communists, American financial assistance to China throughout the years is a diabolical means to enslave the country, whereas the miserly Russian loan of $300 million to the Communist government is a tremendous contribution to reconstruction; or, American technical experts in Asia are invariably spies or saboteurs, whereas Russian technicians in China are selfless servants of modernization; or, American troops in Japan are colonizers, whereas Russian troops in Port Arthur are guardians of the peace.

Obviously, Communist doctrine on international relations is a poor guide to predicting the foreign policy of Communist China, except perhaps within a framework too broad to be of practical value and from a standpoint too long-term to be of any assistance in the day-to-day conduct of international relations. There are few things indeed the Chinese Communists could not fit into their doctrine, and many things they are claiming to say and do in the name of the doctrine have been said and done by Chinese governments for decades.[12] In the evaluation and interpretation of Communist China's foreign policy it seems safer to rely primarily on the traditional and basic factors determining the international behavior of nations, such as national security, geography, or resources, and to realize that Chinese Communist policy, like any other foreign policy, is as much reaction as it is action. Every nation must take into account the foreign policies of other nations and is under the constant necessity of adjusting itself to them, whatever its ideology. The Chinese Communists seem to be aware of this situation, for one of their spokesmen pointed out that their foreign policy must adapt itself to the "objective realities" of the "immediate international situation." Even on the theoretical level the result of this awareness is discernible to some extent in the basic program outlined by the Communists for their foreign policy.

The Common Program of the People's Consultative Conference of September 1949 lays down these points for Communist China's foreign policy:

Article 54. The principle of the foreign policy of the People's Republic of China is protection of the independence, freedom, integrity of territory and sovereignty of the country, upholding of lasting international peace and friendly cooperation between the peoples of all countries, and opposition to the imperialist policy of aggression and war.

Article 55. The Central People's Government of the People's Republic of China shall examine the treaties and agreements concluded between the Kuomintang and foreign governments, and shall recognize, abrogate, revise, or renegotiate them according to their respective contents.

Article 56. The Central People's Government of the People's Republic of China may, on the basis of equality, mutual benefit and mutual respect for territory and sovereignty, negotiate with foreign governments which have severed relations with the Kuomintang reactionary clique and which adopt a friendly attitude towards the People's Republic of China, and may establish diplomatic relations with them.

Article 57. The People's Republic of China may restore and develop commercial relations with foreign governments and peoples on the basis of equality and mutual benefit.

Article 58. The Central People's Government of the People's Republic of China shall do its utmost to protect the proper rights and interests of Chinese residing abroad.

Article 59. The People's Government of the People's Republic of China protects law-abiding foreign nationals in China.

Article 60. The People's Republic of China shall accord the right of asylum to foreign nationals who seek refuge in China because they have been oppressed by their own governments for supporting the people's interests and taking part in the struggle for peace and democracy.

These rules are preceded by and officially said to be merely explanations of the "principle of principles" contained in Article 11 of the Common Program, which reads: "The People's Republic of China shall unite with all peace-loving and freedom-loving countries and peoples throughout the world, first of all, with the USSR, all People's Democracies and all oppressed nations. It shall take its stand in the camp of international peace and democracy, to oppose jointly imperialist aggression and defend lasting world peace."

Naturally the foreign-policy program must be presented as immutable, when it supposedly flows from the general doctrine. Nevertheless a Communist writer has repeated that the seven articles of the Common Program constitute the highest guiding principles for the foreign policy pursued "at present" by the People's Republic of China.[13]

This foreign-policy program, he says, "writes an entirely new leaf in the diplomatic history of China. It has wiped out all the diplomatic disgraces of China for the past 150 years, ended all privileges of the imperialists in China, and marked the beginning of the independence and self-governing diplomacy based on the territory and sovereignty of China and on the interests of the Chinese people." This "brand new" foreign policy, he continues, can only be found in and executed by the People's Republic of China, because it has overthrown the "rule of imperialism in China," and abolished the "domestic feudal system and bureaucratic capitalist system."[14] This interpretation is, of course, not only a gross exaggeration but a falsification of Communist China's foreign relations.

The "rule of imperialism" had been overthrown by the Nationalist government, beginning with the "diplomatic revolution" in the 1920's and ending during the Second World War when China obtained equal status and was proclaimed one of the Big Powers. Some special rights of foreigners had been abandoned in the 1920's. Tariff autonomy had been granted to the Chinese early in the 1930's, although full-fledged autonomous administration was delayed by the Japanese invasion. During the Second World War the Japanese abandoned extraterritoriality, a step in which they were followed by the Western powers. The United States signed a treaty with China on January 11, 1943, relinquishing extraterritorial and related rights. Great Britain signed a similar treaty on the same day and other nations followed, among them Canada, France, Belgium, the Netherlands, Norway, and Sweden. The result of these treaties was the abolition of extraterritoriality, of the Concessions and Settlements, and of the leased ports; the return of Kwangchowwan by France and of British rights in Weihaiwei; and the relinquishing of the right of foreign powers to have naval vessels in Chinese waters and troops in the Peking Legation Quarter.[15] In other words, the inequalities of the early treaties were eliminated before the Communists obtained power in China. Indeed, it was the Communist government which applauded and confirmed the reinstatement of the Soviet Union in many of the special rights and privileges which tsarist Russia possessed in 1904.

22

The Hate-America Campaign

F ROM the enormous wordiness of Chinese Communist dogma, doctrine, program and propaganda, tedious in its repetitiousness and repugnant in its emphasis on hate, there emerge a few main lines of foreign policy as "at present" developed, which are selectively applied to three major categories of nations. One category is typified by the United States. She is the archenemy. With her are classified all other "imperialist" powers, such as Great Britain and France, though these may for tactical reasons occasionally be treated with slightly less vituperation. The Soviet Union is the great and highly venerated friend, the senior partner in the Communist enterprise, the recognized "leader of the camp of peace, democracy, and socialism." All other Communist states belong to this category, though in a carefully graded hierarchy. Finally, notwithstanding Mao's contention that neutrality is "camouflage," the Chinese Communists recognize in fact a third category of states, composed of those standing between the two major camps in present world politics. These are sometimes wooed, sometimes rejected, according to the dictates of circumstances. India best represents this category, and many of the free Asian nations belong to it.

The official Communist view of the United States is determined by the doctrinaire interpretation of the social order with which the United States is identified. American actions, whatever their nature objectively, are therefore explained and treated as manifestations of the despised order. This puts a priori an odium upon them from which the United States can hardly escape. America is pictured as the implacable and immutable enemy not only of China but of all "free" peoples.* She is the prototype of "imperialist" nations and hence stands for everything that is evil in the Communist's world. She is portrayed as the successor

* In Communist language, "free," "democratic," "peace-loving," "popular," and similar adjectives mean Communist exclusively, while the terms "masses," "the people," refer either to Communists or to the people in non-Communist countries as distinct from their leaders.

to the fascist powers, with their ambition for world domination, which must be fought by the Communists of all countries. If the United States as the leader of the imperialist camp is defeated, so the Communists argue, all imperialists will be defeated, for they are merely the "lackeys" and "running dogs" of the American imperialists, or "Wall Street."

Consequently the United States is the primary subject of Chinese Communist propaganda, and her defeat a major aim of foreign policy. The most far-fetched occasions are used to hit out at her. For years the front pages of all newspapers in Communist China have been filled with vituperative attacks. Not a day passes in which the Chinese citizen is left without some reminder that most of his ills are due to American machinations. He must be under the impression that American-Chinese relations are closer and more intense — though much worse — than they have ever been before. The opposite, in fact, is true.

The breakdown of American–Communist Chinese relations began before V-J Day. Pronouncements by the Chinese Communist leaders, though mostly theoretical and abstract, indicated that the chances for friendly relations between the United States and a Communist China would be poor. American efforts to bring internal peace to China in the immediate postwar period were met by the Communists with suspicion first, then with outright opposition. The basic cause of this attitude was a difference between the Communists and Americans in their approach to the peace efforts. The Americans regarded the National Government of Chiang K'ai-shek as the government with which international relations were properly to be conducted. The Communists demanded recognition as more than just an opposition party and refused to separate American peace efforts from the official conduct of American-Chinese relations.* They felt therefore greatly antagonized by the military, economic, and technical aid extended by the United States government to the government of China. The feelings resulting from this situation reinforced the distrust and hatred the Communists harbored on general, ideological grounds and affected the relations which developed between the United States and the Communists in areas under their control.

By the time the Communist victory approached, the United States

* Some authors might argue that this distinction is too legalistic to mean anything to the "Chinese mind." The answer is that the Communist Chinese, like the Nationalists, have shown a perfect understanding of the Western concept of law when it was to their interest to do so.

government had reason to be hesitant about recognizing the Communist regime. America had become the target of the most severe propaganda attacks. American officials (for example, Angus Ward) and American citizens had been badly treated in Communist territory. The Communists had announced that they would not necessarily recognize treaties entered into by preceding governments.

The pattern which had been set before the victory of the Communists continued thereafter. Together with their request for recognition, the Communists hinted at dire consequences if the conditions under which they would accept recognition were not fulfilled, and their anti-American propaganda continued ceaselessly. Severe restrictions were imposed upon American (and other) citizens, especially diplomats and newspaper reporters. Many American citizens were held incommunicado in prisons. Others were denied exit permits except upon extortionary payment of large sums of money.[1] American property in Peking was seized on very flimsy or no grounds. The result of this treatment was that the United States withdrew her last diplomatic and consular officials from the mainland in April 1950.[2] On the other hand, the continued and increased American support of Chiang K'ai-shek's government on Formosa was greatly resented by the Chinese Communists and accepted as substantiation of their charge that the United States was the archenemy of the Chinese people. What peaceful, direct contacts remained between the United States and the mainland of China, especially in the economic field, were broken off when the Chinese joined in the Korean aggression. The United States declared an embargo on any materials whatever to Communist China, and none were shipped there after December 1950.* At the same time all Chinese assets in the United States were put under the control of the American government, while the Chinese Communist government applied the same measure to American assets in China. After October 1950 Chinese and American soldiers faced each other on the battlefield.

Within one year of the establishment of the Communist regime peaceful relations between the United States and the Chinese mainland ended.

* Exports from the United States of arms, ammunition, implements of war, and atomic energy materials to North Korea and Communist China have not been authorized at any time. Exports of other strategic materials to North Korea and Communist China had been severely restricted and in some instances embargoed for some time before June 1950. After the end of June 1950 the list of strategic materials which might not be exported to Communist China was greatly expanded.

The change seems rapid from the days in 1945 when Mao Tse-tung wrote that the Chinese were "grateful to Britain and the United States, particularly the latter, for their immense contribution to the common cause — the defeat of the Japanese aggressors. We are grateful to the governments and the peoples of both countries for their sympathy with the Chinese people and their help." [3] However, the change is less real than it seems. The main course of American–Communist Chinese relations has never been seriously modified since the time, long before V-J Day, when tension began. Complimentary statements by Communist leaders have always been rare and have never inaugurated friendlier contacts. By 1949 they were forgotten and not permitted to be quoted in Communist China. The very facts and occasions to which they referred were then either suppressed or represented as part of the American "plot" to conquer China.

There has never been any change in the attitude of the Communist Chinese toward the United States or in their propaganda, except for an increase in intensity and extremism over the period of years. The propaganda is designed to discredit the United States with the Chinese people and to destroy the sympathy which once existed between the two nations. The task of this propaganda is therefore to create the idea in the minds of the Chinese people that American policy toward their country has always been in the past and is in the present inimical. Another task was added when the success of the Chinese Communists acquired implications beyond the Chinese area — when the Chinese Communists, having secured their position within the country, began to look to other Asian areas. Their propaganda then had to assume a more cosmopolitan character, had to appeal to at least all Asians as well as the Chinese. This was achieved by adapting its major themes.

At first the three main themes of the Hate-America Campaign were (1) American "imperialism" and "aggression" in China, Japan, and Europe, especially American instigation of the Chinese civil war; (2) prediction of the "inevitable collapse" of the American capitalist system, hastened by the victory of the "united liberation forces" and a "correct" policy of the Chinese people; and (3) the "undemocratic nature" of the American political and social system.[4]

By 1950 the new version of these three themes was (1) "Hate the United States, for she is the deadly enemy of the Chinese people"; (2) "Despise the United States, for she is a rotten imperialist nation, the

287

headquarters of reactionary degeneracy in the whole world"; and (3) "Look with contempt upon the United States, for she is a paper tiger and can be fully defeated." [5]

The method used to prove American enmity in the past is the selective rewriting of history. Facts are reinterpreted, singled out, exaggerated, and occasionally invented to point up only the worst aspects of America's policy over the last one hundred years. Sloganwise the Chinese people are informed that "ever since the Opium War, American Imperialism has consistently encroached upon our country." They can read in their most recent history books that much of the opium burned in Canton in 1839 was American-owned; that an American naval squadron helped the British navy in the war against China; that United States warships participated in the war of 1857–1860; that American citizens helped in the suppression of the "revolutionary movement" of the T'ai-p'ings (now represented as a precursor of the Communist revolution); that the Open Door policy was a move to eliminate competitors and permit the creation of an American commercial monopoly in China; that the United States helped in the May 30, 1925, incident; that from 1931 to 1933 the United States assisted Chiang K'ai-shek in his attack upon the "Chinese workers' and peasants' red army"; that the medical and educational work of American foundations in China was part of "cultural imperialism"; that China's food problem is due to American interference with dykes and irrigation systems under the technical aid program; * that the defeat of Japan was the work of the Chinese Communists and the Soviet Union.†Even Florence Nightingale is described as a servant of American "imperialism." [6]

Against this background today's American policy in the Far East and Asia is presented by the Communists as a continuation of the same evil purposes. The concentration is on three main issues: the recognition of Communist China, American policy in Japan, and the Korean War.

---

* There are remarkable parallels between this type of propagandistic interpretation and falsification of American-Chinese relations and that perpetrated by the Chinese regime of the Japanese occupation during World War II. See T'ang Leang-li, *American Imperialism in China* (Shanghai, 1943). The Nationalists themselves, however, are not guiltless of some measure of distortion, witness the historical sections of Chiang's *China's Destiny*.

† When the attack on Pearl Harbor "forced" the British and Americans to fight, so the Communists argue, "they were not active from beginning to end, and it was only after the Soviet Union scored important victories in the Northeast that the U.S. hurriedly dropped atomic bombs to make a show and to usurp the fruits of victory."

The refusal of the United States to recognize the Communist government and her endeavor to keep Communist China out of the United Nations are taken by the Communists as proof that she will not recognize "popular" governments but, on the contrary, will actively intervene against them by supporting their "reactionary" and "feudalistic" opponents. This she is doing, so the Communists feel, because the "reactionaries" are willing to do her bidding and help her "imperialistic" designs. "During the people's war for liberation in China, the American government has always sided with the enemies of the Chinese people," said Foreign Minister Chou En-lai, "and has diligently assisted, and still assists, Kuomintang reaction in the struggle against the Chinese people." * He warned that "anyone who attempts to oust China, with a population of approximately 500,000,000 people, from the United Nations Organization, anyone who disregards or undermines the interests of one-fourth of mankind, anyone who rashly endeavors to find a unilateral solution for any Oriental problem directly affecting China, will inevitably come to grief." [7]

The fact is that when the representation of China was debated in the Security Council, the United States announced that she considered the question procedural, not substantial, which meant that she would not use her veto to prevent the Communist government from representing China. However, in spite of an ardent Russian campaign in favor of seating the Communist representative and ousting the Nationalist, there was a persistent majority in favor of letting the Nationalist representative continue to speak on behalf of China.[8]

This decision created resentment among the Communists at not being acknowledged victors in the Chinese civil war. Chou En-lai's words indicate hurt pride and prestige. But they also show the long-standing Chinese grievance at being slighted, and they will for that reason find a strong echo among many Chinese. A similar Chinese, not merely Communist, grievance underlies the Communist criticism of America's policy in Japan, a criticism which was begun by the Nationalists, though they were less polemic and more truthful in formulating it — and eventually more understanding as well!

---

* In 1946 Chou had expressed appreciation of American efforts to arrange a temporary truce period in Manchuria and had written to General Marshall, urging him to continue his and Ambassador Stuart's "fair and impartial efforts for the peace of China." — Department of State, *United States Relations with China*, pp. 194, 642, 667.

The Communists accuse the United States of restoring fascism in Japan, of using that country as a springboard for an attack upon the Asian mainland, of turning her into an aggressor by remilitarizing her, and of reviving the idea of a co-prosperity sphere by actively tying her industrial potential to the raw materials of Southeast Asia.[9] The United States is held responsible for preventing a Sino-Japanese peace treaty by stifling "the voice of the Japanese people." Chou En-lai stated in 1950 that "the American government not only plans to disrupt the procedure of a Japanese peace treaty, but has gone one step further in planning to overthrow the foundations of a common peace with Japan."

As a substitute for a treaty, the Communists perennially express their friendship for the Japanese people, assure them that they are "keenly interested in the liberation of the people of Japan," and advise them that "only by means of a stubborn revolutionary struggle against American imperialism and Japanese reactionary forces can the people of Japan secure an earlier end to American occupation, to the domination of reaction, and build a democratic Japan." * They even hinted on one occasion that they might help the Japanese as they were helping the Koreans.[10]

When the United States, Great Britain, and other nations began to negotiate peace terms to circumvent the opposition of the Soviet Union and Communist China, the Communists opened a barrage of propaganda attacks. They warned that a peace treaty without Russian and Chinese participation could only be null and void, that it would mean "war and ruin for the Japanese nation," a threat to the peace of Asia, a "deed of sale of national subjugation and extermination" for Japan. "The day when America signs the peace with Japan will be the day when the Japanese nation actually ceases to exist," affirmed the Communists, and ever after that day they have spoken of Japan as a colony.

On legal grounds the Communists declare the peace treaty null and void because it violates the principle of the Four-Power Agreement, because it ignores the agreements reached at Cairo, Yalta, and Potsdam, because Formosa would not be immediately returned to China, because American troops would be retained in Japan, and because Japan would be rearmed.[11] They ignore the case of the Western and other powers which signed the treaty.

* This advice was directed especially at Nozaka, a Japanese Communist, to correct his "erroneous" policy of winning power by peaceful means.

290

Upon the coming into effect of the treaty early in 1952, Chou En-lai engaged in a bitter denunciation of this "illegal" fruition of the preceding negotiations. He accused the Tokyo government of preparing a new war. The whole sequence of recent events in regard to Japan, he stated, was a series of "serious, flagrant acts of provocation" which aroused the "insurmountable indignation" of the Chinese people. He restated all his previous arguments against the treaty and described it summarily as an extremely hostile act against China and the Soviet Union. The separate peace treaty between the government of Chiang K'ai-shek and Japan was to Chou merely additional proof of the "war-like aims" of the combined "reactionary" forces of the United States, Japan, and the Kuomintang.[12]

Agitation against the treaty is continuing. The Chinese Communists are unwilling to let the issue die. By making it a key item on the agenda of the Asian and Pacific Peace Conference at Peking late in September 1952, they were giving their complaints Asian-wide publicity. They knew, of course, that this was an effective move because some aspects of America's policy in Japan are criticized by many groups in various countries of Asia and the Pacific. But even while these groups remain anxious about the prospects of a rearmed Japan, they are beginning — with the exception of the Communists among them — to see the need of enlisting the aid of a democratized Japan in the containment of Communist, specifically Russian, expansionism. The fears of a rearmed Japan on the part of the Chinese Communists spring from the fact that they are less interested in the defense of their own country than in that of the Fatherland of Communism.

The war in Korea was used by the Chinese Communists to drive their Hate Campaign against the United States to its greatest heights. With complete disregard of the findings of the United Nations Commission in Korea (that there was a clear-cut case of aggression by North Korea), of the many attempts by the United Nations and individual powers to end the struggle, and of the military course of the war, the Communists used the war to demonstrate the three themes of their propaganda : American policy in Korea is directed against China; but it is also a step toward the domination of Asia; and the military action shows that the United States is "a paper tiger and can be fully defeated."

It may be well at this point briefly to recall the background and the main events of the Korean War. Mostly as a matter of military expediency, Korea was divided into a northern and a southern section at the Thirty-eighth Parallel by the Soviet and United States governments at the end of World War II. Thanks to the inability of the two governments to reach political agreement, Korea remained divided into two zones. All attempts to unite it failed because both governments feared an accretion of power to the other in case of unification. The northern zone quickly developed into a Soviet satellite; the southern had some of the trimmings of democracy but was largely under the stubborn and very conservative rule of Syngman Rhee. The economy of Korea, weak to begin with, suffered greatly from this division, to which there had been no logic whatsoever. The south depended on the north for electric power and semifinished raw materials. The north needed consumer goods from the south. The south shipped some food to the north, produced partly with the help of northern-manufactured fertilizers.

The division probably hurt the south more than the north. For the lack of power and resources in the south and the loss of its northern market had to be made up by overseas relations, while the north could turn to Manchuria and Siberia. A Soviet–North Korean agreement of March 21, 1949, provided for economic and cultural cooperation between the two countries. This treaty formalized the integration of the Korean economy into the Soviet bloc. The major importance of Korea to China lay in the supply of raw materials and electric power which China received from the plants on the Korean side of the Yalu River dams.

The division of Korea was accompanied by an increasingly strong and bitter propaganda on both sides for unification, each regime claiming to be the legitimate government of all Korea. Border incidents were frequent and it was known that the North Koreans received military aid from the Soviet Union. The situation had become extremely tense when the war broke out.[13]

On the day of the attack, June 25, 1950, the Security Council, thanks to the absence of the Soviet Union, acted swiftly, declaring the North Korean action a breach of the peace and calling for an immediate cessation of hostilities. Two days later the Security Council in a resolution called upon all United Nations members to give such assistance to the Republic of Korea as might be necessary to repel armed attack on her territory. As a result of these resolutions, many nations, the United States foremost among them, contributed to the building up of an international army which could be used to enforce the decisions of the United Nations against the aggressor. On July 7 the Security Council established a unified command for all United Nations forces in Korea and requested the United States to designate the commander of these forces. General MacArthur was appointed to this post one day later.

During the first two to three months of the fighting, the United Nations was engaged in organizing machinery for conducting the war and assisting Korean civilians. The campaign went in favor of the North Koreans, who achieved their greatest advance during the first week of September 1950. Thereafter they were thrown back, and the first United Nations troops reached the Thirty-eighth Parallel on September 29. Early in October all territory south of the parallel was recaptured by the United Nations. The North Koreans rejected General MacArthur's ultimatum for unconditional surrender, and on October 9 United Nations forces crossed the Thirty-eighth Parallel, reaching the Manchurian border on October 26, 1950.

On November 5 General MacArthur reported that from August 22 on the Chinese Communists had been giving support to the North Korean forces. This support was evident first in the form of antiaircraft fire from the Chinese side of the Yalu River, then in the form of Chinese troops on the battlefield. From that moment on Communist China was directly involved in United Nations policy toward the Korean aggression.

On November 8 Communist China was invited to discuss the Korean problem in the United Nations. In December a Chinese mission arrived in New York and left again on the 19th. The war continued, notwithstanding attempts, especially by India and the Asian and Arab nations, to obtain a cease-fire.

On February 1, 1951, the General Assembly declared Communist China an aggressor in Korea by a vote of 44 to 7, with 9 abstentions. All attempts to reach a peaceful settlement having failed, the General Assembly on May 18, 1951, recommended an embargo upon war munitions and strategic materials to Communist China and North Korea.

On June 23, 1951, the Russian representative on the Security Council, Jacob Malik, made a statement which eventually led to the armistice negotiations between the United Nations and the North Koreans, which began in July 1951 and ended successfully in July 1953.

Communist China was involved in these events long before her troops actively engaged in the fighting. Chinese propaganda was part of global

Communist propaganda on the Korean situation before aggression took place, and it served to encourage the North Korean aggressors. When, in 1949, the North Korean army was increased in strength with the assistance of the Soviet Union, two divisions of former Korean "volunteer" groups* — Chinese of Korean origin who were part of the Communist Chinese army — were moved into North Korea.[14] Early in 1950, when the North Korean army was mobilized, 10,000 more veterans from the Communist Chinese army were moved to North Korea.

Just exactly what role the Chinese Communists played in the invasion of South Korea is as yet difficult to determine with absolute certainty. There are a few facts which might indicate that the Chinese government was not expecting the invasion at the moment it actually took place. A major part of the Communist army was at the time massed opposite Formosa; as a result there were persistent rumors, and, on the part of the Nationalist Chinese, certainty, that Formosa was to be invaded.[15] Had the Communists expected the Korean invasion, it might be argued, they would have concentrated more troops along the Manchurian border, as they did later on. Yet it may equally well be argued that the threat against Formosa was a diversionary move, that the Communists were confident of a quick North Korean victory in view of the long preparation of the North Korean army and the unpreparedness of the South Koreans. A second, and much more important fact, appears to be the disarray of the Chinese Communist press when the invasion took place. For the first twenty-four hours after the event, the press did not know what stand to take, an uncertainty which permits the conclusion that at least the lower echelons in the Communist hierarchy were unprepared for the event.[16] But again this argument is not necessarily absolutely convincing. The Communist leaders may have expected the press to know what stand to take in view of the general line on the Korean question, and they may have been hesitant to give out information on the top secret event.†

But the part played by the Chinese Communists in the actual invasion of South Korea is not very important. Much more important is their support of the developments in Korea leading up to the attack and above all the part they played after the attack had taken place. Against all

---

* On the nature of these "volunteers" see below.

† According to Carsun Chang China's entry into the war was probably due to Russian pressure between August and October 1950. — *Third Force in China*, pp. 285–288.

arguments supporting the innocence of the Chinese Communists in the original attack and their purely defensive intentions later on stands the fact that the strategic position of China would have enabled the Communist government to halt the war at any moment it had wanted to do so. All Chinese actions subsequent to the attack indicate that the government had no intention of using the possibilities at its disposal to settle the Korean question peacefully.

The Chinese Communists felt themselves directly involved in the Korean War through United States (as distinct from United Nations) action in regard to Formosa.[17] Two days after the invasion of South Korea, President Truman ordered American naval forces to neutralize Formosa by preventing an attack upon it and by preventing the Nationalists from using it as a base of operations against the mainland. He also pointed out that "the determination of the future status of Formosa must await the restoration of security in the Pacific, a peace settlement with Japan, or consideration by the United Nations," thus failing to reaffirm that Formosa would become a part of China.

The Chinese Communists seized upon this statement in order to whip up their anti-American campaign to unprecedented heights. President Truman's order was explained to the Chinese people as an attempt to prevent the "emancipation of our own Formosa" and as the beginning of "military aggression against Chinese territory." The Communists argued that the order violated the Cairo Declaration, which promised the return of Formosa to China, violated the Potsdam Proclamation, which declared that the Cairo Declaration would be carried out, and violated the President's announcement of January 5, 1950, that the United States had no designs on Formosa.

The argument was erroneous. The Cairo Declaration was implemented when the United States forces enabled the legitimate government of China to accept the surrender of the Japanese and establish a Chinese administration on Formosa. This administration has not been interfered with by the United States or any other foreign power. That this *de facto* control over Formosa could not be turned into *de jure* sovereignty was due to differences in policy among the foreign powers regarding the recognition of the National and the Communist governments.*

* The course of events in the Korean War changed the situation somewhat. General MacArthur's message to the Veterans of Foreign Wars of August 1950 (withdrawn by order of the president) advocated that the United States should not permit Formosa to fall into Communist hands, and this policy was eventually

America's Formosa policy was related by the Communists to her Korean policy, and both appeared in their eyes as a coordinated scheme of "imperialism." The Korean fighting was described as a civil war, provoked by the South Korean government, in which the United States was intervening as an aggressor. On June 28, 1950, Mao Tse-tung gave an address in which he remarked that the United States had now "exposed its own aggressive nature," that "the entire country . . . is solidly uniting and making thorough preparations to defeat the American imperialists in any quarrels they may provoke." He almost welcomed America's action, he said, because the exposure of America's true nature in Korea was "greatly advantageous to the peoples of China and Asia."

On the same day Chou En-lai elaborated on this theme by informing his people that the American move was no surprise "because the Chinese people have long been ceaselessly exposing the secret plot of American imperialism to invade China and to occupy all of Asia." This "American-directed attack," he continued, was only the first step "in a prearranged series of actions whose purpose it is to create a pretext for the American invasion of Formosa, Korea, French Indo-China and the Philippines; and it is also a further step in American imperialist intervention in Asian affairs." [18]

With amazing rapidity the campaign for the "liberation of Taiwan" and against the "American aggressors" got under way. As could be expected, the several assurances by the American government that Chinese territory would not be invaded, that neither the United States nor the United Nations had any aggressive designs against China — assurances fully supported in fact by the strict limitation of military action to Korean territory — had no effect upon China. The government organized "spontaneous" rallies, pledges, campaigns in every village and hamlet of China in preparation for the National Campaign Week Against United States Aggression scheduled for July 17–24, 1950. An accumulation of hate was produced which must have been a record even for a Communist country.

The slogans for the week, announced for many days in succession all over the country were: (1) Oppose the United States imperialist ag-

decided upon by the United States government. But even this step does not imply a severance of Formosa from China, quite apart from the fact that the government recognized by the United States continues to administer the island. See Harold M. Vinacke, *The United States and the Far East* (Stanford, 1952), pp. 122–129; Joseph W. Ballantine, *Formosa* (Washington, D.C., 1952), p. 175.

gression on Taiwan and Korea. (2) Oppose the United States imperialist disruption of peace in the Far East and of world peace. (3) Oppose the unlawful resolution adopted by the United Nations Security Council under United States manipulation. (4) United States imperialism, in launching oppression on Taiwan and Korea, merely presents a bold front void of inherent strength. (5) People of the whole world unite! Defeat the criminal aggression of United States imperialism. (6) Salute the Korean people and the Korean People's Army fighting against the United States imperialist aggression. (7) Salute the people in the East and West opposing the United States imperialist aggression. (8) Stand by the Korean people in their righteous war for national liberation and unity. Defend world peace. (9) People of whole Asia, rally round the world peace camp headed by the Soviet Union. Defeat the imperialist aggression. (10) Unite, consolidate our force and get ready to defeat imperialist provocation. (11) Intensify our work, consolidate our force, defend world peace with actual deeds. (12) Intensify our preparation for the liberation of Taiwan — our own territory. (13) Long live the unity and victory of the world peace.[19]

The possibility of a Chinese "volunteer" force to assist the North Koreans could be foreseen in this appeal. When such a force was about to be created in November 1950, allegedly as a reaction to the United Nations crossing of the Thirty-eighth Parallel, Chinese propaganda concentrated upon the theme that American action in Korea was aimed at China, that the country had to be defended.

On November 4, 1950, all newspapers carried editorials on Chinese "volunteers." A Joint Declaration of All Democratic Parties and Groups appeared on November 5 which stated, after a general attack upon the United States, that "the United States imperialists are copying the old trick of the Japanese bandits — first invading Korea and then invading China." Korea was an insignificant country except from the strategic standpoint, the declaration explained; the main object of the United States was not Korea but China. "History shows us that the existence of the Korean People's Republic and its fall and the security or danger of China are closely intertwined. The one cannot be safeguarded without the other." Helping Korea, the Declaration concluded, is self-defense.

This appeal to the historical fears of the Chinese was further strengthened by Chinese allegations that American airplanes had machine-gunned and bombed the territory and invaded the air of the People's

Republic of China, killing and wounding a number of civilians. Nevertheless it does not appear to have been as successful as the Communist leaders must have anticipated. Enthusiasm for "voluntarily" joining the fighting forces seems to have been mild. The people were told that the historical parallel ended with the "invasion" of Korea by the United States, that action was needed promptly. Unlike Japan, which had waited from 1894 to 1931 to invade China, the United States would not wait. And China this time would not need a breathing spell to strengthen herself. For in 1931, with China under Chiang K'ai-shek and the young Soviet Union weak, there was no way of resisting. But now the "Democratic Peace Camp" of the Soviet Union, the Chinese People's Republic, and the Korean Democratic People's Republic could defeat the United States.

The campaign for the enlistment of "volunteers" was conducted under the slogans "Resist American Aggression and Aid the Korean People" and "In Defending Korea You Defend Your Own Home." And the "volunteers" were told that their mission was to save the Korean people, the Chinese people, and "the peoples of Asia and the whole world." [20]

All through the war the Chinese people were told that the campaign was going in favor of the Communists. The limiting of the United Nations forces to Korean territory, in spite of considerable provocations from across the Yalu River, was never recognized by the Communists as a desire to limit the war and facilitate its ending, but was explained as due to Communist military efficiency.* Perhaps the Communists believed this themselves, which would explain their refusal to respond to the many peace proposals periodically suggested by the United Nations and many nations individually. They were flushed with victory. They had defeated the Nationalists, they had humiliated the Americans and the British, they had annexed Tibet in the late fall of 1950. They were backed by the mighty Soviet Union. This attitude was evident also in the long speech made by the Chinese Communist delegate Wu Hsin-chuan when he appeared before the Security Council on November 28, 1950.

The Chinese had cavalierly refused to discuss the Korean problem because, in their view, the whole United Nations action was based on the "illegal" vote of June 27 — illegal because of Russia's absence. Mr. Wu came to the United Nations not to settle a dangerous conflict peacefully,

* Quite possibly to make this patently absurd claim more plausible, the Chinese may have invented the germ warfare against Manchuria.

298

but to accuse the United States of aggression against Chinese territory. He repeated the whole Chinese Communist case against the United States and warned the United Nations that whatever decision it took would in no way shake the resolve of the Chinese people to liberate Taiwan or prevent action by the Chinese people to this end. A similar reaction took place in Communist China to President Eisenhower's announcement in his State of the Union message early in 1953 that restrictions on Nationalist attacks against the mainland from Formosa would be lifted. The people were told that this was a result of the American "defeat" in Korea. "Staggering under the deadly blows dealt by the people's forces in Korea, American aggressors now cast their hopes on the miserable mob ousted from the Chinese mainland," declared the Peking radio, and called upon the listeners to redouble their efforts to defeat the "imperialists." [21]

In keeping with this superior and arrogant attitude, the Chinese Communists immediately interpreted as a sign of weakness and a desire to sue for peace the favorable response of the United Nations to Russian hints in June 1951, and again after Stalin's death in March 1953, that the Korean War might be settled by peaceful negotiation. And, logically, the armistice in 1953 was celebrated in North Korea as a victory. The difference between the two periods was that in 1953 Communist propaganda on the world level seemed to become less harsh toward the West, particularly the United States. The Chinese Communists, however, were slow in falling into line. They continued much of their anti-American agitation. And the Cominform "peace offensive" was no embarrassment to them. They simply maintained that this had been Communist policy all along, that the new peace "atmosphere" was due to American, not Communist changes of policy. The increasing strength of the Communist world, the Chinese explained, had at last forced the United States to pay "lip service to peace" and would eventually force her to make "actual concessions to peace." [22]

While the question of the recognition of Communist China, the Japanese peace treaty, and the Korean War are the main topics of discussion by the Chinese Communist leaders, they are not the only ones. There is a clearly evident endeavor to make the Chinese case an Asian case. This, the Communists seem to feel, can be done more effectively by drawing into the discussion other aspects of American foreign policy which are not so directly or exclusively related to the Far East. Behind this endeavor lies first of all the Communist policy of creating a united Asian front of "free peoples." But a more specifically Chinese motivation can also be discovered. In stating that "to seize China is to seize the whole of Asia," [23] in stressing the Asian-wide implications of American "aggression" against China, in posing as the defenders of all Asia, the Chinese Communists are in reality making a bid for leadership in Asia, not dissimilar to the practice of their predecessors in power. The more they can show the involvement of all Asia in America's "aggressive policy," the more convincing, of course, can they make their case and the better can they disguise their own ends.

The technique the Communists are using to achieve this goal is to try to convince others that United States policy aims at dominating the whole world. In the process they cite real or alleged American practices; they select and often misinterpret or distort aspects of American policy to make them fit their purpose. Occasionally they are able to draw upon American actions which have been widely criticized also by non-Communists, within and without the United States. The support given to Franco and Rhee and the toleration of Nazis in Germany or reactionaries in Japan belong here, as possibly also the often equivocal stand of the United States on colonial questions. More frequently they twist and invent the facts. For instance, they point to the "armed invasion" of Korea and Formosa; the American "orders" to Great Britain, France, Canada, Australia, Italy, and others to forbid or suppress Communists and their parties; the American economic "penetration" of other countries by giving aid; the "forcing" of other nations into such "American instruments of aggression" as the North Atlantic Treaty Organization, the Middle East Command, and the Anzus Pact.[24]

Lest some states might conclude that it would be hopeless to oppose a United States which has the power to do all this, the Communists simultaneously emphasize their thesis that the United States is a "paper tiger." And they are trying to prove it by pointing to the alleged inherent weakness of capitalist states and their relative weakness compared to the "camp of peace" of the Communist states.

The "ruling class" in America is split, so the Communists maintain, on internal and external matters, and a concentrated effort is further hampered by the ever present threat of the "inevitable" collapse of the capitalist system. Militarily the United States is weak for a number of reasons, they argue: American battle lines are overextended; manpower is lacking and what there is has low morale; American allies are weak, apathetic, and unwilling to fight; American bases across the world are not impregnable; possession of the atom bomb is not a monopoly and, besides, atom bombs cannot win wars; America's industries are geographically concentrated and easy to destroy; and the material resources of the "peace camp" are almost equal to America's. In other resources the "peace camp" is superior — in manpower, productive capacity, and strategic position, and above all in the morale due to the social system.[25]

If comparisons of this sort were only propagandistic in purpose, they could be and indeed are being counteracted with some promise of success. But the aggressions in Korea and Tibet, the appeals to other Asian peoples to revolt and to rely upon the strength of the "peace camp," the disdain of methods for the peaceful settlement of disputes, and, generally, a haughty attitude in communicating with non-Communist nations seem to indicate that the Communist leaders have talked themselves into believing all these things themselves. Some success with their methods and the backing of the Soviet Union may well induce them to continue their campaign for the "liberation" of Asian peoples. In the past the Chinese have many times shown great boldness in words; they may now want to demonstrate their prowess. That they should have picked the United States as the object of this demonstration is a sad ending to a long, though by no means selfless and high-minded friendship. Of all the important powers with which China has had relations during the last hundred and ten years, this much at any rate can be said, that those with the United States have been the least unpleasant.

The government of Chiang K'ai-shek on Formosa and the few million inhabitants and refugees on that island remain the only Chinese with whom the United States and the many other nations which still recognize the National Government can maintain peaceful relations. For a few months after the Communists gained power on the mainland even that possibility was doubtful.

Chiang's government had meager resources to guarantee its own survival and keep Formosa out of Communist hands. At the sacrifice of some islands, Hainan most prominent among them, the Nationalists concentrated all their forces and equipment on the island of Formosa.[26] But it is quite probable that at the beginning of 1950, if the Communists had decided upon a determined attempt to capture Formosa, the Nationalists could not have held out for long. Apparently the Communists did not make such a decision or did not implement it until early in the summer of 1950. It was only then that rumors of an intended invasion and reports of troop accumulations opposite the island began to spread and increase in intensity.

The United States was the only country from which any help could be expected. The Nationalists looked with anxious eyes to Washington. Their close American friends argued for immediate and full support. They wanted the United States to guarantee the safety of the National Government and of Formosa. But President Truman decided differently. He announced on January 5, 1950, that the United States would not give military aid to the Nationalists, had no predatory designs on Formosa or any other Chinese territory, and had no desire to acquire special rights or privileges or to establish military bases on Formosa.[27] This was bad news to the Nationalists. But the picture was not altogether black. Chiang's fight for continued recognition at the United Nations indicated that the Nationalists had not been forsaken by all the nations of the world, that indeed a sufficient number were on their side to make their struggle successful. American economic aid continued to flow to Formosa, and the Nationalists expressed confidence that if enough of it arrived, they could hold Formosa against Communist attacks. This confidence, however, did not prevent them from periodically asking publicly for a common front to defeat communism or for increased economic aid, or even for military advisers. Furthermore the many visits of American officials to Formosa and the many calls of Chinese officials in the United States on American officials and friends indicated that Chinese diplomatic activity was intense.

For a while it had no visible success. The American debate over policy in regard to Formosa grew increasingly bitter, but the Administration stood fast by its refusal to give military assistance or support to the Nationalists. A statement by Secretary of State Dean Acheson on June 2, 1950, to the effect that the United States must prevent the further spread of communism may have foreshadowed the change in policy which came on June 27 with President Truman's order neutralizing Formosa. The development of American policy toward Formosa from that moment on led eventually to military as well as economic support for the National Government.

The Chinese on Formosa were not altogether happy with the president's order. They welcomed it, in the words of Foreign Minister George

Yeh, as "a most welcome sign of comradeship in the fight against communism." But they had some fears. The president's statement accompanying his order seemed to leave open the future status of Formosa, and this was as disturbing to the Nationalists as to the Communists. There was mention of the possibility of making Formosa a trust territory under the United Nations, to which the Nationalists strongly objected.* Above all, the neutralization prevented the Nationalists from attacking and eventually invading the mainland, prevented them, in other words, from realizing their most intense desire. The Nationalists made their position clear. Foreign Minister Yeh stated that the president's order did not affect the status of Formosa as determined in the Cairo Declaration nor China's authority over it. The order was an emergency measure, Yeh pointed out, which he hoped would succeed in ending the Korean War, but if it did not, other and stronger measures would have to be taken.[28]

Most of the Chinese fears were allayed after numerous diplomatic contacts and the organization of expanded American support for the National Government on Formosa began. Following a recommendation by General MacArthur, a group of American military officers made a report on the military situation on the island. In accordance with the report, and after the behavior of the Chinese Communists before the United Nations in November 1950 had indicated that the chances of peace in Korea were extremely poor, the United States government resumed shipments of military supplies in December 1950. Even then this action was kept secret for a few months, so that no remotest chance to settle the war might be missed.[29]

The supply of weapons and other military equipment was formalized in an American note to the National Government on January 30, 1951. In it the United States offered military aid to the Chinese on four conditions: (1) the supplies were to be used only for the island's "internal security or its legitimate self-defense"; (2) classified material and information were to be kept secret; (3) American personnel was to be received on the islands to see that the supplies were used properly; and (4) no military materials were to be transferred or sold by the National Government without previous consultation with the United States government. The Chinese accepted this offer on February 9.[30] Together with

* The same idea was mentioned in the halls of the United Nations in April 1953 and was characterized by T. F. Tsiang of Nationalist China as "too ridiculous to consider." — New York Times, April 9, 1953.

the arms and other matériel a military mission (assisting, not advisory, it was remarked officially) of several hundred Americans was sent to Formosa in April 1951. The Chinese received them with good grace, and President Chiang pledged his cooperation, which presumably meant that the usual resentment of the Chinese officers at foreign interference would not be permitted to lead to friction.[31]

The arrival of the military mission lifted the morale of the Nationalists. They took it as definite proof that the "neutralization" of the island would not be permanent. The constant American stress upon the purely defensive purposes for which military aid was given was not taken very seriously. The Chinese felt that the Seventh Fleet was a perfect protection of the island and that no further defense was necessary. They liked to believe that the strengthening of their army was therefore for different purposes: the invasion of the mainland.[32] In spite of increasingly larger American supplies to the island,[33] there was, however, no evidence that American policy would support such a step. When President Eisenhower took office, American policy changed. The "deneutralization" of Formosa early in 1953 freed the Nationalists to raid and, if they could, invade the mainland, though apparently not without prior consultation with American authorities. By their own admission in February 1953, Nationalist armed forces were not yet adequately equipped for a full-scale invasion, but the president's move was a great help to the morale of the Nationalists and taken by them as aligning American opinion with their own conviction that only pressure on the mainland could solve the problem of peace in the Far East.[34]

Parallel with military assistance, economic assistance is now being given in large measure to the Chinese on Formosa. Until the United States took positive action to ensure the island's security, the main purpose of the ECA program was to assist in current economic needs, to put the island's economy back on its feet, and to strengthen the confidence of its inhabitants. Thereafter the program was greatly enlarged and based on long-range planning, with a view to making the island self-sufficient. Since 1950, about $100 million worth of goods and services — half the amount of military aid — has been supplied annually. Assistance has been directed toward four basic needs: (1) immediate requirements, especially in commodities; (2) increased farm productivity and improved rural welfare; (3) reconstruction of war-damaged industries and their further development; and (4) technical advice.

There is widespread agreement that the program has been very successful.[35]

Compared to American–Nationalist Chinese relations, the relations between Formosa and other nations are insignificant. Toward those nations which have recognized the Communist regime, the Nationalists are naturally very bitter. Madame Chiang K'ai-shek, for instance, in an outburst of great anger, attacked Great Britain as a "moral weakling who has bartered her soul for thirty pieces of silver." [36] With the exception of Japan, relations of the Nationalists with the nations other than the United States with which they continue to have dealings are somewhat devoid of substance and take place mostly in the United Nations.

The major issue that was to be settled between China and Japan was the signing of a peace treaty. This had become a very complicated affair in view of the existence of two Chinese governments, each of which had been recognized by a number of the nations participating in the San Francisco conference dealing with a peace treaty for Japan, and neither of which was invited to participate in the conference. It was left to the Japanese government to determine with which Chinese government it wanted to sign a treaty, and its choice was the National Government on Formosa.

Negotiations began early in 1952. Three points in the proposed treaty emerged immediately as difficult of settlement. The first was the exact title of the treaty. The Chinese insisted adamantly that the title had to make clear that the treaty was a full-fledged peace treaty, while the Japanese hoped to avoid the use of the word peace in the title. The second point was the extent of the territory to which the treaty should apply. The Japanese insisted that the treaty could cover only those territories under the actual control of the National Government at the signing of the treaty or coming under its control thereafter. The Chinese insisted that China was a sovereign entity and the National Government its legal representative, that therefore there should be no provision in the treaty regarding the scope of its territorial applicability. The third point referred to reparations and the date from which Japan's liability was to begin. The Chinese maintained that the state of war began on September 18, 1931, when Mukden was attacked and Manchuria occupied, whereas the Japanese suggested July 7, 1937, when the incident at Lukouchiao renewed the war between the two powers.[37]

After several months of sometimes bitter negotiations, a Treaty of

Peace was signed in Taipei on April 28, 1952. Peace was thus introduced into the official title of the treaty. On the other hand, there is no specific reference to its territorial scope. In an exchange of notes accompanying the signing of the treaty, however, the two powers agreed that its terms "in respect to the Republic of China, be applicable to all the territories which are now, or which may hereafter be, under the control of its Government." [38] In many respects, the treaty follows the San Francisco Treaty of September 8, 1951. In essence it eliminates the special rights and privileges which Japan had gained during the past fifty years by her ruthless methods. It leaves details of the new Chinese-Japanese relations to subsequent agreements. One of these, regarding trade, was concluded, after some difficult negotiations, on December 13, 1952. It foresees a considerable expansion of trade with Japan, which is already Nationalist China's biggest customer and supplier of commodities.[39]

The relations between Nationalist China and the Western powers and Japan are friendly, as they are bound to be. Formosa would have no chance of survival without foreign, especially American, help. The National Government therefore has no bargaining power at all and is dependent upon the good will of the United States. The development of American policy toward Formosa indicates that American support is not a matter of love but of strategic considerations, as of course the Nationalist Chinese realize. They do not hesitate occasionally to point out some of their grievances. Chiang K'ai-shek, on Christmas Day 1952, gave vent to feelings of bitterness dating from the early postwar years when he recalled — for no apparent reason — that the Western powers "kicked us while we were down, encouraged the enemy to knock us out, and rejoiced at our defeat." The objective of Foreign Minister Yeh's speech on November 1, 1952, at the United Nations was clearer when he warned: "If, in our anxiety to conclude an armistice in Korea,* we

* The final truce terms since agreed upon were approved by Chiang K'ai-shek, but only with the warning that the Communists could not be trusted and that they sought, not peace, but rather a breathing-spell to prepare for attacks elsewhere in Asia. He expressed his conviction that in the end the Communist menace could be eliminated only by a victory, not by a compromise. If United States policy was "really aimed" at the elimination of communism, he felt, such a victory could be achieved. The desiderata would be a security pact in the Pacific, the granting of all his requests for matériel from the United States, full support of Syngman Rhee, and a "strong" policy — short of war — toward the Chinese Communists. — New York Times, July 21, 28, 1953.

The signing of the armistice, of course, is making it more difficult for the generalissimo to obtain outside help, without which he cannot hope to invade the mainland.

should unwittingly provide the aggressors with the opportunity to prepare themselves for further acts of aggression, we would be defeating
the very purpose for which we entered into the truce talks." [40] Remarks
of this kind are a reflection of the well-justified distrust the Chinese have
developed in dealings with the big powers and show their fear of being
treated as pawns. That the Chinese Nationalists should in their present
condition have this fear and distrust to a heightened degree is easily understandable. That the Communist Chinese should no longer harbor
the same feelings toward the Russians is almost impossible to believe.

23

The Alliance with the Soviet Union

JUDGING by appearances, the friendship and sympathy between the Soviet Union and Communist China can hardly be surpassed. Just as in Communist eyes the United States represents everything that is evil in the world, so the Soviet Union represents everything that is good. The Soviet Union has always been recognized by the Chinese Communist leaders as the spiritual home and the political progenitress of their China. But she has not been this for the mass of the Chinese people. To them, more often, Russia — tsarist or Communist — has represented a threat to the independence of their country. To the Communist leaders the task of destroying sympathy for the United States has therefore the correlate of creating sympathy for the Soviet Union. The means by which they have undertaken to create such sympathy is to build up the Soviet Union in the minds of their people as the ideal state.

Praise of the Soviet Union is a daily ritual in Communist China. The Chinese press and radio are filled with descriptions of every aspect of Soviet life in the most glowing and tempting terms. Just as the United States is damned as responsible for everything that troubles the Chinese, so the Soviet Union is lauded for everything that pleases them. There are unending expressions of gratitude for Soviet aid in building up the New China. The Chinese Communist citizen is constantly reminded of his indebtedness to the Soviet Union for his country's economic advances, cultural improvements, and "brand new" foreign policy.

The Soviet Union reciprocates to some degree. But Russian assurances of friendship and promises of aid are kept, presumably deliberately, in a different tone. They lack the fervor and eagerness of the Chinese and there is no trace of thankfulness. The Chinese declarations resemble loyalty oaths; the Russian, gracious acceptance. The Soviet Union is the senior partner and acts the role. This is proper form according to the Communist code. As the only nation that has attained the socialist stage, the Soviet Union has a primacy that China, only in the transitional stage of a People's Republic, must accept. Presumably to avoid a second Yugoslavia, however, the Soviet Union pays her respects to Chinese pride and Maoist ambition and gives China a status just a notch above that of the European satellites.[1] This dissimilarity in treatment and, of course, in the nature of the countries involved has often provoked the question of Chinese "Titoism."

There are some passages in the history of the Chinese Communist party that, merely from the standpoint of the inner structure and functioning of Communist organization, permit speculation whether Mao possesses the temperament permanently to make impossible a split between Peking and Moscow. The defeat by the Kuomintang of the Moscow-directed urban Communist movement in 1926 and 1927 might have led to the extinction of communism in China but for Mao's work with the peasants in the provinces of Hunan and Kiangsi. This was work he undertook in despite of Leninist theory and Moscow's policy that "liberation can be achieved only under the leadership of the proletariat." He organized guerrilla activity which was only reluctantly approved by the Sixth National Congress of the Communist Party in September 1928. He insisted that nobody interfere with the activities of his local peasant associations when, in 1927, Stalin still decreed that land reforms should be introduced by the Kuomintang-Communist coalition. To the Comintern's order in the same year to curb "peasant excesses," Mao answered that a revolution was no activity for Confucian gentlemen. He called for the organization of soviets before they were authorized by the Comintern. And he conducted the Autumn Harvest Uprisings of 1928 without the urban proletariat, contrary to what the Central Committee of the party had demanded. After Mao had established his power, such examples of independence and disrespect on his part became less common. But as late as 1950 the Indian Communists called him a deviationist and placed his "New Democracy" on a par with Tito's "Trotskyism" and Browder's "Reformism."

The party's Central Committee was removed from Shanghai to Mao's headquarters in Juichin in the fall of 1932. This may have been a step to control Mao's growing strength. More probably it was an indication of the committee's dependence upon Mao and a bow to him as the outstanding leader of Chinese communism. In either case it showed where the real power in the Chinese Communist movement was located. To concede such power is not the Cominform's ordinary way of doing things. Yet if any striking difference in policy between Mao and the Cominform should ever again arise, it is difficult to imagine the concession coming from Mao's side.

China's advancement from the status of "quasi colony" to the status of a "liberated"— that is, a Communist — country was accomplished, moreover, not according to the orthodox pattern of Communist events. Almost to the end the Chinese Communists lacked outside aid; yet basic Communist doctrine has it that "liberation" should have been impossible without the hegemony of the Chinese proletariat and its cooperation with the proletariat of the Soviet Union and of the world. Mao's proof to the contrary had to be argued out of existence. This was done by pretending that there were proletarians in the leadership, by making honorary proletarians out of nonproletarians, and by overemphasizing the aid the Soviet Union had given the Communists in the last few years of their struggle for power. Mao was probably a willing cooperator in this propaganda. For if China, a "quasi colony," could "liberate" herself without the aid of the proletariat elsewhere, other Asian colonies might emulate the feat. The door would then be opened for a number of independent Asian Communist states and a serious blow administered to Chinese Communist expansionist ambitions.

All these events — from the standpoint of Communist discipline — indicate considerable independence on the part of Mao. He does not seem to have been a yes-man to Moscow even while Stalin was alive. If this was true during the period of his struggle for power and recognition, when compliance with Comintern instructions might have gained him much, now that Stalin is dead and he holds a most powerful position, it should be truer still.

On the other hand, Mao has always wanted to be a good Marxist-Leninist and has thought of himself as such. Instead of altering orthodox doctrine, he claims to have expanded and reinterpreted it. Instead of deviating from it, he thinks he has only "adapted" it to the unique conditions of China. Viewed objectively, his contribution to Communist doctrine is not very striking, and once the Chinese Communists returned to the cities, they returned also to complete orthodoxy. But whatever the extent and the originality of Mao's contribution, the important fact is that he and the Chinese Communists think it has been considerable. The 1945 Constitution of the Chinese Communist party speaks reverently of "the ideas of Mao Tse-tung," and the pride of the Chinese Commu-

nists is a weighty factor in China's relations with the Soviet Union.*
Though there is no evidence that Mao's ideas are considered contrary
to Marxism-Leninism, respect for them as a further development of the
Communist gospel is expected by the Chinese.[2] This respect is paid by
Moscow through approval of Mao's writings as consistent with Marxism-
Leninism-Stalinism.

Ideological considerations aside, the relations between Communist
China and Russia seem to be entirely without friction. The aim of the
Chinese Communist leaders in impressing upon their people the friendship and achievements of the Soviet Union is to stimulate a desire to
imitate Soviet practices. This aspect is greatly emphasized in all Communist propaganda. The Chinese citizen is exhorted to emulate the
Russian example in his private and social life. Considerable pressure is
exerted upon him to familiarize himself with the Soviet way of life and
to learn from Soviet experience, for "Russia's Today is Our Tomorrow."

Among the slogans announced for the Sino-Soviet Friendship Month,
November 1952, was this: "Let all the people throughout the country
study hard advanced experiences of the Soviet people in building their
country, and prepare for the forthcoming large-scale economic and
cultural construction; let us fight for the industrialization of our motherland."

Thereafter followed twelve slogans, each appealing to a different
group — workers in state enterprises, peasants, animal breeders, workers
in state commercial enterprises and cooperatives, civil servants, youth,
women, educational workers, scientific and technical workers, medical
and health workers, literary and art workers, and industrialists and busi-
nessmen — to learn from "advanced" Soviet experience and knowledge
in their respective fields.[3]

This is the continuation of the search by so many Chinese leaders for
the philosopher's stone, for the "secret" of Western success. The endeavor of the Communist leaders may, in part, be based on ideological
affinity with the Russians, but in part it must also be based upon the
career of the Soviet Union from an underdeveloped country to a most
powerful nation within one generation, an achievement which has fas-

---

* It should be borne in mind that Mao's "contributions" lie entirely in the field
of internal Chinese strategy and developments, though they may be applied to other
"quasi-colonial" and colonial areas. Nowhere in Chinese Communist literature has
there ever been any criticism or questioning of Communist theory or practice as
they refer to external affairs, particularly Russian foreign policy.

cinated almost all Asian leaders and many of their peoples and which they all wish to emulate.

The propaganda campaign is conducted on two levels, the official, governmental one and the officially unofficial, "private" one.

The governments of Communist China and the Soviet Union use every conceivable opportunity, such as national anniversaries, army days, the birthdays of heroes, inauguration days and anniversaries of treaty signatures, to exchange greetings, expressions of mutual admiration, delegations, and toasts, and generally to engage in celebrations. The result is that a pretext can be found to remind the Chinese citizen almost every day of the "lasting, powerful, and unbreakable Sino-Soviet Friendship and Alliance."

Among the "private" organizations engaged in propagating friendship between the Soviet Union and Communist China, the Sino-Soviet Friendship Association is the most important. Although the promotion of cultural relations is its primary task, politics is inevitably mixed with its activities.

The association has many millions of members distributed all over China. It reports boundless enthusiasm among the citizens for its aims. The whole population of villages sometimes joins. The "volunteer" army in Korea solicited membership *in toto* by cable and was so admitted.

Between 1950 and 1952, among other activities the association sponsored 23 visits to China by Russian individuals or groups concerned with cultural life and 14 return visits by Chinese. It arranged the translation into Chinese of nearly 800 books on Marxism-Leninism and on the Soviet Union as well as of all literary works receiving the Stalin prize. It organized 7,400 showings of Soviet films to 17 million Chinese, the exhibition of 14,000 photographs on the Soviet Union to 3 million Chinese, and the performance of 50 educational Russian films in schools, colleges, and other institutions. It arranged for 28 broadcasts of Soviet Music Appreciation Hours and 60 meetings for the same purpose.[4]

At the first national conference of the association in October 1951 it was decided to shift from slogans to "the phase of intensification and concrete work with rich contents." In practice this meant an order to the 1,300 branches of the organization to begin "ideological education on internationalism and Soviet experience." The purpose of this education was to be to "absolutely liquidate all vestiges of anti-Soviet thoughts, rebut the viewpoint of narrow nationalism in relation to Sino-Soviet relations, and eliminate the masses' misgivings and worries with regard to Soviet Union and question of Sino-Soviet friendship." [5]

Apparently enthusiasm for the Soviet Union and her new relations with Communist China was not yet complete. Other evidence to this effect emerged from official criticisms that the "Resist US–Aid Korea" campaign was not sufficiently tied in with the Sino-Soviet friendship propaganda.[6] More specifically the complaint was that too many Chinese still ignored the nature of "proletarian internationalism" and were taking too much credit for "resistance to aggression" in Korea instead of giving it to the Soviet Union (whose soldiers were staying safely at home). The Sino-Soviet Friendship Association was assigned the task of clarifying these things.

A principal object of all this propaganda is to create the atmosphere in which close political and economic relations between the two countries can be conducted. There were at the beginning of this new era of friendship still many Chinese who thought these relations were too one-sided and who could not detect much difference between the tsarist and the Soviet Russian position in Manchuria, Mongolia, and Sinkiang. In spite of the Marxist-Leninist-Maoist rationalization of the treaty and the agreements of 1945, sanctioning Russian expansionism at China's expense, enough Chinese asked questions about Russia's "special position" in the northeast (Manchuria) to worry the party leaders. They called a special-delegate conference to make clear once more that, being a socialist state, Russia cannot be imperialistic and that Russian policy in the Far East can be explained satisfactorily from the Chinese Communist standpoint. What they were in fact asking once more was acceptance of the dogma that anything originating in the Soviet Union must be good. Partly in order to lay at rest all doubts, a series of new treaties and agreements were signed between the Soviet Union and Communist China in February 1950.[7]

These treaties laid the foundation for the relations between the two Communist countries.* Their conclusion was hailed by both sides as the greatest contribution to the welfare of the Soviet Union, China, Asia, and the world ever made by two nations in the history of mankind. They

---

* Upon signing the new treaties the Soviet government announced that the 1945 treaties were abrogated. The National Government abrogated the 1945 treaties by formal action in February 1953. This was essentially a gesture for the diplomatic record, though it allows the Nationalists to attack the Russians in Port Arthur and Dairen. — *New York Times*, February 24, 25, 1953.

were praised not as ordinary treaties — "international" relations in the ordinary sense do not exist between Communist states according to Communist doctrine — but as agreements confirming "new" and "special" relations. In Chou En-lai's words: "This great alliance is an alliance between brothers." [8] Every anniversary of its conclusion is the occasion for extensive celebrations. Nothing seems to have been allowed to interfere with it. All speculation abroad on Stalin's death about the possibility of Chinese Titoism was cut short by the Chinese Communist government, which was quick to reaffirm its solidarity with the Soviet Union "indefinitely, forever, and with maximum resoluteness." In a special article for *Pravda* Mao Tse-tung wrote on March 10, 1953, that the Communist Party of the Soviet Union "has been and is for us a model. It will be also a model for us in future." He assured his and the Russian people that Sino-Russian friendship is unbreakable.[9] He has written in a similar vein elsewhere. In July 1953 the Central Committees of the Chinese and Russian Communist parties reaffirmed their "complete unity."

In the Treaty of Friendship, Alliance, and Mutual Assistance of 1950, the two powers agreed to prevent a repetition of aggression by Japan or any other state (since admitted to be the United States) by joint measures. If one of them was attacked by Japan or states allied with her and became involved in a state of war, the other was to render all assistance, including military. They also agreed to work for an early conclusion of the peace treaty with Japan, to consult with each other on all important international problems of common interest, to participate in all international actions aimed at securing peace and security throughout the world, and to establish close economic and cultural ties.

In an agreement on the Chinese Changchun (formerly the Chinese Eastern) Railway, Port Arthur, and Dairen, the two powers agreed that the Soviet Union should return all rights in the joint administration of the railroad to China by the end of 1952 at the latest; that Russian troops should be withdrawn from Port Arthur and the installations there returned to China against compensation by the end of 1952, with the qualification that in case of aggression the base should be used jointly; and, finally, that the question of Dairen should be further considered upon the conclusion of a peace treaty with Japan, but that in any case the civil administration there belongs to China.

In another agreement a credit of $300 million at 1 per cent interest

314

per annum was provided for China, payable in five annual installments over a period of four years and repayable in ten annual installments beginning December 31, 1954. The credit is to be used for the purchase of equipment and supplies from the Soviet Union. Repayment is to be made by deliveries of raw materials, tea, gold, and United States dollars.*

An exchange of notes ensured the "independent" status of Outer Mongolia, and another arranged for the return without compensation of property "acquired by Soviet business organizations from Japanese organizations in Manchuria and buildings of former Soviet military settlements in Peking."

A month later, on March 27, 1950, agreements were signed † for the establishment of joint stock companies for the exploitation of oil and nonferrous metal resources in Sinkiang and the running of civilian airlines between China and the Soviet Union.[10]

The details of the execution and implementation of the political and military clauses of the Treaty of Friendship are largely unknown. To all appearances, perfect harmony is being maintained. In international councils to which Communist China is not admitted, the Soviet Union takes up the Communist Chinese cause. Reports of joint defense arrangements by the two countries are presumably correct. Their cooperation is obvious in the Korean War, both in the sending of physical supplies to the Communist troops and in psychological warfare.

In the late summer of 1952 the highest officials of Communist China and the Soviet Union met in Moscow. It was announced then that a mixed Sino-Soviet commission would arrange for the return of the Chinese Changchun Railway and all property belonging to it to the

* Implementing protocols to these two agreements were signed on June 15, 1951, and April 12, 1952. In 1953 an additional agreement, for a loan and the supply of Russian machinery, was signed.

† When these agreements were announced, many reports emanated from Formosa, Hongkong, and Tokyo about additional secret treaties concluded between the two parties. These would give the Soviet Union an extremely favorable position in China and a much more dominant one than would appear from the published texts. In Peking, on the other hand, there were reports of a telegram which Chou En-lai had sent to Mao, negotiating in Moscow, reminding him that any agreement reached by him was subject to confirmation by the government in Peking. There were further reports that while Mao was in Moscow, he was to be condemned as a deviationist by Stalin but that this plan was scotched when it was found out how important he was for maintaining discipline in the Chinese Communist party. One fact which gives credibility to this last report is that the Indian *Communist* in its February–March 1950 issue called Mao a deviationist, an accusation which it had to retract in the next issue of July–August 1950.

Chinese People's Republic not later than December 31, 1952. This arrangement was completed on December 31, 1952, when the railway and its property were returned to China in conformity with the basic agreement concluded on February 14, 1950.[11]

On the occasion of the same conference, a Chinese note to Moscow was published in which it was stated that the conclusion of a peace treaty between Japan and the United States and several other states and the "seeming" wish of Japan not to conclude a treaty with China and the Soviet Union, had created conditions "dangerous for peace and favorable for a repetition of Japanese aggression." Therefore the Chinese government requested the Soviet government to delay the withdrawal of Soviet troops from the "jointly used" naval base at Port Arthur until a peace treaty between Japan, China, and the Soviet Union should be concluded. The Soviet Union granted the request. The Communist Chinese greeted the two agreements with such enthusiastic comments as that "they greatly inspire peace-loving people the world over while delivering telling blows at US criminal plots to collaborate with the Japanese militarist forces." [12] They also praised the return of the railway without charge to China as a most magnanimous Soviet gesture. The facts are that the Chinese government never agreed to the sale of the railway to Japan in 1935 because that sale was contrary to the Sino-Soviet agreement of 1924, and that the Soviet Union sold the railway to Manchukuo and Japan for a price.[13]

What unpublished agreements of a political and military nature may have been reached by the Soviet Union and Communist China or just how those published will be executed is difficult to know. There is much speculation and little information. More is known, though not by any means everything, about economic relations, but most of this information is of Communist origin, hence of doubtful validity.

Generally speaking, the economic relations between the Soviet Union and Communist China have expanded greatly since their foundation was laid in the basic treaty of 1950 and in various subsequent supplementary agreements. The reasons are easy to find. Ideological affinity may have given an impetus to closer relations generally, including economic. Common support of aggression in Korea and other border areas of China has increased the flow of equipment and resources from the Soviet Union and has furthered Chinese armaments production, especially in Manchuria. Owing to governmental policy and to embargoes and counterembargoes on trade with the non-Communist world after the aggression in Korea, Chinese trade has changed its direction and is now mainly with the Soviet Union. The Soviet Union has also become the main source of China's badly needed financial and technical assistance. It is difficult to believe that the Chinese Communists cherish this dependence upon the Soviet Union or that they find the relatively meager assistance satisfactory. Nevertheless, in the absence of any alternative which would fit their politics, the Chinese Communists are jubilant over the "brotherly help," the "precious assistance," obtained "unselfishly" from the Soviet Union, without which, so they claim, the "tremendous accomplishments" of the New China would not have been possible.[14] At the same time they point out that economic relations with the Soviet Union are based on "reciprocity" and "mutuality." *

The four major types of economic relations of which the Chinese Communists speak are finance, joint enterprises, commerce, and technical aid.

The most prominent case of financial aid is the grant of the $300 million loan in the agreement of 1950. This amount is called a "large sum" in Chinese propaganda; yet from any objective standpoint, and considering China's needs, it is totally inadequate. Annually the two governments sign an agreement for the delivery of goods against the loan.

"Cooperative assistance" is the second type of economic relations. This refers essentially to the continuation of Sino-Russian "joint" enterprises, which have been a feature of Russian economic penetration in China since the days of the tsars. However, the Chinese Communists explain that this cooperation is altogether different from similar practices by the "imperialists," in whose hands such enterprises were merely instruments of "plunder and exploitation." Now they serve to hasten the pace of China's industrialization, are indeed what makes it possible at all. Since the areas in which the "joint" enterprises were established — Sinkiang, the Liaotung peninsula (South Manchuria), and Manchuria — are also those in which Russia has traditionally had expansionist ambitions, the similarity to the tsarist institutions becomes unmistakable.

* This acknowledgment of great indebtedness to Russia at the same time that the economic relations are admitted to be (as such relations frequently are) of mutual benefit is presumably a reflection of Communist protocol, which requires that the Soviet Union be above all other Communist states, for no such gratitude is expressed by Russia. There is good reason to believe that China's exports are considerably in excess of her imports; in other words, that the trade is disadvantageous to China. — *New York Times*, February 28, 1953.

The types of privileges sought and granted are in essence those requested by the Soviet Union from the Nationalist government and refused because they were incompatible with China's national interests. According to the agreements signed in Moscow on March 21, 1950, three "joint" corporations were established: a Sino-Russian Petroleum Corporation for the prospecting, production, and refining of oil in Sinkiang, a corporation for the mining of nonferrous and rare metals in Sinkiang, and a Sino-Russian Civil Aviation Corporation, flying the routes Peking-Chita, Peking-Irkutsk, Peking–Alma Ata.

The formal basis of these corporations, which does not necessarily describe the actual working of their administration, is as follows. Expenses, profits, and products are shared half and half. The leading positions are alternated every three years. During the first three years the chairman of the management committee is a Chinese, the vice-chairman, a Russian; the general manager, a Russian; the assistant general manager, a Chinese. Half the number of employees are Russian, the other half Chinese. The Chinese praised this system as based "on the mutually profitable basis of equal shares in stock, equal rights, and respect for each other's sovereignty." [15]

In Dairen and also in Manchuria many of the industries once developed by the Japanese and unsuitable for transplantation to the Soviet Union were appropriated by the Russians and then converted into "joint" enterprises, such as a glass factory, an electrical equipment plant, and a cement plant in Dairen (hailed as a "concrete" example of Sino-Soviet cooperation).[16] Whenever the Russians, in conformity with the treaty and agreements of 1950, returned any enterprises and buildings in Manchuria and Peking instead of making them "joint" property, they were hailed as the truest and greatest friends China ever had.[17]

Trade — the third area of economic relations — between the two countries has reached considerable proportions. The Soviet Union is both the most important customer of Communist China and her most important source of imports. About 70 per cent of China's trade is with Russia, and this trade has been rising in volume and value ever since 1950.* The nature of China's exports has not changed much compared to pre-Communist days; soybeans, tea, silk, wool, agricultural by-products,

* According to the *Far Eastern Economic Review*, XIII (1952), 684, Russia is buying Chinese goods at "give-away" prices and reselling them at high profit in the European market, whereas China has to pay prices for Russian goods far above world market prices.

and some metals represent the bulk. Her imports, however, are different. Industrial raw materials, machinery, industrial equipment, machine parts, and communications equipment and parts account for about 97 per cent of them — an interesting change from pre-Communist days, when China imported great quantities of consumer goods. Occasionally the Soviet Union supplies sugar, high-quality cotton, fertilizer, and other goods.[18]

The fourth type of economic relations is technical assistance from the Soviet Union. There are many hundreds of advisers in China, mostly in Manchuria. They are helping in the development of railways, agriculture, water conservation, and sewage systems, in road building and traffic control, and in many similar areas. At the same time they assist in the training of Chinese experts and skilled workers, including the "inculcating of the outlook" necessary to do a job perfectly. The Chinese government has also announced that Russians are aiding in the improvement of the administration. Extreme claims are made for the results of this Soviet assistance. Agricultural production and lumber production are said to have increased by many times; zinc plants, lying idle because they were "misguided" by Americans, are announced to have resumed production since Soviet experts redesigned them; even the "procreative ability of studs" has tripled with the expert help of the Russians.[19]

To make sure that aid from the Soviet Union is not confused by the Chinese citizen with the past "imperialist penetration" of the Western powers, explanations are provided periodically. Sometimes they are short, merely to the effect that Soviet help is "entirely different" from American "aid." Sometimes they are more complex: "A basic difference exists between the Sino-Soviet relations and those between China's reactionary governments and the imperialist countries. This difference stems from the fact that imperialism is a system of exploitation of labouring people in other countries, whereas the economic system of Socialism is controlled by the labouring people themselves and is non-exploiting." The Chinese citizen is further told that the Soviet Union, as the first state to have a dictatorship of the proletariat, "is imbued with the consistent internationalism of the working class. It is in sympathy with and eager to help all proletarian dictatorships, and all nations in which the working class occupies the dominant position."[20] This is, of course, no explanation, but merely another reminder that the same phenomena mean different things according to where they originate. If the origin is the Soviet Union, the Communist Chinese is expected to accept them as beneficent.

On the surface the political, economic, military, and, it might be added, cultural relations between the Soviet Union and Communist China are such as to indicate that the two countries live together in friendship and that the many points of friction existing in the past have been eliminated. What is happening under the surface one cannot know with certainty. One may express doubt whether the many aspects of Russian expansionism that so thoroughly aroused the Chinese in the past and instilled in them such suspicion and hatred can have a completely different effect now, at least among those Chinese who are not Communists. Potentially, at any rate, a number of friction areas can easily develop.

There could be rivalry for leadership in the Communist expansion drive. There could be dispute over methods and strategy in common action. There could be dissension over the sharing of sacrifices and benefits in the execution of joint policies. There could be splits over policy. Whose satellite North Korea is to be is apparently already a touchy issue. On the other hand, for the present, there is a vast area of parallel (presumably not common) interests whose existence will prevent the breakdown of good relations, and for whose maintenance Moscow has made some small, and Peking some huge, concessions.

Communist China can give full support to Russian ambitions in Europe because China has few interests there, while the involvement of the Western world in Europe will give Communist China a freer hand in Asia. The Soviet Union can support Communist China in Asia because in most respects, and for the time being, what benefits Chinese interests also benefits Russian interests.[21] The Soviet Union has little to fear from Communist China as long as that country engages in a policy which makes her deeply dependent upon the Soviet Union in every respect. In whatever way this dependence may be evaluated by the Chinese Communist leaders, they may consider it to have compensations. They no longer have to rely upon a precarious balance of power for security; they have Russian support against a feared repetition of Japanese aggression; they have a freer hand than ever before in South and Southeast Asia; they are eliminating all Western powers from China and in the end will have to deal with only one — Russia — instead of all; and they are managing somewhat to balance the loss of economic ties with Western powers by the creation of new ones with the European satellites of the Soviet Union. Most of these advantages, at one time or another, Chinese governments before the Communists have tried to obtain.

When the fog of Communist verbiage is cleared away from Sino-Soviet relations, a situation emerges which is not so radically new or specifically Communist as might at first appear. As far as Russia is concerned, the reference in the Yalta Agreement to the *status quo* of 1904 would alone suffice to indicate a clear desire to continue traditional expansionism. As far as China is concerned, an appeasement of Russian imperialist ambitions has been advocated more than once in the past by Chinese statesmen, Li Hung-chang and Chiang K'ai-shek among them. Pro-Russian and anti-Russian factions have been permanent fixtures in Chinese governmental councils. The motives behind the desire to appease may have varied — sometimes they were ideological, more often political — but at any rate the payment of a price for Russian restraint or friendship has often been considered worth while. The very important difference under the Chinese Communist regime is not only that a policy of complete appeasement has been consummated, but that the situation thus created is no longer represented to the people as a necessary evil, but as most desirable and beneficial for China. A particularly unhappy and dangerous concomitant is that Communist China is using her newly won sense of strength to employ the unscrupulous and ruthless methods of Communist politics in the pursuit of her policies toward other powers.

Because of the close relations with the Soviet Union, entirely new contacts have been established between Communist China and the Communist states of Eastern Europe. In principle these relations are like those with Russia, except that they are adapted to the hierarchy prevailing among Communist states in their interrelations. This means that China and the Eastern European states are on an equal basis with China as *primus inter pares,* and that all join on various occasions in affirming their common allegiance and gratitude to the Soviet Union as the leader of them all.

The nations involved are introduced to China, and vice versa, by the preferred Communist means of cultural relations. There is a steady flow between China and the People's Republics of theatrical, musical, folk-dancing, acting, and athletic groups. Students are exchanged, exhibits are organized, and newspapers have regular supplements dealing with the culture of the other countries. Films are shown, gifts exchanged, and Friendship Months organized. Communist China signed agreements for cultural exchange with the Democratic Republic of Germany (Communist) in October 1951, with Rumania early in December 1951, with Bulgaria on July 14, 1952, with Czechoslovakia on May 6, 1952, with Poland on April 3, 1952, and with Hungary on July 11, 1951. Each signature, and the anniversary of each signature, is the occasion for great festivities. Even Albania, which signed no agreement, felt that these cultural contacts create an affinity among the nations. To quote her minister of education: "Albania is far away from China, yet we feel that China is so near to us." The Communist leaders explain to their people that there is nothing dangerous to China in these close cultural contacts. China rejects only the "degraded elements" of Western culture; she enthusiastically welcomes its "progressive features," and those coming from Albania, for instance, are considered "progressive." Indeed, Mao Tse-tung told his people, "China must absorb abundantly from foreign progressive culture the nourishing material for her own culture." [22]

Of greater importance to Communist China are the trade relations with the Communist countries of Eastern Europe. These too are innovations. China concluded trade agreements with Poland in February 1950, on January 29, 1951, and July 11, 1952; with Communist Germany on October 10, 1950; with Czechoslovakia in June 1950, on June 21, 1951, and July 15, 1952; with Hungary on January 22, 1951, and July 21, 1952; and with Bulgaria on July 21, 1952. In many cases agreements referring to postal and tele-communications and technical aid have also been signed.

In general, China imports metal products, industrial goods, chemicals, paper, cars and trucks, dyes, fertilizer, and some raw materials from these countries, while her exports to them are of the traditional kinds. To a considerable degree this trade has become possible through the rapid industrialization of the Eastern European countries, and has been made necessary through the falling off of trade with non-Communist countries. Much of this trade is conducted on the basis of direct barter, for, as the Foreign Trade Control Conference in Peking in 1951 decided, "the age of the capitalist world's 'free exchange' and 'free markets' has passed." [23]

Shipping between East Europe and China arose immediately as a serious problem. The passage is long, the ships are few, and the cargo is small. In the absence of available Western ships, which, besides, the

Communists were reluctant to use, the solution was found in an agreement between Poland and China, signed in Moscow in February 1950 and January 1951. The Sino-Polish Sea Transport Company was established, with headquarters in Gdynia and Peking. Each side promised to contribute twelve ships, and Poland further agreed to train Chinese crews. When the first group of thirty arrived in Poland, they could speak nothing but Chinese, disliked the traditional food, and distrusted the Poles. Since the Chinese could not supply any ships anyway, Poland took over the whole burden of supplying ships as well as crews. For a while, during the summer of 1951, traffic slowed down and fewer than twelve ships were needed. But traffic increased again in the fall of 1951, so that additional ships were bought in Panama and some were chartered. The Soviet Union and Czechoslovakia also occasionally provide one of their vessels.[24]

Sino-Soviet relations also determine the nature of China's relations with the Mongolian People's Republic. Having been obliged to recognize the "independence" of the Mongolian People's Republic, which, in fact, meant Russian domination, China has continued ever since the fiction that the Republic is indeed an independent nation. On October 16, 1949, China established diplomatic relations. Friendship missions of various kinds have visited back and forth. Mongolian representatives have been present at important Sino-Russian conferences, and occasionally high officials of both states visit each other. With the usual celebrations the signing of a Sino-Mongolian economic and cultural cooperation agreement was announced in Peking on October 4, 1952. The agreement was very brief. It stipulated the establishment of cooperation in the economic, cultural, and educational fields; the future signing of an implementing agreement; and the duration of the agreement for ten years.[25]

The nature of the relations between China and other Communist states of the world indicates clearly that the Communists are trying to establish a formidable unit from the Elbe to the Pacific. Political relations are close, thanks to strict coordination with, or, better, subordination to, the Soviet Union. They are cemented by the strong emphasis upon cultural relations and the effort to bring together important sections of the population from the various nations. Their substance is provided by the rapidly developing economic relations which have become vital to China's economy and the ambitious plans of the Communist leaders for her development. To judge by appearances, China has for the first time in modern history created the kind of bloc at which her policy has aimed on several occasions in the past, so that in reliance upon the strength of this bloc she can conduct a foreign policy of her own. Whether the kind of strength she has now acquired and the kind of political relations she has developed are pleasing to the Communist leaders, not to speak of the Chinese people — whether they really feel that the tremendous price they have had to pay is worth while — is a matter of speculation.

24

The Bid for Asian Leadership

COMMUNIST China's policy in Asia is active and aggressive. These qualities make it appear to be a deviation from what has been typical of China's modern past. In reality, the Communists in many ways are continuing the pursuit of traditional goals. The difference from preceding regimes is that this pursuit is now facilitated by the application of Communist methods and the constellation of world politics. Asia in general has moved closer to the center of world political interest. The changes taking place there lend themselves well to political maneuvering, especially of the Communist kind. The position of the China inherited by the Chinese Communists no longer requires a major expenditure of effort upon the achievement of equality and upon defense against external enemies. Above all, Communist China has the advantage of working in a field carefully prepared for thirty years by the world Communist movement, though this preparation was not equally successful everywhere in Asia or designed to serve specifically Chinese purposes.

This preparatory work was begun immediately upon the birth of the Soviet Union. Major attention was then paid to Europe. Asia was considered merely a supplemental factor in the expected revolution of the West, but it was by no means forgotten. Many Asian Communist leaders received training in Moscow. An attempt was made to identify nationalist movements in Asia with the Communist movement. A Far Eastern Bureau was created at Shanghai in the 'twenties for the coordination of Communist activities throughout Asia. The development of Asian communism was fostered in the periodical meetings of the Comintern and through the organization of Asian congresses, unions, and leagues under various labels. The strategy and tactics were adapted to Asian conditions, though always with an eye to European developments. Underground activity was resorted to almost all the time; terroristic methods were for the most part used at crucial moments only, in the face of governmental attempts to suppress communism or when splits occurred within the

Communist movement. The movement could not be destroyed, and the Stalinist faction always emerged victorious.

When the Second World War approached, the Communist parties in Asia were disciplined and well enough organized to follow the Moscow line in every detail. They hampered the war effort during the period of the Nazi-Soviet Pact after August 1939. They switched with Moscow when Germany attacked Russia in June 1941 and the "imperialist" war became the great "patriotic" war to Communists all over the world. Their tight organization and long training in underground activity enabled them to take the lead in guerrilla activities against the Japanese and so make plausible their propaganda that their aims and those of local nationalism were identical. As a reward for their support of the war effort, they were legalized and began to work with Popular Front groups for their cause. For a while they were successful almost everywhere in drawing genuine nationalists into their ranks. Their true character was revealed after colonialism as the common enemy had been defeated. Then nationalist leaders, eager to establish independent regimes, found that the Communists were anxious to exchange Western dependence for Soviet dependence.[1]

At this point the Communists reverted to their former revolutionary and terroristic tactics wherever they felt this to be advantageous. Stalin's policy advocated in 1925 was declared applicable again in 1948: liberation can come only through victorious revolution; independence can be achieved only by isolating the "compromising section" of the bourgeoisie and organizing "the advanced elements of the working class" in an independent Communist party; victory can be lasting only if the liberation movements establish firm links with the "proletarian movement of the more advanced countries of the West."[2] Although China could hardly be categorized as an "advanced" country from the Communist or any other standpoint, she became the country toward which the Asian Communist parties, at least those of the south and southeast were increasingly oriented.

Most of these parties either had had only indirect ties with the Chinese Communists or none at all. There can be little doubt, however, that after the seizure of power, the Chinese Communist party became the directing office as far as they were concerned. The two permanent liaison bureaus created, the one as a result of the Peking conferences of the Asian and Australasian trade unions in 1949 and the other, of the Asian and Pacific peace councils in 1952, are presumably the equivalent of a Far Eastern Cominform. The first bureau can be used for the "revolutionary proletarian solidarity" line, the second when the "united front" line is applied. Which of these lines is chosen depends on the world strategy of communism as mapped out by the Cominform in Moscow. But the choice is not always applied rigidly everywhere in Asia. Chinese propaganda is flexible and takes into consideration in each country the sensitivities of the people, the position of the Communists, the influence of the Western powers, and the effect of the Cold War. How much concrete support the Asian Communists receive from China in addition to directives and moral encouragement is of course difficult to determine. In some cases, as for instance the Indochinese, considerable support is evident; in others, as for instance the Burmese, it appears to be slight. In all cases the threat of potential support is ever present and cleverly used by the Chinese in their dealings with the governments of Asia.

The main addressees of Communist Chinese propaganda are the countries of South and Southeast Asia. They are traditionally the area of primary Chinese interests and, as colonial or ex-colonial territories, they are, according to Communist theory, also the "weak" spots in the capitalist world.[3] They are being told that they are still under the "yoke of imperialism." Whether colonies or free, they are all considered to be in need of "liberation" from "imperialist" or "feudal" domination, which in Communist parlance means they all need Communist regimes. The grant of freedom to a former colony is consistently described as a sham, a mere disguise of the actual perpetuation of foreign control. Thus, according to Communist literature, Ceylon is engaged in a struggle for "true national liberation"; the Philippine Republic's government is a "puppet of the American imperialists" and the islands have been "completely transformed" into a "military base for aggressive American imperialism"; Indonesia is fighting for "real freedom." In the colonies, Great Britain is engaged in a "criminal war" in Malaya for continued "exploitation and oppression," while France is fighting an "aggressive war" in Indochina; Thailand, finally, has been turned since World War II into "an American colony and war base in Southeast Asia."

Quite logically the Communists can thereafter describe the governments of these countries as "puppets," "lackeys," "fascists," and "feudalists," and justify their moral and material support of the side of "the people," fighting in civil wars for "liberation" from their evil masters.[4]

327

The neutrality of several of these governments in the Cold War and their refusal to vote against Communist China's admission to the United Nations or to participate in an embargo on war materials have not helped to make them more acceptable to the Chinese Communists.

The governments of the countries of western Asia, which have been independent for some time or always were, are occasionally considered "colonial appendages of the leading capitalist powers." Of them it is sometimes said that the "Anglo-American imperialists are taking every measure to strengthen the authority of their protégés . . . to preserve the reactionary order there, a régime of colonial slavery, to crush the people's national liberation movement, and to draw these countries into the orbit of their military adventures." [5] But more often the Near and Middle Eastern countries are considered to be under potential rather than actual "imperialist" domination. They are being warned daily that the Americans and the British are concentrating their efforts on enslaving them for purposes of economic exploitation and military development.

The reason for the different status assigned to western Asian countries is that some of these have a policy toward Great Britain and the United States that suits the purposes of the Communists very well; they cannot therefore be written off as altogether "imperialist-dominated." Communist analysis explains that "as regards the national bourgeoisie, one portion of it has made a direct deal with the imperialists and fulfills the role of their agent, while the other portion, although not consistently, opposes the imperialist yoke." With this second portion the "toiling masses," under the leadership of the Communist party, may cooperate in the struggle for liberation and, indeed, are encouraged to do so. The existence of this useful "portion of the national bourgeoisie" and the absence of any sharp lines as yet between the "imperialists" and the "anti-imperialists" enable the Chinese Communists to applaud from time to time the policies of some of the western Asian nations — especially, of course, when these are directed against the United States or Great Britain, as in the Iranian oil dispute or over the Suez Canal and Sudan questions.[6]

The correlate of "proving" the existence of capitalist "imperialism" is an invitation to form a "united aggressive front" against it. Specifically the Asian nations are invited to oppose the "aggressive" policies and machinations of the "imperialist" powers. In this category belongs almost everything the United States and other powers are doing in Asia, particularly their support of non-Communist governments, the conclusion of military agreements, and the institution of economic aid and technical assistance.*

In contrast to this dark picture of the "imperialist" powers, China represents herself to the Asian peoples as the savior of all Asia, leading its peoples to a glorious future.[7] In the struggle for independence, which is always identified with the struggle for communism, China is in the van. Those who "volunteered" in Korea did so for the sake of all Asians. Communists participating in civil wars in Asia are encouraged by the promise of aid and comfort from their Chinese brethren. And the great internal improvements of which Communist China boasts are held out as the reward at the end of the common struggle in which all are asked to share.

When special circumstances require, this aggressive and pugnacious line is changed back again to the much more peaceful one of the United Front. On such occasions local Communists become publicly less active, and the barrage of propaganda from the Chinese government subsides to an occasional spurt or dies down altogether. Communist front organizations, such as peace councils or friendship societies, take over and fulfill the purposes of the Communists.[8]

The need of these United Front tactics occasionally arises in Asia for mainly two reasons. The first is that in many areas violent methods are not popular. The second, and more important, is that genuine nationalism is strong in Asian countries. If the Communists want to be successful in enlisting its strength for the Communist cause, they must eliminate suspicion that they are a foreign-directed group. "Proletarian internationalism" — the idea that the Soviet Union must, if necessary, be preserved at the expense of one's own country — does not appeal very much to many people in Asia who have just emerged from a long struggle for the freedom of their own country. In Asia more than in Europe the Com-

* The appeals are successful to some degree when they concern the regimes of men like Chiang and Rhee, who are disliked in Asia, and to a lesser degree when they concern military arrangements, which are widely suspect. When they concern economic measures, they are hardly successful at all. On the contrary, delegates to Asian conferences have often remarked that neither Communist China nor Soviet Russia has ever made a constructive, altruistic contribution to the alleviation of misery in Asia. As Nehru pointed out once, all that the Communists have contributed to Asia is chaos and strife. — Since Stalin's death this situation has changed slightly. In conjunction with the "peace offensive" the Soviet Union has offered a small amount to the technical-assistance program of the United Nations.

munists must appear as patriotic citizens and their movement as an indigenous one.*

All the customary techniques of propaganda are used in this area. Broadcasts are beamed to all Asian countries from China. Books and pamphlets about Communist China and her leaders can be had cheaply and in abundance. Cultural, economic, educational, and peace missions are exchanged in great numbers, and conferences are held at periodic intervals.†

In Southeast Asia, China has a special and effective means of propaganda at her disposal in the form of the large Chinese minorities domiciled there. For the purpose of collecting contributions and spreading influence, the Kuomintang had created an overseas organization, which the Communist government took over and is using for the same purpose. The Communist Overseas Chinese Affairs Commission competes with the original Kuomintang organization, now reconstructed on Formosa, for the loyalty of Chinese in other countries. Chou En-lai has pledged the government's support to the ten million Chinese abroad and has on several occasions interfered in their behalf with foreign governments. Not to be outdone, the Nationalists on Formosa held an Overseas Chinese Affairs Conference in October 1952, which was well attended, mainly by the representatives of the white-collar class among the Chinese abroad.[9]

Which side is winning the battle for the loyalty of the overseas Chinese is difficult to determine. While the Nationalists make a clear-cut anti-Communist appeal, the Communist government seems anxious to attract all classes and sections. Ho Hsiang-ning, as director of Overseas Chinese Affairs in the Communist government, assured all returning Chinese of a hearty welcome. "All overseas Chinese," he said, "should unite, support the motherland, and strengthen their unity. Strong and broad patriotic unity among all overseas Chinese, irrespective of class, occupation, political views or religious beliefs should be developed."[10]

At first a considerable number of the overseas Chinese in Southeast Asia seem to have been willing to follow the Communist government. Their antipathy to communism apparently was overcome by loyalty to

* In contradistinction to European Communist leaders, the Asian leaders originate almost invariably from the locality in which they are active.

† Among the more spectacular postwar conferences were the regional meeting of the World Federation of Democratic Youth at Calcutta in 1948, the Asian and Australasian Trade Union Conference at Peking in 1949, and the Asian and Pacific Peace Conference in Peking in 1952.

the homeland, the need of support from the stronger government, economic considerations, and probably also Communist pressure and blackmail. But the large group among them belonging to the middle class became disillusioned rapidly by the fate of their class in Communist China and swung back to (or remained with) the Nationalists. The Chinese community in every country of Southeast Asia is split. In some countries, for instance Burma and Malaya, the two factions have actually been fighting each other. In others the Chinese are trying to turn with the wind. In yet others they are not disclosing their political loyalty.*

Regardless of the size of the Communist groups among the overseas Chinese, their existence in any number at all is sufficient for the political purposes of the Communist government. They can be used to foment unrest and civil strife, as for instance in Malaya, where almost all the Communist guerrillas are Chinese. They can be used as pioneers for Communist movements, as in Thailand. They can be used as contact men with local native Communists, as in Burma, Indochina, and elsewhere. They can always and everywhere be used as a pretext for the interference of the Chinese government in the affairs of the countries of Southeast Asia. They are, in other words, regardless of their actual numbers, useful tools for the pursuit of Chinese expansionism.

* The number of Chinese in the countries of Southeast Asia is as follows: Burma, 300,000; Thailand, 2,500,000; Indochina, 850,000; Malaya, 2,615,000; British Borneo, 220,000; Indonesia, 1,900,000; Philippines, 120,000. These figures are taken from Victor Purcell, *The Chinese in Southeast Asia* (London, 1951), p. 2. — The tendency of the overseas Chinese to rely upon the Chinese embassies for support is with many states an important consideration in the question which Chinese government should be recognized and admitted to the United Nations. See *New York Times*, August 22, 1953.

25

Realizing Ambitions in Asia

THE most striking aspect of Communist China's program for Asia is that the area of major interest, Southeast Asia, is also the area in which imperial China had or claimed a paramount position, in which large Chinese communities exist, and in which all regimes succeeding the Manchu dynasty have sought to expand Chinese influence. There can be no doubt that the program corresponds faithfully to Marxist-Leninist doctrine. But at the same time it can satisfy every Chinese chauvinist, from the Manchus down to the Nationalists. In this dual attraction it has a great and important advantage over the similar program of previous regimes, an advantage which will contribute considerably to its chances of success.

The Nationalists, in the absence of force, can use only the subversive qualities of the Chinese minorities in the area for the achievement of their program. This method is not very effective because of the widespread hostility toward the Chinese and toward anything coming from China. The activity of the Nationalists, moreover, has always been hampered by their friendship with the West. They can hardly openly propagandize in a way embarrassing to their Western friends in the area. The Communists are under no such obligation. On the contrary, and until the line is changed again to a more peaceful one, embarrassment of the West is a most useful feature of their program. It fits very neatly into the pattern of Sino-Soviet friendship, and may even gain the Chinese some sympathy among anti-Western Asians. By representing communism as an indigenous and international — at any rate, not specifically Chinese — movement, the Communists have a group of native sympathizers to rely on. And they have, of course, the same Chinese minorities as the Nationalists have for the promotion of their aims.

Thus the political conditions in Southeast Asia are favorable to the realization of the Chinese Communist program. Having few scruples about methods and acting under the influence of a highly developed sense of mission, the Communists are fully utilizing their advantage. The Nationalists never had the same opportunity. This is probably the reason why the Chinese Communists appear to have inaugurated a "brand new" policy, as they boast they have done. The fact nevertheless is that fundamentally they are merely expanding and invigorating a program whose basic goals are of long standing and whose realization had been begun by the Nationalists or even, in some cases, by their predecessors. The long life these goals have had is particularly evident in Tibet, Indochina, and Burma, but to a lesser degree also in the other states of the area.

The Chinese Communists, like many other Chinese, maintain that Tibet is an integral part of China. The Tibetans have always had the opposite conviction. The situation which the Communists found in 1949 had developed over a period of many decades and had been formalized in 1906 when Great Britain and China signed a convention in which China's suzerainty over Tibet was recognized.[1] This convention did not, however, settle the triangular relationship of China, Great Britain, and Tibet. Tibet remained an object of Chinese imperialist ambition. Its importance was not only in its strategic situation, but also in the fact that its worldly ruler, the Dalai Lama, had considerable spiritual influence in Manchuria and Mongolia as well. The Chinese implemented their suzerainty in 1908 by seizing administrative power in Tibet, leaving the Dalai Lama little more than his titles. When they also brought in troops in 1910, the Dalai Lama fled.

Taking advantage of the unrest caused by the revolution in 1911, the Tibetans expelled the Chinese forces. The Dalai Lama declared Tibet to be independent. Yuan Shih-k'ai, however, declared it to be an integral province of China and tried to enforce his order by military force. But he was unsuccessful and agreed to a British suggestion embodied in a convention initialed in April 1914. Chinese suzerainty over all Tibet was confirmed. For administrative purposes Tibet was divided into Outer Tibet, containing Lhasa, and Inner Tibet, the area adjoining China. The autonomy of Outer Tibet was recognized, and China promised not to interfere in its administration, not to have it represented in the Chinese parliament, not to send troops or to station civil servants there, and not to establish a Chinese colony in the territory. The Chinese refused to ratify this convention because they disagreed with the boundary line between Inner and Outer Tibet, maintaining that some territory of Outer Tibet, including Chiamdo (Changtu), Litang, and Batang, belonged to China. Ever since, that area has remained in dispute.[2]

In 1933 a mission from the National Government arrived in Lhasa asking the Tibetan government to let the Chinese handle Tibet's foreign affairs and have a considerable share in its internal administration. The Tibetan government refused these requests and went one step further, declaring it would not even recognize Chinese suzerainty unless certain territory was ceded to Tibet. In 1939 the National Government made a new attempt, politically and militarily, to extend its control over Tibet. It failed. After that the Japanese advances in China and the outbreak of World War II brought about improved, almost cordial, relations between China and Tibet. The nature of these relations again became a subject of discussion in the fall of 1945. A Tibetan good-will mission to Chiang K'ai-shek requested the return of all Tibetan territory occupied by the Chinese and the recognition of Tibet's independence. From the reaction of the National Government it was clear that not only would these requests be refused but that Tibet was considered a part of the Republic.

Even while it was in its last gasps on the mainland, the National Government tried to make Chiang's statement come true that "the frontiers of China lie in Tibet." For this purpose it exploited the difficulties which had arisen in the early 'twenties between the Dalai Lama, the more worldly and more powerful leader of the Tibetans, and the Panchen Lama, their more spiritual leader. As a result of these difficulties, the Panchen Lama had fled Tibet in 1923, accompanied by influential monks, and had settled in China. Although in 1932 he had been given permission to return to Tibet, he did not do so, and he was still in China when he died in 1937. In 1944 it was announced that a new Panchen Lama had been found and enthroned in the Chinese province of Chinghai. The Tibetan government did not recognize this reincarnation. In 1949 the National Government enthroned him a second time in Chinghai province, presumably as a countermove to the activities of the Tibetans, who had used the weakening of the Chinese government to get rid of the Chinese and Chinese influence in their country. The enthronement came too late to help the Nationalists. Instead it provided the Communists with a wonderful weapon for their conquest of Tibet.

The Communists had never left any doubt that they too considered

334

Tibet an integral part of China. They had carefully propagandized and indoctrinated Tibetan monks in China and some even in Tibetan monasteries, readying them for the time when Tibet should be "liberated." That time came in the spring of 1950, when an excellently organized propaganda campaign against Tibet began. The Tibetan people were described as suffering under the yoke of Takta Rimpochi, the regent of Tibet, whose government was said to "dance to the tune" of the Anglo-American "imperialists" * who supplied Tibet with arms against their "liberators." [3]

The Tibetan people, so the Communists announced, were yearning to be freed by the Chinese People's Army of Liberation. In support of this contention, Tibetan Communists in China made ardent appeals to the Peking government to rejoin Tibet to the "motherland." "Plant the five star national flag on the Himalayas," was their plea.[4] Tibetan "patriots" in China called on their people to achieve a peaceful liberation. The Chinese Communist government supported these activities by subtle threats and open seductions. The Tibetan people should have no illusions that the People's Liberation Army could not penetrate Tibet. Tibetans were reminded of the Long March of the Communists in 1935 and other deeds which proved that snow, mountains, and grasslands were no barriers to Communists. They should happily look forward to their "liberation," for the present Chinese government was "absolutely loving and protecting the minority nationalities"; religions would be respected, and Tibet would have autonomy "under unified control of the Central People's Government." [5]

The Tibetan government was determined to resist a Chinese invasion of the country. While making preparations for resistance, it sent a mission to China in February 1950 to negotiate a peaceful arrangement. This mission stayed in India until October, partly because of inability to obtain transit visas through Hongkong. In September they began conversations with the Chinese ambassador in India, and while these were proceeding, the Communists began to move their troops toward disputed territory in Outer Tibet. They occupied and established bases in the provinces of Sikang and Chinghai, where the Panchen Lama got under their control and cooperated with them. In October 1950 they

---

* A Tibetan delegation under H. E. Shāgappa arrived in Washington in July 1948 to ask for assistance; they failed in their mission, apparently because they could not submit the statistics required of them. — "Tibet Today," *World Today,* VIII (1952), 205.

began the march into Tibet in order, they announced, to free three million Tibetans from imperialist aggression and improve the defenses of China. They battled Tibetan troops in a campaign which was extremely expensive and difficult. Winter stopped their steady advance in January 1951. It was clear that the Tibetans could offer no serious resistance. They were inferior in everything. Outside aid was not to be expected. An appeal by the Tibetans themselves and by San Salvador to the General Assembly led to no action, largely because the Indian government reported in December 1950 that the Chinese invasion had been halted and because the Tibetans did not follow up their appeal. Instead of appearing at Lake Success, a Tibetan delegation appeared in Peking on April 22, 1951, just before the arrival of the Panchen Lama, to negotiate with the Chinese.

On May 23, 1951, an agreement was signed * between the Communist government, the Dalai Lama's group, the Panchen Lama's group, and the Communist-sponsored People's Government for the Autonomous Tibet, which regulates the integration of Tibet into the governmental and administrative structure of Communist China.[6]

According to this agreement the Tibetans must help in the complete "liberation" of Tibet so that Tibet may be able to return to the "mother country," China. The Tibetan people may exercise "national regional autonomy under the leadership of the Central People's Government." They may retain their political system, the Dalai Lama, and various officials. The Panchen Lama is reinstated in the position he held before 1923. Tibet's religion, traditions, and customs will be respected. Tibetan troops will become part of the Chinese army. There are some vague statements about the development of a Tibetan language and the welfare of the people. The Chinese will use no coercion in bringing reforms to Tibet; these are to be effected voluntarily by the local government. But when "the people demand" these reforms they will be decided "through consultation with prominent Tibetan figures." Officials who have broken their former "imperialist" and Kuomintang ties may stay in office. The Chinese government will control the foreign affairs of Tibet. So that the conditions of the agreement may be properly fulfilled, a military administration will be established in Tibet, staffed by personnel sent by the Chinese government and supplemented by Tibetan personnel,

* There is evidence that this agreement was dictated to the Tibetans and that they had to accept it as it was given to them by the Chinese.

whose appointment must be approved by the Central People's Government.

What this agreement means in effect is that Tibet is under the complete control of the Communist government. For, even though in appearance certain minor matters remain within the bailiwick of local Tibetan authorities, it must be assumed that these authorities will be loyal to the Communist government. The agreement was announced in the usual manner, with all the bombast and fanfare of Communist propaganda. For days newspapers devoted pages to the description of Tibet's "liberation." The Chinese people were so happy, the newspapers reported, that they danced in the streets.[7] Reports from Tibet indicated that the Tibetan people were less happy. In spite of efforts by the Chinese Communists to win over the population by correct behavior, friction has not been avoided and clashes have occurred. There is evidence that the Tibetans are not meekly surrendering to their new masters. However, Tibet has been completely *gleichgeschaltet* and militarized, and the Tibetans are in no position to give effective expression to their opposition. How little autonomy is left to Tibet even by official admission is indicated by the statement of the head of one of the many Tibetan "friendship" missions to Peking in April 1953 to the effect that "the new Tibet is an integral part of our mighty Motherland."

In Indochina the Chinese Communists have not yet been as successful as in Tibet. Signs indicate, however, that they hesitate to relax their effort to integrate it into the Communist world. But here again, as in Tibet, the old and the new Chinese imperialism melt into one. Tonkin especially has long been an object of Chinese expansionist ambition, though Annam and Cochinchina have not been ignored. The only parts of Indochina that have been mostly outside the range of this ambition are the remaining two, Laos and Cambodia. The alleged justification of the Chinese wish to integrate Vietnam* into the Chinese Empire is the fact that it was under Chinese suzerainty for centuries until the French took it from China in the Treaty of Tientsin in 1885. The Chinese have never reconciled themselves to this loss, and many Frenchmen have considered them the worst enemy of French sovereignty over the colony.[8] Devoid of any means to recover the territory, all the Chinese could do was to permit Vietnamese nationalist refugees of various polit-

* Tonkin, Annam, and Cochinchina are known as Vietnam.

ical complexions freedom of organization and agitation in south China. Though there has not been much sympathy between the Vietnamese and the Chinese, the one fearing imperialism, the other nationalism, for the purpose of embarrassing the French they concluded this marriage of convenience, which lasted until the Communists took over in China.

When the Vietnamese nationalists first began to organize themselves, the Chinese did not participate in any activities; they merely tolerated them. In the early 1920's the Vietnamese Revolutionary Youth League was created. Nguyen Ai Quoc became its leader after he returned from training in Moscow. In 1930 he presided over the formation of the Indochinese Communist party in Hongkong. In 1927 the Vietnam Nationalist party (the V.N.Q.D.D.) was formed, inspired by the ideals of Sun Yat-sen and patterned after the Kuomintang. From bases in south China, both organizations agitated in Indochina. Their activities were suppressed by the French in 1930 and 1931, and for a few years afterward little was heard of them. After 1933 the Communists resumed their activities, in cooperation with the world Communist movement and in close contact with the Chinese Communists. Small nationalist parties also developed in great numbers, but they were less active and poorly organized. All of these groups became useful to the Chinese during the Second World War.

The outbreak of the war provided the golden opportunity for the Chinese to take a hand in Indochinese affairs. The Japanese occupation of Indochina, the split of the French into a Vichy and Free French section, the factionalism among the Vietnamese nationalists, the antagonisms between the various regions of Indochina, and finally the occupation of the colony by British and Chinese troops after the surrender of Japan, created an almost impenetrable jungle of political intriguing in which the Chinese found ample opportunity for maneuver.*

Active Chinese interference in Indochinese politics began in 1941. Communist-nationalist activities in Indochina had been suppressed by the French and Japanese garrisons in Tonkin. Communists and nationalists in considerable numbers had been forced to flee to China. Nguyen Ai Quoc negotiated with the Chinese authorities of Yunnan and Kwangsi with a view to organizing resistance groups. In conformity with the Comintern directives, the Communist party's policy was to assume lead-

---

* The extremely complex situation in Indochina will be considered here only insofar as the Chinese role in it is concerned.

ership of the national liberation movements by enlisting the aid of all nationalist and socialist organizations and to prepare for the day when the victorious United Nations should abolish colonialism.

Nguyen Ai Quoc's aim was to form a broad front organization among the Vietnamese refugees in China. He called a congress in Tsingsi, Kwangsi province, in May 1941, which was camouflaged as a meeting of many resistance groups but which was in fact a meeting of the Central Committee of the Indochinese Communist party. The Congress decided to unite on a platform of integral nationalism and to underplay the class struggle. Such a program would attract Indochinese nationalists and prevent them from collaborating with the Japanese against the French, and it would allay the fears of the anti-Marxist Kuomintang. The Congress founded the Viet Nam Doc Lap Dong Minh Hoi, Viet Minh for short, which was designed to be the organizational vehicle for the popular front. Its program was general enough to appeal to all Indochinese. The organization which it envisaged and soon created in Indochina enabled it to be victorious over all rival groups soon after the end of the war.

The Chinese National Government recognized at once the true, predominantly Communist nature of the Viet Minh and feared it. The organization was harassed by Chinese authorities, and Nguyen Ai Quoc was imprisoned in southern China as a French spy! Upon the suggestion of an anti-Communist Vietnamese nationalist the Chinese created another organization which was ideologically less distasteful. In the summer of 1942 the military governor of Kwangsi, Chang Fa-kwei, brought together a large number of refugees and trained them for resistance activity. In October 1942 he engineered a coalition between the Viet Minh, the Vietnam Nationalist party, and the Dong Minh Hoi, a group of eight small nationalist parties.* The leader of the coalition was a trusted friend of the Kuomintang, Nguyen Hai Than. The Chinese felt happier now, believing that the coalition group would be more subservient to them than the Communist-dominated Viet Minh.

The group received a monthly subsidy of 100,000 Chinese dollars for the organization of espionage and sabotage in Indochina. But since the nationalists in the coalition had no organization in the colony, they could do no effective work, while the Viet Minh with its excellent organization

* Dong Minh Hoi was at first the name of the coalition organization, but later was used only for the smaller nationalist parties.

reaped for itself whatever prestige was to be gained from the existence of the coalition. Chang Fa-kwei was blamed by the Chinese government for the failure of the group and even suspected of cooperation with the Chinese puppet government in Nanking. Nguyen Ai Quoc, still in prison, came to his rescue. In return for freedom, he offered Chang to organize an espionage system in Tonkin. Chang accepted the deal. But since Nguyen Ai Quoc as a Communist was anathema in Chungking, he informed the government that he had an able Annamite revolutionary, by name Ho Chi Minh, who was willing to work for the Chinese in Tonkin. Ho was appointed chief of the coalition group. He received the financial and moral support of the Chinese, and later of some American and Free French groups; this he used for the further development of his Viet Minh Front.

Ho did such effective work that the Chinese became slightly more sympathetic toward the Viet Minh, while the French, even the Free French, became worried over possible Sino-Vietnamese cooperation after the war. Countermeasures were taken, and the Viet Minh was forced to withdraw into the remote regions of Tonkin. The French discovered the identity of Ho Chi Minh and informed the Chinese government, expecting that it would disavow him as a Communist. But they were disappointed. All the Chinese did was to try once more to force him into the coalition group with the nationalists. At a congress in March 1944 at Liuchow, under strong Chinese pressure, the coalition group formed a provisional republican government for liberation, which presumably the Chinese would control and use for the expulsion of the French from Indochina. Once more, however, the nationalist section of the coalition disintegrated, and the Viet Minh was left in control of the provisional government and furnished with another useful front organization.

The genius and the popularity of Ho Chi Minh, the discipline and the program of the Viet Minh, and the singleness of purpose and lack of scruple of the Communists brought the first victory at the end of the war. Ten days after the surrender of the Japanese, on August 25, 1945, the Viet Minh dominated all Vietnam. By negotiation, intrigue, subversion, propaganda, intimidation, murder, effrontery, the benevolent "neutrality" of the withdrawing Japanese, and sheer good luck, they had cleared their road to power. Emperor Bao Dai had abdicated. The nationalist competitors were eliminated. On September 2 the independent Democratic Republic of Vietnam was proclaimed. It was supposedly based upon a broad national front of many political parties. In reality it was completely under the control of the Communists within the Viet Minh. The revolution was thus begun under the leadership of the Viet Minh. But the party still had to prove that it could lead the revolution to a successful conclusion. Many barriers had yet to be overcome.

One of the most formidable had been built at the conference of the Allies at Potsdam, in 1945. It was decided at that conference that in the absence of French troops, Japanese troops should be disarmed and Allied prisoners liberated by British troops south and Chinese troops north of the Sixteenth Parallel in Indochina.

In the British zone things went fairly well for the French, though not without serious friction and some bloodshed. Cochinchina was returned to France by March 1946, while fighting was still raging throughout the countryside. In Cambodia French control was re-established in January 1946. In Laos, under Chinese control until August 1946, the French restored their protectorate without very great difficulty because the nationalism there was moderate and the influence of the Viet Minh weak. But in Vietnam north of the Sixteenth Parallel things were different.

The Chinese armies, accompanied by women and children, moved in at the end of August 1945. They made themselves most unpopular by living off the land, exploiting the country and its population, buying up goods and enterprises at artificially low rates fixed by them, and generally behaving like conquerors, not liberators. They were apparently determined to compensate themselves at the expense of the Indochinese and the French for their losses to the Russians in Manchuria.

Together with their armies, the Chinese brought their Indochinese protégés, the nationalist groups of the provisional republican government, and used them wherever possible to replace the Viet Minh administration. In October 1945 Ho Ying-chin, Chinese commander in chief, arrived in Hanoi and announced that China had no territorial ambitions in Vietnam. On the contrary, she would help to bring independence to the colony in accordance with the principles established by the big powers. No French vessels would be permitted in the area without Chinese approval.

The Viet Minh was pleased, but not for long. It became clear that the Chinese would use their power to strengthen the nationalist parties at the expense of the Viet Minh. They demanded a place for them in the

341

Viet Minh Front government. Ho Chi Minh, extremely flexible as always, in order to retain the appearance of leading a broad nationalist front and to gain, he hoped, the support of vast sections of the public as well as that of foreign powers, appeared to give in. He dissolved the Communist party and replaced it by the Indochinese Marxist Study Association for those interested in the "theoretical study" of communism. At the same time, he assured the public of his democratic intentions, promised the promulgation of a constitution, and announced the first nationwide elections for an Assembly. These promises did not satisfy the Chinese. Under their instigation and protection the nationalist parties formed a Nationalist Bloc, created a militia, and continued to agitate for participation in the government.

Under Chinese auspices the Viet Minh and the Nationalist Bloc agreed to a truce, a fusion of their militias, and the formation of a National Union government. But two weeks later Ho Chi Minh announced that, in view of the forthcoming elections, there was no point in changing the government for just a few weeks. Yet this is exactly what the Chinese wanted. They, and their protégés, did not trust any elections arranged by a Viet Minh government. They did not get their way, but under tremendous Chinese pressure Ho Chi Minh promised the nationalist parties a guaranteed minimum representation of 70 members in the future Assembly of 350. The elections on January 6, 1946, resulted in the expected overwhelming and apparently unmanipulated victory of the Viet Minh.* The Viet Minh could now claim that it ruled on the basis of broad popular support, and the Assembly gave it the requisite respectable democratic front.

Also in January 1946, Sino-French negotiations began over the evacuation of Indochina and other problems concerning the two powers. The Chinese could now foresee the time when they would have to leave the colony and would lose their influence upon its politics. This prospect affected the Indochinese parties as well, all of which could play the Chinese against the French, and some of which, the nationalist, owed their power to the Chinese. For all these reasons the recovery of Indochina by the French assumed special importance. A truly frantic political activity developed among these various groups.

The Chinese put enormous pressure on the Viet Minh government to

* However, the elections were manipulated before they took place in the sense that persons not approved by the Viet Minh hardly had a chance of becoming candidates. Opponents of the Viet Minh branded the elections a farce.

include the nationalists. They recognized the Viet Minh as an extremely effective instrument and did not intend to antagonize it, but only to circumscribe its political power by introducing the more docile nationalists. The wish for continued relations was mutual, for the Viet Minh wanted to use Chinese support in negotiations with the French — quite apart from the fact that hitherto China had been the only power lending support to Indochinese independence. The French approached the nationalist parties. But these, being much more anti-French than the Viet Minh, refused all contacts. The Viet Minh was willing to negotiate with the French, partly to counteract Chinese pressure, and simultaneously continued conversations with the Chinese. The Viet Minh knew that there was no choice but to come to terms with the French; the question was merely one of holding out for the best possible terms. But whatever they should be, any agreement with the French would be a compromise of the original Viet Minh position of independence for Vietnam and would need a good explanation to the public. Foreseeing difficulties, Ho agreed to the creation of a coalition government on February 20 and announced its creation on the 24th. This took the Chinese pressure off the Viet Minh and increased its bargaining position with the French. Above all, the extremist nationalist parties now had to share in the responsibility for the inevitable agreement with the French.

Two days later, on February 26, Ho disclosed that he had negotiated with the French and that an accord might be possible. The need of such an accord became more plausible to the nationalists and the public when France and China announced the signing of a treaty on February 28, 1946, in which France granted considerable concessions in return for the evacuation of Indochina.*

As a result of this treaty, the French fleet appeared off Haiphong on March 5, 1946. But there was still no agreement between the French and the Chinese on the details of the evacuation or on the relations between the Vietnamese and the French. There was some last-minute bargaining by all concerned to get the most out of their opponents. On March 6 Ho and the French signed an agreement which was expected to lay the foundation for the eventual integration of a free Indochina into the French Union. But there was no agreement with the Chinese. They

---

* The French surrendered extraterritoriality and other special rights; they gave up their holdings in the Yunnan Railway; they granted free passage of Chinese goods through the port of Haiphong; and they guaranteed special rights to the Chinese in Indochina.

started bombarding the French fleet and continued until orders finally came from Chungking to let the French land.

At last, in June 1946, the Chinese reluctantly withdrew their last troops.* With them left the leaders and some followers of the Dong Minh Hoi. The leaders of the Nationalist party (the V.N.Q.D.D.) stayed behind. But the Viet Minh soon forced them also to flee to China, leaving the field to the Viet Minh in most of Vietnam. To maintain the popular front and perhaps to obtain American or Chinese support in their quest for independence,† the Viet Minh government invited some of the nationalist leaders to return and join the government. But the Chinese government prevented this. It was unwilling to support a Communist government in the south while it was fighting its own Communists in the north. The nationalist United National Vietnam Front, created in Nanking in February 1947 and composed of the refugee nationalists and nationalists from Cochinchina, was informed that the conditions of Chinese support were (1) the Front must remain anti-Communist and (2) Bao Dai must be restored to power. In a congress at Canton in March 1947 the Front complied. It withdrew all support from Ho Chi Minh and acknowledged the leadership of Bao Dai (who was still "supreme political adviser" in the Ho cabinet and hoping to become the mediator between the various Indochinese parties). Thereafter the refugee nationalists maintained some tenuous contacts with nationalists in Cochinchina, where the French were strong and the Viet Minh was weak. Internal dissension among the refugee nationalists made them ineffective. They attached themselves increasingly to the Chinese Nationalists who, however, became increasingly preoccupied with their own fate. The Viet Minh retained the field for itself until the Communists came into power in China. The result of Chinese policy was a favorable treaty with the French and a weakening of the position of the Chinese in Indochina. Considering the close ties which developed between the Chinese Communists and the Viet Minh, it is doubtful whether, looking back, the Chinese Nationalists on Formosa can consider their policy beneficial to their interests.

As soon as the Chinese Communists seized power on the mainland, the nature of the Viet Minh regime as a Communist regime became obvious. Ho congratulated Mao Tse-tung on the occasion of the establish-

---

* One division remained in Haiphong until August.

† The Indochinese Communists felt very lonely. None of the big powers, not even the Soviet Union, supported at that time their bid for independence.

ment of the Communist regime.* On January 14, 1950, the Viet Minh government asked for recognition. Communist China recognized it on January 16. The new Democratic Republic of Vietnam indicated by its international actions and foreign policy as well as by its internal reorganization that it was an orthodox Communist state which had joined the "camp of freedom and democracy led by the Soviet Union." It was used immediately, as it had been used, though less efficiently, by the Nationalists, for Chinese expansionist purposes.[9] The Indochinese Communists now receive from China moral support, advisers, and the sinews of war. The Chinese themselves boast that the Vietnamese people "have received all-out support from Soviet Russia, China, and other people's democracies," as distinct from the "sympathy" received by Communists elsewhere. So far, Chinese "volunteer" troops in Indochina are reported only rarely, or, on the occasions when they are, they are described as "bandits" donning Chinese uniforms. The French authorities are desperately trying to prevent an expansion of the conflict and are avoiding everything that might antagonize the Chinese. They are hopeful that they may be able to defeat the Viet Minh troops if the Chinese stay across the border. For not only do they become stronger, thanks to increasing American help, but the true Indochinese nationalists are increasingly opposed to the Communists. Nevertheless Chinese Communist supplies to the Viet Minh troops are sufficiently large to enable these troops to conduct a campaign against the French and the Vietnamese nationalists which has made Indochina a most serious issue in world politics and a potential area of Communist conquest.[10]

The Chinese Communists have so far shown little interest in Burma; in fact, less than the Nationalists. This may be due to the ruggedness and inaccessibility of the border region between Burma and China or, more likely, to an endeavor to maintain friendly relations with India. It

* The New York *Daily Worker* of May 31, 1953, described the following ceremony which took place after Stalin's death: "Try to visualize this scene in the heart of the forest; the candelabra made of bamboo illuminate the portrait of the Soviet leader, in front of which are green-leafed wreaths of white and violet flowers. The 500 cadres as well as all governmental leaders stand silently as President Ho speaks briefly. He hails the greatness, the universal significance of Stalin's leadership, and he leads the whole audience in a solemn oath. Each right hand rises high over the shoulder and each voice repeats hoarsely the pledge of solidarity with the world-wide fight for peace and the liberation of all peoples. Group by group, the Government leaders rise from their rude benches to bow three times before the portrait of the Soviet leader as the burning incense perfumes the heavy night air of the jungle and two violins play softly."

is also true that communism came to Burma relatively late, never got a strong foothold among the masses, and was weakened by factionalism within the Communist group.

The main issues between Burma and China have been the Chinese minority and the course of the border line between the two countries. The second, however, has been much more important than the first. For there are only about 200,000 Chinese in Burma, and they are greatly outnumbered by the Indian minority. Nevertheless there has periodically been friction and occasionally bloodshed between the Burmese and the Chinese. To the usual causes of antipathy to the Chinese in Southeast Asia has been added here the experience with Chinese troops during the war, which was none too pleasant.

The building of the Burma Road in 1937 caused fears in Burma that it might involve the country in the Sino-Japanese War and might be a standing invitation to the Chinese to infiltrate into the country.[11] This it has indeed turned out to be. For in the immediate postwar years, and much to the chagrin of Burmese nationalists, the Chinese population in Upper Burma increased rapidly. Burmese anxiety referred not so much to Chinese infiltration as to Chinese conquest. And at this point the issues of the Chinese minority and the border line merged into one.

The border issue dates back to 1885, when Great Britain occupied Upper Burma. The first border convention was drawn up in 1894. This convention was inconclusive and led to differences regarding the border line as well as to the triangular northern tip of Burma bordering on Yunnan and comprising about 75,000 square miles. Throughout the period of British rule in Burma negotiations regarding the border line proceeded between China and Great Britain. When the war interrupted these negotiations in 1941, much of the line was settled, but a long stretch north of 25° 35′ north latitude remained unsettled and has since become a bone of contention.[12]

On the Chinese side the negotiations have been accompanied, since the 'twenties, by nationalist agitation. Sun Yat-sen claimed the whole of Burma as Chinese territory.[13] Beginning with 1931, and perhaps as a reaction to the loss of territory in Manchuria, Chinese nationalists have engaged in the pastime of tracing historical claims to territories which were once under Chinese suzerainty or connected by even more nebulous ties. This northern Burmese area became one of their pet objects. Public agitation ceased when the Second World War and the Japanese

346

occupation of Burma made close relations between Burma and China mandatory. But the frequent exchange of gifts and good-will missions between the two governments merely covered up temporarily Burmese suspicions and Chinese expansionist ambitions.

The fight against the Japanese and the protection of the Burma Road gave the Chinese a legitimate opportunity to occupy just those territories to which they laid claim. Some of the troops there behaved as if China already owned them. When the time came for evacuation, the troops moved out most reluctantly. Under the pretext of looking for deserters, they came back for a month in 1946 and left only after they were threatened with air action.[14]

A year later the Chinese government took the occasion of Burma's becoming independent to congratulate her and express the hope that the fifty-three-year-old boundary issue might be settled "amicably." In elaboration Fu Chio-chin, territorial commissioner in the Ministry of Interior, voiced China's claim to Burmese territory north of 25° 35' north latitude, basing it on the fact that the area was part of a state which had paid tribute to China since the Tang dynasty in the seventh century.

The Burmese public was greatly aroused; the government suggested that it remain cool until there was an official statement from China. Seeing the Burmese reaction, the Chinese government was not long in making the statement. It assured the Burmese that no unilateral action or declaration by "either" party could be binding, that the issue would be settled by diplomacy according to international law. The Burmese government took an unyielding stand on this statement. It asserted that the boundary line was clear, that there was no international problem, and that Burma would defend her territory "without any hesitation." Further trying to allay Burmese fears, high Chinese officials, attending the independence festivities in Rangoon, repeated the assurance that Chinese aggression against Burma was not "likely," yet they remained evasive regarding the territorial claim.[15]

The Chinese Communists did not maintain the claim of the Nationalists; neither did they renounce it unequivocally. The Burmese prime minister announced the receipt of a note from Communist China stating that China had no territorial ambitions in Burma; that as there had not yet been time to draw new maps, the old maps, showing an undemarcated border region, were reproduced; and that there would be no difficulty in reaching an agreement. The prime minister published this note in answer to rumors in February and March 1951, which he branded as an attempt to disrupt the "most cordial" relations with Communist China, that Chinese Communist troops were roaming freely in Upper Burma and that the Burmese government was afraid to protest. At the same time the Burmese Embassy in Washington announced that there existed "complete understanding" between the two countries regarding the future of the northern border areas. What this understanding is was not announced.[16]

An issue that appears to worry the Burmese government much more is the Kuomintang troops that settled in northern Burma along China and Thailand when they retreated before the Communists. They are estimated to number about 12,000 men, about 7,000 to 8,000 of them being organized, at first under the command of General Li Mi, and more recently under that of General Liu Kuo-chuan. They call themselves the Yunnan Anti-Communist and National Salvation Army. Their main base is Kengtung, one of the Shan states, with an airfield at Mongh-sat. They live off the land, requisitioning what they can get and sometimes paying with slips of papers that say, "The Americans will pay." There is considerable evidence that their military supplies are coming from Formosa through Thailand.*

The troops prove most embarrassing to the Burmese government. They have joined the Karens, one of the many Burmese rebel groups, in a common fight against the government, and at times they have even worked with the Burmese Communists against it. They are pillaging and burning Burmese villages. They occasionally foray into Communist China and could serve the Chinese Communists as a good pretext — if one were needed — for an invasion of Burma. So far, the Communists have been surprisingly restrained. They have assured the Burmese government that they would not violate Burma's border unless Burmese territory were used by the Nationalist troops as a base of attack against them. They have, however, used the presence of these troops in their propaganda campaign against the United States — until the "peace offensive" began after Stalin's death — describing them as American-trained and equipped and as being trained for an American-engineered invasion

* The Thais may be willing to permit this traffic because (1) they still resent having been forced to return to Burma after the war two Shan states which the Japanese had permitted them to annex, and (2) they have 2,500,000 Chinese in their midst whom they wish to keep loyal to the National Government, which the Thais recognize.

348

of Communist China. The State Department has denied any American contacts with these troops and, on the contrary, has tried, in cooperation with India, to persuade Chiang K'ai-shek to withdraw them from Burma. The Burmese government has agreed that the American government has nothing to do with the Nationalist troops. But in March 1953 the Burmese defense minister stated that he had "conclusive proof" that a "few" Americans had been training and arming these troops and he vaguely involved the "China Lobby" in the Nationalists' activities.[17]

American endeavors to reconcile the Burmese and the Chinese Nationalist points of view remaining without much success, the Burmese government finally brought its case before the General Assembly of the United Nations in March 1953. It introduced a sharply worded resolution in which the Assembly was asked to recommend to the Security Council that the "Kuomintang Government of Formosa" be condemned for its aggression and that all steps be taken to stop that aggression. The spokesman for the Formosa regime denied any control over the troops in Burma,* and the mood in the Assembly did not favor such a strong resolution. Toward the end of April, to the satisfaction of the Burmese, a resolution was passed unanimously, with Burma and Nationalist China abstaining, "deploring" the situation, condemning the presence of "foreign forces" in Burma and their hostile acts, and demanding their disarmament and evacuation. But the implementation of this resolution is causing many difficulties and lengthy discussions. A commission composed of officials from the United States, Burma, Thailand, and Nationalist China reached an agreement on June 22, 1953, on the evacuation of the Nationalist troops. But when it consulted with the field commander of these troops, it found out that these refused to recognize either the United Nations resolution or the agreement for evacuation. The only concession they were willing to make was to stop fighting and remain in a neutral zone along the Burma-China border created for them by the four-power commission. Their main arguments were, first, that evacuation of the troops would be contrary to the principle of "voluntary repatriation" as developed in the Korean truce talks and, second, that they could not leave undefended the thousands of non-Chinese anti-Communist troops which had joined them. This attitude of the Chinese

---

* Chiang K'ai-shek's chargé d'affaires at Bangkok stated, however, that the Chinese troops in Burma were under Chiang's command and that their operations were part of Formosa's war against China. — *New Statesman and Nation*, XLV (1953), 386.

Nationalist troops made the evacuation agreement inapplicable. The Burmese government feels that the government on Formosa could exert stronger pressure upon these troops and is considering further steps in the United Nations.[18]

In spite of potential dangers from China and the perpetual war with Burmese Communist rebels and other insurgents, the Burmese government has pursued an independent policy toward Communist China. It has supported United Nations resolutions declaring North Korea an aggressor and calling for the support of South Korea. It has put an embargo on oil to China and has accepted aid from the Western world. On the other hand, Burma was the first non-Communist country to recognize the Communist regime in China, and she has on her soil a Russian Embassy with a staff of over fifty members, a Chinese Communist Embassy known to maintain close relations with local Chinese Communists and left-wing Burmese, and the main overseas mission of the Viet Minh government. The presence of these agencies, the existence of Burmese Communist and other rebels, and the threat on the border will not, in the judgment of J. S. Furnivall and other competent observers, prevent Burma from continuing her neutral policy. In Furnivall's words, "The danger is not Communism but anarchy," if — a big if — the Chinese Communists do not cross the border.*

The relations between China and Thailand (Siam) have been bad for a long time. The issue here is the large Chinese minority, which has a strong influence on the Thai economy. The National Government had for many years regularly sent protests to Siam against the treatment of the Chinese and against the legislation to curb their further immigration. The collaboration of the Thais with the Japanese during the Second World War and the rise of China into the ranks of the big powers gave the National Government the opportunity to take a stronger stand. This stand provoked stronger Thai nationalism, and the result was street riots in Bangkok at the conclusion of the war. To overcome the tension and generally to ingratiate itself with the United Nations, the Thai government made a number of concessions to the big powers. It settled a dispute with France over territory along the Indochinese border. It

---

* This judgment seems to be based largely on the supposed incompatibility of Buddhism and communism. Similar arguments, however, have proved woefully wrong in other parts of Asia. Cf. J. S. Furnivall, "Burma, Past and Present," *Far Eastern Survey*, XXII (1953), 25.

established diplomatic relations with the Soviet Union. It signed a treaty of friendship with China, in January 1946, by which for the first time diplomatic relations between the two countries were established. But this treaty failed to settle the many problems regarding the Chinese in Thailand satisfactorily to both countries. The rapid weakening of the National Government encouraged the Thais to solve some of the problems one-sidedly, to the disadvantage of the Chinese.

The change of governments in Thailand, following a *coup d'état,* affected Sino-Thai relations very little. The anti-Chinese feeling of the Thai people and government found expression in an increasing restriction of all Chinese activities, Nationalist or Communist. The Thai government showed little interest in close relations with China or, for that matter, with any Asian state. It was more eager to be on friendly terms with the big Western, particularly the anti-Communist, powers, but not so much as to become involved in an open conflict with any Communist state.[19]

The arrival of the Communist regime in China did not materially change the country's relations with Thailand. The Thai government maintains diplomatic relations with the Nationalists and continues very strict controls upon the Chinese community. The warnings and threats of the Communist government against the banning of Communist Chinese newspapers and the rounding up of suspect Chinese Communists do not appear to intimidate the Thai government.[20] So far the Chinese government has limited itself to verbal blasts against what it calls the "fascist satellite" of the American and British "imperialists."

Malaya, Indonesia, and the Philippines play a role in Chinese Communist propaganda, but hardly any in China's international relations. The inaccessibility of these countries from the Chinese standpoint is probably mostly responsible for this situation. It probably also explains the absence so far of any sizable material assistance to the Communist guerrillas in Malaya, the Hukbalahaps in the Philippines, and the Communists in Indonesia, who have to be satisfied with the strong moral support they receive from Chinese Communist propaganda.

As the details of Communist China's policy in Asia emerge, even Asian nations not directly involved become apprehensive. This has been particularly true of India. The aggression in Korea and especially in Tibet has brought about a distinct change in the Indian attitude toward

Communist China. Benevolent interest and sympathy on the part of many Indians accompanied the Communist seizure of power. The Communist Chinese had a good opportunity of establishing excellent relations with Free India. But their aggressive actions and their treatment of India have dissipated much of the existing good will and have reduced relations to cautious friendliness. Their true feelings toward India are difficult to fathom. They have blown both hot and cold, in rapid succession, on the Indian government, and in their relations with it seem to be in a state of suspended judgment.*

The Chinese Communists have used much of their vile vocabulary against the Indian government and against Prime Minister Nehru personally. The members of the government have been called "bourgeois reactionaries," "running dogs of Anglo-American imperialism," "lackeys," and "stooges of capitalism." They have been accused of "complicity" in the American government's "aggression" against Tibet and Afghanistan and of permitting India to be converted into "an Anglo-American gendarme in the East."

This vilification is never quite balanced by an equivalent degree of enthusiastic praise. But the Communists occasionally condescend to approve some of India's actions. And there always are the usual affirmations of friendship on diplomatic occasions and, for obvious propagandistic purposes, the frequent exchanges of missions, exhibits, and cultural visits. Communist China is cleverly using the mixture of admiration and fear exhibited by many Indians toward her by reciprocating with a mixture of threats and wooing.

India is still useful to Communist China, and the maintenance of good relations pays. India is a champion of Communist China's admission to the United Nations. She has refused to declare China an aggressor in Korea and to put an embargo on war materials to China. She has given comfort to China by refusing to sign — for reasons of her own — the Japanese peace treaty at San Francisco. The use of the Indian Embassy in Peking as a go-between seems to be desired by the Chinese; it is one of the few non-Communist contacts Communist China has with the free world.

Chinese reaction was very sharp when India's neutral independence worked against China, as it did in the Tibetan invasion. On that occasion

* The details of Indian-Chinese relations, especially from the Indian standpoint, can be found in Werner Levi, *Free India in Asia* (1952), pp. 79–112, 131–145. They will not be discussed here.

the Indian government expressed regret in a note to Peking, calling the action an "invasion" and contrary to the interests of China and peace. The answer from China was that her action was a domestic affair and that India's representation must have been affected "by foreign influence hostile to China." [21] The reaction of the Chinese press was even less diplomatic,[22] though considering how unbridled it can be, it was relatively mild. The Indians took little comfort in this restraint. On the contrary, they have continued to be worried by subsequent Chinese actions. The militarization and fortification of Tibet, the Communist infiltration into Nepal, and the tremendous Communist propaganda effort in India have seemed to indicate further aggressive intentions.

Behind the day-to-day contacts and relations between India and China lies the rivalry for leadership in Asia which permeates their actions, though it is hardly ever visible to the naked eye. In fact, both states deny such ambition, as they must according to diplomatic practice and wisdom. But at the All-Asian Conference in Delhi in 1947 this rivalry became clear to most observers, and it has been discoverable in their policies ever since. The smaller Asian states, particularly those sandwiched in between the two giants, do not relish the thought of becoming satellites. Their nationalism is directed against Asian imperialism as much as it is against Western imperialism. Though the Chinese, especially the Chinese Communists, could for a while use this nationalism for the promotion of their own ambitions, they are beginning to find out that nationalists react to Communist expansionism as much as to any other. Except where the Communists have been able to overcome it by brute force, as in Tibet, they have found that local nationalism has so far meant the frustration of their aims in Asia. For, although in some areas such as Malaya and Indochina, resistance was first offered by Western powers, the vast majority of the peoples of Southeast and South Asia have not yet been won over to the Communist cause.

Notes and Index

NOTES

In THE citations that follow, brief notes have been combined wherever clarity and convenience would permit; hence the sources mentioned under any one reference number may pertain to facts given earlier than in the sentence to which the reference number is attached. The source first mentioned is the one from which any verbatim quotation occurring in the text covered by the note is taken.

The abbreviation DS is used throughout for the United States Department of State; the combinations DSDD and DSDI signify U.S. Dep't of State Diplomatic Despatches and U.S. Dep't of State Diplomatic Instructions respectively. Other citations are given in full once for each chapter; after the first occurrence of a name or title, a shortened form is used.

Chapter 1. The Inadequacy of Old Practices

[1] Cf. Mary Gertrude Mason, *Western Concepts of China and the Chinese, 1840–1876* (New York, 1939), pp. 64–89, 115–173. There is a considerable literature trying to analyze Asian mentality and suggesting means for the meeting of East and West; see, e.g., F. S. C. Northrop, *The Meeting of East and West* (New York, 1947) and *The Taming of Nations* (New York, 1952); Lily Abegg, *The Mind of East Asia* (London, 1952); Richard Wilhelm and C. G. Jung, *Das Geheimnis der goldenen Blüte* (Zürich, 1944), pp. 1–19; Chiang Monlin, *Tides from the West* (New Haven, 1947), pp. 237–260; Gustav Amann, *Im Spiegel Chinas* (Berlin, 1925).

[2] Ming Kao-chao, *Essays on Chinese and Foreigners* (Mukden, 1930), p. 21.

[3] T. F. Tsiang, "Origins of the Tsungli Yamen," *Chinese Social and Political Science Review*, XV (1931), 92.

[4] Huang Yen-yü, "Viceroy Yeh Ming-ch'en and the Canton Episode (1856–1861)," *Harvard Journal of Asiatic Studies*, VI (1941), 71.

[5] Pao Chao Hsieh, *The Government of China (1644–1911)* (Baltimore, 1925), pp. 235–238, 244–246; H. S. Brunnert and V. V. Hagelstrom, *Present Day Political Organization of China* (Shanghai, 1912), p. 104; W. A. P. Martin, *A Cycle of Cathay* (New York, 1897), p. 152; "North China Herald" Office, *A Retrospect of Political and Commercial Affairs in China during the Five Years 1868–1872* (Shanghai, 1873), p. 43.

[6] Nathan A. Pelcovits, *Old China Hands and the Foreign Office* (New York, 1948), pp. 11–31.

[7] On rewards and punishments as a system of social control see Hellmut Wilhelm, *Gesellschaft und Staat in China* (Peking, 1944), pp. 33–35.

[8] Ssu-yu Teng, John K. Fairbank, and E-tu Zen Sun, *China's Response to the West, A Documentary Survey (1839–1923)* (mimeographed, Harvard University, 1950), pp. 33–34; cf. Abegg, *Mind of East Asia*, pp. 18–19, 212.

[9] John K. Fairbank, "Chinese Diplomacy and the Treaty of Nanking, 1842," *Journal of Modern History*, XII (1940), 1–30; Yen-chen T. H. Tchang, "Le Traité de Whampoa 1844," *Yenching Journal of Social Studies*, V (1950), 31–58.

[10] This opinion was expressed by all contemporary foreign consuls, merchants, ministers, and journalists in China. For some literature see Archibald R. Colquhoun,

China in Transformation (New York, 1898), pp. 199–208; John W. Foster, *American Diplomacy in the Orient* (Boston, 1904), pp. 203–255; Chester Holcombe, *The Real Chinese Question* (London, 1901), pp. 186–187.

[11] T. F. Tsiang, "The Secret Plan of 1858," *Chinese Social and Political Science Review*, XV (1931), 293; John K. Fairbank, "The Manchu Appeasement Policy of 1843," *Journal of the American Oriental Society*, LIX (1939), 469–484; also in Teng, Fairbank, and Sun, *China's Response*, p. 90.

[12] Fairbank, "Chinese Diplomacy."

[13] Teng, Fairbank, and Sun, *China's Response*, pp. 45, 51–52; G. W. Overdijkink, *Lin Tse-hsu, Een Biographische Schets* (Leiden, 1938), p. 90; Angelus Grosse-Aschhoff, *The Negotiations between Ch'i-Ying and Lagrené 1844–1846* (St. Bonoventure, N.Y., 1950), pp. 133–134.

[14] Fairbank, "Manchu Appeasement Policy." For an example of Chinese cleverness in talking in Western terms when Western help was wanted see Hyman Kublin, "The Attitude of China during the Liu-ch'iu Controversy, 1871–1881," *Pacific Historical Review*, XVIII (1949), 213–231; on Chinese morality see Max Weber, *Gesammelte Aufsätze zur Religionssoziologie* (Tübingen, 1922–1923), I, 513–532, in the translation by Hans H. Gerth (Glencoe, Ill., 1951), *The Religion of China*, pp. 236, 241; Talcott Parsons, *The Structure of Social Action* (Glencoe, Ill., 1949), pp. 550–551; G. Margouliès, *Anthologie raisonnée de la littérature chinoise* (Paris, 1948), p. 136.

[15] For some examples of proceedings within the government and for the ineptitude with which the new problems were tackled see Ssu-yü Teng, *Chang Hsi and the Treaty of Nanking 1842* (Chicago, 1944); Kublin, "Attitude of China during the Liu-ch'iu Controversy"; Tsiang, "Secret Plan of 1858"; Fairbank, "Chinese Diplomacy."

[16] Great Britain, F. O. 228/280, Shanghai, June 26, 1860.

[17] Holcombe, *Real Chinese Question*, p. 189.

[18] Teng, Fairbank, and Sun, *China's Response*, p. 38; Overdijkink, *Lin Tse-hsu*, p. 91.

[19] On the meaning and significance of the tribute system see John K. Fairbank and S. Y. Teng, "On the Ch'ing Tributary System," *Harvard Journal of Asiatic Studies*, VI (1941), 135–246; T. C. Lin, "Manchuria Trade and Tribute in the Ming Dynasty: A Study of Chinese Theories and Methods of Control over Border Peoples," *Nankai Social and Economic Quarterly*, IX (1937), 855–892; T. F. Tsiang, "China and European Expansion," *Politica*, II (1936), 1–18; Martin, *Cycle of Cathay*, p. 19.

[20] Ping Chia Kuo, "Caleb Cushing and the Treaty of Wanghia, 1844," *Journal of Modern History*, V (1933), 34–54; see also Kenneth Ch'en, "The Cushing Mission, Was it Necessary?", *Chinese Social and Political Science Review*, XXIII (1939), 3–14.

[21] Tsiang, "China and European Expansion," p. 3.

[22] Tsiang, "China and European Expansion."

[23] Earl H. Pritchard, "The Kowtow in the Macarthney Embassy to China in 1793," *Far Eastern Quarterly*, II (1943), 196–200; W. S. Ridge, "K'ot'ow in Chinese Diplomacy; Centenary Reflections on the War of 1839–42," *Chinese Social and Political Science Review*, XXIV (1941), 357–382.

[24] *Real Chinese Question*, p. 84.

[25] John K. Fairbank, *The United States and China* (Cambridge, Mass., 1948), p. 157; Holcombe, *Real Chinese Question*, p. 84; Demetrius C. Boulger, *The History of China* (London, 1898), II, 202; Arthur H. Smith, *Chinese Characteristics* (London, n.d.), pp. 58–64, 98–106.

[26] E.g., Kung Tzu-chen, Pao Shih-ch'en; see Arthur Hummel, ed., *Eminent Chinese of the Ch'ing Period, 1644–1912* (Washington, D.C., 1943), *sub* Kung and Pao.

[27] Teng, Fairbank, and Sun, *China's Response*, pp. 41–45; Gideon Chen, *Lin Tse-hsu, Pioneer Promoter of the Adoption of Western Means of Maritime Defense in China* (Peiping, 1934), pp. 51–58.

[28] Great Britain, F. O. 228/280.

[29] For details on the governmental system of the Manchus see Fairbank, *United States and China*, pp. 98–112; Hsieh, *Government of China*; Kenneth S. Latourette, *The Chinese: Their History and Culture* (New York, 1943), II, 27–44; cf. also *U.S. Foreign Relations, 1863*, Part 2, p. 940.

[30] Stanley F. Wright, *Hart and the Chinese Customs* (Belfast, 1950), p. 146; Tsiang, "Origins of the Tsungli Yamen"; John K. Fairbank and S. Y. Teng, "On the Types and Uses of Ch'ing Documents," *Harvard Journal of Asiatic Studies*, V (1940), 5; Wolfgang Franke, "Chinesische Quellen zur auswärtigen Politik des 19. und frühen 20. Jahrhunderts," *Sinologica*, I (1948), 210; S. Couveur, *Choix de documents* (Ho Kien Fou, 1894), p. 7.

[31] Knight Biggerstaff, "The T'ung Wen Kuan," *Chinese Social and Political Science Review*, XVIII (1934), 307–340; Li Hung-chang, "Memorial on the School," in Teng, Fairbank, and Sun, *China's Response*, pp. 170–171.

[32] For a description of official meetings see Sir Rutherford Alcock, "The Chinese Empire and Its Foreign Relations," *Fortnightly*, XXV (1876), 652–670; *London Times*, October 31, 1884. For details on the Tsungli Yamen see Hsieh, *Government of China*, pp. 238–242; Holcombe, *Real Chinese Question*, pp. 192–197; Colquhoun, *China*, pp. 208–214; Valentine Chirol, *The Far Eastern Question* (London, 1896), pp. 45–61; Brunnert and Hagelstrom, *Present Day Political Organization*, p. 105; Martin, *Cycle of Cathay*, pp. 338–342. On the organization of relations before the creation of the Tsungli Yamen see M. G. Pauthier and M. Bazin, *Chine moderne* (Paris, 1853), pp. 207–219. For a general description of Chinese administration at that time see Tuan-sheng Ch'ien, *The Government and Politics of China* (Cambridge, Mass., 1950), pp. 30–48.

[33] For examples see "North China Herald" Office, *A Retrospect*, pp. 8, 9, 19.

[34] Pelcovits, *Old China Hands and the Foreign Office*, pp. 11–31.

[35] On the Chinese press during that period see Colquhoun, *China*, pp. 228–247; Lin Yu-t'ang, *A History of the Press and Public Opinion in China* (Chicago, 1936), pp. 77–93; Roswell S. Britton, *The Chinese Periodical Press 1800–1912* (Shanghai, 1933), pp. 2–15. For examples of placards see S. Lane-Poole and F. V. Dickins, *The Life of Sir Harry Parkes* (London, 1894), I, 165, 226.

[36] "North China Herald" Office, *The Anti-foreign Riots in China in 1891* (Shanghai, 1892), pp. 81–228, provides a good contemporary discussion of the causes of the riots.

Chapter 2. Developing a Foreign Policy

NOTE. The citations in this and subsequent chapters from the *Papers on China* mimeographed for private distribution by the Committee on International and Regional Studies, Harvard University, have been made possible through the courtesy of Professor John K. Fairbank of Harvard in making the *Papers* available.

[1] Thomas Taylor Meadows, *Desultory Notes on the Government and People of China and on the Chinese Language* (London, 1847), p. 231. On Prince Kung see Arthur Hummel, ed., *Eminent Chinese of the Ch'ing Period, 1644–1912* (Washington, D.C., 1943), *sub* Prince Kung.

[2] Richard Wilhelm, *Die Seele Chinas* (Berlin, 1926), p. 37; "North China Herald" Office, *Anti-foreign Riots*, p. 106; Franz Michael, "Revolution and Renaissance in Nineteenth Century China: The Age of Tseng Kuo-fan," *Pacific Historical Review*, XVI (1947), 144–151. On the T'ai-p'ing Rebellion in general see Ssu-yu Teng, *New Light on the Taiping Rebellion* (Cambridge, Mass., 1950); Stanley F. Wright, *Hart and the Chinese Customs* (Belfast, 1950), pp. 88–117; Vincent Yu-

chung Shih, "Interpretations of the Taiping Tien-kuo by Noncommunist Chinese Writers," *Far Eastern Quarterly*, X (1951), 248–257, and "The Ideology of the Taiping Tien-Kuo," *Sinologica*, III (1951), 1–15; Eugene P. Boardman, "Christian Influence upon the Ideology of the Taiping Rebellion," *Far Eastern Quarterly*, X (1951), 115–124, and *Christian Influence upon the Ideology of the Taiping Rebellion 1851–1864* (Madison, 1950); M. N. Roy, *Revolution and Counter-Revolution in China* (Calcutta, 1946), pp. 129–165; George E. Taylor, "The Taiping Rebellion," *Chinese Social and Political Science Review*, XVI (1933), 545–614; Ssu-yu Teng, John K. Fairbank, and E-tu Zen Sun, *China's Response to the West, A Documentary Survey (1839–1923)* (mimeographed, Harvard University, 1950), pp. 119–124; Yeh Ting-yi, "How American Imperialists Assisted Manchus in Frustrating T'ai-p'ing T'ien-kuo Revolutionary Movement," American Consulate General, Hong-Kong, *Current Background*, No. 85, June 19, 1951; M. A. Baranovsky, "The Anglo-American Capitalists Throttle the Taiping Rebellion," *Soviet Press Translations*, VII (1952), 227–237.

[3] Teng, Fairbank, and Sun, *China's Response*, p. 90.

[4] Knight Biggerstaff, "The Secret Correspondence of 1867–1868: Views of Leading Chinese Statesmen Regarding the Future Opening of China to Western Influence," *Journal of Modern History*, XXII (1950), 122–136.

[5] John K. Fairbank, "Chinese Diplomacy and the Treaty of Nanking, 1842," *Journal of Modern History*, XII (1940), 1–30.

[6] Knight Biggerstaff, "The Establishment of Permanent Chinese Diplomatic Missions Abroad," *Chinese Social and Political Science Review*, XX (1936), 1–41; also "The First Chinese Mission of Investigation Sent to Europe," *Pacific Historical Review*, VI (1937), 307–320.

[7] Franz Michael, "Military Organization and Power Structure of China during the Taiping Rebellion," *Pacific Historical Review*, XVIII (1949), 469–483.

[8] Hellmut Wilhelm, "The Problem of Within and Without: A Confucian Attempt in Syncretism," *Journal of the History of Ideas*, XII (1951), 48–60.

[9] Otto Franke, *Ostasiatische Neubildungen* (Hamburg, 1911), pp. 22–25. For a most recent statement of the Chinese obsession with Western materialism and Eastern spirituality see Chang Hsin-hai, *Letters from a Chinese Diplomat* (Shanghai, 1948).

[10] The best sources are, of course, the writings of the individuals involved, some of which have been translated into Western languages. For a general survey see Paul S. Reinsch, *Intellectual and Political Currents in the Far East* (Boston, 1911), pp. 151–159; E. V. Zenker, *Geschichte der Chinesischen Philosophie* (Reichenberg, 1927), II, 311–322; Yu-hao Tseng, *Modern Chinese Legal and Political Philosophy* (Shanghai, 1930), pp. 39–86; Joseph R. Levenson, "The Breakdown of Confucianism: Liang Ch'i-ch'ao before Exile — 1873–1898," *Journal of the History of Ideas*, XI (1950), 448–450; Teng, Fairbank, and Sun, *China's Response*, pp. 150–169, 221.

[11] Wing-tsit Chan, "Neo-Confucianism," in Harley F. MacNair, *China* (Berkeley, 1946), p. 263.

[12] Chester Holcombe, *The Real Chinese Question* (London, 1901), p. 84.

[13] R. H. Tawney, *Land and Labour in China* (London, 1932), pp. 122, 196; Gideon Ch'en, *Tso Tsung T'ang, Pioneer Promoter of the Modern Dockyard and the Woollen Mill in China* (Peiping, 1938). To speak of this industrialization as the "first stage" in the reform movement seems somewhat exaggerated; see Ku Hung-ming, *Chinas Verteidigung gegen europäische Ideen* (Jena, 1921), p. 54; cf. Meribeth E. Cameron, *The Reform Movement in China, 1898–1912* (Stanford University, 1931), p. 11.

[14] Hummel, *Eminent Chinese*, pp. 296, 643, 721, 765.

[15] Holcombe, *Real Chinese Question*, pp. 143–145; Demetrius C. Boulger, *A Short History of China* (London, 1900), pp. 311–313; Wright, *Hart and the Chinese*

Customs, pp. 225–252; John L. Rawlinson, "The Lay-Osborn Flotilla: Its Development and Significance," *Papers on China (vol. 4) from the Regional Studies Seminars*, Mimeographed for private distribution by the Committee on International and Regional Studies, Harvard University (April 1950), pp. 58–93.

[16] J. O. P. Bland and E. Backhouse, *China under the Empress Dowager* (London, 1910), pp. 65–67; Alexander Michie, *The Englishman in China* (London, 1900), II, 412.

[17] Thomas Meadows, *The Chinese and Their Rebellions* (London, 1856), p. 160.

[18] Henri N. Frey, *L'Armée chinoise* (Paris, 1904); William Leslie Bales, *Tso Tsungt'ang, Soldier and Statesman of Old China* (Shanghai, 1937), pp. 37–52; C. P. Dabry, *Organisation militaire des Chinois; ou, La Chine et ses armées* (Paris, 1859); "The Chinese Army," *Saturday Review*, XC (1900), 167; Holcombe, *Real Chinese Question*, pp. 115–147; *U.S. Foreign Relations, 1881*, pp. 244–254; E. T. C. Werner, *Chinese* (London,1910), p. 117, in Herbert Spencer, *Descriptive Sociology; or Groups of Sociological Facts*, No. IX; Michael, "Military Organization and Power Structure of China," and "Die Ära Tseng Kuo-fan's," *Sinologica*, I (1947), 46–52. On the important role of Tseng Kuo-fan see further Gideon Ch'en, *Tseng Kuo-fan, Pioneer Promoter of the Steamship in China* (Peiping, 1935); Hellmut Wilhelm, "The Background of Tseng Kuo-fan's Ideology,"*Asiatische Studien*, III (1949), 90–100; Teng, Fairbank, and Sun, *China's Response*, pp. 126–149; see also Ralph L. Powell, "The Rise of Yüan Shih-k'ai and the Pei-yang Army," *Papers on China (vol. 3) from the Regional Studies Seminars* (May 1949), pp. 225–256; and William J. Hail, *Tseng Kuo-fan and the Taiping Rebellion* (New Haven, 1927), pp. 329–363.

Chapter 3. Foreign Impact and Reform

[1] T. F. Tsiang, "Sino-Japanese Diplomatic Relations, 1870–1894," *Chinese Social and Political Science Review*, XVII (1933), 4–16; T. C. Lin, "Li Hung-Chang: His Korea Policies 1870–1885," *Chinese Social and Political Science Review*, XIX (1935), 208–210; cf. also Hoshien Tchen, *Les Relations diplomatiques entre la Chine et le Japon de 1871 à nos jours* (Paris, 1921), pp. 13–20.

[2] Cf. Chu Djang, "War and Diplomacy over Ili," *Chinese Social and Political Science Review*, XX (1936), 369–392.

[3] Tsiang, "Sino-Japanese Diplomatic Relations," pp. 16–106; Yuan Tao-feng, "Li Hung-Chang and the Sino-Japanese War," *T'ien Hsia Monthly*, III (1936), 14; Hyman Kublin, "The Attitude of China during the Liu Ch'iu Controversy, 1871–1881," *Pacific Historical Review*, XVIII (1949), 213–231; Lin, "Li Hung-Chang: His Korea Policies 1870–1885," pp. 202–233; Henri Cordier, *Histoire des relations de la Chine avec les puissances occidentales* (Paris, 1901–1902), III, 219; London *Times*, January 19, 1895.

[4] J. O. P. Bland and E. Backhouse, *China under the Empress Dowager* (London, 1910), pp. 115–117. On the diplomatic and political background of the war see Stanley F. Wright, *Hart and the Chinese Customs* (Belfast, 1950), pp. 639–652; Payson J. Treat, "The Cause of the Sino-Japanese War, 1894," *Pacific Historical Review*, VIII (1939), 149–158; "Russian Documents Relating to Sino-Japanese War, 1894–'95," *Chinese Social and Political Science Review*, XVII (1933–1934), 480–515, 632–670; Robert T. Pollard, "American Relations with Korea 1882–1895," *Chinese Social and Political Science Review*, XVI (1932), 425–471.

[5] G. N. Curzon, *Problems of the Far East: Japan, Korea, China* (London, 1896), pp. 366–368.

[6] Wright, *Hart and the Chinese Customs*, p. 646.

[7] For examples of ideas among the reformers see Ssu-yu Teng, John K. Fairbank, and E-tu Zen Sun, *China's Response to the West, A Documentary Survey (1839–1923)* (mimeographed, Harvard University, 1950), pp. 390–502.

[8] London *Times*, April 27, May 6, 31, July 17, 1895. For Chinese efforts to get

the intervening nations France, Germany, and Russia also to regain Formosa for China see G. Germain and Kao Kien-long, "En marge du traité de Shimonoseki," *Bulletin de l'Université l'Aurore,* Ser. 3, VI (1945), 497–516.

⁹ London *Times,* March 5, 1895.

¹⁰ Quoted in Lin Yu-t'ang, *A History of the Press and Public Opinion in China* (Chicago, 1936), p. 95. For the condition of the press at this time see the same, pp. 94–102; Roswell S. Britton, *The Chinese Periodical Press* (Shanghai, 1933), pp. 86–101.

¹¹ London *Times,* September 26, 1895.

¹² London *Times,* September 26, 1895.

¹³ Meribeth E. Cameron, *The Reform Movement in China, 1898–1912* (Stanford University, 1931), p. 28; Otto Franke, *Ostasiatische Neubildungen* (Hamburg, 1911), p. 93; London *Times,* July 17, 1895.

¹⁴ Hosea Ballou Morse, *International Relations of the Chinese Empire* (Shanghai, 1918), III, 132. See also *Krasnyi Arkhives* (Moscow, 1922), II, 287–293.

¹⁵ Morse, *International Relations,* III, 137–139; London *Times,* October 7, 1898; Franke, *Ostasiatische Neubildungen,* pp. 136–157.

¹⁶ Seiji Hishida, *Japan among the Great Powers* (New York, 1940), p. 115; Auguste Moireau, "Les Boxeurs," *Revue Bleu,* Ser. 4, XIII (1900), 739.

¹⁷ For the text of the reform edicts see "North China Herald" Office, *The Emperor Kuang Hsü's Reform Decrees, 1898* (Peking, 1900).

¹⁸ Cf. Franke, *Ostasiatische Neubildungen,* pp. 72–95, who gives a description and interpretation of the *coup d'état* (based on Chinese sources) which appear more convincing than those of most other authors. See also Albert Maybon, *La Politique chinoise* (Paris, 1908), p. 32; Ch'en Ch'iu, "The Political Thoughts of the Anti-Reformists during the Time of 'The Hundred Days of Reform'," *Yenching Journal of Chinese Studies,* XXV (1939), 263–265, and Kenneth Ch'en, "Yuan Shih K'ai and the coup d'état of 1898 in China," *Pacific Historical Review,* VI (1937), 181–187.

¹⁹ London *Times,* September 26, 1895.

²⁰ London *Times,* January 23, 1899, and many similar reports in the press.

²¹ London *Times,* April 17, 1895.

²² Chang Chih-tung, *China's Only Hope* (New York, 1900), Chap. 10; *Boston Evening Transcript,* November 1, 1899. Cf. George N. Steiger, *China and the Occident* (New Haven, 1927), pp. 99–106; London *Times,* September 18, 1899, February 1, 1900.

²³ H. Frey, *L'Armée chinoise* (Paris, 1904), pp. 34–45; P. Dabry, "The Chinese Army," *Saturday Review,* XC (1900), 201.

²⁴ London *Times,* October 11, December 12, 1898; July 27, September 2, October 25, 1899; January 16, 1900; *Kobe Weekly Chronicle,* June 4, p. 501, June 25, p. 549, 1898.

²⁵ London *Times,* October 21, November 30, December 26, 1898; May 15, June 27, August 15, 1899; France, Ministère des affaires étrangères, *Documents Diplomatiques* (Livres Jaunes), *Affaires de Chine, 1898–1899,* No. 73, pp. 128, 135.

²⁶ London *Times,* September 27, 1899.

²⁷ Westel W. Willoughby, *Foreign Rights and Interests in China* (Baltimore, 1920), p. 114. The Chinese employed these tactics, for instance, when Italy demanded Sammun Bay; London *Times,* March 9, 1899. In 1905, when the viceroy of Szechwan heard that a new railway was to end at Wanhsien and when he was expecting that foreigners would therefore demand the opening of that city, he decided to open it himself "to preserve Chinese territorial integrity," *North China Herald,* October 13, 1905, p. 63.

²⁸ Cf. the fate of the Americans in the Anglo-American syndicate of 1899; London *Times,* July 15, 1899.

²⁹ London *Times,* May 13, 1899.

[30] London *Times*, February 27, March 1, July 24, 27, November 11, 1899; *Boston Evening Transcript*, November 7, 1899.

[31] London *Times*, July 24, 27, August 9, 12, 26, October 25, 1899; *Kobe Weekly Chronicle*, November 1, 1899, p. 336; *New York Daily Tribune*, September 2, 1899.

[32] Chang, *China's Only Hope*.

Chapter 4. Territorial Integrity or the Open Door?

[1] London *Times*, March 20, 1901; *Journal des Débats*, August 13, 1898. Victor A. Yakhontoff, *Russia and the Soviet Union in the Far East* (London, 1932), claims to have seen the original text of the agreement in the Moscow archives and reprinted it on pp. 365–366. This does not exclude that additional secret agreements were reached which remained unpublished; *The Memoirs of Count Witte* (New York, 1921), pp. 87–94.

[2] *Boston Evening Transcript*, November 4, 7, 8, 9, 1899; *New York Herald*, November 5, 1899.

[3] DSDD, China, December 21, 1899, No. 297; DSDI, China, November 20, 1899, No. 217.

[4] *New York Herald*, November 8, 1899. For a recent interpretation of the Open Door policy see Paul H. Clyde, "Historical Reflections on Continuity in United States Far Eastern Policy," in Philip W. Thayer, ed., *Southeast Asia in the Coming World* (Baltimore, 1953), pp. 17–32.

[5] This interpretation is based on the reading of the notes, Hay's acknowledgments of receipt of answers to the notes, letters from Rockhill to Hay suggesting an Open Door policy, and on the American attempts immediately following the sending of the notes to expand the meaning of the policy. Cf. especially the documents reprinted in Alfred L. P. Dennis, *Adventures in American Diplomacy 1896–1906* (New York, 1928), p. 212; John V. A. MacMurray, *Treaties and Agreements with and concerning China 1894–1919* (New York, 1921), p. 228.

[6] London *Daily Chronicle*, November 10, 1899; *New York Daily Tribune*, November 10, 1899; *Boston Evening Transcript*, November 10, 1899.

[7] *U.S. Foreign Relations, 1899*, pp. 150–153.

[8] T. F. Tsiang, "The Extension of Equal Commercial Privileges to other Nations than the British after the Treaty of Nanking," *Chinese Social and Political Science Review*, XV (1931), 423.

[9] Great Britain, *China No. 1 (1900)*, p. 406; London *Times*, November 24, 1900.

[10] *U.S. Foreign Relations, 1915*, p. 114 (cf. also Seward W. Livermore, "The American Naval-Base Policy in the Far East, 1850–1914," *Pacific Historical Review*, XIII (1944), 113; *U.S. Foreign Relations, 1901*, p. 39; *1902*, p. 275; *1909*, p. xviii; *1912*, p. xi; Carnegie Endowment for International Peace, Division of International Law, Pamphlet 40, *The Consortium*, pp. 4, 15.

[11] See Paul A. Varg, "The Foreign Policy of Japan and the Boxer Revolt," *Pacific Historical Review*, XV (1946), 279–285.

[12] France, Ministère des affaires étrangères, *Documents Diplomatiques* (Livres Jaunes), *Affaires de Chine, 1899–1900*, No. 74, pp. 42–64.

[13] Cf., for example, *Verhandlungen des Reichstages*, November 19, 1900, 10th Period, 2nd Session, I, 22–23; *Public Opinion* (London), LXXVII (1900), 418; Leonida Bissolati, *La politica estera dell'Italia dal 1897 al 1920* (Milano, 1923), p. 36; G. Ricchieri, "L'Italia in Cina," *Rivista d'Italia*, I (1899), 630; Prussia, *Berichte des Hauses der Abgeordneten*, April 17, 1899, 57th Session, p. 1862; France, *Journal Officiel*, Chambre, Débats, July 3, 1900, p. 1752.

Chapter 5. Rebellion against the West

[1] London *Times*, January 12, 1901.

[2] Mgr. Favier, *Le Temps*, January 10, 1901; London *Times*, October 4, 1900;

Sir Robert Hart, *These from the Land of Sinim: Essays on the Chinese Question* (London, 1901), p. 118.

[3] London *Times*, September 5, 1900.

[4] Albert Maybon, *La Politique chinoise*, pp. 122–142; George N. Steiger, *China and the Occident* (New Haven, 1927), pp. 247, 251; Isaac Taylor Headland, *Court Life in China* (New York, 1909), p. 54.

[5] Robert B. Sheeks, "A Re-examination of the I-ho Ch'uan and Its Role in the Boxer Movement," *Papers on China from the Regional Studies Seminars*, Mimeographed for private distribution by the Committee on International and Regional Studies, Harvard University, December 1947, pp. 85–87, 101–111. On various aspects of the Boxer Rebellion cf. J. O. P. Bland and E. Backhouse, *China under the Empress Dowager* (London, 1910), pp. 166–241; P. H. Clements, *The Boxer Rebellion: A Political and Diplomatic Review* (New York, 1915).

[6] *New York Daily Tribune*, June 9, 1900; France, Ministère des affaires étrangères, *Documents Diplomatiques* (Livres Jaunes), *Affaires de Chine, 1899–1900*, No. 74, pp. 26, 30. Cf. also *U.S. Foreign Relations, 1900*, p. 140; *North China Herald*, May 21, 1900, p. 527.

[7] *U.S. Foreign Relations, 1900*, pp. 139, 140; Sheeks, "Re-examination of the I-ho Ch'uan," pp. 84–100; J. J. L. Duyvendak, *The Diary of His Excellency Ching-shan* (Lugduni Batavorum, 1924).

[8] *North China Herald*, July 7, 1900, p. 58.

[9] *U.S. Foreign Relations, 1900*, pp. 248–249; Great Britain, *China No. 1 (1901)*, p. 1; *Documents Diplomatiques* (Livres Jaunes), *Chine, 1899–1900*, No. 74, p. 58; London *Times*, August 3, 16, 1900; *New York Daily Tribune*, June 27, 30, 1900.

[10] *Staatsarchiv*, LXV (1902), No. 12327, p. 197; *Documents Diplomatiques* (Livres Jaunes), *Chine, 1899–1900*, No. 74, p. 58; *New York Daily Tribune*, August 12, 1900; Great Britain, *China No. 1 (1903)*, p. 13; DS, Consular Despatches, Shanghai, July 17, 1900, No. 276.

[11] London *Times*, August 6, 13 (R. S. Gundry), 15, 1900; Great Britain, *China No. 1 (1901)*, pp. 85, 100.

[12] *Staatsarchiv*, LXV (1902), No. 12425, p. 258; Great Britain, *China No. 1 (1901)*, pp. 3, 49, 54, 99, 117; *New York Daily Tribune*, July 6, 8, 1900; London *Times*, August 3, 6, 11, 20, 1900. The British occupied Shanghai without formal agreement with the viceroys.

[13] *U.S. Foreign Relations, 1900*, pp. 265–266; Great Britain, *China No. 1 (1901)*, pp. 17, 117; *No. 5 (1901)*, p. 90; London *Times*, August 20, 1900; DS, Consular Despatches, August 18, 1900, No. 300.

[14] See Great Britain, *China No. 1 (1900)*, p. 3, for examples.

[15] Great Britain, *China No. 1 (1900)*, p. 89; London *Times*, August 6, 1900.

[16] London *Times*, August 6, 13, 1900; Great Britain, *Parliamentary Debates*, March 21, 1901, col. 707; *U.S. Foreign Relations, 1900*, pp. 219–221.

[17] *New York Daily Tribune*, June 8, 9, 10, 12, 13, 15, 19, 20, 22, July 11, August 3, 19, 1900; *Kobe Weekly Chronicle*, August 7, 1901, p. 128.

[18] *Documents Diplomatiques* (Livres Jaunes), *Chine, 1899–1900*, No. 74, p. 70; see *North China Herald*, July 11, 1900, p. 61.

[19] *New York Daily Tribune*, July 11, 1900; *Documents Diplomatiques* (Livres Jaunes), *Chine, 1899–1900*, No. 74, p. 65.

[20] Great Britain, *China No. 1 (1901)*, pp. 30, 45, 48, 49, 54, 82; London *Times*, August 14, 1900.

[21] London *Times*, December 28, 29, 1900; August 24, 1901.

[22] London *Times*, September 24, 25, 27, October 5, 14, November 6, 1900; February 7, 16, April 26, 29, July 22, September 4, 1901; January 3, 16, 1902.

[23] London *Times*, February 25, April 26, 1901; January 30, 1902; Great Britain, *China No. 1 (1901)*, p. 113; *China No. 5 (1901)*, p. 90.

[24] London *Times*, September 17, December 12, 1900; February 15, 1901.

[25] London *Times*, February 25, March 22, 1901; *U.S. Foreign Relations, 1901*, Appendix, pp. 159, 170, 171, 181.

[26] London *Times*, December 29, 1900, September 30, 1901; *Kobe Weekly Chronicle*, September 4, 1901, p. 227; *North China Herald*, September 19, 1900, p. 609.

[27] London *Times*, November 13, 1901, April 10, 1902; *North China Herald*, January 15, 1904, p. 73.

[28] *Le Temps*, January 10, 1901.

Chapter 6. Threatened Loss of Manchuria

[1] The exact text was first published in *Krasnyi Arkhives*, reprinted by B. A. Romanov, *Rossii v. Manchzhurii, 1892–1906* (Leningrad, 1928), and by W. H. Langer, *The Diplomacy of Imperialism, 1890–1902* (New York, 1935), pp. 714–716. For details on the Manchurian problem see Paul H. Clyde, *International Rivalries in Manchuria, 1689–1922* (Columbus, 1928), pp. 81–101.

[2] *Die Grosse Politik der Europäischen Kabinette, 1871–1914* (Berlin 1921–1927), XVI, 336.

[3] London *Times*, April 4, October 26, November 9, 19, 1901.

[4] Cf. Otto Franke, *Ostasiatische Neubildungen* (Hamburg, 1911), p. 38; DSDD, China, November 29, 1904, No. 1755. On the taxes see Shao-Kwan Chen, *The System of Taxation in China in the Tsing Dynasty, 1644–1911* (New York, 1914), pp. 42–45; Kinn Wei Shaw, *Democracy and Finance in China* (New York, 1926), pp. 146–147; Pao Chao Hsieh, *The Government of China (1644–1911)* (Baltimore, 1925), pp. 203–204; E. T. C. Werner, *Chinese* (London, 1910), p. 90.

[5] London *Times*, April 2, 4, 6, 1901.

[6] London *Times*, April 3, July 24, 1901.

[7] London *Times*, September 17, 1900.

[8] *Kobe Weekly Chronicle*, April 10, 1901, p. 316; J. J. Gapanovich, "Sino-Russian Relations in Manchuria, 1892–1906," *Chinese Social and Political Science Review*, XVII (1933), 459. Chang offered concessions to Russia in Chinese Turkestan and Ili in return for a Russian withdrawal from Manchuria; London *Times*, November 22, 1901.

[9] *Grosse Politik*, XVI, 326, 331, 333.

[10] France, Commission de publication des documents relatifs aux origines de la guerre de 1914, *Documents Diplomatiques Français*, Ser. 2, I, 168, 195.

[11] Cf. *Grosse Politik*, XVI, 334–335, 340; *Documents Diplomatiques Français*, Ser. 2, I, 168–169.

[12] London *Times*, April 3, 1901.

[13] London *Times*, April 3, 1901; see also March 4, 1901; *Kobe Weekly Chronicle*, April 10, 1901, p. 316; Alfred L. P. Dennis, *Adventures in American Diplomacy 1896–1906* (New York, 1928), p. 242.

[14] Great Britain, *China No. 2 (1904)*, p. 8; London *Times*, April 2, October 25, 1901.

[15] London *Times*, April 5, 6, 1901.

[16] London *Times*, March 14, April 8, 9, November 13, 1901; *Kobe Weekly Chronicle*, April 3, 1901, p. 316; "On the Eve of the Russo-Japanese War," *Chinese Social and Political Science Review*, XIX (1935), 239.

[17] London *Times*, October 24, November 6, 1900; April 4, 8, 11, 1901; *New York Herald*, April 3, 1901; *Staatsarchiv*, LXVI, 158; *Grosse Politik*, XVI, 336.

[18] "On the Eve," pp. 130, 239–266; *Documents Diplomatiques Français*, Ser. 2, I, 224; London *Times*, March 26, April 5, 8, 9, 1901.

[19] London *Times*, April 8, 1901; *Kobe Weekly Chronicle*, April 10, 1901, p. 308.

[20] London *Times*, May 6, August 5, 19, 1901; Great Britain, *China No. 2 (1904)*, pp. 25–27; Gapanovich, "Sino-Russian Relations," p. 462. On the Tibet incident see *Wiener Zeitung*, July 9, 1901; London *Times*, July 6, 8, 9, 19, 1901; *Kobe Weekly*

Chronicle, July 17, p. 70, August 14, p. 167, September 4, p. 244, 1901; Great Britain, *Parliamentary Debates,* August 12, 1901, col. 425.

[21] Gapanovich, "Sino-Russian Relations," pp. 462–464; cf. London *Times,* October 24, November 9, 1901; Edward H. Zabriskie, *American-Russian Rivalry in the Far East* (Philadelphia, 1946), p. 77.

[22] *Frankfurter Zeitung,* February 7, 1902.

[23] DSDD, December 4, 1901, No. 836; *Frankfurter Zeitung,* February 13, 14, 1902; Gapanovich, "Sino-Russian Relations," p. 463; G. P. Gooch and H. W. V. Timperley, eds., *British Documents on the Origins of the War, 1898–1914* (London, 1926–1938), II, 126; *Documents Diplomatiques Français,* Ser. 2, II, 100; London *Times,* February 13, 1902; *Japan Weekly Chronicle,* February 19, 1902, p. 165.

[24] *Japan Weekly Chronicle,* March 5, 1902, p. 212; London *Times,* March 7, 1902.

[25] DSDD, December 12, 1901, No. 846; January 29, 1902, No. 898; February 4, 1902, No. 905.

[26] Gooch and Timperley, *British Documents,* II, 201.

[27] *Documents Diplomatiques Français,* Ser. 2, III, 292; IV, 150, 168; *U.S. Foreign Relations, 1903,* p. 54; DSDD, June 18, 1903, No. 1327.

[28] London *Times,* May 2, 26, June 19, 23, 30, December 29, 1903; *U.S. Foreign Relations, 1903,* p. 66; *Documents Diplomatiques Français,* Ser. 2, III, 585.

[29] *Japan Weekly Chronicle,* September 30, 1903, p. 317; London *Times,* October 2, 10, 12, 1903.

[30] London *Times,* November 2, 3, 6, 9, 13, 14, December 7, 9, 12, 19, 1903; *Japan Weekly Chronicle,* November 11, p. 493, November 18, pp. 520, 521, 1903; *Documents Diplomatiques Français,* Ser. 2, IV, 88.

[31] *New York Herald,* January 13, 1904, and following days; London *Times,* January 13, 15, 1904; *Documents Diplomatiques Français,* Ser. 2, III, 307.

Chapter 7. Nurturing Nationalism

[1] DSDD, January 30, 1904, No. 1490; France, Commission de publication des documents relatifs aux origines de la guerre de 1914, *Documents Diplomatiques Français,* Ser. 2, IV, 280, 292, 311.

[2] *North China Herald,* January 8, p. 50, January 22, p. 124, February 5, p. 264, 1904; *Documents Diplomatiques Français,* Ser. 2, IV, 308; *Die Grosse Politik der Europäischen Kabinette, 1871–1914* (Berlin, 1921–1927), XIX(1), 113.

[3] *Documents Diplomatiques Français,* Ser. 2, IV, 308; *North China Herald,* January 22, 1904, p. 111.

[4] Alfred L. P. Dennis, *Adventures in American Diplomacy 1896–1906* (New York, 1928), p. 400; *Documents Diplomatiques Français,* Ser. 2, IV, 230, 231, 308; V, 68; VI, 22, 207; *North China Herald,* September 15, 1905, pp. 591, 634; *U.S. Foreign Relations, 1905,* pp. 816–818; *Grosse Politik,* XIX(1), 112; J. J. Jusserand, *What Me Befell* (London, 1933), p. 116; Stephen Chao-ying Pan, *American Diplomacy concerning Manchuria* (Boston, 1938), p. 112.

[5] *Documents Diplomatiques Français,* Ser. 2, VII, 68; London *Times,* September 27, 1905, February 6, 1906; *North China Herald,* September 15, pp. 591, 634, September 22, p. 694, September 29, p. 705, 1905; *Grosse Politik,* XIX(2), 544.

[6] *North China Herald,* October 6, 1905, pp. 2, 3, 4.

[7] *North China Herald,* October 6, pp. 4, 41, October 13, p. 102, October 20, p. 118, 1905. On the influence of some Yale professor on the Treaty of Portsmouth see G. Germain, "Autour du traité de Portsmouth," *Bulletin de l'Université l'Aurore,* Ser. 3, IX (1948), 326–331.

[8] *North China Herald,* October 27, p. 178, 1905; September 7, pp. 554, 561, 1906; *Documents Diplomatiques Français,* Ser. 2, VIII, 243; John V. A. MacMurray, *Treaties and Agreements with and concerning China 1894–1919* (New York, 1921), 1905/18, pp. 549–551.

⁹ For details of these reforms see Meribeth E. Cameron, *The Reform Movement in China, 1898–1912* (Stanford University, 1931), pp. 65–99, 136–180; Harold M. Vinacke, *A History of the Far East in Modern Times* (New York, 1941), pp. 208, 254–298; Otto Franke, *Ostasiatische Neubildungen* (Hamburg, 1911), pp. 106–135.

¹⁰ Smith, *Chinese Characteristics*, pp. 107–114.

¹¹ E-tu Zen Sun, "The Chinese Constitutional Mission of 1905–1906," *Journal of Modern History*, XXIV (1952), 251–268; Vinacke, *History of the Far East*, p. 209. On the history of modern constitution-making see Pan Wei-tung, *The Chinese Constitution* (Washington, D.C., 1945); W. Y. Tao, *The Constitutional Structure of Modern China* (Melbourne, 1947), pp. 1–22; Harold M. Vinacke, *Modern Constitutional Development in China* (New York, 1920).

¹² On the relation between family loyalty and nationalism see Bertrand R. Russell, *The Problem of China* (New York, 1922), pp. 36–38; Lin Yutang, *My Country and My People* (New York, 1935), pp. 176–186; Max Weber, *Gesammelte Aufsätze zur Religionssoziologie* (Tübingen, 1922–1923), in the translation by Hans H. Gerth (Glencoe, Ill., 1951), *The Religion of China*, pp. 236, 241; Paschal M. d'Elia, ed., *Le Triple Démisme de Suen Wen* (Shanghai, 1930), p. 12; also Lin Yueh-hwa, *The Golden Wing* (London, 1948), on the nature of the modern Chinese family.

¹³ *U.S. Foreign Relations, 1904*, pp. 153–155; *North China Herald*, October 13, pp. 59, 63, 78, October 20, pp. 119, 165, November 10, p. 296, 1905; London *Times*, January 6, 1906; "Le Nationalisme économique en Chine," *L'Asie française*, VI (1906), 430, 432.

¹⁴ *North China Herald*, October 6, pp. 44, 46, October 13, pp. 76, 78, October 20, p. 166, November 10, pp. 324, 334, December 8, p. 573, 1905; May 18, p. 350, 1906; London *Times*, January 6, 1906; "La Direction des douanes impériales," *L'Asie française*, VII (1907), 175. On Young China see Jean Rodes, *La Chine et le mouvement constitutionel* (Paris, 1913), pp. 207–251. For some results of the new policy in China's relations with Japan and Russia see Shuhsi Hsu, *China and Her Political Entity* (New York, 1926), pp. 299–316; Michel N. Pavlovsky, *Chinese-Russian Relations* (New York, 1949), pp. 40–43.

¹⁵ "The Foreign Policy of the United States," *Current History*, January 1924, XIX, 577; *Conference on the Limitation of Armament*, Senate Document No. 126, 67th Congress, 2nd Session (Washington, D.C., 1922), p. 636.

Chapter 8. Alignment with Germany and America

¹ A. M. Pooley, ed., *Memoirs of Count Hayashi* (New York, 1915), p. 216; A. Gérard, *Ma Mission au Japon* (Paris, 1919), p. 18.

² France, *Journal Officiel*, Chambre, Débats, June 17, 1907, p. 1389; London *Times*, May 7, 9, 1907; *U.S. Foreign Relations, 1907*, II, 756; Bernhard Heinrich Schwertfeger, *Zur Europäischen Politik* (Berlin, 1919), II, 176.

³ London *Times*, May 9, August 24, 1907; *North China Herald*, August 9, pp. 321, 343, August 23, p. 432, 1907.

⁴ Pooley, *Memoirs of Count Hayashi*, p. 221.

⁵ *U.S. Foreign Relations, 1907*, p. 758; *Grosse Politik*, XXV(1), 69; London *Times*, August 24, 1907.

⁶ Edward H. Zabriskie, *American-Russian Rivalry in the Far East* (Philadelphia, 1946), p. 137.

⁷ *Grosse Politik*, XXV(1), 86.

⁸ *Grosse Politik*, XV(1), 68, 71, 74, 78, 79, 80, 81, 93, 95.

⁹ DS, Division of Far Eastern Affairs, Memorandum, December 5, 1908, 2413/—; Herbert Croly, *Willard Straight* (New York, 1924), Chaps. 7 and 8.

¹⁰ DSDD, November 29, 1909, 2413/188–189; Croly, *Willard Straight*, p. 274.

¹¹ DSDD, November 25, 1908, 16533/13; December 3, 1908, 16533/46; see also A. Whitney Griswold, *The Far Eastern Policy of the United States* (New York,

1938), Chap. 4; Philip C. Jessup, *Elihu Root* (New York, 1938), p. 38; Sir John T. Pratt, *War and Politics in China* (London, 1943), p. 163.

[12] *Grosse Politik*, XXV(1), 97, 98.

[13] DSDD, July 16, 1908, 2413/146–148, No. 966, and the notes of W. Phillips and Adee attached; July 30, 1908, 2413/151, No. 973; August 1, 1908, 2413/146–148; *U.S. Foreign Relations, 1908*, pp. 67–68.

[14] DS, Division of Far Eastern Affairs, Memorandum, December 5, 1908, 2413/—; December 5, 1908, 2413/219; interview between Mr. T'ang Shao-yi and the Secretary of State, December 9, 1908, 2413/—.

[15] DSDI, December 11, 1908, 2413/213A.

[16] Details of T'ang's visit to the United States can be found in DS, 2413.

Chapter 9. Strengthening the Empire

[1] *North China Herald*, August 21, p. 442, September 18, pp. 666, 667, September 25, p. 709, October 21, p. 162, December 30, p. 767, 1910; John Gilbert Reid, *The Manchu Abdication and the Powers, 1908–1912* (Berkeley, 1935), p. 77; Herbert Croly, *Willard Straight* (New York, 1924), pp. 306–308; Owen Lattimore, *Manchuria Cradle of Conflict* (New York, 1932), p. 70.

[2] DSDI, January 7, 1910, 5315/670, telegram; *U.S. Foreign Relations, 1910*, p. 245.

[3] Croly, *Willard Straight*, p. 301; cf. *North China Herald*, July 3, 1909.

[4] DSDD, August 20, 1909, 5767/88, August 23, 1909, 5767/89; *Japan Weekly Chronicle*, August 4, 1910, p. 205; *North China Herald*, August 21, 1909, p. 442.

[5] DSDD, December 19, 1909, 5315/705.

[6] DSDD, January 10, 1909, 5315/773.

[7] DSDD, January 19, 1910, 5315/691; DSDI, January 22, 1910, 5315/704; A. Gérard, *Ma Mission au Japon* (Paris, 1919), p. 124.

[8] DSDD, January 20, 1910, 5315/697, January, 1910, 5315/722.

[9] DSDD, February 5, 1910, 5315/746; DSDI, February 8, 1910, 5315/746; *North China Herald*, October 21, 1910, pp. 145, 161.

[10] DSDD, May 28, 1909, 4002/186/187/188; March 3, 1909, 5767/39; September 7, 1909, 5767/65/66.

[11] DSDD, March 3, 1909, 5767/39; February 27, 1909, 4002/177/178.

[12] DSDD, July 30, 1910, 794.611; DSDI, August 17, 1910, 711.93/15; *North China Herald*, October 21, 1910, p. 161; cf. B. von Siebert, ed., *Benckendorffs diplomatischer Schriftwechsel* (Berlin, 1928), I, 409, II, 87–89.

[13] Von Siebert, *Benckendorffs*, I, 380.

[14] Von Siebert, *Benckendorffs*, I, 401, 409; cf. Aitchen K. Wu, *China and the Soviet Union* (London, 1950), pp. 27–46; Michel N. Pavlovsky, *Chinese-Russian Relations* (New York, 1949), pp. 39–43, for a survey of Russian-Chinese friction over Mongolia.

[15] Archibald Rose, "Chinese Frontiers of India," *Geographical Journal*, XXXIX (1912), 203; Charles Monrey, "La Politique chinoise au Tibet et au Yuannan," *L'Asie française*, XII (1912), 190.

[16] DSDD, August 22, 1910, 741.93/67; *L'Asie française*, XII (1912), 371; Great Britain, *Parliamentary Debates*, July 25, 1912, col. 1325; July 30, 1912, cols. 1978ff; *Grosse Politik*, XXXII, 421, 442; John V. A. MacMurray, *Treaties and Agreements with and concerning China 1894–1919* (New York, 1921), p. 581.

[17] *Grosse Politik*, XXXII, 448–449; "L'Angleterre et la politique des zones d'influences en Chine," *L'Asie française*, XIV (1914), 53.

[18] *Grosse Politik*, XXXII, 3, 6.

[19] "L'Angleterre et la politique . . .," p. 52; London *Daily Telegraph*, February 25, 1914; Great Britain, *Parliamentary Debates*, June 15, 1910, col. 1390.

[20] DSDD, August 17, 1910, 893.00/429, August 25, 1910, 893.00/437, September

7, 1910, 893.00/442; *North China Herald*, January 1, 1908, p. 169; *Grosse Politik*, XXV(1), 76, XXXII, 164; Henry F. Pringle, *The Life and Times of William Howard Taft* (New York, 1939), II, 691; von Siebert, *Benckendorffs*, I, 403, III, 213.

[21] Von Siebert, *Benckendorffs*, I, 402–405; *Grosse Politik*, XXXII, 29.

[22] DSDD, August 17, 1910, 893.00/429; August 25, 1910, 893.00/437.

[23] *Grosse Politik*, XXXII, 152.

[24] *Grosse Politik*, XXXII, 154–155; *North China Herald*, October 7, p. 6, October 14, p. 106, 1910.

[25] Pringle, *Taft*, II, 684–686.

Chapter 10. Revolution and Foreign Money

[1] *The Invasion of China by the Western World* (London, 1937), p. 131. See, e.g., the observations noted in Great Britain, *Parliamentary Papers, Affairs of China*, No. 3 (1912), pp. 134, 180, 185, 188, 206; Albert Maybon, "La Révolution chinoise," *L'Asie française*, XII (1912), 10; Jean Rodes, *La Fin des Mandchous* (Paris, 1919), pp. 85, 138; and the remarks of T'ang Leang-li, *China in Revolt* (London, n.d.), p. 101.

[2] From the vast literature covering this period in Chinese history, the following works have been especially consulted, in addition to the diplomatic reports of the American, British, German, and French ministers: Albert Maybon, *La République chinoise* (Paris, 1914); André Duboscq, *L'Elite chinoise* (Paris, 1945); Rodes, *La Fin des Mandchous*; Jean Rodes, *Le Céleste Empire avant la révolution* (Paris, 1914); T'ang Leang-li, *The Foundations of Modern China* (London, 1928); Fernand Farjenel, *Through the Chinese Revolution* (New York, 1916); John Gilbert Reid, *The Manchu Abdication and the Powers, 1908–1912* (Berkeley, 1935); J. O. P. Bland, *Recent Events and Present Policies in China* (London, 1912); Harley Farnsworth MacNair, *China in Revolution* (Chicago, 1931); Arthur N. Holcombe, *The Chinese Revolution* (Cambridge, Mass., 1931); M. N. Roy, *Revolution and Counter-Revolution in China* (Calcutta, 1946), pp. 216–223; Tyan Ling, *Beiträge zur neuesten Geschichte Chinas* (Berlin, 1917), pp. 16–51.

[3] Hosea B. Morse, *The Trade and Administration of the Chinese Empire* (London, 1913), p. 81.

[4] There is a large literature on Chinese finances and loans. For the essential details see Meribeth E. Cameron, *The Reform Movement in China, 1898–1912* (Stanford University, 1931), pp. 161–171; Bland, *Recent Events*, pp. 391–395; J. W. Jenks, "Monetary Conditions in China," in George H. Blakeslee, *China and the Far East* (New York, 1910), pp. 121–132; Frederick V. Field, *American Participation in the China Consortiums* (Chicago, 1931), pp. 55–66; Edward H. Zabriskie, *American-Russian Rivalry in the Far East* (Philadelphia, 1946), pp. 171–179; T. W. Overlach, *Foreign Financial Control in China* (New York, 1919), pp. 234–236.

[5] Mongton Chih Hsu, *Railway Problems in China* (New York, 1915), pp. 108–120; Cameron, *Reform Movement*, pp. 186–195; Reid, *Manchu Abdication*, in the Index under Railway references to Szechuan; Rodes, *La Fin des Mandchous*, pp. 33–39; Willard Straight, "China's Loan Negotiations," *Journal of Race Development*, III (1913), 384, 386.

[6] T'ang, *Foundations of Modern China*, p. 149; Roy, *Revolution and Counter-Revolution*, p. 223; Maybon, *République chinoise*, pp. 149–152.

[7] *North China Herald*, September 28, 1912.

[8] For statements and manifestoes friendly to foreigners see London *Times*, November 16, 23, 1911; *North China Herald*, January 20, p. 167, September 14, p. 754, 1912; Paul S. Reinsch, *An American Diplomat in China* (Garden City, 1922), p. 73. For loans to the revolutionaries see *North China Herald*, January 20, p. 167, February 3, p. 306, February 10, p. 364, 366, 367, February 17, p. 438, 1912; and generally the *Far Eastern Review* covering this period.

[9] See DSDD, December 6, 1911, 893.00/745; December 11, 1911, 893.00/759; also Willard Straight, "China's Loan Negotiations," in G. H. Blakeslee, ed., *Recent Developments in China* (New York, 1913), pp. 132, 136.

[10] France, Commission de publication des documents relatifs aux origines de la guerre de 1914, *Documents Diplomatiques Français*, Ser. 3, II, 391.

[11] *North China Herald*, March 29, 1913, p. 947; Tien-yi Li, *Woodrow Wilson's China Policy, 1913–1917* (New York, 1952), pp. 23–48.

[12] On recognition policy see Li, *Woodrow Wilson's China Policy*, pp. 57–84.

[13] *Far Eastern Review*, VIII (1912), 374; IX (1912), 163–164, 199–200; *North China Herald*, March 23, 1912, p. 752. For details of some of these loans see Overlach, *Foreign Financial Control*, pp. 238, 241–247, 252–256; Harold M. Vinacke, *A History of the Far East in Modern Times* (New York, 1941), pp. 233–240; Westel W. Willoughby, *Foreign Rights and Interests in China* (Baltimore, 1920), pp. 497–499, 506–507; *Documents Diplomatiques Français*, Ser. 3, IV, 233; V, 316, 328; Li, *Woodrow Wilson's China Policy*, pp. 163–195.

[14] *Documents Diplomatiques Français*, Ser. 3, VI, 275; France, *Journal Officiel, Chambre, Débats*, December 24, 1921, pp. 5252, 5260; March 30, 1914, pp. 2060, 2064; *L'Asie française*, XIII (1913), 487; London *Times*, February 14, 1914.

[15] Robert de Caix, "La Question des emprunts chinois," *L'Asie française*, IX (1909), 374.

[16] For details on these treaties and the admission of Russia and Japan to the Consortium see Ernest B. Price, *The Russo-Japanese Treaties of 1907–1916 concerning Manchuria and Mongolia* (Baltimore, 1933); Zabriskie, *American-Russian Rivalry*, p. 187; A. Whitney Griswold, *The Far Eastern Policy of the United States* (New York, 1938), pp. 171–172; Field, *American Participation*, pp. 101–109.

[17] DSDD, October 31, 1913, 761.93/107; November 18, 1912, 893.002/29, No. 676; December 20, 1912, 893.51/1243, No. 694.

[18] For the text of the agreements see John V. A. MacMurray, *Treaties and Agreements with and concerning China 1894–1919* (New York, 1921), 1912/12, 1913/11, 1915/10. For the diplomacy see Michel N. Pavlovsky, *Chinese-Russian Relations* (New York, 1949), pp. 44–67; Aitchen K. Wu, *China and the Soviet Union* (London, 1950), pp. 41–46; "Krasny Archiv, Tsarist Russia and Mongolia in 1913–1914," *Chinese Social and Political Science Review*, XVI (1934), 632–688, XVII (1934), 170–205.

[19] DSDD, December 2, 1913, 893.00/2050; Charles F. Remer, *Foreign Investments in China* (New York, 1933), pp. 125–130, 249–265, 338. On President Wilson's relations with Yuan Shih-k'ai see Li, *Woodrow Wilson's China Policy*, pp. 139–159.

Chapter 11. "Theoretical" Ally in World War I

[1] Paul S. Reinsch, "Secret Diplomacy and the Twenty-One Demands," *Asia*, XXI (1921), 937–943; cf. *North China Herald*, August 8, 1914, p. 399; Otto Hoetzsch, ed., *Die Internationalen Beziehungen im Zeitalter des Imperialismus* (Berlin, 1934), I, v, 272, II, vi, i, 179; *Japan Weekly Chronicle*, August 13, 1914, p. 324.

[2] *U.S. Foreign Relations, 1914*, Suppl., p. 190; also pp. 165, 168, 186, 187.

[3] *U.S. Foreign Relations, 1914*, Suppl., pp. 172–183; Hoetzsch, *Die Internationalen Beziehungen*, II, vi, i, 94–96; John V. A. MacMurray, *Treaties and Agreements with and concerning China 1894–1919* (New York, 1921), 1154, 1367; Nagao Ariga, *La Chine et la grande guerre européenne au point de vue de droit international* (Paris, 1920), pp. 19–30; Thomas F. Millard, *Democracy and the Eastern Question* (New York, 1919), pp. 84–90; Russell H. Fifield, *Woodrow Wilson and the Far East* (New York, 1952), pp. 14–24. For details on China in the war see Thomas E. LaFargue, *China and the World War* (Stanford University, 1937); Robert T. Pollard, *China's Foreign Relations* (New York, 1933), pp. 8–49.

[4] For details on the Twenty-One Demands see G. Z. Wood, *Twenty-One Demands*

(New York, 1921); Smimosa Idditti, *The Life of the Marquis Shigenobu Okuma* (Tokyo, 1940), pp. 380–389.

⁵ Earl Albert Selle, *Donald of China* (New York, 1948), pp. 153–169; Tien-yi Li, *Woodrow Wilson's China Policy, 1913–1917* (New York, 1952), pp. 105, 133; Paul S. Reinsch, *An American Diplomat in China* (Garden City, 1922), p. 131.

⁶ Cf. *U.S. Foreign Relations, 1915*, p. 87.

⁷ *North China Herald*, February 27, 1915, p. 591; cf. also February 13, pp. 490, 492, February 27, pp. 584, 620, March 6, pp. 676, 716, March 13, pp. 774, 797, March 20, pp. 821, 840, March 27, p. 891, 1915.

⁸ *North China Herald*, February 27, p. 584, March 6, p. 722, March 27, pp. 896, 897, 1915; *Japan Weekly Chronicle*, May 6, 1915, p. 684.

⁹ *Japan Weekly Chronicle*, May 6, p. 684, May 13, p. 724, 1915.

¹⁰ *U.S. Foreign Relations, 1915*, p. 91.

¹¹ *U.S. Foreign Relations, 1915*, pp. 149–150; B. L. Putnam Weale, *The Fight for the Republic in China* (New York, 1917), p. 121; *Japan Weekly Chronicle*, May 13, 1915, p. 727. Accounts of the episode are contradictory.

¹² *Japan Weekly Chronicle*, May 6, p. 686, May 13, pp. 712, 726, 1915. Fifield, *Woodrow Wilson and the Far East*, pp. 24–32, 36.

¹³ J. E. Spencer, "On Regionalism in China," *Journal of Geography*, XLVI (1947), 132; R. H. Tawney, *Land and Labour in China* (London, 1932), p. 165; O. M. Green, *The Story of China's Revolution* (London, n.d.), pp. 76–86; Harold Isaacs, *The Tragedy of the Chinese Revolution* (London, 1938), pp. 22–23; Sir Meyrick Hewlett, *Forty Years in China* (London, 1944), pp. 84–135. On the internal situation during this period see also Harley Farnsworth MacNair, *China in Revolution* (Chicago, 1931), pp. 46–64; Jermyn Chi-hung Lynn, *Political Parties in China* (Peking, 1930); Stephen Chen and Robert Payne, *Sun Yat-sen: A Portrait* (New York, 1946), pp. 146–158; J. O. P. Bland, *China, Japan, and Korea* (New York, 1921), pp. 89–112; Jean Marques-Rivière, *La Chine dans le monde* (Paris, 1935), pp. 44–49.

¹⁴ For the American diplomacy see Fifield, *Woodrow Wilson and the Far East*, pp. 62–73; A. Whitney Griswold, *The Far Eastern Policy of the United States* (New York, 1938), pp. 199–205.

¹⁵ *U.S. Foreign Relations, 1917*, Suppl. 1, pp. 404–407.

¹⁶ For a contemporary account of this event see Weale, *Fight for the Republic in China*, pp. 309–369.

¹⁷ Gilbert Reid, *China Captive or Free?* (New York, 1921), pp. 110, 84–120. On some aspects of foreign activity in China to draw the nation into war see in addition to the literature quoted in the immediately preceding notes: *Le Journal* (Paris), August 4, 1917; *New Republic*, X (1917), 184; Weale, *Fight for the Republic in China*, p. 343; Reinsch, *American Diplomat*, pp. 261–271; K. K. Kawakami, *Japan and World Peace* (New York, 1919), pp. 125–142; Samuel G. Blythe, "The First Time in Five Thousand Years," *Saturday Evening Post*, April 28, 1917, pp. 28–34; Patrick Gallagher, *American Aims and Asian Aspirations* (New York, 1920), pp. 169–180.

¹⁸ *U.S. Foreign Relations, 1918*, p. 106; *1917*, Suppl. 1, p. 435; Suppl. 2, Part 1, pp. 694, 702; Suppl. 2, Part 2, p. 694; *L'Asie française*, XVII (1917), 115; *Le Figaro*, August 15, 1917; *North China Herald*, April 21, p. 101, December 22, p. 732, 1917.

¹⁹ T'ang Leang-li, *The Inner History of the Chinese Revolution* (London, 1930), p. 130; *U.S. Foreign Relations, Paris Peace Conference, 1919*, I, 241, 242, 306, 348, 355, 490; DSDD, Quarterly Report, November 29, 1918, 893.00/2925, No. 2348; *North China Herald*, November 30, 1918, p. 504; Fifield, *Woodrow Wilson and the Far East*, pp. 179–181.

²⁰ *U.S. Foreign Relations, 1919*, I, 280, 333; *Paris Peace Conference, 1919*, II, 491–511; David Hunter Miller, *My Diary at the Peace Conference of Paris* (New York, 1924), II, 332; Gallagher, *American Aims*, pp. 351–364.

²¹ *L'Asie française*, XIX (1919), pp. 197, 225–227; *Millard's Review*, VII (February

15, 1919), 374, 377, 379; *U.S. Foreign Relations, Paris Peace Conference, 1919*, II, 491–498, 521, IV, 556; *U.S. Foreign Relations, 1919*, I, 275, 278, 280, 282; MacMurray, *Treaties*, 1918/13, 1445; Liang Chi-chao, "Causes of China's Defeat at the Peace Conference," *Millard's Review*, IX (July 19, 1919), 263–265; Senate Document No. 106, 66th Congress, 1st Session, 1919, pp. 450, 526. Cf. also Robert Lansing, *The Peace Negotiations* (New York, 1921), p. 254, and Balfour's interesting reaction in Blanche E. C. Dugdale, *Arthur James Balfour* (New York, 1936), II, 332.

[22] The most detailed account of the Shantung negotiations in Paris can be found in Fifield, *Woodrow Wilson and the Far East*, pp. 218–287. Ray Stannard Baker, *Woodrow Wilson and World Settlement* (Garden City, 1922), III, 316; Lansing, *Peace Negotiations*, p. 265; Liang, "Causes of China's Defeat," p. 263. Cf. also Thomas F. Millard, *Conflict of Policies in Asia* (New York, 1924), pp. 85–86.

[23] The best source for a description of the events following the Treaty of Versailles is the local newspapers. See also Bland, *China, Japan, and Korea*, pp. 68–83; T'ang Leang-li, *The Foundations of Modern China* (London, 1928), pp. 106–107; Hewlett, *Forty Years in China*, pp. 129–135; Reinsch, *American Diplomat*, pp. 358–359, 368–374; E. H. Hume, "Young China," *Foreign Affairs*, V (1927), 446–458; Stanley High, *China's Place in the Sun* (New York, 1922), pp. 119–138.

[24] Cf. *New Statesman*, XIII (July 5, 1919), 339.

[25] Cf. Hollington T. Kong, "Significance of China's Refusal to sign the Peace Treaty," *Millard's Review*, IX (July 12, 1919), 216.

Chapter 12. The Washington Conference, 1921

[1] *U.S. Foreign Relations, 1921*, I, 323–325, 348–349, 351–352; *1922*, I, 688; London *Times*, November 3, 19, 1921.

[2] London *Times*, January 30, 1922.

[3] *U.S. Foreign Relations, 1921*, I, 337–339; *North China Herald*, October 1, 1921, p. 33; January 21, p. 150, February 4, p. 288, 1922; London *Times*, November 10, 1921.

[4] *U.S. Foreign Relations, 1921*, I, 29, 35–37, 52, 82.

[5] *North China Herald* (Lennox B. Simpson), January 28, 1922, p. 250. For the vast literature on the proceedings of the Washington Conference see the references cited by Harold M. Vinacke, *A History of the Far East in Modern Times* (New York, 1941), p. 436. For some interpretations of Conference results see Geoffrey F. Hudson, *The Far East in World Politics* (London, 1939), pp. 202–204; Sir John T. Pratt, *War and Politics in China* (London, 1943), p. 195; Harold Isaacs, *The Tragedy of the Chinese Revolution* (London, 1938), p. 63; O. M. Green, *The Story of China's Revolution* (London, n.d.), pp. 127–129; Putnam Weale, *An Indiscreet Chronicle from the Pacific* (New York, 1922), pp. 152–233. For Chinese reactions to the Conference see the contemporary *North China Herald* and *China Weekly Review*; also London *Times*, November 4 and 29, 1921; *U.S. Foreign Relations, 1921*, I, 57, 352; *1922*, I, 684.

[6] *U.S. Foreign Relations, 1920*, I, 816.

[7] For some details on the Shantung negotiations see Westel W. Willoughby, *China at the Conference* (Baltimore, 1922); Yamato Ichihashi, *The Washington Conference and After* (Stanford, 1928), pp. 267–288; Ge-Zay Wood, *The Shantung Question* (New York, 1922), pp. 237–277.

[8] *North China Herald*, February 18, 1922, p. 435.

Chapter 13. Turning from the West to Russia

[1] On the cultural changes see Harold M. Vinacke, *A History of the Far East in Modern Times* (New York, 1941), pp. 275–298; Dryden L. Phelps, "Letters and

Arts in the War Years," in Harley Farnsworth MacNair, *China in Revolution* (Chicago, 1931), pp. 406–409; Hu Shih, *The Chinese Renaissance* (Chicago, 1934); John K. Fairbank, *The United States and China* (Cambridge, Mass., 1948), pp. 179–183; E. V. Zenker, *Geschichte der Chinesischen Philosophie* (Reichenberg, 1927), II, 322–329; André Duboscq, *L'Elite chinoise* (Paris, 1945), pp. 83–99; T'ang Leang-li, *The New Social Order in China* (Shanghai, 1936), pp. 127–156; Wen-Han Kiang, *The Chinese Student Movement* (New York, 1948), pp. 21–45; John de Francis, *Nationalism and Language Reform in China* (Princeton, 1950), pp. 211–254.

² On the early labor movement see the *China Year Book, 1926*, pp. 1002–1008; Harold Isaacs, *The Tragedy of the Chinese Revolution* (London, 1938), pp. 56–57; Vinacke, *A History of the Far East*, pp. 269–274, and the literature cited there; P. W. Kuo, "Political, Economic, and Social Tendencies in Modern China," in *Oriental Interpretations of the Far Eastern Problem* (Harris Foundation Lectures, 1925) (Chicago, 1925), pp. 122–123; Fairbank, *The United States and China*, pp. 177–178; R. H. Tawney, *Land and Labour in China* (London, 1922), pp. 150–160; T'ang, *The New Social Order in China*, pp. 196–214; Min-Ch'ien T. Z. Tyau, *China Awakened* (New York, 1922), pp. 225–243; Sir Meyrick Hewlett, *Forty Years in China* (London, 1944), p. 130.

³ Cf. Nathaniel Peffer, *China: The Collapse of a Civilization* (New York, 1930), pp. 141–190.

⁴ On Kuomintang-peasant relations see Arthur Ransome, *The Chinese Puzzle* (London, 1927), pp. 98–105; T. C. Woo, *The Kuomintang and the Future of the Chinese Revolution* (London, 1928), p. 247; Stephen Chen and Robert Payne, *Sun Yat-sen: A Portrait* (New York, 1946), p. 204. On the development of the Kuomintang up to that point see Tuan-sheng Ch'ien, *The Government and Politics of China* (Cambridge, Mass., 1950), pp. 86–88.

⁵ Quoted by Alfred Sze, "The Present Position in China," *Asiatic Review*, N. S., XVII (1921), 10–15.

⁶ Ch'ien, *Government and Politics of China*, p. 363; see also Benjamin Schwartz, "Ch'ên Tu-hsiu and the Acceptance of the Modern West," *Journal of the History of Ideas*, XII (1951), 61–74; Hans Kohn, *A History of Nationalism in the East* (London, 1929), pp. 125–173.

⁷ For various views on early Kuomintang-Communist relations see Kiang, *Chinese Student Movement*, pp. 75–78; Isaacs, *Tragedy of the Chinese Revolution*, pp. 41–65; Arthur N. Holcombe, *The Chinese Revolution* (Cambridge, Mass., 1931), pp. 156–161; Sir John T. Pratt, *War and Politics in China* (London, 1943), pp. 195–199; Harry Gannes, *When China Unites* (London, 1937), pp. 46–68; Agnes Smedley, "The Social Revolution," in MacNair, *China*, pp. 168–169; M. N. Roy, *Revolution and Counter-Revolution in China* (Calcutta, 1946), pp. 327–338; Fairbank, *United States and China*, pp. 185–188; Aitchen K. Wu, *China and the Soviet Union* (London, 1950), pp. 309–331; Freda Utley, *Last Chance in China* (New York, 1947), pp. 170–189; David J. Dallin, *The Rise of Russia in Asia* (New Haven, 1949), pp. 272–279; Benjamin I. Schwartz, *Chinese Communism and the Rise of Mao* (Cambridge, Mass., 1951), pp. 37–78. Percy Finch, *Shanghai and Beyond* (New York, 1953), has material on the history of the Chinese Communist movement.

⁸ Shu-chin Tsui, "The Influence of the Canton-Moscow Entente upon Sun-yat Sen's Political Philosophy," *Chinese Social and Political Science Review*, XVIII (1934), 96–145, 177–209, 341–388; XX (1936), 101–139.

⁹ Shu-chin Tsui, "The Influence of the Canton-Moscow Entente," p. 127.

¹⁰ *North China Herald*, February 20, 1926, p. 318; Hewlett, *Forty Years in China*, p. 202.

¹¹ For some literature on the cooperation between the Kuomintang and the Communists see *North China Herald*, January 30, pp. 179, 216, February 6, p. 237, 1926;

John B. Powell, *My Twenty-five Years in China* (New York, 1945), pp. 141–160; Conrad Brandt, Benjamin Schwartz, and John K. Fairbank, *A Documentary History of Chinese Communism* (London, 1952), pp. 65–69.

[12] On some of the background of the campaign see Jean Rodes, *La Chine nationaliste 1912–1930* (Paris, 1931), pp. 101–120; A. Karup-Nielsen, *The Dragon Awakes* (London, 1928), pp. 99–110, 203; Lao P'ong-yo, *Le Double Dragon chinois, jaune ou rouge?* (Paris, 1927), pp. 115–117; H. Owen Chapman, *The Chinese Revolution 1926–27* (London, 1928), pp. 17–27; R. Y. Lo, *China's Revolution from the Inside* (New York, 1930), p. 158.

[13] Gustav Amann, *Chiang Kaishek* (Heidelberg, 1936), pp. 5–12.

Chapter 14. Diplomatic Successes

[1] Harold Isaacs, *The Tragedy of the Chinese Revolution* (London, 1938), p. 87; *China Year Book, 1926*, p. 1011; John B. Powell, *My Twenty-five Years in China* (New York, 1945), p. 145; Dorothy Borg, *American Policy and the Chinese Revolution 1925–1928* (New York, 1947), pp. 23–29 (on the May 30, 1925 incident); T'ang Leang-li, *The Foundations of Modern China* (London, 1928), pp. 221–226; Geoffrey F. Hudson, *The Far East in World Politics* (Oxford, Clarendon Press, 1937), pp. 214–215; Nathaniel Peffer, *China: The Collapse of a Civilization* (New York, 1930), p. 160.

[2] For details of the Russo-Chinese relations at this time see Aitchen K. Wu, *China and the Soviet Union* (London, 1950), pp. 118–133.

[3] For details see, e.g., Leo Pasvolsky, *Russia in the Far East* (New York, 1922), pp. 71–137.

[4] For Russo-Chinese relations during this period see Robert T. Pollard, *China's Foreign Relations 1917–1931* (New York, 1933), pp. 115–204; Harold M. Vinacke, *A History of the Far East in Modern Times* (New York, 1941), pp. 406–412; Harold S. Quigley and George H. Blakeslee, *The Far East* (Boston, 1938), pp. 16–31; Wu, *China and the Soviet Union*, pp. 123–157; Victor A. Yakhontoff, *Russia and the Soviet Union in the Far East* (London, 1932), pp. 252–253; Michel Pavlovsky, *Chinese-Russian Relations* (New York, 1949), pp. 68–97; Harley F. MacNair and Donald F. Lach, *Modern Far Eastern International Relations* (New York, 1950), pp. 255–266; Iwan Z. Korostovets, *Von Chinggis Khan zur Sovietrepublik* (Berlin, 1926), pp. 286–343.

[5] Great Britain, *Parliamentary Debates*, June 18, 1925, col. 919.

[6] Summaries of these events can be found in the *China Year Book* and Arnold J. Toynbee, *Survey of International Affairs* (Published under the Auspices of the British Institute of International Affairs), for the years in question.

[7] *U.S. Foreign Relations, 1925*, I, 763–764.

[8] DSDD, December 3, 1924, 893.00/5814; September 23, 1924, 893.00/5558; September 27, 1924, 893.00/5575; October 20, 1924, 893.00/5659–60; October 24, 1924, 893.00/5674; DSDI, October 1, 1924, 893.00/5575.

[9] *U.S. Foreign Relations, 1925*, I, 767, 779, 781, 792, 831.

[10] Sir John T. Pratt, *The Expansion of Europe into the Far East* (London, 1947), p. 177; George W. Keeton, *China, the Far East and the Future* (London, 1949), p. 93; Geoffrey F. Hudson, *The Far East in World Politics* (Oxford, Clarendon Press, 1937), p. 223; H. Owen Chapman, *The Chinese Revolution 1926–1927* (London, 1927), pp. 117–147; Wesley R. Fishel, *The End of Extraterritoriality in China* (Berkeley, 1952), pp. 132–144; Borg, *American Policy and the Chinese Revolution*, pp. 227–241.

[11] On the Peking Tariff Conference see M. T. Z. Tyau, *The Special Conference on Chinese Customs Tariff, October, 1925–April, 1926* (Peking, 1928); Stanley F. Wright, *China's Struggle for Tariff Autonomy* (Shanghai, 1938), pp. 461–600; Borg, *American Policy and the Chinese Revolution*, pp. 95–121; Pollard, *China's Foreign Relations*, pp. 330–369; also Fishel, *End of Extraterritoriality*, pp. 90–100.

[12] Fishel, *End of Extraterritoriality*, pp. 109–126; Borg, *American Policy and the Chinese Revolution*, pp. 154–182; Pollard, *China's Foreign Relations*, pp. 281–287; Keeton, *China, the Far East and the Future*, pp. 80–81.

[13] Cf. *Chinese Affairs*, July 7, July 14, #6, August 11, #10, 1928.

[14] *Chinese Affairs*, December 31, #62, 1929; cf. also Quigley and Blakeslee, *The Far East*, pp. 135–150; *La Revue nationale chinoise*, V (1931), 40–43, 237–239.

[15] British Chamber of Commerce, Shanghai, *The Nanking Government's Laws and Regulations Affecting Trade, Commerce, Finance, etc.* (mimeographed), VII (1931), 74–76.

[16] *U.S. Foreign Relations, 1925*, I, 849.

[17] *U.S. Foreign Relations, 1927*, II, 363.

[18] *U.S. Foreign Relations, 1925*, I, 801; *1928*, II, 410, 415.

Chapter 15. *"Incident" with Japan and Reconstruction*

[1] Facts on Communist-controlled areas are difficult to ascertain. The statements in the following accounts can all be substantiated by the findings of people strongly opposed to communism as well as those in sympathy with the Communists. They should be correct. See, e.g., Freda Utley, *Last Chance in China* (New York, 1947), pp. 170–218; V. K. Wellington Koo, *Memoranda Presented to the Lytton Commission* (New York, 1932), II, 753–777; George E. Sokolsky, *The Tinder Box of Asia* (New York, 1934), pp. 320–348; Gustav Amann, *Bauernkrieg in China* (Heidelberg, 1939); Victor A. Yakhontoff, *The Chinese Soviets* (New York, 1934), pp. 80–99; Aitchen K. Wu, *China and the Soviet Union* (London, 1950), pp. 186–197; O. M. Green, *The Story of China's Revolution* (London, n.d.), pp. 136–153.

[2] Utley, *Last Chance in China*, p. 175.

[3] For the activities of the National Government in the first years of power see Amann, *Bauernkrieg in China*, pp. 9–22; J. B. Condliffe, *China Today: Economic* (Boston, 1932), pp. 71–74, 88–96; Min Ch'ien Tyau, *Two years of Nationalist China* (Shanghai, 1930); Maurice Lachin, *La Chine capitaliste* (Paris, 1938), pp. 138–169; Utley, *Last Chance in China*, pp. 310–326; Nathaniel Peffer, *China: The Collapse of a Civilization* (New York, 1930), pp. 231–259; Harold Archer van Dorn, *Twenty Years of the Chinese Republic* (New York, 1932); T'ang Leang-li, *Reconstruction in China* (Shanghai, 1935).

[4] On the condition of the army see the relevant issues of the *China Year Book*, and Tyau, *Two Years of Nationalist China*, pp. 130–137; Sir Eric Teichman, *Affairs of China* (London, 1938), pp. 30, 259–264; *North China Herald*, July 15, 1930, p. 79; February 3, 1931, p. 148; *China Year Book, 1931–1932*, p. 427; Anatol M. Uotenev, *The Chinese Soldier* (Shanghai, 1937), pp. 128–140. For documents on the disbandment of the army see *Chinese Affairs*, 1929, #44–45.

[5] *U.S. Foreign Relations, 1931*, III, 647; see also Paul K. Wang, "China's Stand toward Japanese Recognition of Manchukuo," *China Weekly Review*, October 8, 1932, p. 232; DSDD, June 24, 1931, 893.00/11544; *U.S. Foreign Relations, 1931*, III, 805.

[6] *U.S. Foreign Relations, 1931*, III, 126, 145, 647, 714, and many others.

[7] DSDD, telegram from T'ang Shao-yi, handed President Hoover, June 11, 1931, by Dr. C. C. Wu, 893.00.

[8] On the Russian attitude toward the Manchurian incident see the details cited by Pauline Tompkins, *American-Russian Relations in the Far East* (New York, 1949), pp. 247–253; Frederick L. Schuman, *Soviet Politics at Home and Abroad* (New York, 1948), pp. 235–239; Victor A. Yakhontoff, *USSR Foreign Policy* (New York, 1945), pp. 101–104); Harriet Moore, *A Record of Soviet Far Eastern Relations* (New York, 1943), pp. 4–8; and *Soviet Far Eastern Policy 1931–1945* (Princeton, 1945); Wu, *China and the Soviet Union*, pp. 213–221; *U.S. Foreign Policy, 1931*, III, 27, 29, 68, 99, 104, 105, 371, 391, 416, 443; *1932*, III, 25; IV, 6, 70, 142, 297, 420, 440, 446.

[9] *U.S. Foreign Relations, 1931*, III, 104, 189, 190, 196, 219; *1932*, III, 4; see also *1933*, III, 134.

[10] *U.S. Foreign Relations, 1933*, I, 99. These attitudes become generally obvious from a reading of the dispatches from Geneva in *U.S. Foreign Relations, 1931*, III, and *1932*, III. See Sara R. Smith, *The Manchurian Crisis 1931–1932* (New York, 1948), for the United States and the League in the affair.

[11] *U.S. Foreign Relations, 1931*, III, 496.

[12] *U.S. Foreign Relations, 1931*, III, 673; see also p. 104.

[13] *U.S. Foreign Relations, 1932*, III, 25–26.

[14] *U.S. Foreign Relations, 1931*, III, 19, 38. From the vast literature on the Manchurian incident, the following may be cited: Harold S. Quigley and George H. Blakeslee, *The Far East* (Boston, 1938), pp. 103–119; Sir John T. Pratt, *War and Politics in China* (London, 1943), pp. 208–229; Edward S. Rubinow, *Sino-Japanese Warfare and the League of Nations, Geneva Studies*, May 1939; Smith, *The Manchurian Crisis, 1931–1932*; Westel W. Willoughby, *The Sino-Japanese Controversy and the League of Nations* (Baltimore, 1936); Pen-chung Wu, *La Vérité sur la Mandchourie* (Paris, 1936); Ernest R. Perkins, "The Non-application of Sanctions against Japan, 1931–1932," in Dwight E. Lee and George E. McReynolds, *Essays in History and International Relations in Honor of George Hubbard Blakeslee* (Worcester, Mass., 1949); the volumes *U.S. Foreign Relations, 1931*, III, and *1932*, III, IV; *The Memoirs of Herbert Hoover: The Cabinet and the Presidency* (New York, 1952), pp. 362–378; Henry L. Stimson, *The Far Eastern Crisis* (New York, 1936).

[15] See, e.g., Hoh Chih-hsing, "The Lytton Report Viewed through Chinese Eyes," *China Weekly Review*, October 15, 1932, p. 278; *North China Herald*, December 1, 1931, p. 299; Arnold J. Toynbee, *Survey of International Affairs, 1931* (Published under the Auspices of the British Institute of International Affairs), p. 523; G. E. Hubbard, *British Far Eastern Policy* (New York, 1943), p. 40; *Chinese Affairs*, IV (1932), 227–236.

[16] DSDD, January 26, 1932, 793.94/3642; January 27, 1932, 793.94/4656.

[17] See Harold S. Quigley, *Chinese Politics Today* (Minneapolis, 1934), p. 21. See the resolutions of the plenary sessions of the Kuomintang's Central Executive Committee in 1934, *North China Herald*, October 10, p. 42, December 19, p. 442, 1934; *U.S. Foreign Relations, 1933*, III, 183.

[18] See Richard Wilhelm, *Chinese Economic Psychology* (mimeographed, New York, 1947), pp. 5–6; Eduard Erkes, *China und Europa* (Leipzig, 1947), p. 24; Max Weber, *Gesammelte Aufsätze zur Religionssoziologie* (Tübingen, 1922–1923), I, 532; Lily Abegg, *The Mind of East Asia* (London, 1952), p. 244.

[19] League of Nations, Council Committee on Technological Cooperation between the League of Nations and China, *Report of the Secretary to the Council Committee on His Mission in China* (Geneva, 1935), General 5; Tze-hsiung Kuo, "Technical Cooperation between China and Geneva," Council of International Affairs, Nanking, *Information Bulletin*, I (1936), #6; Heinrich Schmitthenner, *China im Profil* (Leipzig, 1934), pp. 28–37; *North China Herald*, December 19, 1934, p. 442; J. M. D. Pringle, *China Struggles for Unity* (Harmondsworth, England, 1939), pp. 93–116.

[20] F. C. Remer, *Foreign Investments in China* (New York, 1933); Chang Kia-ngau, *China's Struggle for Railroad Development* (New York, 1943), p. 76.

[21] Harold S. Quigley, *Far Eastern War 1937–1941* (Boston, 1942), pp. 40–42, and "The Open Door Policy and Peace in the Pacific," *Southern Review* (1936), I, 745; *North China Herald*, March 14, 1934, pp. 397, 412.

[22] British Chamber of Commerce, Shanghai, *The National Government's Laws and Regulations Affecting Trade, Commerce, Finance, etc.* (mimeographed), XVIII (1936), 41; *Chinese Affairs*, V (1933), 80.

[23] *Chinese Affairs*, V (1933), 75, 87. For a typical expression of suspicion about foreign aid see *People's Tribune*, N. S., XI (1935), 7–12.

[24] For the text of the notes, some Chinese reactions, and details of the episode

see W. H. Ma, "Sino-Japanese Relations since Tangku," International Relations Club, Nanking, *Bulletin on China's Foreign Relations*, II (1934), #6, 6–10; Quigley and Blakeslee, *The Far East*, pp. 90–102.

[25] Pan Chao-ying, *China Fights On* (New York, 1945), p. 67; *New York Times*, March 24, 27, 1934.

[26] *Oriental Economist*, IV (1937), 385.

[27] Albert T. Lu, "Hirota's Three Principles vis-a-vis China," Council of International Affairs, Nanking, *Information Bulletin*, I (1936), #7; Hu Shih, "The Readjustment of Sino-Japanese Relations," *People's Tribune*, N. S., XIII (1936), 169–173; Tien-tsung Sih, "Sino-Japanese Economic Cooperation in North China," Council of International Affairs, Nanking, *Information Bulletin*, III (1937), 175–194.

[28] *Oriental Economist*, II (March, July 1935), 5–6, 16–17.

[29] On British and United States policy toward China at this time see *New York Times*, April 25, May 12, July 17, 1934; *North China Herald*, December 26, 1934, p. 482; Quigley and Blakeslee, *The Far East*, pp. 179–223; J. O. P. Bland, "What are we doing in China?" *English Review*, LXI (1935), 566; Irving S. Friedman, *British Relations with China 1931–1939* (New York, 1946), p. 63; Hubbard, *British Far Eastern Policy*, p. 48; A. Whitney Griswold, *The Far Eastern Policy of the United States* (New York, 1938), pp. 444–446.

[30] *People's Tribune*, N. S., XII (1936), 17–27; Hubert Freyn, *Prelude to War, The Chinese Student Rebellion of 1935–1936* (Shanghai, 1939).

[31] *China Today*, I (1935), 90, 132.

Chapter 16. Renewed Aggression and Internal Discord

[1] Cf. *Ostasiatische Rundschau*, XIX (1938), 339.

[2] For a survey of Kuomintang-Communist relations at this time, written by authors of various political views, see DS, *United States Relations with China* (Washington, 1949), pp. 45–54; Lawrence K. Rosinger, *China's Wartime Politics 1937–1944* (Princeton, 1944), pp. 25–44; Lawrence K. Rosinger, *China's Crisis* (New York, 1945), pp. 11–30; Stuart Gelder, *The Chinese Communists* (London, 1946), pp. 1–60; Mao Tse-tung et al., *China, The March toward Unity* (New York, 1937); Henry Casseville, *De Chiang Kai Shek à Mao Tse Tung* (Paris, 1950); *China Handbook 1950* (New York, 1950), pp. 260–283. The *North China Herald*, February 9, p. 194, and March 16, p. 406, 1938, has two typical statements from both sides showing the fundamental nature of their conflict.

[3] Chang Peng-chun, "The Second Phase of China's Struggle," *International Affairs*, XVIII (1939), 221.

[4] *Documents on German Foreign Policy 1918–1945* (Washington, 1949), Ser. D, I, 741.

[5] For Communist policy in general see Freda Utley, *Last Chance in China* (New York, 1947), pp. 188–197; Martin Ebon, *World Communism Today* (New York, 1948), pp. 370–374. For the details mentioned in the text see Wallace C. Merwin, "Can China trust Russia?" *Christian Century*, LX (1943), 1099–1100, and "The Chinese Communists," *Christian Century*, LXII (1945), 366; Wang Ming, *The Revolutionary Movement in the Colonial Countries* (New York, 1935), pp. 12–19; T'ang Leang-li, *Fundamentals of National Salvation* (Shanghai, 1942), p. 79; "Chinese Communists," *China Weekly Review*, XCVI (1941), 258; Lin Yu-tang, "Conflict in China Analyzed," *Far Eastern Survey*, XIV (1945), 191–195. The Communist manifesto on the Russian-Japanese pact is printed in *Amerasia*, V (1941), 113.

[6] Frank W. Price, "The Outlook for Unity and Democracy in China," *China Information Service*, March 4, 1941, #59, pp. 10–11.

[7] For a variety of views on the army and its new relations with the population see Evans Fordyce Carlson, *The Chinese Army* (New York, 1940); Lily Abegg, *Chinas Erneuerung* (Frankfurt a. M., 1940), pp. 142–173; Jean-Jacques Brieux,

La Chine du nationalisme au communisme (Paris, 1950), pp. 235–246, 371–383; Haldore Hanson, *"Humane Endeavour"* (New York, 1939), pp. 352–362; *North China Herald*, February 15, 1939, p. 266; John K. Fairbank, *The United States and China* (Cambridge, Mass., 1948), pp. 203–206; Rosinger, *China's Crisis*, pp. 124–138; Guenther Stein, *The Challenge of Red China* (New York, 1945), pp. 303–404; Agnes Smedley, *China Fights Back* (New York, 1938); Edgar Snow, *Red Star over China* (New York, 1944, Modern Library), pp. 277–356; Nym Wales, *Inside Red China* (New York, 1939), pp. 33–43.

[8] *Moscow News*, August 31, September 4, September 18, 1939.

[9] Cf. Gerald F. Winfield, *China: The Land and the People* (New York, 1948), pp. 210–243.

[10] See George E. Taylor, *The Struggle for North China* (New York, 1940).

[11] *Japan Weekly Chronicle*, September 16, 1937, p. 398.

[12] *L'Asie française*, XXXVII (1937), 101; Asiaticus, "China's Advance from Defeat to Strength," *Pacific Affairs*, XI (1938), 21–34; Robert Craigie, *Behind the Japanese Mask* (London, 1946), pp. 37–41.

[13] Chiang K'ai-shek, *Resistance and Reconstruction* (New York, 1943), p. 21; see also p. 23 *et al.* for similar expressions.

[14] Chiang, *Resistance and Reconstruction*, pp. 53, 143.

[15] *Memoirs of Cordell Hull* (New York, 1948), p. 557. J. C. Grew, formerly ambassador to Tokyo, maintains that there was unanimity between the Japanese government and the Japanese military in China; Joseph C. Grew, *The Turbulent Era* (New York, 1952), pp. 1035–1041.

[16] G. S. Rubinow, *Sino-Japanese Warfare and the League of Nations* (Geneva, 1938); see also C. Kuangson Young, *The Conflict in the Far East 1937* (Geneva, 1937).

[17] A. Whitney Griswold, *The Far Eastern Policy of the United States* (New York, 1938), pp. 459–461; Herbert Feis, *The Road to Pearl Harbor* (Princeton, 1950), pp. 8–16; DS, *The Conference of Brussels*, Publication 1232, Conference Ser. 37 (Washington, 1938); *Memoirs of Cordell Hull*, p. 553; *Documents on German Foreign Policy* Ser. D, I, 765, 771, 774; Erich Kordt, *Wahn und Wirklichkeit* (Stuttgart, 1948), p. 110; Franklin D. Roosevelt, *Personal Letters*, ed. Elliott Roosevelt (New York, 1950), I, 729.

[18] Cf. *China Weekly Review*, LXXXV (June 4, June 11, 1938), 32, 58; LXXXVI (September 10, 1938), 40; *North China Herald*, January 5, 1938, p. 2. Chiang's interview, *Peiping Chronicle*, September 1, 1937. For Chinese propaganda in general see Bruno Lasker and Agnes Roman, *Propaganda from China and Japan* (New York, 1938).

[19] Chiang, *Resistance and Reconstruction*, p. 165. For a survey of the Far Eastern situation see Harold S. Quigley, *Far Eastern War 1937–1941* (Boston, 1942), pp. 166–262.

[20] *Documents on German Foreign Policy*, Ser. D, I, 734–820; IV, 693; T'ang Leang-li, *Fundamentals of National Salvation*, pp. 27–30, 35–36; Kordt, *Wahn und Wirklichkeit*, p. 110; Feis, *Road to Pearl Harbor*, p. 134; Malcolm Muggeridge, ed., *Ciano's Diplomatic Papers* (London, 1948), pp. 142–143; Roosevelt, *Personal Letters*, II, 741–742; Herbert von Dirksen, *Moscow, Tokyo, London Twenty Years of German Foreign Policy* (London, 1951), pp. 160, 189–191; *North China Herald*, August 30, 1939, p. 350; October 2, p. 3, October 9, p. 42, 1940; James T. C. Liu, "German Mediation in the Sino-Japanese War 1937–1938," *Far Eastern Quarterly*, VIII (1949), 157–171; Charles F. Romanus and Riley Sunderland, *Stilwell's Mission to China, United States Army in World War II, China-Burma-India Theater* (Washington, D.C., 1953), pp. 9–10.

[21] T'ang, *Fundamentals of National Salvation*, pp. 35–36; T. S. Lin, *China Weekly Review*, XC (1939), 285.

[22] Winston Churchill, *The Second World War: II, Their Finest Hour* (London, 1949), pp. 571, 574.

[23] Max Beloff, *The Foreign Policy of Soviet Russia* (London, 1949), II, 184–185; *North China Herald*, May 1, 1940, p. 162. Many other officials repeated this statement, e.g., Chen Hsiao-wei, *Present Military Problems in China* (Hong Kong, 1940), p. 50. Commissar Litvinov told the American ambassador in Moscow that the Soviet Union was "meticulously careful to maintain peace" with Japan; *U.S. Foreign Relations, The Soviet Union 1933–1938*, p. 542.

[24] *Ostasiatische Rundschau*, XVIII (1937), 446.

[25] *Documents on German Foreign Policy*, Ser. D, I, 756–757, 848; *North China Herald*, January 18, 1939, p. 90; March 6, 1940, p. 358; *Japan Weekly Chronicle*, September 9, 1937, pp. 344, 360, 366; *Peiping Chronicle*, August 31, 1937.

[26] *North China Herald*, May 29, p. 322, July 31, p. 154, 1940; *Documents on German Foreign Policy*, Ser. D, I, 748.

[27] *U.S. Foreign Relations, Japan 1931–41*, II, 139.

[28] Romanus and Sunderland, *Stilwell's Mission*, pp. 13–17.

[29] Joseph C. Grew, *Ten Years in Japan* (New York, 1944), p. 362. For more details on this basic American policy see Werner Levi, "American Foreign Policy Interpreted," *Fortnightly*, N. S., MI (1950), pp. 281–288.

[30] E.g., *North China Herald*, July 17, 1940, p. 78.

[31] Feis, *Road to Pearl Harbor*, pp. 316–319; *Report of the Joint Committee on the Investigation of the Pearl Harbor Attack*, 79th Congress, 2nd Session, Senate Document No. 244, pp. 37, 512, 563; Winston Churchill, *The Second World War: III, The Grand Alliance* (London, 1950), pp. 529–532. For a brief survey of American policy see Stanley K. Hornbeck, *The United States and the Far East: Certain Fundamentals of Policy* (Boston, 1942), pp. 30–50.

[32] *North China Herald*, September 11, p. 390, September 25, p. 470, 1940; March 5, 1941, p. 354.

Chapter 17. The Alliance in World War II

[1] Robert W. Barnett, "Isolated China," *Far Eastern Survey*, XI (1942), 167–169.

[2] Chiang K'ai-shek, *All We Are and All We Have* (New York, 1943), p. 22; *Resistance and Reconstruction* (New York, 1943), p. 275.

[3] Charles F. Romanus and Riley Sunderland, *Stilwell's Mission to China, United States Army in World War II, China-Burma-India Theater* (Washington, D.C., 1953), pp. 61–63, 158–159.

[4] *Shanghai Evening Post and Mercury*, March 26, 1943.

[5] T. S. Chien, "New China's Demands," *Foreign Affairs*, XXI (1942), 690–698; Guenther Stein, "Chungking Considers the Future," *Far Eastern Survey*, XI (1942), 190–193; *Shanghai Evening Post and Mercury*, February 19, 1953; Hu Shih, *Requirements for a Just Peace in the Pacific* (mimeographed, Chungking, 1942); Wellington V. K. Koo, "China and the Problem of World Order," *New Commonwealth Quarterly*, January 1942, pp. 183–190; S. R. Chow, *Winning the Peace in the Pacific* (New York, 1944); Pan Chao-ying, *China Fights On* (New York, 1945), pp. 163–176.

[6] Romanus and Sunderland, *Stilwell's Mission*, pp. 50–52.

[7] *London Times*, December 10, 16, 17, 1941; *Facts on File*, January 17, 1942; Barnett, "Isolated China," p. 167; Guenther Stein, "The Chinese Press Weighs Allied Strategy," *Far Eastern Survey*, XII (1943), 117–118; *Contemporary China*, I (December 29, 1941), #16.

[8] Romanus and Sunderland, *Stilwell's Mission*, pp. 172, 177.

[9] This becomes evident from Romanus and Sunderland, *Stilwell's Mission*, pp. 57, 261, 352, *et al.* But see also Ho Yungchi, *The Great Circle* (New York, 1948).

[10] Winston Churchill, *The Second World War: III, The Grand Alliance* (London,

1950), p. 532, and *The Hinge of Fate* (Boston, 1950), pp. 133–134; Robert E. Sherwood, *Roosevelt and Hopkins* (New York, 1948), p. 773. For an example of contemporary debate on that point see *Contemporary China*, III, August 23, 1943; C. L. Hsia's letter, *New York Herald Tribune*, August 2, 1943; and for some of the difficulties involved Henry L. Stimson and McGeorge Bundy, *On Active Service in Peace and War* (New York, 1948), pp. 528–541.

[11] See Knight Biggerstaff, *China: Revolutionary Changes in an Ancient Civilization* (Ithaca, 1945), p. 49; Pan, *China Fights On*, pp. 136–158, for China's contribution to the United Nations. On the state of the Chinese army in the fall of 1941 see Romanus and Sunderland, *Stilwell's Mission*, pp. 32–37, 43.

[12] David Nelson Rowe, *China among the Powers* (New York, 1945), pp. 8–10.

[13] Cf. Chiang, *All We Are*, p. 43; Franz Michael, "Patronage or Partnership for China?" *Amerasia*, VI (1943), 507; *Amerasia*, VI (1942), 415, 425, 439; *New Statesman and Nation*, XXIII (1942), 347; Lawrence K. Rosinger, *China's Crisis* (New York, 1945), pp. 219–226; George E. Taylor, *America in the New Pacific* (New York, 1942), p. 113.

[14] Cf. Vincent Torossian, "Vital Factors of China's Civil War," *China Monthly*, VIII (1947), 191–192; Taylor, *America in the New Pacific*, pp. 114, 127–137.

[15] For a few divergent statements of the reasons for the Communist success at this time see Theodore H. White and Analee Jacoby, *Thunder out of China* (New York, 1946); George Creel, *Russia's Race for Asia* (New York, 1949), p. 88; Freda Utley, *Last Chance in China* (New York, 1947), pp. 147, 158.

[16] For a variety of views on internal conditions, especially Kuomintang-Communist relations, see Lin Yu-tang, *Vigil of a Nation* (New York, 1944), pp. 104–133; Creel, *Russia's Race for China*, pp. 78–88; Rosinger, *China's Crisis*, pp. 97–114; Guenther Stein, *The Challenge of Red China* (New York, 1945), pp. 453–466; Harrison Forman, *Report from Red China* (New York, 1945), pp. 181–190; DS, *United States Relations with China* (Washington, D.C., 1949), pp. 52–58; Hoh Chih-hsiang, *China Belongs to the Chinese People* (Shanghai, 1948), pp. 33–59, 273–370.

[17] See the articles of the *Ta Kung Pao* quoted in *China Weekly Review* at various times, especially CII (August 3, 1946), 231; *New York Times*, May 31, July 15, 23, August 4, 1946; Hoh, *China Belongs to the Chinese People*, p. 34; Dorothy Borg, "America Loses Chinese Good Will," *Far Eastern Survey*, XVIII (1949), 37–45; and Melville T. Kennedy, Jr., "The Chinese Democratic League," *Papers on China (vol. 7) from the Regional Studies Seminars*, Duplicated for private distribution by the Committee on International and Regional Studies, Harvard University (February 1953), pp. 136–175. For American policy toward China since 1945 see Harold M. Vinacke, *The United States and the Far East 1945–1951* (New York, 1952), pp. 11–56; Kenneth S. Latourette, *The American Record in the Far East, 1945–1951* (New York, 1952), pp. 88–138.

[18] *New York Times*, June 8, July 8, 18, August 17, 1946, for examples.

[19] *Military Situation in the Far East*, Hearings before the Committee on Armed Services and the Committee on Foreign Relations, United States Senate, 82nd Congress, 1st Session, pp. 1851, 1857.

Chapter 18. The Aftermath of Yalta

[1] DS, *United States Relations with China* (Washington, D.C., 1949), p. 558.

[2] Joseph C. Grew, *The Turbulent Era* (New York, 1952), pp. 1451, 1465–1467; William D. Leahy, *I Was There* (London, 1950), pp. 445–446.

[3] DS, *United States Relations with China*, pp. 116–120; James F. Byrnes, *Speaking Frankly* (New York, 1947), pp. 42–45, 205; John R. Deane, *The Strange Alliance* (New York, 1947), p. 271; Edward R. Stettinius, *Roosevelt and the Russians* (New York, 1949), p. 97; Stephen C. Y. Pan, "Legal Aspects of the Yalta Agreement," *American Journal of International Law*, XLVI (1952), 40–59; J. Patrick White, "New Light on Yalta," *Far Eastern Survey*, XIX (1950), 105–112.

[4] Gerard M. Friters, *Outer Mongolia and Its International Position* (Baltimore, 1949), pp. 209–216. For more details see Harley F. MacNair and Donald F. Lach, *Modern Far Eastern International Relations* (New York, 1950), pp. 634–635, and literature there; also Yasuo Misshimo and Tomio Goto, *A Japanese View of Outer Mongolia* (New York, 1942); R. Bollenbach, "The Mongol People's Republic (Democracy of a New Type)," *Papers on China (vol. 3) from the Regional Studies Seminars,* Mimeographed for private distribution by the Committee on International and Regional Studies, Harvard University (May 1949), pp. 257–291.

[5] *Chinese News Service,* January 29, 1952; cf. Aitchen K. Wu, *China and the Soviet Union* (London, 1950), pp. 289–292; J. Patrick White, "New Light on Yalta," *Far Eastern Survey,* XIX (1950), 105–112; *Military Situation in the Far East,* Hearings before the Committee on Armed Services and the Committee on Foreign Relations, United States Senate, 82nd Congress, 1st Session, p. 1846; William A. Williams, *American Russian Relations 1781–1947* (New York, 1952), pp. 276–277; George F. Kennan, *American Diplomacy 1900–1950* (Chicago, 1951), p. 85.

[6] Details can be found in the newspapers for the second half of February and the first half of March, 1946; see especially *New York Times,* February 15, 24, 1946.

[7] *New York Times,* March 24, 1946, September 17, 1947. For a view on Sun Fo see *China Monthly,* VIII (1947), 191.

[8] For some examples see *New York Times,* May 22, 1946 (Sun Fo); March 19, 1947 (Wang Shih-chieh); March 22, 1947 (Chiang); March 24, 1947 (Kuomintang Central Executive Committee); May 23, 1947 (People's Political Council); June 8, 1947; June 24, 1947 (Sun Fo); June 27, 1947 (Chiang); June 28, 1947 (Paul Yupin); September 17, 1947 (Sun Fo); September 28, 1947; November 19, 1948 (Chiang); March 25, 1949; *China Weekly Review,* September 13, pp. 41–42, 57, September 27, pp. 98–99, 1947.

[9] Cf. Robert C. North in Nym Wales, *Red Dust* (Stanford, 1952), p. 17; Paul M. Linebarger, "The Problem of China," *Yale Review,* XXXVI (1947), 505; DS, *United States Relations with China,* pp. 72, 562.

Chapter 19. The Loss of Manchuria and Sinkiang

[1] *Nippon Times,* December 4, 1945.

[2] DS, *United States Relations with China* (Washington, D.C., 1949), p. 72; James F. Byrnes, *Speaking Frankly* (New York, 1947), p. 228.

[3] Carsun Chang, *The Third Force in China* (New York, 1952), p. 162.

[4] For details of military developments during the period October to December. 1945, the *New York Times* and the *Nippon Times* have been relied upon.

[5] DS, *United States Relations with China,* pp. 131–132.

[6] David J. Dallin, *Soviet Russia and the Far East* (New Haven, 1948), pp. 331–332. Cf. *New York Times,* February 3, 1948.

[7] Dallin, *Soviet Russia and the Far East,* pp. 333–338; Aitchen K. Wu, *China and the Soviet Union* (London, 1950), pp. 302–306; *New York Times,* January 11, October 30, 1946; March 26, April 17, June 26, August 31, 1947; March 14, 1948.

[8] *New York Times,* March 13, 1946; *Contemporary China,* V (March 18, 1946); *Soviet Press Translations,* VI (1951), 213, 331.

[9] DS, *United States Relations with China,* pp. 596–604; F. C. Jones, *Manchuria since 1931* (London, 1949), pp. 227–230; Freda Utley, *Last Chance in China* (New York, 1947), pp. 219–241; Dallin, *Soviet Russia and the Far East,* pp. 244–245.

[10] Daniel H. Lew, "Manchurian Booty and International Law," *American Journal of International Law,* XL (1946), 584–589.

[11] *New York Times,* September 8, 1949; Otto B. van der Sprenkel, ed., *New China, Three Views* (London, 1950), pp. 74–75.

[12] *Shanghai Evening Post and Mercury,* November 30, 1945.

[13] *Nippon Times,* November 27, 1945; Dallin, *Soviet Russia and the Far East,* pp. 246–247; Chang, *Third Force,* p. 167.

[14] DS, *United States Relations with China*, pp. 596–598.

[15] *Nippon Times*, November 22, 24, 1945.

[16] Jones, *Manchuria*, p. 231.

[17] Dallin, *Soviet Russia and the Far East*, p. 322; Chang, *Third Force*, pp. 168–169.

[18] *New York Times*, October 25, 1945.

[19] *New York Times*, November 3, 7, 1945; Dallin, *Soviet Russia and the Far East*, p. 252; Jones, *Manchuria*, p. 233; Chang, *Third Force*, p. 163.

[20] *Nippon Times*, November 9, 1945.

[21] *Nippon Times*, November 14, 1945.

[22] *New York Times*, November 13, 14, 1945; *Nippon Times*, November 14, 24, 29, 30, December 3, 1945.

[23] Chang, *Third Force*, p. 171.

[24] DS, *United States Relations with China*, p. 314.

[25] Cf. *New York Times*, February 3, 1948.

[26] *New York Times*, March 13, 1946.

[27] On affairs in Sinkiang since 1945 see Owen Lattimore, *Pivot of Asia* (Boston, 1950), pp. 69–102, 214–223; *Current Notes on International Affairs* (Canberra), XX (1949), 463–466; Wu, *China and the Soviet Union*, pp. 261–262; Dallin, *Soviet Russia and the Far East*, pp. 361–368; U.N. Documents, S/C 2/SR 18, July 29, 1947, pp. 8–13; S/P.V. 186, August 18, 1947, pp. 66–80; S/479, August 11, 1947, pp. 8–12, 41–46; *New York Times*, March 13, 1946; June 11, 12, 13, 14, 16, 18, 19, 23, 24, 26, July 5, 10, 12, 18, 29, August 4, 10, 23, 1947; April 22, September 3, 7, 8, 1948; January 29, February 1, 2, 14, 28, March 22, 30, April 6, 20, May 12, September 29, 30, 1949; American Consulate General, Hong Kong, *Survey of China Mainland Press*, No. 297, March 18, 1952; *People's China*, May 16, 1951, pp. 10–12; Max Beloff, *The Foreign Policy of Soviet Russia* (London, 1949), II, 185–186.

[28] For some characteristic opinions see *North China Daily News*, May 23, 1947, and the foreign policy debate reported on March 19, 1947.

Chapter 20. The Collapse of the National Government

[1] DS, *United States Relations with China* (Washington, D.C., 1949), p. 354 and Annex 172; Freda Utley, *The China Story* (Chicago, 1951), pp. 30–54; *New York Times*, January 1, 1949.

[2] Immanuel C. Y. Hsu, "Allied Council for Japan," *Far Eastern Quarterly*, X (1951), 173–178; Werner Levi, "International Control of Japan," *Far Eastern Survey*, XV (1946), 299–302; DS, *Occupation of Japan: Policy and Progress* (Publication 267, Far Eastern Series 17), pp. 7–8, 67–73. See also W. Macmahon Ball, *Japan Enemy or Ally?* (New York, 1949), pp. 14–42; Edwin M. Martin, *The Allied Occupation of Japan* (Stanford, 1948), pp. 7–10.

[3] Cf. *New York Times*, November 2, 1946; May 23, September 10, November 2, 1947.

[4] E.g., *Nippon Times*, August 2, 1947; April 23, June 17, July 3, 1948. For some popular reactions see *Nippon Times*, August 8, December 4, 1947; May 27, June 7, 1948.

[5] *Nippon Times*, September 21, 28, October 2, 11, 14, November 27, December 4, 1947; January 20, February 16, April 16, May 21, June 7, 17, September 7, 12, 30, 1948.

[6] *China Weekly Review*, CII (August 10, 1946), 247; CIII (November 9, 16, 1946), 295, 339; Jean-Jacques Brieux, *La Chine du nationalisme au communisme* (Paris, 1950), pp. 177–180; M. E. Orlean, "The Sino-American Commercial Treaty of 1946," *Far Eastern Quarterly*, VII (1948), 354–367; Charles T. Fox, "The Sino-American Treaty," *Far Eastern Survey*, XVI (1947), 138–142.

[7] Walter Millis, ed., *The Forrestal Diaries* (New York, 1951), p. 285.

[8] *North China Daily News*, August 30, September 7, 10, 11, 1947.

[9] *North China Daily News*, July 8, 1947.

[10] *North China Daily News*, July 22, 24, August 25, 1947.

[11] *North China Daily News*, August 29, September 2, 5, 1947; Thurston Griggs, *Americans in China: Some Chinese Views* (Washington, D.C., 1948), pp. 46–52.

[12] Kenneth S. Latourette, *The American Record in the Far East, 1945–1951* (New York, 1952), pp. 114–116.

[13] DS, *United States Relations with China*, p. 888.

[14] By T. F. Tsiang in the Political and Security Committee of the United Nations General Assembly, *New York Times*, January 27, 1952.

[15] Werner Levi, "Union in Asia?" *Far Eastern Survey*, XIX (1950), 144–145, and "The Chances of an Asian NATO," *Fortnightly*, N. S., MXXXIX (July 1953), 3–8.

[16] These statements by Nationalist officials can be found in *China Information Bulletin*, November 15, 1948; *China Weekly Review*, CXIII (March 12, 1949), 39; *Current Digest of the Soviet Press*, I (May 10, 1949), 47; *New York Times*, March 3, 20, July 12, September 11, October 6, December 14, 1947, May 4, 21, July 11, October 11, November 9, 13, 1948, July 16, August 8, 28, 1949, March 12, 1950, January 20, May 6, November 17, 1951; *North China Daily News*, March 21, August 30, September 7, 10, 11, 1947; Cecil Brown's broadcast, December 26, 1952. See also Hsin Ying, "The Collapse of the Nationalist Regime in China," *Far Eastern Economic Review*, X (1951), 124–129.

[17] On "bureaucratic capitalism" see Harley Stevens, "Business and Politics in China," *Far Eastern Survey*, XV (1946), 296–297; C. Yun, "Government Monopoly in China," *Far Eastern Survey*, XVI (1947), 46–47; on UNRRA in China see George Woodbridge, *UNRRA: The History of the United Nations Relief and Rehabilitation Administration* (New York, 1950), II, 371–393; Pao-Liu Tai, *Summary Report on UNRRA Activities in China* (New York, 1947), p. 6.

[18] As an example of dissatisfaction see Carsun Chang, *The Third Force in China* (New York, 1952), pp. 90–109.

[19] *New York Times*, May 7, 1952. For a discussion of China's postwar economic situation see Chih Tsang, *China's Postwar Markets* (New York, 1945), pp. 3–14; Institute of Pacific Relations, *Problems of Economic Reconstruction in the Far East* (New York, 1949), pp. 21–33; D. K. Lieu, *China's Economic Stabilization and Reconstruction* (New Brunswick, 1948); Ta Chen, "Basic Problems of the Chinese Working Class," *American Journal of Sociology*, LIII (1948), 184–191.

[20] For some discussion of this idea see Wing-tsit Chan, *Religious Trends in Modern China* (New York, 1953), pp. 262–264; Charles P. Fitzgerald, *Revolution in China* (New York, 1952), pp. 146–150; H. G. Creel, *Chinese Thought from Confucius to Mao Tse-tung* (Chicago, 1953), pp. 252–257; George E. Taylor, "The Hegemony of the Chinese Communists 1945–1950," *Annals*, CCLXXVII (1951), 13–21; Percy Finch, *Shanghai and Beyond* (New York, 1953), pp. 189–190; and Benjamin Schwartz's book review of Fitzgerald's book in *Pacific Historical Review*, XXIII (1953), 204–206. For a description of how the Chinese are indoctrinated to become Communists see Edward Hunter, *Brain-Washing in Red China* (New York, 1951); Liu Shaw-Tong, *Out of Red China* (New York, 1953).

Chapter 21. The Theory of Communist Foreign Policy

[1] Newspaper reports are the most detailed source of conditions on Formosa. See also *China Handbook 1950* (New York, 1950), Gung-hsiang Wang, "Nationalist Government Policies, 1949–1951," *Annals*, CCLXXVII (1951), 213–223; *Current Notes on International Affairs* (Canberra), XXI (1950), 191–198; H. Maclear Bate, *Report from Formosa* (London, 1952), pp. 38–67; Fred W. Riggs, *Formosa under Chinese Nationalist Rule* (New York, 1952); Joseph W. Ballantine, *Formosa* (Washington, D.C., 1952).

[2] Article 55; the translation used here can be found in Mao Tse-tung, *On People's Democratic Rule* (New York, 1950).

[3] The more important documents are A/C.1/551 through 556; A/C.1/SR.344;

A/PV.273; A/1236; A/1239; A/PV.314; A/1563; A/2098. For summaries of the debates see *United Nations Bulletin*, VIII (1950), 40–46; IX (1950), 728–733.

⁴ Charles P. Fitzgerald, *Revolution in China* (New York, 1952), pp. 215–219, speculates about some of the motives behind this behavior; cf. also Derk Bodde, *Peking Diary* (New York, 1950), pp. 158, 264.

⁵ Theodore Hsi-En Chen, "Relations between Britain and Communist China," *Current History*, XXIII (1952), 295–299; *Current Digest of the Soviet Press*, II:36 (October 21, 1950), 27–28; *Soviet Press Translations*, V (July 1, November, 1950), 413, 589; *People's China*, June 1, 1950, p. 26; *New China News Agency*, May 21, 31, 1950.

⁶ Almost all of the writings of Mao Tse-tung contain references to foreign affairs. Other high officials of the party have frequently dealt with that topic. See, e.g., Liu Shao-ch'i, "On Internationalism and Nationalism," American Consulate General, Hong Kong, *Current Background*, No. 98, July 15, 1951; this article can also be found in *China Digest*, V (December 14, 1948), 6–9, and in abbreviated form in *Current Digest of the Soviet Press* I:23 (July 5, 1949), 14–17; Liu Ting-yi, "Explanation of Several Basic Questions concerning the Postwar International Situation," *Emancipation Daily*, January 6, 1947. See also H. Arthur Steiner, "Mainsprings of Chinese Communist Foreign Policy," *American Journal of International Law*, XLIV (1950), 69–99; O. Edmund Clubb, "Chinese Communist Strategy in Foreign Relations," *Annals*, CCLXXVII (1951), 156–166. For the Communist view on international relations in general see Frank M. Russell, *Theories of International Relations* (New York, 1936), pp. 507–536; T. H. Teracouzio, *War and Peace in Soviet Diplomacy* (New York, 1940), pp. 19–56.

⁷ "The Foreign Policy of the People's Republic of China during the Past Two Years," *Soviet Press Translations*, VI (1951), 669.

⁸ The translation used here was published in London, 1950. A translation can also be found in *Soviet Press Translations*, IV (1949), 454–461.

⁹ Liu Shi-ch'ao, "Internationalism and Nationalism." The other quotations in this analysis are also from this source.

¹⁰ For a detailed discussion of the nature of ideology and its relation to foreign policy see Werner Levi, *Fundamentals of World Organization* (Minneapolis, 1950), 165–172.

¹¹ Conrad Brandt, Benjamin Schwartz, and John K. Fairbank, *A Documentary History of Chinese Communism* (London, 1952), p. 474.

¹² Cf. on this point Fitzgerald, *Revolution in China*, pp. 31–32, 51.

¹³ Yeh Mang, "Foreign Policy of New China," *Current Background*, No. 65, March 15, 1951.

¹⁴ Yeh Mang, "Foreign Policy of New China."

¹⁵ For the treaties concluded during World War II and shortly thereafter see Chinese Ministry of Information, *China Handbook, 1937–1945* (New York, 1947), pp. 155–186; DS, *United States Relations with China* (Washington, D.C., 1949), pp. 34–37, 514–519; Chiang K'ai-shek, *China's Destiny* (New York, 1947), pp. 141–143; Wesley P. Fishel, *The End of Extraterritoriality in China* (Berkeley, 1952), pp. 214–215.

Chapter 22. The Hate-America Campaign

¹ Cf. DS, *Bulletin*, XXIV (1951), 947.

² DS, *Bulletin*, XXIII (1950), 238.

³ *The Fight for a New China* (New York, 1945), p. 67.

⁴ These themes are outlined in Mao's speech of November 6, 1948, printed in H. Arthur Steiner, *Maoism: A Sourcebook* (Los Angeles, 1952). A summary of the early stages of the campaign can be found in H. Arthur Steiner, "Mainsprings of Chinese Communist Foreign Policy," *American Journal of International Law*,

XLIV (1950), 80–84, and Margaret Stockdale, "Anti-American Propaganda in the Communist Press 1946–1949," a paper written in 1949 for the Far Eastern Seminar at Harvard University.

[5] American Consulate General, Hong Kong, *Current Background*, No. 32, November 29, 1950, and *Soviet Press Translations*, V (1950), 667–675.

[6] The Chinese "historians" are Ch'in Pen-li, Hu Shen, and Liu Ta-nien; see *Soviet Press Translations*, VI (1951), 411–416; VII (1952), 303–304. The article on the T'ai-p'ings can be found in *Current Background*, No. 85, June 19, 1951, and its Russian counterpart in *Soviet Press Translations*, VII (1952), 227–237. *Current Background*, No. 32, November 29, 1950, contains a list of historical events the like of which can be found in many other places. See also *New China News Agency*, May 11, 1950; American Consulate General, Hong Kong, *Survey of China Mainland Press*, No. 165, August 31–September 1, 1951.

[7] *Soviet Press Translations*, V (1950), 590.

[8] For a summary account see Herbert W. Briggs, "Chinese Representation in the United Nations," *International Organization*, VI (1952), 192–209.

[9] Cf., e.g., *New China News Agency*, May 10, 15, 16, 1950; *People's China*, December 1, 1951, pp. 9–11.

[10] *Soviet Press Translations*, V (1950), 151; VI (1951), 210, 558; *New York Times*, August 22, 1951.

[11] E.g., Chou En-lai's statements December 4, 1950, May 24, 1951, and August 15, 1951, published in *Soviet Press Translations*, VI (1951), 48; China Information Bureau, *Daily News Release*, May 25, 1951, and August 16, 1951; *People's China*, September 1, 1951, Supplement. See also China Information Bureau, *Daily News Release*, April 23, 1951; *Shanghai News*, June 11, 1950; *People's China*, December 1, 1951, pp. 9–11; *Soviet Press Translations*, VI (1951), 556–558; *Survey of China Mainland Press*, No. 165, August 31–September 1, 1951.

[12] *New York Times*, May 7, 1952; *Survey of China Mainland Press*, No. 333, May 11–12, 1952.

[13] For details see Lawrence K. Rosinger *et al.*, *The State of Asia* (New York, 1951), pp. 129–154; E. Grant Meade, *American Military Government in Korea* (New York, 1951), pp. 90–96.

[14] Dean Acheson, *The Problem of Peace in Korea*, DS Publication No. 4771, October 1952, pp. 15–16.

[15] *New York Times*, June 3, 1950.

[16] Charles P. Fitzgerald, *Revolution in China* (New York, 1952), p. 220.

[17] For details see Harold M. Vinacke, *The United States and the Far East, 1945–1951* (New York, 1952), pp. 98–106, 121–129; Kenneth S. Latourette, *The American Record in the Far East, 1945–1951* (New York, 1952), pp. 171–195.

[18] *Soviet Press Translations*, V (1950), 419, 590; VI (1951), 672; *Shanghai News*, June 30, July 1, 1950.

[19] Text in *Shanghai News*, July 16, 1950. For details of the campaign see *Shanghai News*, July 14 through 24, 1950.

[20] *Chinese-English Intelligence*, November 7, 10, 1950; *Survey of China Mainland Press*, No. 4, November 5–6, 1950; No. 5, November 7, 1950; *Soviet Press Translations*, VI (1951), 337, 672.

[21] *New York Times*, February 4, 1953; *Survey of China Mainland Press*, No. 506, February 4, 1953.

[22] American Consulate General, Hong Kong, *Review of Hong-Kong Chinese Press*, No. 59/53, March 27, 1953. *Survey of China Mainland Press* is the best source for Chinese comments on the course of the truce negotiations.

[23] So wrote the Communist newspaper Jen Min Jih Pao, *Survey of China Mainland Press*, No. 5, November 7, 1950.

[24] The most complete summary of this line can be found in *Current Background*,

No. 32, November 29, 1950. One or the other aspect of it can be found almost daily in *Survey of China Mainland Press*, and in innumerable articles in *Soviet Press Translations* and *People's China*.

[25] This theme recurs perennially and can be found in many places. See, e.g., *Current Background*, No. 32, November 29, 1950; *Survey of China Mainland Press*, No. 4, November 5–6, 1950; No. 38, December 28, 1950.

[26] Fred W. Riggs, *Formosa under Chinese Nationalist Rule* (New York, 1952), p. 15; H. MacLear Bate, *Report from Formosa* (London, 1952), p. 79.

[27] For United States policy, see Vinacke, *U.S. and the Far East*, pp. 121–129.

[28] Details can be found in the *New York Times*, June 28 and following days, 1950.

[29] *New York Times*, January 7, 1951.

[30] DS, *Bulletin*, XXIV (1951), 747.

[31] *New York Times*, May 3, 1951.

[32] *New York Times*, April 22, 25, May 6, 1951.

[33] Cf. Riggs, *Formosa*, pp. 16–17; *New York Times*, May 27, 1951; January 3, September 14, October 10, 1952; U.P. dispatch, March 18, 1953.

[34] *New York Times*, February 4, 13, March 3, August 19, 23, 1953; *Far Eastern Economic Review*, XIII (1952), 75.

[35] Riggs, *Formosa*, pp. 61–130; Economic Cooperation Administration, *United States Economic Assistance to Formosa, January 1–December 31, 1950*, and its current reports.

[36] Bate, *Report from Formosa*, p. 105.

[37] *Chinese News Service*, February 19, 1952.

[38] *Chinese News Service*, May 5, 1952.

[39] *Chinese News Service*, April 8, September 23, December 16, 1952.

[40] *Chinese News Service*, November 4, 1952; *New York Times*, December 26, 1952.

Chapter 23. The Alliance with the Soviet Union

[1] Cf. Karl Wittfogel, "How to Checkmate Stalin in Asia," *Commentary*, X (1950), 334-341; Max Beloff, "Soviet Far Eastern Policy since Yalta," in William Mandel, *Soviet Source Materials on USSR Relations with East Asia, 1945–1950* (New York, 1950), p. 23.

[2] The facts on this speculation on Maoist "Titoism" can be found in Conrad Brandt, Benjamin Schwartz, and John K. Fairbank, *A Documentary History of Chinese Communism* (London, 1952); Benjamin Schwartz, *Chinese Communism and the Rise of Mao* (Cambridge, Mass., 1951); Robert C. North, *Kuomintang and Chinese Communist Elites* (Stanford University, 1952). Some thoughts on the possibility of Maoist "Titoism" can be found in " 'Titoism' and the Chinese Communist Regime," *World Today*, VIII (1952), 521–532; Wittfogel, "How to Checkmate Stalin"; Shao Chuan Leng, "The Chance for Titoism in China," *Current History*, XXI (1951), 337–344; Max Mark, "Chinese Communism," *Journal of Politics*, XIII (1951), 232–252.

[3] American Consulate General, Hong Kong, *Survey of China Mainland Press*, No. 443, October 31, 1952.

[4] *Survey of China Mainland Press*, No. 275, February 14, 1952; *People's China*, November 16, 1952, pp. 5–10; K. E. Priestley, "The Sino-Soviet Friendship Association," *Pacific Affairs*, XXV (1952), 287–292.

[5] *Survey of China Mainland Press*, No. 195, October 16, 1951.

[6] *Survey of China Mainland Press*, No. 173, September 13, 1951.

[7] Otto B. van der Sprenkel, ed., *New China, Three Views* (London, 1950), pp. 74–75; Derk Bodde, *Peking Diary* (New York, 1950), pp. 156–157.

[8] *Soviet Press Translations*, VI (1951), 670.

[9] *New York Times*, March 9, 11, April 27, 1953; *Survey of China Mainland Press*, No. 527, March 10, 1953.

[10] *Keesing's Contemporary Archives*, May 13–20, 1950, p. 10712.

[11] Chao Ching-lun, "The Transfer of the Chinese Changchun Railway," *People's China*, No. 2, January 1953, pp. 8–9.

[12] *New York Times*, September 17, 1952, January 1, 3, 1953; *Survey of China Mainland Press*, No. 417, September 17, 1952; No. 443, October 31, 1952. For an interpretation of the Moscow agreements see Robert C. North, "Sino Soviet Partnership," *Foreign Policy Bulletin*, December 15, 1952.

[13] For details see Harold S. Quigley and George H. Blakeslee, *The Far East* (Boston, 1938), pp. 69–71.

[14] Cf. *Soviet Press Translations*, VII (1952), 240.

[15] *New China News Agency*, March 30, April 3, 1950. See also April 2, 6, 7, 8, 9, 11, 1950; *Chinese-English Intelligence*, October 4, 1950; *People's China*, May 16, 1951, pp. 10–12.

[16] *New China News Agency*, May 12, June 18, 1950.

[17] *Soviet Press Translations*, VI (1951), 331, also 213; *Survey of China Mainland Press*, No. 64, February 9–11, 1951.

[18] United Nations, *Economic Survey of Asia and the Far East 1951* (E/CN.11/345), pp. 160–164; *Soviet Press Translations*, VII (1952), 294, 296, 307–312; *Survey of China Mainland Press*, No. 311, April 6–7, 1952; No. 314, April 10–12, 1952; No. 315, April 13–15, 1952; *People's China*, October 16, 1952, 16–17, 33–35; *New York Times*, March 26, May 2, 1953; *Far Eastern Economic Review*, XIII (1952), 684.

[19] *Shanghai News*, June 10, 1950; *New China News Agency*, June 9, 1950; *People's China*, February 16, 1952, pp. 5–7, 31; *Soviet Press Translations*, V (1950), 681; *China Weekly Review*, CXVII (March 11, 1950), 23.

[20] *New China News Agency*, March 19, April 6, 1950; *Soviet Press Translations*, VII (1952), 240; Liu Shao-chih's speech, *New China News Agency*, May 2, 1950.

[21] For some discussion of this point see Charles P. Fitzgerald, *Revolution in China* (New York, 1952), pp. 225–253; Freda Utley, *The China Story* (Chicago, 1951), pp. 219–241; George Creel, *Russia's Race for Asia* (New York, 1949), pp. 173–184; van der Sprenkel, *New China*, pp. 71–77, 113–116, 140–144; Michael Lindsay, "China: Report of a Visit," *International Affairs*, XXVI (1950), 22–31.

[22] *Survey of China Mainland Press*, No. 28, December 12, 1950; No. 31, December 15–16, 1950; No. 39, December 28, 1950; No. 51, January 18, 1951; No. 57, January 26–27, 1951; No. 62, February 2–4, 1951; No. 70, February 20, 1951; No. 91, April 4–5, 1951; No. 104, May 11–15, 1951; No. 111, June 6–7, 1951; No. 123, June 24–25, 1951; No. 190, October 7–9, 1951; No. 192, October 11, 1951; No. 196, October 17, 1951; No. 202, October 25, 1951; No. 227, December 2–3, 1951; No. 232, December 9–10, 1951; No. 245, December 30–31, 1951; No. 258, January 18–19, 1952; No. 277, February 17–18, 1952; No. 303, April 1, 1952; No. 309, April 3, 1952; No. 315, April 13–15, 1952; No. 338, May 18–19, 1952; No. 341, May 22, 1952; No. 363, June 26, 1952; No. 373, July 13–14, 1952; No. 378, July 20–21, 1952; No. 399, August 21, 1952; No. 400, August 22–23, 1952; No. 417, September 17, 1952; No. 419, September 19–20, 1952; No. 420, September 21–22, 1952; No. 441, October 28, 1952; No. 455, November 19, 1952; No. 521, February 28–March 2, 1953; Sidney Shapiro, "Cultural Relations with Eastern Europe," *China Monthly Review*, CXXIII (1952), 161–165.

[23] *Survey of China Mainland Press*, No. 20, November 30, 1950; No. 42, January 5–6, 1951; No. 55, January 24, 1951; No. 63, February 5–8, 1951; No. 122, June 22–23, 1951; No. 193, October 12–13, 1951; No. 311, April 6–7, 1952; No. 314, April 10–12, 1952; No. 331, May 8, 1952; No. 358, June 19, 1952; No. 377, July 18–19, 1952; No. 382, July 25–26, 1952; No. 384, July 29, 1952; No. 416, September 16, 1952; No. 438, October 23, 1952; No. 444, November 1–2, 1952; *Soviet Press Translations*, VI (1951), 311–313; VII (1952), 294.

[24] Ivar Buxell af Riksvyl, "Die Polnisch-chinesische Schiffahrtslinie," *Osteuropa*,

II (1952), 302–303; *Survey of China Mainland Press*, No. 378, July 20–21, 1952.

²⁵ *Survey of China Mainland Press*, No. 427, October 1, 1952; No. 429, October 5–7, 1952; No. 433, October 14–15, 1952; No. 434, October 16–17, 1952.

Chapter 24. The Bid for Asian Leadership

¹ For brief summaries of the history of communism in Southeast Asia see Virginia Thompson, Richard Adloff, *The Left Wing in Southeast Asia* (New York, 1950), pp. 221–227; Milton Sacks, "The Strategy of Communism in Southeast Asia," *Pacific Affairs*, XXIII (1950), 227–236; Martin Ebon, *World Communism Today* (New York, 1948), pp. 379–400.

² R. Palme Dutt, "Right Wing Social Democracy in the Service of Imperialism," *For a Lasting Peace, For a People's Democracy*, November 1, 1948.

³ For a brief survey see Charles A. Fischer, "China and her South-Western Neighbours," *World Affairs*, IV (1950), 139–153.

⁴ For examples see *China Monthly Review*, CXXII (June 1952), 582–589; CXXIII (July 1952), 92; *Survey of China Mainland Press*, No. 15, November 22–23, 1950; No. 241, December 21–22, 1951; No. 334, May 13, 1952; *Soviet Press Translations*, VI (1951), 275–277, 691–693. For a discussion of possible Chinese plans for Southeast Asia see Maurice Qéguiner, "Sud-est Asiatique: Zone névralgique," *Etudes*, CCLXXII (March 1952), 385–389.

⁵ *Soviet Press Translations*, V (1950), 136.

⁶ For examples see *Survey of China Mainland Press*, No. 196, October 17, 1951; No. 207, November 1, 1951; *Soviet Press Translations*, VI (1951), 531–533, 593–595; VII (1952), 11–13.

⁷ E.g., *Shanghai News*, August 5, 1950; *Survey of China Mainland Press*, No. 334, May 13, 1952.

⁸ *New York Times*, September 26, 1952.

⁹ *New York Times*, October 22, 25, 31, 1952; *Far Eastern Economic Review*, XIV (1953), 9–12.

¹⁰ *New China News Agency*, May 2, 9, 11, 1950; *Shanghai News*, August 13, 1950; China Information Bureau, *Daily News Release*, October 9, November 3, 1951. For a survey see Claude A. Buss, "Overseas Chinese and Communist Policy," *Annals*, CCLXXVII (September 1951), 203–212.

Chapter 25. Realizing Ambitions in Asia

¹ John V. A. MacMurray, *Treaties and Agreements with and concerning China 1874–1919* (New York, 1921), pp. 576–577. For a detailed history of the relations between Tibet and pre-Communist China see Yao-ting Sung, "Chinese-Tibetan Relations 1890–1947," unpublished Ph.D. thesis, University of Minnesota, 1949; for Yuan Shih-k'ai's Tibet policy see Tyan Ling, *Beiträge zur neuesten Geschichte Chinas* (Berlin, 1917), pp. 125–131.

² MacMurray, *Treaties*, pp. 582–583.

³ *New China News Agency*, May 13, 1950; *Soviet Press Translations*, VI (1951), 103.

⁴ *Shanghai News*, August 4, 1950.

⁵ *Chinese-English Intelligencer*, May 25, 1950.

⁶ For these events see *Current Notes on International Affairs* (Canberra), XXIII (1952), 23–32; *New York Times*, May 27, 1951; "Tibet Today," *World Today*, VIII (1952), 202–209; *Soviet Press Translations*, VI (1951), 367–371; *Neue Zürcher Zeitung*, May 16, 1951; Tsung-Lien Shen and Shen-Chi Liu, *Tibet and the Tibetans* (Stanford, 1953), pp. 52–65.

⁷ China Information Bureau, *Daily News Release*, May 28, 30, 1951.

[8] J. Decoux, *A la barre de l'Indochine* (Paris, 1949), p. 258.

[9] The account of Chinese policy in Indochina is based mainly on the following sources: Philippe Devillers, *Histoire du Viet-Nam de 1940 à 1952* (Paris, 1952); Institut Franco-Suisse d'Etudes Coloniales, *France and Viet-Nam* (Paris, 1947); Lawrence K. Rosinger *et al.*, *The State of Asia* (New York, 1951), pp. 221–267; Virginia Thompson, Richard Adloff, *The Left Wing in Southeast Asia* (New York, 1950), pp. 21–50; Harold R. Isaacs, *No Peace for Asia* (New York, 1947), pp. 134–178; Milton Sacks, "Strategy of Communism in Southeast Asia," *Pacific Affairs*, XXIII (1950), 236–244; *Current Notes on International Affairs*, XXI (1950), 9–21; XXII (1951), 255–266; XXIII (1952), 494–509; Ellen J. Hammer, *The Emergence of Viet Nam* (New York, 1947).

[10] *New York Times*, April 13, 1951, February 4, August 30, 1953; *Soviet Press Translations*, VII (1952), 170.

[11] John L. Christian, *Burma and the Japanese Invader* (Bombay, 1945), p. 229.

[12] Christian, *Burma*, pp. 271–278; Victor Purcell, *The Chinese in Southeast Asia* (London, 1951), p. 98.

[13] Paschal M. d'Elia, ed., *Le Triple Démisme de Suen Wen* (Shanghai, 1930), p. 95.

[14] Purcell, *Chinese in Southeast Asia*, p. 98.

[15] Purcell, *Chinese in Southeast Asia*, p. 99; *New York Times*, December 2, 1947.

[16] *New York Times*, February 1, February 26, March 9, 1951.

[17] *New York Times*, January 29, 1952; January 17, 20, March 12, 1953; *Keesing's Contemporary Archives*, March 1–8, 1952, p. 12063; *Economist*, CLXII (1952), 203.

[18] *New York Times*, March 27, 28, 29, 31, April 8, 11, 14, 18, 20, 22, 23, May 22, June 8, 10, 17, 21, 23, 29, 30, July 13, 24, 31, August 1, 1953.

[19] Purcell, *Chinese in Southeast Asia*, pp. 189–206; Rosinger, *State of Asia*, pp. 268–291; Charles P. Fitzgerald, *Revolution in China* (New York, 1952), pp. 246–247.

[20] *New York Times*, December 9, 1952.

[21] The text of the notes can be found in *India News*, November 4, 1950.

[22] For some examples see *People's China*, December 1, 1950, p. 4; *Chinese-English Intelligencer*, November 21, 1950.

INDEX

Administrative integrity; *see* Integrity
Alliances: advocated Sino-British, 42; attempted Sino-Japanese, 50–51, 55, 86, 89; alleged Sino-Russian, *1896*, 52; alleged Sino-British-American, 52, 54; Anglo-Japanese, 81, 82, 88, 108, 160; of France, 100; attempted Sino-German-American, 101–105, 117, 118; advocated Sino-German-American, 114, 117, 118; attempted Sino-Soviet, *1931*, 200; Anti-Comintern Pact, 212, 214; German-Italian-Japanese, *1940*, 223; proposed Asian, 266–267; Sino-Soviet, 313–314
Allied Council for Japan, 262–263
Amau, Eiji, statement on Japanese policy, 207–208
Anglo-Japanese Alliance: political effect, 81, 82; China's attitude, 88–89, 108, 160
Annam: Chinese administration, 4; French acquisition, 21, 36; *see also* Indochina
Anti-Comintern Pact, *1936*, Chinese Communist reaction, 212, 214
Anti-Communist policy: of foreign powers, 184–185; of Anti-Bolshevik League, 194; of National Government, 196, 198, 204, 212
Anti-foreignism: of imperial court, 15, 23, 45, 70; of public, 19, 263; causes, 21; and T'ai-p'ing Rebellion, 24; and Boxer Rebellion, 60; and nationalism, 94, 95, 142, 169, 182, 193, 219; and revolution of *1911*, 122, 129; and Paris Peace Conference, *1919*, 155; and Nationalist revolution, 171, 176, 178
Armed forces: popular attitude toward, 91, 217–218, 219; governmental attitude, 99; imperial, character, 30, 31–34, 45–47, 91; imperial, strength, 33–37; Nationalist, 195, 196–197, 203, 213, 215–216, 235, 269, 270; Communist, 195, 197, 216–217, 269; "volunteers" for Korea, 297–298

Asian and Australasian Trade Unions Conference, *1949*, 326–327
Asian and Pacific Peace Conference, *1952*, 291, 327
Asian Conference, Delhi, *1947*, 353
Asian union, 266–267

Balance-of-power policy; *see* Foreign policy: methods
Bannermen; *see* Armed forces: imperial
Banque industrielle de la Chine, and Consortium, 132, 133
"Blue Express" incident, 182
Blythe, Samuel G., and World War I, 148
Borodin, Michael, in China, 174
Boxer Rebellion: settlement, 55, 66–69; nature, 58, 59, 61; causes, 59–62; politics, 60–61, 64–65, 73; U.S. policy, 65; British policy, 65–66; effect on modernization, 66, 90, 91; indemnity, 68, 103, 105, 149, 150, 182
Boycott, as political weapon, 141, 156, 183, 200
Braves; *see* Armed forces, imperial
Brussels Conference, on Sino-Japanese War, *1937–1941*, 220–221
Bryan, William J., notes exchanged with Japan, 144, 148
"Bureaucratic capitalism," 271
Burlingame mission, 34
Burma: British acquisition, 21; Chinese support of Communists, 327, 350; Chinese political ambitions, 345, 346–347; Chinese minority, 346; fear of Chinese political ambitions, 346–347; border dispute with China, 346–347; Chinese occupation, 347; Nationalist guerrilla troops, 348–350
Burma Road: Japanese attacks, 223; closing, 226, 227; as China's lifeline, 226; Burmese fears, 346

C. C. Clique, criticizes National Government, 268